HERMANN HESSE'S
FICTIONS OF THE SELF

HERMANN HESSE'S
FICTIONS OF THE SELF,

Autobiography and the Confessional Imagination

EUGENE L. STELZIG

PRINCETON UNIVERSITY PRESS   PRINCETON, NEW JERSEY

Library of Congress Cataloging-in-Publication Data
Stelzig, Eugene L.
    Hermann Hesse's fictions of the self :
autobiography and the confessional imagination /
Eugene L. Stelzig.
        p. cm.
    Includes index.
    ISBN 0-691-06750-3 (alk. paper)
    1. Hesse, Hermann, 1877-1962. 2. Authors,
German—20th century—Biography.
3. Autobiographical fiction, German—History and
criticism. 4. Autobiography. 5. Self in literature.
I. Title.
PT2617.E85Z937 1988
833'.912—dc19
    [B]   88-12556
                                                      CIP

FOR ELSJE

CONTENTS

Preface   ix

Abbreviations   xiii

I   THE CONFESSIONAL IMAGINATION   3

II   LIFE *AS* WRITING   25

III   SELF-WILL   43
The Politics of Conscience   45
A Child Possessed   54
The Religion of Dissent   71

IV   AUTOBIOGRAPHICAL BEGINNINGS   80
Romantic Apprenticeship   80
Peter Camenzind   87
Beneath the Wheel: Hesse's Past Redux   95

V   DOMESTIC FICTIONS   105
Some Prewar Stories   107
Knulp   117
Two Art Novels   119

VI   HESSE'S MARRIAGE OF HEAVEN AND
     HELL   130
     Several Mother *Märchen*   135
     Demian   139
     Demian and "The Decline of Europe"   150
     A Child's Soul   154

VII TICINO LEGENDS OF SAINTS AND
     SINNERS   159
     The Psychomachia of *Klein and Wagner*   162
     Klingsor's Self-Portrait in an Expressionist
       Mirror   169
     Siddhartha   173

VIII LIVE(D) FANTASIES   188
     Hesse's *Piktor* Fable   190
     Living/Writing on the Horizon of the
       Steppenwolf   193
     The Making of *Steppenwolf*   201
     The Magic Mirrors   208
     Narcissus and Goldmund   224

IX   HOME TO THE UN-BECOMING SELF   238
     The Journey to the East   239
     The Riddling "Bird" of Montagnola   250
     The Long Making of *The Glass Bead Game*   253
     Knecht's Non-Castalian Lives   269
     Introductory Matter to *The Glass Bead
       Game*   280
     Hesse's Bridging of Polarities   286

     EPILOGUE: WHO IS HE?   311

     Notes   315

     Index   337

PREFACE

This book has been a long time in the making. Its beginnings coincide with my teaching, during the mid-1970s, a course on Hesse and Lawrence that soon evolved into a course strictly on Hesse. Because from the first my interest in this writer has been psychological *and* literary, my reading of his works has turned as much on their auto/biographical as on their formal aspects. My original plan, which was to analyze his fiction in terms of his root-concept of "self-will," soon led to the larger issue of Hesse the confessional writer—and this in turn opened my eyes to autobiography criticism, which had then just acquired real momentum but which has grown exponentially in the intervening years. My introductory chapter, with its larger reflection on the problematic relationship between Poetry and Truth in the modern confessional imagination, is a kind of dialogue with this burgeoning field to which my discussion of Hesse's writings in subsequent chapters is also indebted. However, several important books that are in different ways related to my concerns appeared only after this study was already in its final stage—the most recent are Jerome Hamilton Buckley's *Autobiography and the Subjective Impulse Since 1800* (1984) and Paul John Eakin's *Fictions in Autobiography* (1985)—so that I was not able to make substantive use of them. In any event, if I had paused to reconceptualize my project with the publication of every relevant book and article, I would never have been able to finish.

My aim throughout has been to examine what it means to be an "autobiographical writer" by considering Hesse's fictions of the self as exemplary instances of the relationship between life and art, biography and autobiography, in the subjective tradition of modern literature. The intended audience of this book comprises students of autobiography, readers and critics with a psychological and biographical interest in literature, and readers of Hesse. Though what follows is neither an "influence" nor a comparative study, I have not ignored the literary and intellectual sources of an author who was very widely read and whose vision of literature was not a national but a global one; nor have I hesitated to let my interests as a Romanticist draw me into pointing out occasional parallels and affinities between Hesse and several major English writers with whom many of my readers will surely have a more than nodding acquaintance.

All quotations of Hesse's writings are given in English: for the most part, and when possible, I have used existing translations, though these are not always as good as one might wish. Since I make extensive use of Hesse's (published) letters and journals, and since these are not available in English, I have had to do a good bit of translating. Even though German is the first language I learned to speak as a child, I did not find this an easy task. My rendering of Hesse may not capture the rich register of his highly-nuanced, yet crisp and lucid German prose, but I hope I have at least managed to avoid the pitfalls of obvious mistranslation.

My obligations in writing this book are many and a pleasure to acknowledge. The Hesse scholar-critics to whom I owe the most—more than my notes can indicate and even where I disagree with them— are Hugo Ball, Mark Boulby, George Wallis Field, Ralph Freedman, Volker Michels, Joseph Mileck, and Theodore Ziolkowski. Indeed, without the biographies of Freedman and Mileck (published in the same year) this book would not have been possible in its present form. My work has also been much facilitated by Volker and Ursula Michels's collected edition (especially the first two volumes) of Hesse's letters, which, though it is not a truly complete gathering, is the best we are likely to have. Michels's documentary companion volumes to Hesse's major novels (*Materialen zu . . .*) have also been an invaluable help, as has been Siegfried Unseld's *Werkgeschichte*.

For offering encouragement and sometimes helpful criticisms in different forms and at different stages of this project, I am indebted to George Wallis Field, Volker Michels, Don Norford, Henry Remak, James Olney, and most recently, Paul John Eakin. As for institutional support, I owe the most to the National Endowment for the Humanities: research for this book was pursued as the independent project in three of its Seminars for College Teachers, whose topics also proved stimulating for my work ("Modern Literary Criticism," "European Romanticism," "The Forms of Autobiography"). And an NEH Fellowship for College Teachers during 1985–1986 allowed me to complete my rough draft and revise it for publication. I must also acknowledge the assistance of the SUNY Research Foundation (for a faculty research fellowship during summer 1978) and SUNY Geneseo (for a sabbatical leave during spring 1980). And I would be remiss in not mentioning the friendly staff of the Schiller-Nationalmuseum in Marbach am Neckar who helped me on my "fishing expedition" to the Hesse archive in July 1978.

On a more personal level, I want to thank my colleagues in the Geneseo English Department, including three past chairmen, Paul Stein, Bill Rueckert, and Jim Scholes, as well as the current one, Donald Watt, for encouraging their junior and then senior Romanticist in his quixotic pursuit of a twentieth-century German writer. Finally, my greatest debt is to my wife, to whom this book is dedicated, and who helped me keep faith with and see it through to its completion.

Three sections of this book have appeared in slightly different form before: Chapter I, in *University of Toronto Quarterly*, vol. 54, no. 1 (1984) and is reprinted here with permission of University of Toronto Press; a part of Chapter III ("A Child Possessed: *Eigensinn* as Hesse's Identity Theme") in *The Germanic Review*, vol. 56, no. 3 (1981), 111–118 (published by Heldref Publications, 4000 Albermarle St., N.W., Washington, D.C. 20016) and is reprinted here with permission of the Helen Dwight Educational Foundation; a part of Chapter IX ("*The Journey to the East*: Autobiography à Clef and Symbolic Prolegomenon to *The Glass Bead Game*") in *Monatshefte* 79, no. 4 (1987), copyright by the Board of Regents of the University of Wisconsin System and is reprinted here with permission of University of Wisconsin Press.

Excerpts of Hesse's poetry from the German text (translated by me) are reprinted with the kind permission of Suhrkamp Verlag, Frankfurt am Main. The poetry excerpt from *Siddhartha* (copyright 1951 by

New Directions Publishing Corp.) is reprinted by permission of New Directions.

These acknowledgments would be incomplete without my thanking the friendly and helpful editorial staff of Princeton University Press, especially Robert Brown for his encouragement of and patience with this project, and Charles Ault for his eagle-eyed and judicious copyediting of my manuscript.

ABBREVIATIONS

AB   Hermann Hesse. *Ausgewählte Briefe*. Ed. Hermann and Ninon Hesse. 2nd ed. 1964; rpt. Frankfurt: Suhrkamp Verlag, 1967.

AS   Hermann Hesse. *Eigensinn: Autobiographische Schriften*. Ed. Siegfried Unseld. Frankfurt: Suhrkamp Verlag, 1972.

AW   Hermann Hesse. *Autobiographical Writings*. Ed. Theodore Ziolkowski. Trans. Denver Lindley. New York: Farrar, Straus and Giroux, 1973.

Ball   Hugo Ball. *Hermann Hesse: Sein Leben und sein Werk*. 1927; rpt. Frankfurt: Suhrkamp Verlag, 1972.

Boulby   Mark Boulby. *Hermann Hesse: His Mind and Art*. Ithaca: Cornell University Press, 1967.

Field   George Wallis Field. *Hermann Hesse*. New York: Twayne Publishers, 1970.

Freedman   Ralph Freedman. *Hermann Hesse*: *Pilgrim of Crisis, A Biography*. New York: Pantheon Books, 1978.

GB I   *Hermann Hesse: Gesammelte Briefe, Erster Band 1895–1921*. Ed. Ursula and Volker Michels. Frankfurt: Suhrkamp Verlag, 1973.

GB II   *Hermann Hesse: Gesammelte Briefe, Zweiter Band 1922–1935*. Ed. Ursula and Volker Michels. Frankfurt: Suhrkamp Verlag, 1979.

GW (vols. 1–12)   *Hermann Hesse: Gesammelte Werke.* Werkausgabe
                  edition, 12 vols. Frankfurt: Suhrkamp Verlag, 1970.
MB   Hermann Hesse. *My Belief: Essays on Life and Art.*
                  Ed. Theodore Ziolkowski. Trans. Denver Lindley
                  and Ralph Manheim. New York: Farrar, Straus and
                  Giroux, 1974.
Mileck   Joseph Mileck. *Hermann Hesse: Life and Art.* Berke-
                  ley: University of California Press, 1978.
Unseld   Siegfried Unseld. *Hermann Hesse: Eine Werkge-
                  schichte.* Frankfurt: Suhrkamp Verlag, 1973.
Ziolkowski   Theodore Ziolkowski. *The Novels of Hermann Hesse:
                  A Study in Theme and Structure.* Princeton: Princeton
                  University Press, 1965.

HERMANN HESSE'S
FICTIONS OF THE SELF

CHAPTER I

THE CONFESSIONAL

IMAGINATION

Confession and the lie are one and the same. In order to be able to confess, one tells lies.—Franz Kafka

The German critic Friedrich Schlegel signaled towards the close of the eighteenth century the subjective character of much Romantic literature with the observation that "the modern poet must create all things from within himself . . . each poet separately and each work from its very beginning, like a creation out of nothing." Yet the Romantic work is not necessarily a production *ex nihilo*; unlike "ancient poetry" it is "based entirely on a historical foundation," for it has "a true story at its source, even if variously reshaped."[1] Much Romantic and post-Romantic literature aims for a definition of the self in historical terms, as a process of becoming.[2] This process has been enacted in literary form since the Romantics through autobiography as well as fiction, with confessional fiction forming a prominent and problematic middle term. Modern autobiography first found its self-referential voice in the self-serving *Confessions* of Rousseau (1782–1789), and the self-advertising adventures of the letter "I" have held a center-stage position in much writing since 1800. Indeed, what Schlegel observed about the relationship between writers of fiction and their works seems to hold substantially true nearly two hundred years later: "What is best in the best novels is nothing but a more or less veiled confession of the author."[3]

With the rise of Romanticism in the late eighteenth century, the drive to literary confession was able to find an outlet through a variety of established forms that it could make over or adapt to meet its formal and psychological requirements. In each case a distinctive new type or subspecies was likely to emerge. As Roy Pascal has concluded, the great age of autobiography is the late eighteenth century and the early nineteenth: the "search for the true self" is the new element in Rousseau's *Confessions*; in Goethe's *Poetry and Truth* it is the sense that being *is* becoming.[4] For Karl Weintraub, "the full convergence of all the factors constituting this modern view of the self occurred only at the end of the eighteenth century," as manifest in Goethe's autobiography.[5] The *Bildungsroman* and the *Künstlerroman* are closely allied forms that represent Romantic refashionings of the novel and whose modern prototypes are to be found in Goethe's *Wilhelm Meister* volumes and *The Sufferings of Young Werther*, respectively. Jerome Buckley has underscored the fact that the *Bildungsroman* draws extensively on autobiographical material turned into fiction, as the examples of Joyce's *Portrait of the Artist as a Young Man* or Lawrence's *Sons and Lovers*—amalgams of the education and the artist novel—will attest.[6]

And in poetry, the Romantic turn to the lyric allowed for an intense overflowing of powerful feelings, evident in the prolific lyrical production of the early Goethe and Wordsworth. The long poem in the Romantic age and beyond came readily to serve as a vehicle for the direct or veiled self-exploration of inward-gazing writers, as can be seen in such otherwise different works as Byron's *Childe Harold's Pilgrimage*, Shelley's *Alastor*, Wordsworth's *Prelude*, Novalis's *Hymns to Night*, Rimbaud's *Drunken Boat*—all of them highly subjective ventures of the confessional imagination. Then, too, the essay, or essayistic prose—not to mention the letter, diary, and journal—could easily be put to the uses of a new-found inwardness, as in France in Rousseau's *Reveries of a Solitary Walker* and in England in the form of the familiar or personal essay of leading men of letters like De Quincey, Hazlitt, and Lamb. Last and probably least successfully, Romantic drama could take upon itself the burden of disguised autobiography, as is apparent in different ways in Goethe's *Faust*, Byron's *Manfred*, and Shelley's *Prometheus Unbound*, mythic cosmodramas that soar beyond the limitations of the stage and in which the extended dramatic monologues tend to become the focal point of the author's fictionalized self-regard.

What these different genres that I have passed in such brief review have in common is of course the confessional impulse, and the reflection of the writer in his work that is a fundamental feature of Romantic literature. Ironically, the "confession" is frequently a fictional device, as it is, in varying degrees, in Goethe's *Werther*, Chateaubriand's *René*, Hogg's *Private Memoirs and Confessions of a Justified Sinner*. From the Romantic age down to the present, confession is not only a vigorous psychological impulse that informs many important works, from Rousseau's and Gibbon's autobiographies to probably even such an ostensibly scientific treatise as Freud's *The Interpretation of Dreams*; it is also a fairly consistent literary technique employed by canny fiction writers to achieve authenticity in the depiction of characters, and vividness and immediacy in the fabrication of scene and situation. A mode of first-person narrative, confession is a sophisticated strategy that can make for a highly effective—and affective—bond, or even identification, between audience and character, by diminishing or collapsing the fictive gap between them, so that life and art, the reader's and the speaker's experience, appear to be aligned on the same plane. In some respects it matters very little whether the confessional voice can be equated with an actual historical personage, such as the "I" of Rousseau's *Confessions* or Wordsworth's *Prelude*, or whether we are presented with the formal pretext of autobiography (as in *Jane Eyre*, subtitled *An Autobiography*), or with an imaginary confessor of one sort or another. The last is a rich first-person mine in the prose fiction of the last two hundred years, one that has produced such different works as Blicher's *Journal of a Parish Clerk*, Gogol's *Diary of a Madman*, Mary Shelley's *Frankenstein*, Dickens's *Great Expectations*, Constant's *Adolphe*, Dostoevsky's *Notes from Underground*, Twain's *Huckleberry Finn*, Camus's *The Stranger*, Salinger's *The Catcher in the Rye*, Plath's *The Bell Jar*, not to mention such a recent hybrid of poetry and truth as Styron's *Confessions of Nat Turner*, which incorporates some of the historical records into the narrative. Ironically, fictitious confessions—which always purport to be "true confessions"—can be even more vivid and convincing than the veritable and verifiable sort: so art triumphs over life.

The title of Goethe's autobiography, *From My Life: Poetry and Truth* (1811–1833), harbors an issue that modern readers have sometimes preferred to approach in disjunctive terms: poetry *or* truth. Is the genre a mode of historiography, and is the story of a person's life as written by himself to be evaluated as a kind of first-person biography? Should what I am calling actual confessions be judged by or held accountable to strict standards of truthfulness? If so, then many of the famous autobiographies come off as flawed performances, displaying such lapses as prevarication, omission, distortion, self-aggrandizement, and general plea bargaining with posterity. Jean Guéhenno concludes that Rousseau may have always been sincere, but he certainly wasn't always telling the truth about himself.[7] Wordsworth in the books of *The Prelude* dealing with his stay in France mentions neither his romantic liaison with Annette Vallon nor the illegitimate daughter who was its result; Goethe fails consistently to explain why a number of his youthful affairs of the heart were so abortive. Clearly these works fall short of the rigorous standards of modern history writing or biography. But—so goes the other side of the argument—the fault lies not in the works but in the misplaced expectations of the reader-critic, for autobiography is not principally or only historiography, but a literary art like poetry and fiction.

Many of the leading twentieth-century considerations of autobiography as a genre have emphasized or allowed for the play of the confessional imagination in organizing the life-story presented into a coherent literary structure. Thus the first and greatest scholar of the history of autobiography, Georg Misch, argues in his discussion of Rousseau that "an autobiography which is a great and enduring work of art cannot at bottom be untrue," even though its truth is subject to the principles of a recreative process, according to which "the contents of consciousness are not reproduced mechanically, but re-experienced, reshaped according to conditions of the present state of mind." This reconstitutive agency is Rousseau's "Phantasie" (fantasy/imagination)—a hypothesis that also permits Misch to conceive of *The Confessions* as "the highest stage which the *Bildungsroman* has attained in Rousseau." Misch locates the agency of the autobiographer's imagination in the moment of writing, because such an artful shaping of lived experience "can only express the author's present understanding of life."[8] The view of autobiography as an imaginative reconstruction of the past accepts as legitimate the incorporation of insights occurring at the moment of writing, which retroactively alter the significance of previously recounted experience.

A number of later students of autobiography follow Misch's lead here. In what is still the best short treatment of the problems inherent in the autobiographical venture, Georges Gusdorf stresses that it is a second reading or recomposition of experience, that the dilemma of lived versus remembered experience renders objectivity impossible, and that the true significance of the genre is to be sought "beyond the true and the false," because autobiography is not only "testimony," but also "a work of art." Hence Gusdorf's cachet for autobiography is "making, and in making, making oneself" ("faire et en faisant se faire").[9] While not willing to embrace the autotelic view of Gusdorf, Pascal also asserts that the autobiographer is engaged in a coherent shaping of the past, interpreting it from the standpoint of the present. To Pascal, such shaping means a necessary distortion of experience, since "the completed fact is substituted for the 'fact-in-the-making.' "[10]

These critics make allowance for the writer's imagination in shaping the life-story, and grant autobiography the standing of a literary art, but they do not wish to identify it directly with fiction, or evaluate it according to purely aesthetic criteria, a procedure by which, as Pascal believes, autobiography necessarily falls short of the accomplishments of fiction.[11] More recent discussants, however, take more unequivocal positions, from Alfred Kazin (himself an autobiographer), who in an essay of 1964 seems to endorse autobiographical narrative as fiction, to John Sturrock, who deplores the "formal subordination of autobiography" to the exigencies of history-writing and biography, and who suggests instead that "it would do autobiography . . . a power of good to recognize how close it stands to fiction."[12] Not surprisingly, the impact of structuralist and post-structuralist criticism has carried over into the discussion of autobiography, in order to define, delimit, or deconstruct the subjective contexts of the first-person pronoun in the linguistic functioning of autobiographical texts. Philippe Lejeune's is the most interesting recent work, with its goal to extrapolate the culture and language terms of "the autobiographical pact" and its premise that "the deep subject of autobiography is the proper name."[13] Probably the chief danger of the post-structuralist ventures is that—with a language that is willfully opaque and jargon-ridden—they can problematize the genre to a vanishing point.[14]

As should be apparent from this selective survey, the basic terms of the modern debate about autobiography are implicit in Goethe's *From*

My Life: Poetry and Truth. The title is compactly ambiguous, for it refers simultaneously to the chief concerns of Goethe's life and to the
manner in which he chooses to present them. His larger purpose, as
he explains in a famous passage in Book 7 (1812), is to ground his
literary productions, all of which are confessional in character, back
into the overall context of his life: "all that has become known by me
consists only of fragments of a greater confession, which to render
complete this little book is a bold attempt."[15] To Goethe, the twin
poles of his life are not firm opposites, but provisional oppositions
involved in a dialectical interplay. Here we have an acceptable model
of the manifold possibilities of autobiography as a literary genre, one
elastic enough to allow for the artful merger of experiential fact with
the devices of fiction. Autobiographical composition is imaginative
recomposition according to principles that shape the biographical
matrix into a product that may, under the auspices of the literary
imagination, sometimes play with the biographical *données*, so long
as it preserves—or at its most revealing draws out into the open for
the first time—the inner form and teleology of that life as it emerges
in the aesthetic-psychological dimension of recollective recomposition. Nor is there any reason, as Sturrock has suggested, why the
literary form of a life should be articulated chronologically, as opposed to modally or thematically[16]—for example, De Quincey on the
pains and pleasures of opium. Indeed, if one thinks about it, the literary possibilities for the nonlinear writing of one's life must be myriad. And so are, it should be added, the possibilities of the reader's
reception of that life, which should not be subjected to a single or
simplistic formula.

If the critics' approach should be a flexible one, the generic paradigm of autobiography should nevertheless include some limits and
conditions, for despite its retrospective merging of poetry and truth
there is still a fundamental sense in which the genre cannot be
wholly self-sustaining or autonomous in the way that forms like tragedy, romance, or the epic can. Whereas these may be considerably
clarified by historical and biographical "frames," autobiography in
some respects and at some point has to be considered in relation to
the writer's biography. In the case of the other forms, our ordinary
human curiosity hankers for some information about the author's life
and times, and nearly all criticism has traditionally supplied some of

this, no matter how cursorily. Yet in the case of these modes of imaginative writing, the historical-biographical background is not a sine qua non to our appreciation of the literary foreground of particular works—otherwise "great books" would be a critical fiction. But with actual autobiographies—as opposed to confessional novels, or fictions employing "autobiography" as a formal device—there must be not only the "autobiographical pact" of Lejeune but also some warrant that the life presented is substantially aligned with the author's, or that the text and the *vita* have an inherent similarity, or are at least homologous. Here autobiography demands biography. The former cannot be wholly sundered from the latter, for the text of a life depends to some degree on an extratextual sanction: the author's life. Such a guarantee is not required by the other genres instanced above, although it is possible to cite particular subtypes that call for certain kinds of alignment between life and art—for example, the historical novel and realist-naturalist fiction depend on a credible fit of character and situation with the societies, classes, and periods of history in which they are set. The famous "willing suspension of disbelief" does not cover obvious *mésalliances*, for in reading autobiographers our will to believe is seriously compromised as soon as we sense a glaring discrepancy between the text and the life it purports to present.

These conditions do not counteract what I have described as the complementarity of poetry and truth in autobiography, at least for those who are not too literal-minded readers of the genre and who do not insist on narrow or too-strict standards of autobiographical truth and verifiable correspondence. The requirement of a homological relationship between the author's biography and autobiography does not abridge the freedom inherent in the paradigm of poetry *and* truth, but guarantees the conditions for the success of autobiography, for it honors both the historic and the aesthetic dimension of this hybrid genre. Nor does this proviso ignore how subjective and selective a filter memory can be, and to what extent truth is a matter of perspective. The impossibility of a truly "objective" self-description by no means constitutes an impairment or suspension of the homological requirement, but makes for the creative challenges and problem solving inherent in the autobiographical enterprise, which allows for a good deal of play and flexibility of subjective self-rendering.

The homology between the life lived and the life written is vitiated if the autobiographer sets out with the intention, or succumbs to the (conscious or unconscious) temptation, to misrepresent himself and his life at some fundamental level, and does so in a pervasive manner. At this point autobiography, when considered vis-à-vis the writer's life, becomes what we might (punningly) call "alterbiography." What else it becomes depends upon individual instances, which could range from crude and blatant self-misrepresentation, for whatever reasons—Hitler's *Mein Kampf* may be the most glaring twentieth-century example—to an interesting piece of fiction or fantasy. And the line between autobiography and alterbiography will never be easy to draw, especially as regards boundary or liminal cases, the classic instance of which is surely Rousseau. Nor can the determination be based on too narrow grounds, centering on an evidential debate about particular facts or sections of a book, which could lead to nothing but quibbles and caveats. To demonstrate, for instance, that Rousseau's idyllic Charmettes interlude with Madame de Warens (Book 6) is more fiction than fact is not sufficient to disqualify the *Confessions* as autobiography. The judgment has to be a holistic one, a value judgment arrived at on the basis of responding to the whole work, and with the reader's intuition playing at least as much a part as an analysis or checking of particular instances and episodes. Arriving at such a holistic judgment can involve extratextual and intratextual considerations, or a combination of both. The author's biography can be compared with his autobiography to help make a determination as to whether the homological requirement has been met. And the reader can also ask whether the life-story offered is internally consistent with itself and whether it is credible when viewed against the grain of the manner of its presentation. This is not to imply that we should discredit an autobiography because it seems extraordinary and beyond the pale of anything we have experienced, but rather that we become aware of recurrent signs within the text that point to a pervasive inconsistency between lived and recounted experience. I am not speaking here of the gaps and contradictions inherent in actual living, nor of the necessary distortions of memory and that wide gulf between what Wordsworth calls "the two consciousnesses"

(*Prelude* 2, l. 32, 1805 text)—how we perceived an event *then* as opposed to *now*—but to evidence within the text that points to a thorough falsification of experience, to a will to prevaricate.

Any such discrepancies or inconsistencies that begin to accumulate are fatal to the autobiographical enterprise, because they constitute a breach of trust on the part of the author, a confidence that must be maintained at all costs and that is a primary condition of successful autobiography. The maintenance of this trust is probably essential to any first-person narrative that takes the form of confession. As soon as we have a consistently unreliable narrator, the necessary bond of confidence between the reader and narrator is sundered. In autobiography and confessional fiction, an unreliable narrator can succeed in preserving the premises on which the success of the form is posited only by acknowledging and passing judgment upon his or her unreliability, as is the case in Pip's retrospective confession in *Great Expectations*.

Ironically, Rousseau strives for exactly this sort of confessional self-judgment when he chronicles his various betrayals of himself and others, but his efforts aren't convincing. As apparent in probably his most shameful admission, the false accusation against the servant girl Marion (Book 2), his eloquent avowals of his youthful misconduct always lighten his guilt as much as possible with extenuating circumstances, and usually show more pity for himself than sympathy for his victims. These intimate professions of perfidious acts are meant to convince us of his absolute sincerity, which, as he asseverated in the (canceled) Neuchatel introduction, is the psychological center of his work. And as he explains in Book 7, the test of his sincerity is not his factual accuracy but the authenticity of his feelings: "I may have omitted or transposed facts, or made errors in dates, but I cannot go wrong about what I have felt, nor about that which my feelings have led me to do; and this is what I am principally concerned with."[17] But it is not so much Rousseau's mistaking of fact and chronology that is troubling, nor even his regular penchant for romanticizing his experience, but the conviction that grows on the reader at *some* point that for Jean-Jacques apology or self-vindication coincides with self-deception, in an attempted hoodwinking of himself and his audience. The constant stress on his "sincerity" sounds exaggerated and thus invites suspicion (a defense mechanism?), and his owning-up to a variety of misdeeds, while it may relieve his guilty conscience, does so only at the expense of further self-delusion, which brings on more unconscious guilt, which will have to be purged by further self-serving confession—and so on, in a protracted progress or regress to the prison-house of the paranoid self that Rousseau increasingly inhabits in the later sections of his *Confessions*.

In sum, Rousseau's autobiography reads like alterbiography because the posited homology between the lived life and the recorded version appears to be lacking. His compulsive and successful desire to let himself be taken in by himself operates on a scale so gigantic that in the end it compels a kind of wonder and admiration. To be sure, one could simply say that Rousseau's is the autobiography of a self-deluded man that in spite of its author tells the deeper truth about him—in D. H. Lawrence's well-known formula, never trust the teller, trust the tale. Yet such a protracted self-deception is a major flaw in autobiography—especially if the reader can see through it. And even if we credit the sincerity of Rousseau's professions of sincerity, we must admit the judgment of Guéhenno, that "to be sincere is not enough," for "this man who spoke so much about himself didn't know himself or knew himself poorly."[18] Granted that Rousseau's was a highly complex personality containing a multitude of contradictions that he acknowledged and struggled to understand and that, indeed, there may have been different Rousseaus (as evident even in the title *Rousseau juge de Jean-Jacques*), yet in Guéhenno's characterization of Rousseau we have an account of what, through the analogy of dramatic irony, we might call "confessional irony": it comes into the picture when we begin to feel that in some respects we may understand the confessor better than he understands himself. This situation may be flattering to the reader's self-esteem, but it is not salutary to the purposes of autobiography. Perhaps a measure of confessional irony is inherent in the genre—in the wake of psychoanalysis, such a sense of reader superiority is hard to avoid— and constitutes a problem area for all autobiographers. After all, even that prodigy of the analytic intellect, Freud, when chronicling his own dreams fails signally at times to pursue precisely the sort of interpretation one would expect of a "Freudian."[19] Whenever our reading of a writer's self-reading turns up a real blind spot, the result is a degree of confessional irony.

It is not because Rousseau transposes or distorts facts and episodes that *The Confessions* adds up to something less or more than genuine autobiography. Even his extreme waffling under the promptings of idyll and daydream (whose notes are struck right at the beginning in the account of his family background) is still within the limits of literary autobiography as poetry *and* truth. That model can accommodate even such serious omissions as Henry Adams's silence about the suicide of his wife or Wordsworth's about his French love affair. It allows for the literary stylization of experience, as in Rousseau's fancy of Charmettes or in Goethe's depiction of his wooing of Friederike Brion in hues borrowed from *The Vicar of Wakefield*. It even admits the transposition of episodes or sequences for the sake of a greater unity of design and coherence of form, as in *The Prelude*'s chronological inversion of the Crossing of the Alps and Mount Snowdon "spots of time." But what is beyond the boundaries of autobiography is the whole tenor of *The Confessions* toward a graphic self-misrepresentation, a "sincere" desire to save face by presenting posterity with a fiction of the "correct" or corrected version of himself. Judged either through intratextual or extratextual evidence, it strikes us as a false face: Rousseau erases his true self as he writes about his life, of which his text is too revisionist a reading. Hence his *Confessions* are autobiography crossing over into confessional fiction. Part 1 deserves to be read as a Romantic *Bildungsroman*, a fact that suggests the paradox that failed autobiography can become first-rate fiction—something implicit in Schlegel's observation that "the *Confessions* of Rousseau is in my opinion a most excellent novel, *Heloise* only a very mediocre one."[20]

It poses no problems to draw viable boundary lines between history, biography, and autobiography, but what is the difference—a vexing issue implicit in my comments on Rousseau—between autobiography and fiction? The two have a long-standing affiliation; Misch traces their "permanent connection" back to the sixteenth-century Spanish picaresque novel, and critics have frequently acknowledged the difficulty, in the words of Buckley, of drawing "a sharp line between autobiography and the autobiographical novel."[21] Lejeune deals with "the problems of the difference between the autobio-

graphical novel and autobiography" with his postulate of "the autobiographical pact" ("le pacte autobiographique"): the author's name
on the title page is "the only mark in the text of something indubita-
bly outside the text, referring back to a real person." And in his article on "Autobiography in the Third Person," he observes that the
two "have always developed by a series of reciprocal grafts and exchanges" and points to "fictive fictions," which add another point of
view to the autobiography "by creating a character in a novel" in
order to convey to the reader the idea "the autobiographer has of
someone else's idea of him." His closing question poses the dilemma,
"how do we distinguish between an autobiography employing fictive
fictions and an autobiographical novel?"[22]

As the examples of Goethe, Rousseau, Henry Adams, Twain,
Gide, Sartre, and Nabokov—among others—show, various authors
have, with varying degrees of success, written both autobiography
and fiction. Working in one genre does not preclude working in the
other, although the self-reflexive impulse in our century has found
expression primarily through confessional fiction, and not through
autobiography: Proust, Joyce, Hesse, D. H. Lawrence, Hemingway,
and Bellow are important figures associated with confessional novels
who never wrote an autobiography proper. The practice of the latter
seems to decline around the mid-nineteenth century, just when the
confessional novel begins to flourish in a major way. And in the
twentieth century, next to the daring innovations of the modernist
novel, it appears to be a largely secondary genre. It may be possible
to explain this lopsided situation by considering the question of what
the respective literary and psychological needs are that autobiography and confessional fiction satisfy.

Up to a point these are similar. Since the late eighteenth century,
both forms have answered to a more fluid sense of the self, and have
dramatized a search for that self as an experiential process of becoming. Then, too, the therapeutic function of confession has been a
prominent one, whether to purge a sense of guilt, to vindicate one's
rightness by way of defense or apology, or even to settle some old
scores and get even, as in contemporary bestsellers like Plath's *The
Bell Jar* or French's *The Women's Room*, where confession becomes the
writer's revenge on life or at least on the male gender. Ideally, both
forms transcend self-exploration to attain some type of self-transfor-

mation. Montaigne's celebrated apothegm, "I have no more made my book than my book has made me,"[23] captures the dialectic of such literary self-making. The signified self is changed in the process of signification; confessions are Janus-faced, beholding the past and the future, recreative as well as procreative. The retrospective and proleptic axes intersect in the moment of composition, which may be extrapolated as a moment of self-grasping in the three dimensions of time, but which in actual temporal terms is an extended series of moments ranging from weeks (*Werther*) to years (*Poetry and Truth*).

As for the reception of modern confessional literature, there has been on the one hand a fairly unsophisticated audience-speaker identification (which the mass market exploits), and on the other hand a traditional critical bias against autobiography and confession as being inferior to works of "pure" fiction. Particularly for the Anglo-American modernists, who reacted against what they perceived as the Romantics' overbearing self-expression, the confessional was liable to be downgraded to the level of a literary contaminant. If, as in T. S. Eliot's classic formulation of the "Impersonal theory," poetry is "an escape from personality," then the poet and the person in the same author are in effect split off into different psychic compartments.[24] That pure works of fiction may be a pure fiction is an idea that has gained ground as the formalist stress on impersonality has abated, what with the outpouring, in the postmodern sixties and seventies, of a large quantity of confessional literature. As Alfred Kazin has wryly observed, the lure of "autobiography of one kind or another" in contemporary American writing "has become all too fashionable," and there would not be "so much confessional poetry and fiction" around "if there were not so many readers who seem to read no poetry and prose that is not confessional."[25]

Both autobiography and confessional fiction serve what Buckley has called "the general uses of subjectivity" in "Romantic and modern culture,"[26] and do so under the guise of telling "the whole truth." But the manner in which these truths of the subjective self are presented, and the literary-psychological needs that their expression serves, begin to diverge in autobiography and confessional fiction. The first and most obvious difference here is that confessional fiction allows the writer to use the autobiographical matrix, only to range beyond it at will. Freed from the homological requirement, he can give full rein to the play of the literary imagination in appropriating and transforming elements of his own experience, and in blending these with invented material. The audience of fictional confession, too, is relieved of the burden of considering the veracity of the book when examined in the light of its author's life, so that it is able to let its imagination enter more fully into the story *as* story. Pascal has noted that readers of autobiography tend to take a judgmental stand outside the work, whereas readers of autobiographical novels are more apt to identify with its heroes, and participate in a "dream-alliance" with them. This gain of the fiction writer brings an added responsibility, as both Buckley and Pascal observe, because the novel demands a more firm and coherent narrative structure: fictional narrative must be able to stand on its own, as opposed to being propped up by an extratextual *vita*.[27]

A second difference is that confessional fiction is often an exploration, in one way or another, of what might be called, to quote Robert Frost, "the road not taken." If autobiography is the retrospective chronicle and interpretation of the road already traveled, confessional fiction can luxuriate in what might have been, what might yet be. Somerset Maugham's comment on his procedure in *Of Human Bondage*—"turning my wishes into fiction, as writers will"—might stand as a slogan for confessional fiction, where "fact and fiction are inextricably mingled."[28] It is the literary equivalent of wishing and willing, of imaginative self-projection; its significance is to be found as much in the promptings of pleasure as in the sober restraints of daily life. A literary version of private fantasies made public, it can range from trivial indulgence in Walter Mitty-type daydreams (Thurber's antihero, the henpecked husband, escapes his drab world and timid self through Hollywood-style fantasies in which he single-handedly performs heroic exploits) to the most ineffable yearnings of the human spirit, like those figured in the quest of Novalis's Heinrich von Ofterdingen for the fabulous "blue flower." As a means of psychic compensation for the shortcomings of life, confessional fiction can express itself as mere sentimental escapism, like Emma Bovary's amorous reveries, or as a mode of self-healing through the active exercise of the imagination. Nor is it any accident that the erotic aspect has loomed so large in confessional writing, from Saint Augustine's avowals of youthful lust and Rousseau's romances of the road to Henry Miller in Paris (*Tropic of Cancer*) and Hesse's Harry Haller in the "all girls are yours" fantasia of *Steppenwolf*'s Magic Theater, to the titillating and often pornographic "true confessions" that have become a staple of magazine fiction—for the presiding deity of the confessional imagination, of the self fantasized, is none other than Eros in all his myriad guises.

If everyone were to be held accountable for his innermost wishes and fantasies, none of us, in Hamlet's phrase, could escape whipping. Thus the freedom of the writer of confessional fiction includes that of being able to own up to deeds and desires under the cover of some other name or voice. The manifold contents of the author's consciousness can be represented without his being held responsible for them. He insulates himself from his wishes even as he expresses them in fictional form; this allows him, as the saying goes, to have his cake and eat it too. Here the concept of "confession" can probably be expanded to describe important areas of the relationship, in post-Enlightenment literature, between a writer and his major character(s): Flaubert is and is not Madame Bovary;[29] Paul Morel, Birkin, and Mellors are and are not Lawrence; Raskolnikov is and is not Dostoevsky; Marlow is and is not Conrad; and so on. Since the self of any major writer is likely to be too multifaceted and contradictory ever to be adequately rendered through a single character, the relationship of the author to his confessional persona(s) can obviously never be that of a one-to-one correspondence. As the instances above should suggest, there are degrees of distance and proximity, and levels of ironic detachment and sympathetic attachment. The relationship might be described as the paradoxical one of identity *and* difference, which simply means that the text gives us a version of the writer's larger identity. For that reason the wide spectrum of potential fictional self-incarnations in a confessional persona is more likely to appeal to the artist per se, as opposed to autobiographers, a motley tribe who write for any number of reasons that have nothing whatever to do with the artistic will to form, and who are often motivated (from Saint Augustine to Malcolm X) by a basic ideological drive. Conversely, if confessional fiction as a type of sophisticated playing with elements of the writer's psyche appeals to the creative temperament, when that temperament turns to present itself directly through autobiography, as does Rousseau, it is prone to fall into the temptation of self-fictionalization. One ingenious way to capitalize on this dilemma is that of the German Romantic ironist, Jean Paul Richter, who wrote what he called a "conjectural biography" of his life.[30]

Confessional fiction appeals to the modern writer because it encourages an aesthetic and psychological game-playing with fragments of the self, self-exposure as well as self-masking. Nietzsche's assumption that deep truths are in need of the mask also holds true for the confessional imagination. An artist may not only express himself in his work; he may also hide behind it, or disappear into it. He may become another, or many others, in order to get a better purchase on himself, and to capture the existential sense (to borrow Kierkegaard's title) of "stages on life's way." We must remember that the great autobiographies were not written principally as works of art: Augustine recorded his errant life to celebrate his conversion to God; Goethe wrote his to give its truth a poetic treatment; surely not even Rousseau set out with the purpose of writing autobiography as fiction. But modern confessional fiction differs from these in that it actively seeks out the element of play and playacting. The novelistic aspect takes over, not in spite of itself, but for its own sake.

While I am not sure about the frequent claim that the autobiographer cannot create a perspective in his work that is genuinely different from his own—Pascal has an even stricter formula: he "can neither get inside other people nor outside himself,"[31]—the writer of confessional fiction certainly can. The play element inherent in the form seems positively to encourage such a creation of multiple perspectives. For instance, the novelist may split himself into two or more characters with significantly different outlooks, as with Raskolnikov and Svidrigaylov in *Crime and Punishment*. As Peter Axthelm has pointed out, the use of the double is a characteristic technique of confessional fiction;[32] this is as true of minor or secondary doubles, like Heinrich the mad flower-picker in *Werther*, as of those who are more fully implicated in the fate of the protagonist, like Joan Gilling vis-à-vis Esther Greenwood in *The Bell Jar*, or those who begin to approximate one another in relative importance, like many of the striking binary character pairings in Hesse's fiction. But beyond this division of the author's self into two or more characters, which is still arguably a reflection of his situation, confessional novelists have succeeded in projecting characters and viewpoints that are radically opposed to their own view of things. An excellent example is *Sons and Lovers*, where Lawrence's third-person narrative is modulated largely through Paul Morel's perceptions, but which nevertheless allows the points of view of other characters to contradict, modify, or complement Paul's limited outlook and values—Clara, Miriam, Mr. and Mrs. Morel, even Baxter Dawes. Lawrence's imaginative sympathy allows each of these a distinct perspective of his or her own which may clash with that of his spokesman, Paul, as well as with that of other characters. That this "subjective" mode of writing can seek out a more objective and inclusive sense of individual reality is part of its therapeutic character, as a limited self reaches out to a fuller, healthier, more informed one. In the *Bildungsroman*, of course, this is the burden of *Bildung* (education). An excellent example of the experimental elaboration of a more objective perspective for the purpose of self-growth is the fiction-within-a-fiction of the Steppenwolf Treatise in Hesse's novel, which discusses the suicidal dilemma of Harry Haller with ironic detachment.

The creation of any confessional persona or point of view is an imaginative act of entering one's self by stepping outside of it, which already involves a necessary self-detachment, no matter how subjective the "reflector" may appear to be. This is true even of extreme instances, such as young Werther, or his distant American cousin, Holden Caulfield, whose insistent first-person claims are still countered by secondary revisions of outlook encoded in the text. Albert, Lotte, and the Editor serve as counter-perspectives to Werther's emotionalism; for Holden, the humorous-hilarious tenor of the novel serves as a necessary corrective to his singularity of perception, as do his continual self-contradictions (attacking "phonies" and "actors," while constantly implicated in such behavior himself) and characters like his former English teacher, Mr. Antolini, and his younger sister, Phoebe. In fictions where the author seeks to question the claims of his confessional persona, the introduction of secondary character perspectives can be devastating, as evident in Dostoevsky's Underground Man's encounter with the young prostitute, or, at the conclusion of Chateaubriand's *René*, the priest's severe reprimand to René's self-pitying confession: "Nothing . . . in this story merits the pity which has been extended to you here. I see a young man infatuated with idle fancies, whom everything displeases, and who has withdrawn himself from the demands of society to give himself up to use-less reveries."[33]

There are still other differences between autobiography and confessional fiction: one of these is that the former usually attempts to organize retrospectively the whole configuration of a life from the perspective of the moment of writing, whereas the latter typically aims at the representation of a temporal slice of life, which may range from several days or weeks to a number of years or decades. A re-lated distinction, as Buckley has observed, is that "the autobiogra-pher is typically the older man . . . indulging in fond retrospect . . . the autobiographical novelist is usually the younger man,"[34] whose fund of experience is more limited, and whose identity is more ten-tative and undefined—a fact that would make fictional self-portrai-ture a much more attractive alternative. The last point does not ex-plain the preponderance, noted earlier, of confessional fiction over literary autobiography in the later nineteenth and the twentieth cen-turies. This is where another significant difference between the two forms comes into play. Although both are manifestations of the sub-jective tradition that has predominated since the eighteenth century and are based on a view of the person as a process of becoming, confessional fiction has emerged as the preferred mode because of a changed relationship to this developmental model. Those great Ro-mantic self-chroniclers, Rousseau, Goethe, and Wordsworth, could still try to encompass the whole life-cycle within the bounds of a sin-gle work. They might not succeed in such a grandiose scheme—for different reasons, Goethe and Wordsworth give us only about a third of their lives in their autobiographies—yet the ideal was that of a psy-chological and temporal grasping of the whole self. Later in the nine-teenth century such schemes to get all of the person between the covers of a book begin to be scaled down, as evident in such (still ambitious Romantic) soul-surveys as Whitman's *Song of Myself* or Thoreau's *Walden*.

In his analysis of three types of autobiography, William Howarth identifies the third, the "poetic," with the practice of the genre since Rousseau, and concludes that in post-Romantic exemplars "only the process of *becoming* is essential; if the book reveals that process, it endures, like a poem, forever."[35] If it is true that since the close of the Enlightenment literature has sought to dramatize the process of becoming, since the late eighteenth century that evolutionary sense of personality has shifted to a model of the open-ended, "existential" self. In the dynamics of this more recent view, change does not involve, as in Goethe, Wordsworth, and Rousseau, an inner teleology, an immanent purposiveness that guides us toward some as yet unfathomed goal. This more existential valuation—according to which personal identity is tentative and undefined until the supervention of death, and the self without a fixed center—is strikingly caught, for instance, in Ibsen's parable of Peer Gynt peeling the onion (in the final act), only to discover that it is all layers, and has no core. Our contemporary notion of the protoplasmic and undefinable ego, which Robert Jay Lifton has epitomized as "protean man,"[36] resists or frustrates the autobiographical will to shape the life into a whole, and to unfold retrospectively the indwelling pattern that has informed it throughout its different stages. This may help to explain why autobiography has been an impoverished medium next to confessional fiction, which does not aim to give us the Big Picture, but only an imaginative transformation of a segment or an aspect of a life, a provisional version that can be updated as the self and its settings change. Autobiographical vision inheres in a coherent revision of the whole past; the confessional novelist can present us with a series of successive recastings, incarnations of his variable self, new texts for the self's changing contexts.

A final difference between autobiography and confessional fiction—and one not easy to sort out neatly because it involves the whole problem of the relationship between life and art—is that perhaps certain truths can only be adumbrated or brought out through fiction. To pun on the title of Goethe's autobiography, perhaps the representation of *Wahrheit* (truth) requires the intervention of *Dichtung* (poetry). Certain forms of inner experience may only be conjurable in fantastic form; they need what the poet Klingsohr in his romantic *Märchen* (in Novalis's *Heinrich von Ofterdingen*) calls the handmaiden "Fable." Here the confessional imagination can make tangible through fiction that which exceeds the unmediated reach of autobiography proper. Hence, too, the relationship between poetry and truth in successful confessional fiction is more genuinely dialectical, as can be seen in Goethe's *Sufferings of Young Werther*, which unlike *Poetry and Truth* ranges freely beyond the life/art homology of autobiography. As Goethe acknowledges in his autobiography, the sufferings of young Werther are very close to those of the young storm-and-stress Goethe, including the love for Lotte, which is cut from the cloth of his experience. Yet to render these passionate and chaotic emotions coherent, he felt in need, as he tells us, of a story or "fable." It came to him from real life, ironically, through the news of the death of a young acquaintance, who had killed himself because of his frustrated passion for the wife of a friend. When Goethe heard this, including the account of the attendant circumstances, the plan for his epistolary novel jelled, and he immediately set to work.[37] He had found the fictional framework for the catharsis of confession that is *Werther*.

A major genre since the emergence of Romanticism, confessional fiction employs the "fable" element—story as symbol—to develop those inner truths that resist direct autobiographical presentation. The confessional writer may lie in order to reveal himself more truly: as a reading of Kafka's stories and novels next to his voluminous journals (both of which in a sense go over the same ground) will show, in those fabulous thought-experiments of that modernist forger of autobiographical parables the traumas of the family romance and the spiritual dilemmas of the agonized self are marvelously transfigured through a translucently precise yet ever bizarre confessional fantasy. Such exquisite symbolic self-fictionalizations can cast a spell and speak to a much larger audience than autobiography, for they can seem like echoes from our own depths, tropes of our own experience, ciphers of our own selves.[38]

In this opening chapter I have sought to ground the varied literary manifestations of the post-Enlightenment confessional imagination in the phenomenon of Romantic self-reflexivity, and to signal some important differences between the allied modes of autobiography and confessional fiction. Admittedly the latter is a problematic if not impossible task, and to those critics prone to take only the broadest and most inclusive view of autobiography, an unnecessary one. Yet without a willingness at least to entertain such difficult distinctions we run the risk of collapsing the category of Literature into that of Autobiography.[39] I believe the Goethean model I have proposed of autobiography as poetry *and* truth avoids an excessively determined or rigidly referential view of the genre as biographical-historical truth by allowing for the combination of the *données* of a life with the strategies of fiction within the limits of a homological relationship between the lived and the recorded *vita*. And as I have tried to demonstrate with the classic problem of Rousseau's *Confessions*, the judgment that the avowed project of autobiography has crossed over into alterbiography has to be a holistic one, based not on particular pieces of evidence outside or inside the text, but on an accumulating pattern of persistent prevarication on the confessor's part. With its compulsively defensive and revisionist retouching of the story of his life, Rousseau's alterbiography is really disguised confessional fiction posing as "straight" autobiography, and as such makes for a much less positive—a less flexible and more defensive—exercise in storytelling than the richly creative autobiographical fiction that has positively flourished as the most prolific version of literary subjectivity during the last two centuries or so.

While it is possible and even desirable, as I have argued, to draw some boundary lines between autobiography proper and confessional fiction, it is nevertheless true that we can also choose to view modern confessional fiction as autobiography in an extended or broader context. This view becomes more viable if we place the stress on autobiography not so much as a constitutive and final overview or product of a life, but as an ongoing process and performance of the self in and through the act of writing itself—or, to rephrase Gusdorf's cachet, *to write, and in writing, to write oneself.* The perception of autobiography as an activity rather than as an artifact (or even a genre) has been gaining support in recent criticism in the wake of Elizabeth Bruss's pioneering study of a decade ago.[40] Autobiography in this extended sense as the literary exercise of the confessional imagination allows for a wide range of self-segmentation, self-rearrangement, or both, through the creation of multiple character perspectives. While certain modern autobiographers—the preeminent instance is surely Nabokov in *Speak, Memory*—are willing to exploit their experience for the purpose of psychological and literary gamesmanship, modern confessional fiction has the advantage of being able to capitalize on the appeal of the self fantasized, for our century's open-ended or existential concept of personal identity has resisted the autobiographical will (evident in canonical texts from Augustine up to Rousseau and the Romantics) to shape the life into a whole, finding instead a fictionalized and provisional slice of life more congenial to its protean needs. The final difference I signaled between autobiography proper and confessional fiction—a distinction that now at the close of this introductory chapter I want provisionally to redefine as a *narrower* versus a *broader* view of "autobiography"—brings me back full circle to my title, because the fantastic dimension of the confessional imagination—symbol, parable, metaphor—may be a more substantial adumbration of the deeper truths of a life than can be grasped through the narrative of autobiography proper. Hence the question here is ultimately that of mimesis. What constitutes a truer or more adequate reflection of the self, the fabulous distortions of confessional fiction or the résumé of autobiography proper of the circumstances and exigencies of our actual life-experiences—poetry, truth, or some dialectical synthesis of the two?

CHAPTER II
LIFE *AS* WRITING

There was a time when the artist mobilized all his defects to pro-
duce a work which concealed *himself; the notion of exposing his*
life to the public probably never occurred to him. We do not imag-
ine Dante or Shakespeare keeping track of the trifling incidents of
their lives in order to bring them to other people's attention. Per-
haps they even preferred giving a false image of what they were.
They had that reticence of power which is no longer a property of
the deficient modern. Our confessions, our novels are all charac-
terized by the same aberration. What interest can a mere life af-
ford?—E. M. Cioran

Cioran invokes a prelapsarian art-world in which the artifact could be
kept separate from and uncontaminated by the life of the artificer.
Was there indeed ever such a world, and did Dante and Shakespeare
have the "reticence of power" to keep their lives out of their works,
or did they not, on the contrary—to paraphrase Keats's famous comment on Shakespeare—write allegories of their own experience?[1] In
any case, the plaint above about the "deficient modern" is but one
instance of a persistent refrain since the end of the eighteenth century—from the older Goethe's diagnosis of "subjectivity" as the general disease of his age,[2] to the strongly held impersonality ideals of
modernist writers earlier in our century—of what I have elsewhere
described as the literary fall into subjectivity[3] and of the writer's dependence on his experience for the materials of his work. The various
twentieth-century attempts to formulate aesthetic concepts of objectivity and detachment—persona, mask, objective correlative—are
perhaps themselves manifestations of this dilemma, for it stands to
reason that only a poet struggling in the Nessus shirt of subjectivity
should seek to extricate himself by defining poetry, in T. S. Eliot's
formulation of "the Impersonal theory," as "an escape from personality."[4]

Indeed, the grandfather of modern theories of impersonality, Flaubert, was caught up in such a struggle to get beyond himself. With the claim that "Great Art is scientific and impersonal," his influential pronouncements on *Madame Bovary* fly in the face of the Romantic penchant to subjectivize experience and to exhibit the self confessionally. Yet his objective and anatomical method in his masterpiece of realist fiction is a defense against his autobiographical proclivities: "I have always sinned in that direction myself; that's because I have always put myself into everything I have written." In the light of this avowal, Flaubert's claim about his novel does seem to protest too much: "*Madame Bovary* contains nothing of my life. It is a *completely invented* story. The illusion . . . comes, on the contrary, from the *impersonality* of the work. It is one of my principles that you must not *write yourself*. The artist ought to be in his work like God in his creation, invisible and omnipotent."⁵ In the spirit of James Olney's title we might reply that even professions of impersonality may be "metaphors of self," or, to cite the legendary comment Flaubert is also credited with, "*Madame Bovary, c'est moi.*"⁶ Shown to the front door and rudely ejected, subjectivity may steal in through the back door and take over the house of fiction under the guise of authorial detachment.

Of the leading autobiographical novelists of our century, Hermann Hesse may well be the one whose practice goes most completely against the grain of the Flaubertian and formalist ideal of aesthetic impersonality. Over the course of a long life of self-fictionalizing, from *Peter Camenzind* (1904), the novel that first won him literary acclaim and a larger audience, to *The Glass Bead Game* (1943), the clarified work of his old age that earned him the Nobel Prize, Hesse's books are a perpetual reprise of the same subject—himself—transmogrified into his leading characters. From first to last Hesse was a fabulator who *wrote himself* with single-minded zeal: his narratives are seriated self-inventions, or, to borrow Hazlitt's witticism about Rousseau, in all of his writings he never once lost sight of himself.⁷ While Hesse's critics have observed that, like Goethe, he wrote fragments of a greater confession, some have not hesitated to tag his fiction with the clinical label of narcissism. If we consider Hesse as a modern exemplar of an unrelentingly confessional and subjective fiction, then the answer to Cioran's challenge might be that the interest a mere life affords is the challenge of life lived *as* writing: the adventure of living the text of one's life-in-the-making, of fashioning one's inner experience into a personal myth or metaphor enacted in and through language. Moreover, Hesse was quite cognizant of the questionableness of writing "a mere life," and especially his own, for he carried on a vigorous and sustained critical dialogue with the problems and dilemmas posed by being a confessional writer. This ongoing dialogue caused him to reshape, sometimes radically so, his personal outlook and his literary practice as his perceptions of himself and his artistic goals and limitations became progressively clearer to him.

When in late adolescence Hesse set to work preparing himself for a literary career, his thoughts turned frequently to Goethe, for as he put it, "it is well worth studying the giant who contains everything; one learns to know the world, art, humanity, and above all, oneself." Despite his acknowledgment of the depth and breadth of Goethe's powers, the young Hesse also noted the subjective character of the giant's writings: "Goethe frequently appears to be an eagle who ascends nearly to the sun yet is unable to soar beyond himself." Because of Goethe's subjective bias, Hesse found himself searching in his life and letters for the clue to the relationship between Goethe and his characters, observing for instance that after Goethe's trip to Italy his development shows a multifaceted aspect from which his past appears in an ambiguous light.[8] Hesse's early insight into the complexity of Goethe's confessional art prefigures his own practice later, including his puzzling fictional self-transformations and the concomitant shifts of perspective on his own past. If the acolyte read in Goethe his own embryonic literary concerns, however, he was not yet able to face directly the issue and challenge of being an autobiographical writer. In fact, as he came to realize only after World War I, his popular prose narratives of the decade before the war were based on a critical failure of insight into the sources of his inspiration. At the age of eighteen he was already on the track of Goethe's confessional career, but he failed, ironically, to see its relevance for his own

subsequent literary efforts. He admitted after the war in the introduction to a never-published edition of his early writings ("A Poet's
Preface to His Selected Works," 1921) that he was shocked to discover his prewar fiction was confessional in spite of itself: he had
sincerely thought he was writing the *other* when he had in essence
been writing only *himself*. As he scrutinized his earlier works—"often
with wonder and surprise, often with shame and groans"—Hesse
found to his amazement that "all these stories were about myself,
they reflected my chosen path, my secret dreams and wishes, my
own bitter anguish! Even those books in which, when I wrote them,
I had honestly thought I was portraying alien destinies and conflicts
remote from myself, even these sang the same song . . . my own."
And if his scrutiny showed that much of his fiction was unwitting
confession that "revealed [him] most pathetically, when read with a
sharpened eye," it also showed that even in those writings conceived
in the "desire for pure confession," there were "strange . . . eva-
sions, concealments, extenuations": "No, among these books there
was not one that was not confession and a ringing desire to express
my essential being, but by the same token not one in which the
confession was complete and clean, not one in which the expression
had found its way to deliverance!"[9]

Hesse's belated recognition in his forties of the autobiographical
character of his fiction had the salutary effect of getting him to face
up to himself and consciously to accept the self-reflexive bent of his
imagination as his particular virtue and limitation. The path he
mapped out with his subsequent program of *Kunst als Bekenntnis* (art
as confession) constitutes his insight that his limitation as a writer,
his autobiographical bias, is also the essence of his talent. Beginning
with *Demian* (1919), his abrasively self-confronting books of the
1920s—most sensationally so, *Steppenwolf* (1927)—pursue this goal
under the new confessional banner of honesty and authenticity (*Aufrichtigkeit*). His commitment to a style that will reveal the unvar-
nished and "deep" truth about the self—fiction with a difference—is
also the upshot of his psychoanalytic reading (chiefly Freud and
Jung) and experience dating back to 1916, when he first went through
an extended series of sessions with a Jungian analyst. In his postwar
fiction the Socratic imperative is psychoanalytically redirected into a
multifaceted confession that seeks to avoid the double lure of senti-

mental self-evasion and Romantic prettification, but that comes "clean" in as authentic as possible a rendering of the author's inner experience. If the cumulative impact of Freud and Jung was decisive for Hesse's turn to a more conscious, probing, and sophisticated fictional reprise of his problems and struggles, the encounter with psychoanalysis (which continued through the 1920s) "did not simply produce," as Ziolkowski has put the case, "the incentive for self-analysis: it also provided Hesse with the tools of that analysis."[10]

From the closing years of World War I the direction of Hesse's fiction is the by-then well-traveled Romantic "way within" (*Weg nach Innen*),[11] but wrenchingly redirected through his cathartic encounter with psychoanalysis. Like all revolutions, in other words, what Hesse effected in his style and content in the 1920s is a striking and innovative reconstitution of previously existing elements. The "journey within," to which his fiction had only been feebly and euphemistically committed hitherto, had already been enshrined as the central creed of the German Romantic movement of the 1790s—especially in its leading poet, Novalis, who, next to Goethe, is probably the single greatest literary influence on Hesse's conception of the artist and the role of the imagination. What Hesse relished in the literary milieu of the early German Romantics (of which he was a lifelong student and admirer), was their visionary program of a fantastic psychography of the inner self, whose imaginative energies they intuited as grounded in the cosmic whole. Here Jungian depth psychology, with its twentieth-century romance of the collective unconscious and the stages of individuation (Shadow, Anima/Animus, Self) owes, like Hesse's fiction, a good deal to the mythopoeic modes of German Romanticism. Like Blake, Wordsworth, Shelley, and Keats in England, the German *Frühromantiker* (early Romantics) were engaged in a sustained effort to chart, in the forms of personal myth, the dynamics of the imagination as the mediatrix between subject and object, nature and spirit. To paraphrase Keats, they wished to build a temple to Psyche in some hitherto untrodden region of the human mind. The young Hesse had been enraptured by the subjective and spiritual dreamworld conjured by the *Frühromantiker*, a literary fellowship of kindred souls the foundation of whose "confession" of faith he summed up in 1899 as "devotion to the voice of eternity, attending to the rhythm of the inner life, being-at-home at the hidden sources of the soul."[12] Two decades later, less spiritually and tactfully, Hesse began to attend deliberately to the repressed beat of his inner life and the hidden sources of his soul. His new commitment after *Demian* to an unblinking and unblinkered confessional fiction can still be located on the same literary horizon as Keats's assertion in "To Psyche"—"I see, and sing, by my own eyes inspired"—but if Hesse, too, is Psyche's priest, his confession and the sort of self-examination it generates is now defined as much by the setting of the psychiatrist's couch as by the church's confessional.

Hesse's polemical aesthetic of the 1920s is truth at the expense of the self in order to purge and thus save that self from the deadly lie. For the first time he also owned up to the compulsion of his work, for he writes no longer in order to make a living, but simply to be able to go on living: writing has become a survival need. The radical departure from his earlier outlook and style was akin to a conversion experience, involving a right-angle turn from false to genuine confession. He knew that no matter how painful for him or shocking for his readers, the change was irreversible. As he wrote in a letter of January 5, 1920,

> After the war . . . I couldn't simply pick up again where I had left off . . . I had come to see the world in a new light and had completely reoriented my psychology due to living through these times as well as because of psychoanalysis. If I wanted to continue at all there was nothing left for me but to draw a line under my earlier things and to begin anew. What I am seeking to express now are in part things which have never been represented before.[13]

Yet despite the new impetus, materials, and techniques made available by his psychoanalytically motivated embrace of art as confession, Hesse was beset by nagging doubts, the gist of which was, Is art as confession really art? Conditioned willy-nilly by neo-Flaubertian assumptions that fiction should be objective and impersonal, Hesse even after his turn to unflinching confession could not quite bring himself to accept that his self-involved narratives could pass muster as *Kunst* (art). As he found himself more and more caught up in the psychic momentum of a type of fantastic fictional self-documentation, however, he was willing to choose confession

(*Bekenntnis*) over literary art (*Dichtung*), or as he put it more bluntly, simply to write off "the aesthetic ambition" for the time being.[14] Indeed, to the middle-aged writer who had emerged with a new identity and a new voice (and even, with the pseudonymous author of *Demian*, Emil Sinclair, a new name) after the double shocks of World War I and psychoanalysis, the criteria of artistic objectivity and formal perfection, per se, became increasingly suspect. A new age has to forge a new idiom, and for Hesse the bridge to the literary future lay in a strict adherence to his new confessional ethic of honesty and authenticity. His essential ambivalence about his new creed on the threshold of the 1920s is that his frankly self-exhibiting works are something more or less than traditional fiction—in any event, they are all he is capable of, given the disturbed temper of his life and his age. He did not rule out the possibility—in the larger context of his career it turns out to be a mirage—that, as he confided to Stefan Zweig in 1926, he might aspire "to write 'objectively' and to function and create purely as an artist."[15]

A journal Hesse kept in 1920–1921, on the threshold of his most productive decade, contains some of his most probing reflections on the challenges and problems facing him as a confessional writer. His first dilemma is that of the experiential multiplicity of the self:

> Alas, I should keep ten or more journals. I have already started three or four. One is called "Journal of a Wastrel," another, "Jungle of Childhood," another, "Dream Book." To this should be added the journal of a painter, a music journal, another concerning the old struggle between the desire to live and the longing for death, journal of a suicide, perhaps also a journal of self-recollection, of search for norms: the application of personal reflections to things in general, to nature, politics, history. And then I should have to keep three or more journals to make the attempt at polyphony and bipolarity for a while, to document somehow the fullness and multifacetedness of the soul. It's impossible, even the minutest is too much, the most simple too complicated, the hand would have to have twenty fingers and the day a

hundred hours. O Indian gods with ten and twenty arms, how true you are![16]

To some extent he was able to address this embarrassment of riches with works like *Klein and Wagner* (1920), *Siddhartha* (1922), and *Steppenwolf*, which aim on the level of both theme and style to capture life's polyphony. A second and more difficult conundrum Hesse mentions, however, is "if one considers literature as confession—and only in this manner am I able to conceive of it at present,"[17] what then is the aim or goal of such confession? He concludes that in terms of both its psychological and religious functions confession aims at a therapeutic cleansing of the self. But at this juncture in his meditation, Hesse runs up against a fundamental conflict in his life as well as his writing, namely, the conflict between religion and literature, which goes back to a childhood strongly rooted in the Pietist-Protestant tradition of his missionary family. He is forced to admit to himself that the literary and the religious impulses of confession ultimately lead in diametrically opposed directions: literary confession remains self-attached, whereas religious confession aims at the spirit's elevation through a necessary sacrifice of the ego. To Hesse this crucial difference is exemplified in Augustine's and Rousseau's *Confessions*, respectively:

> The catch lies in the fact that the confession of the artist, no matter what its conscious purpose, is probably never pure confession! Pure confession is simply the breaking out of fermenting juices, the getting rid of something, externalizing, venting it. Artistic confession, on the other hand, always and unmistakably inclines to self-justification. The artist overvalues his confession, he devotes a love and a care to it unlike anything else in the world; and the more honest, careful and complete, the more reckless the confession, the greater is the danger that it will again become all art, all design and self-purpose. The artist is forever prone to lose himself in his work, to shift his task and achievement entirely to his confession, and thus to get trapped in the magic circle of his individual concerns. For the artist is in any case a being who has to exaggerate the significance of his work, because he has relegated all the achievement of his life and along with it all of his self-justification to his work. One has

only to compare the confessions of a saint with those of a man of letters, and the difference is immediately apparent: Augustine versus Rousseau. The one gives himself away, because he has offered himself up to God; the other justifies himself. Beginning with the same motive they end at exactly opposite poles: the one as a saint, the other as a poet: the one overcomes the person he is and becomes a great human being; the other remains caught up in his complexes and is unable to get beyond being an interesting person.[18]

Hesse concludes that the path of Augustine—the "Imitatio Jesu" and the sacrifice of "the empirical I"—is most attractive to him, for his most tempting self-image, as he frankly admits, is that of the saint.[19] But he also knows that his wish-image is not a viable alternative, for his is the road of Rousseau, on which the goal of confession is not so much self-transcendence as a compulsive devotion to the work itself. As he put it in a letter of April 30, 1921, the artist's vanity keeps him from trying the steep road to beatitude, which would require nothing less than the willing sacrifice of his literary vocation.[20] In a sense the result of Hesse's never fully resolved conflict between literary-artistic and religious confession is a type of autobiographical fiction that gives us a modern secular approximation of his favorite medieval genre, the saint's life. What in turn has made Hesse's autobiographical fiction so appealing to a broad reading public is that it is a compelling version of a preoccupation very much with us at least since the subjective proclivities of the Romantics, in literature as well as in life: the search for salvation introjected and translated into a search for the self, for one's "true" identity. Hesse's journal of 1920–1921 shows that he was honest enough to admit his strong hankerings after sanctity; his literary career as a whole demonstrates that he was able to exploit the cross-pull in his life between art and religion for the purposes of a secular confession.

With its assertion that the artist shifts the meaning of his life to his work, the previously quoted excerpt from Hesse's journal signals yet another important truth about his confessional career and perhaps about the tribe of modern autobiographers. As recent autobiography

criticism has increasingly granted in the wake of Gusdorf's pioneering article,[21] the truth of autobiography rests not in some finished
and sealed-off past, but primarily in the self-constituting moment of
writing. This moment is the autobiographer's psychic focal point,
and Hesse knows as much when in a letter of August 16, 1919, he
concludes that his writing has become a survival need and the center
of his life: "If I now seek to make my mental and poetic work . . .
entirely and exclusively the center of my life, I do so because without
it I could not go on living."[22] It is no exaggeration to say that for the
modern confessional writer of Hesse's type, his biography is not
merely the material for his autobiography, but rather his autobiography creates his biography, for the process of writing himself is his
most satisfying and complete mode of being.

    That there is a loss as well as a gain inherent in displacing the ex-
istential center from unreflective living to self-reflexive writing Hesse
knew only too well. Through his narrator H. H. in *The Journey to the
East* (1932) he noted the phenomenon, disconcerting to the naive,
that famous authors in the flesh can appear paltry and diminished
next to their literary offspring, "only half real, only half there, not
quite solid, not quite genuine."[23] For the author who experiences
himself most fully in and through his books, who lives his life *as* writing, the mere biographical contingencies and mundane clutter of his
experience simply become the material out of which his work is fashioned. A writer of autobiographical fiction such as Hesse in a way *de*-
realizes his ordinary self so as to re-realize and textualize it in and
through his work. The data of his life are reconstituted as a text, with
the result that if he is a good writer, the latter is more integral and
interesting than the former. This is the triumph of art over life, for
even in autobiography, the *bios* is swallowed up by the *graphe*.[24] For
the genuine writer, his texts are more "real" than anything else he
can say or do: artists live primarily in and through their artifacts, and
not their other transactions and deeds, which are in a sense quite
beside the point. Insofar as their works represent them most art-
fully—"Find What the Sailor Has Hidden," Nabokov teases at the
end of *Speak, Memory*[25]—their biographies are superseded by their autobiographies. The too-exclusive or literal-minded concentration on
an author's life as opposed to his writings is also a major flaw of that
exhaustively practiced modern genre, those formidable writers' biographies that with painstaking effort and at epic length reconstruct

the mere biographical circumstances of a life without ever accounting for what makes it worthy of our interest in the first place. Hesse himself expressed such a valuation when he praised Hugo Ball, whose short and readable Hesse biography was commissioned by Hesse's publisher, Samuel Fischer, to honor him on the occasion of his fiftieth birthday, for having captured "not the banal history, but the legend of this life."[26]

Perhaps another way to frame the issue of the literary use of personal experience and of writing itself as a mode of being is to assert that confessional writers at once live and create the shapes of their lives through their works. What matters most from a literary viewpoint is not the "actual" life behind the work, but how this is made over into literature—though, in order to appreciate the latter, it is obviously helpful to have some ancillary biographical information. The thing made, the text, acquires an a posteriori ascendancy over the maker. Hesse may be suggesting as much with a witty parable in his essay, "Life Story Briefly Told" (1925), where the biographical account of his life veers off at the conclusion into sheer fantasy. He imagines that at the age of seventy he will be in prison "for seduction by magic of a young girl." On the wall of the cell he paints a landscape with a train in it, and then calls to mind the "Chinese formula": "I made myself small and stepped into the picture, got aboard the little train, and rode in the little train to the little black tunnel. For a while the sooty smoke continued visible, pouring out of the round hole, then the smoke dispersed and with it the entire picture and I with the picture." Hesse's redaction of the Chinese legend of the painter vanishing into his painting can be read as his sly comment on the relationship in his fiction between experience and art, biography and autobiography. "The guards" who "remained behind in great embarrassment" can be taken to stand for the too-literal-minded reader-critics who wish to capture and imprison the autobiographical writer in the biographical frame of his work, and who are unable or unwilling to appreciate the prime importance of the magical act of literary artifice and textual self-fashioning at the heart of Hesse's confessional project.[27]

The ironic parable above also signals a prime motive of Hesse's fiction, namely, to achieve a kind of invisibility and anonymity. As he informs us in another autobiographical essay, "Childhood of the Magician" (1923), his favorite childhood wish was to be a magician with the power of making himself invisible, and that later as a writer, "I frequently tried to disappear behind my creations, to rechristen myself and hide behind playfully contrived names." He sums up "the real content of his life's story" as the aspiration "to replace the crude invisibility of the magic cloak with the invisibility of the wise man who, perceiving all, remains always unperceived."[28] In this regard his autobiographical fiction is, paradoxically, self-expression as self-disguise for the purpose of achieving anonymity. Such is the psycho-literary charade Hesse played out in language for half a century, the emperor in the realm of his imagination with an entire wardrobe of different costumes, reinventing himself from book to book. As he wrote to his analyst and friend, Josef B. Lang, in 1920 when the secret of the identity of the true author of *Demian* was beginning to unravel, "I would much prefer to issue each new work under a new pseudonym. I am really not Hesse, but have been Sinclair, Klingsor, Klein, etc., and will be much else besides."[29]

Hesse's self-fictionalizing involves the projection of symbolic self-images, or, to use his own description of the process in "A Work Night," an essay written in 1928 when he was working on *Narcissus and Goldmund*, every new fiction is "a new incarnation, a somewhat differently blended and differentiated embodiment of my being in words." His narratives jell around such "incarnations," which dramatize in fantastic form those concerns currently uppermost in his experience:

> For me a new work begins to emerge at the moment when a figure becomes visible to me that can become for a time the symbol and bearer of my experience, thoughts, and problems. The appearance of this mythic person (Peter Camenzind, Knulp, Demian, Siddhartha, Harry Haller, etc.) is the creative instant from which everything else takes its being. Nearly all the works of prose fiction I have written are soul-biographies; all of them are concerned not with stories, [plot] complications and suspense, but are fundamentally monologues in which a single person, precisely this mythic figure, is considered in its relation to the world and to itself.[30]

Though these legendary self-images may loom larger than life, they are nevertheless considerably less than that complex individual, Hermann Hesse, for they incorporate only parts of a greater whole that remains hidden like the sage who, perceiving all, is unperceived. Hesse's development as a writer can be seen as his attempt to progressively express and clarify different areas of this shadowy entity, which for the lack of a better word we can call the mystery of the self. Through his playfully self-reflexive fiction he sought to reconcile the conflicting psychic drives to manifest *and* to hide himself, to continually exhibit yet also to mask that strange being he spent a lifetime trying to fathom. Hesse's fictional self-incarnations are in a sense both self-reflections and self-inventions, and in his best work—*Steppenwolf*, for instance—it is impossible to tell where the former leaves off and the latter begins. This fusion of inner and outer, of biographical fact and autobiographical fantasy, so reminiscent of the milieu of early German Romanticism from Novalis to E.T.A. Hoffmann in which Hesse felt most at home as a writer, makes these fictional alter egos ambiguous and Janus-faced—the very features the fledgling poet had admired in Goethe's work. Nor should it surprise us that Hesse's self-inventions should be retrospective as well as proleptic, looking to the past as well as to the future. Because his leading fictional "incarnations" both recapitulate growth and anticipate future possibilities of growth, they are at once the product and the producers of his self in a process enacted in and through language. If that sounds obvious, we should remember that the longstanding metaphor of autobiography as self-portrait is in some respects substantially off the mark, because autobiography is writing and not painting, and there is a world of difference between language and pigment. Although both writing and painting can be subsumed under such concepts as "style" and "representation," self-portraiture and literary confession are radically different to the extent that paint simply cannot fabricate a self with the complexity that language so indisputably can.

In autobiography and confessional fiction, the author to some degree makes his book, but as Montaigne already observed, the book also makes the man. Hesse's larger achievement demonstrates that literary confession is purgative as well as self-transforming, because in a reciprocal movement, as the self fashions its language, that language helps to produce the self. His autobiographical fiction is not merely narcissistic or self-indulgent, but entails a rigorous commitment to an ideal of art, as Hesse put it memorably in the Journal of 1920–1921, "as a long, diverse, and winding path, whose goal it would be to express the personality, the 'I' of the artist so completely, so minutely in all its branchings . . . that this 'I' would in the end be as it were unreeled and finished, that it would have raged and burned itself out."[31] In traveling this demanding road, from the sentimental and neo-Romantic narratives of the pre–World War I years, which leave so much unsaid or euphemized, to the crisis of confession of the 1920s when he dedicated himself to a confessional *oeuvre* that would force into language and consciousness the most repressed and unflattering truths of his inner experience, to—finally—the many-layered refractions of his last period and *The Glass Bead Game*, Hesse managed to live out and to rise above the limitations inherent in being a subjective writer.

That Hesse knew what interest a mere life can afford—to return to the prefatory quotation at the head of this chapter—is suggested very nicely by a retrospective piece that he wrote in 1953 at the age of seventy-six, "Events in the Engadine," and that constitutes a sort of farewell to his autobiographical art. He mentions rereading *Narcissus and Goldmund*, something he had not done since its publication in 1930. With wry humility he observes that "it was a friendly and beneficent reunion" that did not spare him, as he puts it,

> a recurrent and rather shaming insight into my lack of talent and ability: this reading was a self-examination that once more showed me clearly my limitations. It struck me again most forcibly that most of my longer works of fiction do not, as I believed during their writing, present new problems and portraits of people in the way true masters do but only repeat variations of the few problems and types congenial to me, though at new stages of life and experience.

But if this textual self-encounter brought home to him once more the limits of his literary imagination, it also made him see more clearly his particular virtue, for in the wise words of that foolish counselor, Polonius, he had been true to his own self:

But this insight did not pain me, it meant no more than simply a reduction and curtailment of my self-esteem, which before, to be sure, had been appreciably greater; it meant something good and positive as well, it showed me that in spite of many ambitious wishes and efforts, on the whole I had remained true to my nature and had not abandoned the path of self-realization even at times of crisis and constraint.

It is also fitting that Hesse should add, "it was the language far more than the content of the book that I retained true and undisturbed in memory,"[32] for in the end the language that it has generated and that had generated it remains as the truest reminder and remainder of the autobiographer's self.

It is indeed a remarkable phenomenon that a writer whose sources of inspiration were so highly personal has been able to achieve a much larger resonance and relevance and to speak, in different ways in different decades, in something approaching a universal idiom. In the sixties and seventies he became a runaway bestseller in the U.S. and Japan; and though the Hesse "wave" has certainly peaked in the West, in more recent years the Hesse reception has apparently also begun to flourish in the Eastern-bloc countries. The reason for the extraordinary appeal of such intensely introspective narratives can be explained in part through the fact, noted at the close of the previous chapter, that confessional fiction can make for a particularly strong reader-author bond or even identification. As Joseph Mileck has reminded us, the clue to Hesse's huge international audience is that "life transfigured—fantasized, poeticized, dramatized, and symbolized—becomes art with universal implications."[33]

Certainly a part of Hesse's success in addressing an international audience, particularly among the young, is that his major works, revolving as they do around searching or questing heroes, obviously hold a strong and often larger-than-literary appeal for those who are themselves beset by uncertainty, confusion, doubt, and anxiety. As noted earlier, the quest for the "true" self in Hesse's novels correlates readily with the needs of readers who turn to them for succor or guidance, and who find in them a validation of their innermost concerns. And in times of social stress and cultural crisis—the sixties, for instance—when rapid social change on a large scale and the clash of fundamental value systems (for example, political and religious) among different generations, classes, and groups are undermining the sense of cultural security, what is usually a small minority of searchers and doubters can turn into a much larger cohort. It is frequently to such an audience that Hesse's soul-searching romances have spoken with all the fervent appeal of a gospel of the inward way. Among the many who read Hesse in the scriptural mode on the college campuses of the sixties and the seventies, as a writer of wisdom books or a religious guru—and sometimes with a copy of *Siddhartha* in one pocket and *The Prophet* in the other—there was not likely to be much critical sophistication about Hesse's literary art. Conversely, the fact that Hesse qua counterculture Pied Piper had such a large and uncritical following was enough for many literary highbrows to downplay or write him off disdainfully as a writer of adolescence, or worse yet, *for* adolescents.

Thus Peter Gay opened his 1979 review of Ralph Freedman's Hesse biography with the wholesale dismissal, "to many literate Americans, Hermann Hesse is little more than an exhibit of what went wrong with America's youth in the 1960s." Gay proceeded to debunk Hesse as "a fanatical scribbler" who wrote "autobiography practically undisguised" because "the hand of art, which converted, say, Proust's memories and experiences into an immortal masterpiece, lay lightly on Hesse's memories and experiences."[34] A clever put-down like this, however, is as much of a misprision as is the gospel-truth worship of Hesse by the more devotional and unliterary readers. A balanced critical evaluation of Hesse the confessional writer will show him to be neither a saint nor a scribbler. In any event, a common trait of both the hagiographic and the debunking receptions is what appears to be a limited acquaintance with his works: those who turn to literature for edification or wisdom don't need too many such texts, and those who don't like an author from the start don't want to punish themselves by reading very much of him. Hesse the writer is in fact more sophisticated, playful, and *literary* than either his debunkers or his boosters of the more uncritical sort have been willing to grant or able to discern.

Finally, why did Hesse the subjective writer never write an autobiography? For beyond his prose fiction, his self-reflexive impulses spilled over into a huge body of poetry, personal essays, private journals and diaries, and an ever-active correspondence, not to mention a number of compact autobiographical sketches. Given this large and diverse body of autobiographical matter, it is remarkable that, unlike a Rousseau or a Goethe, he never sat down to compose a full-scale retrospective or overview of his life. Actually, the thought seems never to have even occurred to him, which suggests that such a venture would have been uncongenial or incongruous to him. Although he made a successful career out of mining his life for his art, and although he did not suffer from any shortage of vanity or self-regard, I suspect that in some respects he was humble enough to believe that his person and his life per se were not of sufficient interest to warrant the treatment of a full autobiography. Presumably he found confessional fiction so attractive because it shifts the reader's attention and scrutiny away from the actual or historic person of the author to his fictional (dis)guise. Moreover, as I sought to indicate with the generic differentiations of Chapter I, confessional fiction meets creative needs other than those autobiography proper does, chief among them the aesthetic penchant for play, fantasy, masking/unmasking, and wish-fulfillment.

Another reason why the writing of a full-fledged autobiography would have been unattractive if not impossible for Hesse is that the classic project of autobiography appears to be correlated with a normative overview of the autobiographer's life at the moment of writing. Such a conclusive retrospect was beyond Hesse's confessional reach or inclinations, for his self-mirroring narratives give us instead the temporally self-segmenting metamorphoses of a writer whose sense of his identity was constantly changing. As Hesse was fond of underscoring, he was a man of variable, evolving selfhood, "a man of becoming and of changes."[35] As his identity and his outlook transformed, so did his fictional self-incarnations; nor did he ever come to rest with a conclusive or "closed" overview of the stages of his life. Instead, he maintained into old age that proto-existential and fluid sense of the self forever permeable and open to redefinition, something wonderfully summed up in that representative late Hesse poem affirming the process of change and the hazards of the venturing self, "Stages" (1941):

> As every blossom fades and all youth
> gives way to age, so every stage of life,
> so all wisdom and all virtue also blooms
> in its own time and may not last forever.[36]

To such a post-Romantic sense of the protean and "open" self, confessional fiction is a much more attractive and viable alternative than the perspectival closure of classic autobiography.

CHAPTER III

SELF-WILL

I trust that there are many [readers] ... who are willing to consider an author like me as an attorney of the individual, of the soul and of conscience, without subordinating themselves to him as to a catechism ... No doubt I have sometimes erred ... and have occasionally been too passionate so that some young readers have been confused and endangered by my words. But if you consider the inhibiting powers which the contemporary world has marshaled against the development of the individual ... into a full human being ... then you will not find it difficult to muster some understanding and forbearance for the bellicose gestures of the little Don Quixote against those huge windmills.—Hesse in a 1954 letter to a German student

So far my discussion of Hesse the autobiographical writer has not dealt with a central element that helps to define Hesse's self-reflexive personality as well as the subjective character of his fiction and that runs like a leitmotif through his life: *Eigensinn* (self-will). Hesse's beloved voice from within, a secularized version of the Protestant stress on individual conscience, gives a distinctive coloration to his political, religious, and aesthetic outlook. Self-will is Hesse's chief article of faith, his ethical touchstone for value and integrity in all areas of human life. The center of his mature self-concept, it also represents the core of whatever teachings he wished to impart in his writings. Sometimes he preached the gospel of *Eigensinn* with a measure of proselytizing self-righteousness worthy of the missionary zeal of his Protestant forbears. As he summed it up in the opening of his 1919 essay on the subject,

> There is one virtue that I love, and only one. I call it self-will. I cannot bring myself to think so highly of all the many virtues we read about in books and hear about from teachers. True, all the

virtues man has devised for himself might be subsumed under a single head: obedience. But the question is: *whom* are we to obey? For self-will is also obedience. But all the other virtues, the virtues that are so highly esteemed and praised, consist in obedience to manmade laws. Self-will is the only virtue that takes no account of these laws. A self-willed man obeys a different law, the one law I hold absolutely sacred—the law in himself, his own "will."[1]

Although the latter part of World War I represents the vocal high point of Hesse's pronouncements on self-will—in a rhetorical mode that combines a Nietzschean contempt for the conformity of the herd with a Jungian romance of individuation and a quest for the deep self, as evident in the political tract, *Zarathustra's Return*, and in the novel, *Demian*—Hesse never wavered during the remainder of his long career in his protest on behalf of the person vis-à-vis the pressure of collective norms. As his voluminous letters, fiction, criticism, journals, personal and political essays all show with an almost compulsive concern, his advocacy of the sanctity of the individual remained his highest good as a writer and a moralist. The positive aura of his ideal of *Eigensinn* is evident in his quasi-hagiographic gallery of fictional characters who choose to go their own way; in his political writings, the stress on the primacy of the individual conscience emerges as a positive counter and psychic defense against the dire manifestations in the public realm of what Freud (in *Group Psychology and the Analysis of the Ego*, 1922) describes as the herd-instinct and its blind identification with an external authority figure or *Führer*.

As Hesse points out in his "Eigensinn" essay in a tone sometimes strongly reminiscent of Nietzsche, the virtue of attending to one's inner voice can put one in conflict with one's fellow citizens, who regard self-will "as a vice or at best a deplorable aberration." Self-will provokes "antagonism and hatred"—"witness Socrates, Jesus, Giordano Bruno, and all other self-willed men" (*War*, 79), adds Hesse in a Blake-like gloss. His ideal of the inner-directed person is not just a quaint or quirky cult of "character" or "personality," but involves a devout attentiveness to "the mysterious power in himself which bids him live and helps him to grow" (*War*, 83). Like Emerson's "self-reliance," with which it has significant affinities,[2] Hesse's favorite vir-

tue is a transcendental or theologically based version of individualism: in harkening to this "mysterious power" within ourselves we
are also observing the promptings of a higher moral law, a divine
principle that is the supratemporal and transcultural source of human conscience. And like Thoreau's "civil disobedience," Hesse's
self-will or inner dictate can bring one into conflict with the laws and
mores of society. Indeed, like Blake's, Emerson's, Thoreau's,
Nietzsche's, and D. H. Lawrence's radical ethics of individual conscience, Hesse's model of the self-willed person is but one distinctive
version of a Romantic individualism that always involves (implicitly
or explicitly) a marked degree of self-conscious differentiation from
the mentality of the group and a strong measure of contempt for the
conformity of the masses and its lowest embodiment, the psychology
of the mob.

Like Emerson's self-reliant man, Hesse's self-willed individual has
an essential trust in himself; he does not pursue the worldly goals of
money and power, because these are "the inventions of distrust" and
compensations or poor substitutes for "the life-giving force within"
(*War*, 83). For the apostle of *Eigensinn*, the commonly praised virtues
begin to appear questionable, especially the perennial favorite of the
masses and their manipulators, patriotism, which "for the individual
. . . substitutes a larger complex," and which is most prized "when
the shooting starts" (*War*, 82). The soldier who kills at the behest of
the state cannot be a hero, for "the obedient well-behaved citizen
who does his duty is not a 'hero'. Only an *individual* who has fashioned his 'self-will', his noble, natural and inner law, into his destiny
can be a hero" (*War*, 82). In ringing Nietzschean accents, "Eigensinn" preaches a late-Romantic ethic of the great-souled individual
who lives for and by "the silent, ungainsayable law in his own
heart," which to "the self-willed man is destiny and godhead" (*War*,
85).

The Politics of Conscience

The references to shooting, soldiers, and unquestioning obedience of
social authority are not accidental, of course, for like *Demian* and the
essays on Dostoevsky, "Eigensinn" champions the primacy of conscience and the inner voice against the xenophobic rhetoric of World

War I, which had poisoned the mental atmosphere of Europe. The most coherent and convincing political statement during the *Demian* period of Hesse's concern with *Eigensinn* is to be found in *Zarathustra's Return* (1919, issued under the signature, "A Word to German Youth by a German"), Hesse's "confession of an unpolitical person," which he wrote "almost unconsciously" and "explosively" in "two days and nights under the pressure of world events."[3] Hesse's jeremiad to the returning veterans is imbued with the same visionary urgency as *Demian*, but its language and tone are more rhetorically controlled, perhaps in part because of the distinctive Nietzschean persona he chose to address his young audience. The powerful message of this compact and highly stylized performance is direct and—in Hesse's view—most timely: the primacy of the inner voice and of individual conscience. Hesse's blunt lecture is directed against the foremost enemy, in the country of his birth, of individual moral accountability—unthinking obedience of and blind submission to external authority, which in his view is one of the root causes that made possible the horror unleashed by World War I. As he undiplomatically reminds his readers, "you Germans more than any other people are accustomed to obedience" (*War*, 115). In the Preface to the second, signed edition (1920), he calls attention to a different and more honorable German spirit:

> There was once a German spirit, a German courage, a German manhood that did not express themselves in the uproar of the herd or in mass enthusiasm. The last great vehicle of this spirit was Nietzsche, who, amid the business boom and sheep-like conformism that characterized the beginnings of the German Empire, became an antipatriot and anti-German. In this little book I wish to remind the young German intellectuals of that man, of his courage and solitude, and in so doing turn their minds away from the herd outcry (whose present whining tone is not a jot more pleasant than the brutal, bullying tone it assumed in those "great days") to a few simple facts and experiences of the soul. (*War*, 86)

The Preface also offers a concise formulation of Hesse's Romantic humanism with regard to the issue of political action: "Only a few suspect how deeply the German mind had degenerated long before the war. If we wish once again to have minds and men capable of securing our future, we must not begin at the tail end, with political methods and forms of government, but at the beginning, with the building of the personality" (*War*, 86–87). In *Zarathustra's Return*, the emphasis on the independent individual and the integrity of the self is developed, appropriately enough considering the title and speaker, in the Nietzschean triad of fate, solitude, and suffering. The impulses of *Eigensinn* represent an internalized version of fate—Nietzsche's *amor fati*—which if embraced in solitary suffering, leads to a higher humanity. Like Demian, Hesse's Zarathustra is an ideal self-image and symbolic carrier of his profoundest spiritual experiences. And for Hesse the Romantic hierophant, the deeper self is transpersonal and, indeed, in touch with the divine. Thus the voice of his prophetic persona resounds "like a voice that comes not from men but from stars or gods or, still more, like the voice that every man hears secretly in his own heart at times when God is with him" (*War*, 91).

The point of Hesse-Zarathustra's ministry is to teach in order to strengthen the individual sense of self and self-responsibility:

> [Zarathustra] has learned only one thing, he prides himself only on one bit of wisdom. He has learned to be Zarathustra. And that is what you want to learn from him, yet so often lack the courage to learn. You must learn to be yourselves, just as I have learned to be Zarathustra. You must unlearn the habit of being someone else or nothing at all, of imitating the voices of others and mistaking the faces of others for your own. (*War*, 92)

Viewed spiritually, the great war represents the dire consequences of a collective and mindless flight from the demands of individual conscience. Against the basic human urge to find security in the group, Hesse insists on the essential internality of the highest of all authority figures, God. The external God of the herd who sanctions war and the gross inhumanities that men commit en masse under the dispensation of His high name is, like Blake's Old Noboddady, an insidious human fiction. Thus in his "leave-taking," Hesse pointedly admonishes his readers: "O young men of Germany . . . you have always looked for God, but never in yourselves. He is nowhere else. There is no other God than the God within you" (*War*, 116). In his parting shot, he preaches a message that is to resound in different voices and styles in his writings henceforth—the highest "teacher" is one's self: "listen to the voice that comes from within yourself! When that voice falls silent, know that something is amiss, that something is out of joint, that you are on the wrong road" (*War*, 117).

What Hesse's friend and biographer, Hugo Ball, summed up as his "revolutionary testament, a confession of faith to the inner *civitas dei*"[4] appears not to have found much of a response among the German youth to whom it was addressed. But then, as Hesse came to recognize over the years, his pleas for *Eigensinn* would be ignored or misunderstood by the majority of his readers, and thus in his later years he concentrated his pedagogic hopes on a minority responsible and thoughtful enough to become inner-directed individuals. In any case, *Zarathustra's Return* presents with a prophetic voice uncannily like Zarathustra's the larger sociopolitical implications inherent in an "unpolitical" man's (Hesse's ironic self-description) ideal of self-will. Although the Nietzschean mask was to be discarded almost entirely in the coming decade, Hesse for the remainder of his career never swerved from the "unpolitical" political stance of his Zarathustra confession. On the contrary, he elaborated and even harped upon it on countless occasions in his subsequent writings. The two-volume collection of his political writings assembled by his German publisher under the apt title, *Politics of Conscience*,[5] documents both the richness and the lifelong consistency of a political outlook founded on the Romantic-transcendental perspectives of *Eigensinn* and the ethical primacy of the person above and beyond any ideological or partisan calculus of political means and ends.

Hesse's belief in self-will, which was both tested and strengthened in the crisis year 1916 in the crucible of psychoanalysis and the mounting nightmare of World War I, led him to speak out against the war hysteria and propaganda—at least, after his initial ambivalence and ambiguity in 1914–1915, when, as a native German, his sympathies still lay with the German side.[6] This creed, however, also kept him, then and later, from aligning or allying himself with any political party or program. Remaining so much his own man he was usually also very much a man on his own, and, during the long crisis years of World War I and again during the Nazi era, sometimes a man caught in the crossfire of the politics of Right and Left—though as someone making his permanent home in neutral Switzerland since 1912 his personal safety was never in question. During the Hitler period, however, he developed a considerable degree of sympathy for the goals of socialism and even of left-wing revolutionaries, yet without ever approving of the tactics or the world-view of the latter. In 1930 he wrote to one of his sons that although he was no socialist, he considered socialism the only serious critique of "our false society."[7] He summarized his mixed feelings about the Marxist agenda in another letter to the same son: "In my *thinking* I am as far to the left as the most leftish Bolshevik . . . but in my innermost feelings I am no revolutionary, and do not believe that man has been endowed with a mind so that proletarians can have bread."[8] Though intellectually he can endorse the Marxist critique of capitalism, he cannot accept for himself its program of revolutionary violence, something he tried to crystallize in a poem written in 1933 in response to repeated queries why he did not commit himself to the Communist cause:

> Better to be killed by the Fascists
> Than to be a Fascist oneself!
> Better to be killed by the Communists
> Than to be a Communist oneself![9]

In the letter to his son quoted above, he counseled a religiously grounded pacifism, not as a general solution, but only as a tenable posture for himself, a point he elaborated in another letter of 1933:

> I experienced the 1914–1918 war so intensely and nearly to my destruction that since then I have been completely and unalterably clear about one thing: that for my own person I reject and refuse to support all schemes to change the world through violence, not even the socialist one, not even the apparently desirable and just one. The wrong people always get killed, and even if it were to be the right ones: I simply cannot believe in the progressive and avenging force of killing.[10]

He knows that his choice of nonviolence is "probably the path of a Don Quixote," but he will stick by it: adverting again to revolutionary violence in the name of justice and humanity, he asserts, "As far as I am concerned I am not prepared for that, under no circumstances; and am a Christian to the extent that if it comes down to it I certainly would choose being killed over killing; but I have never sought to influence others, not even my sons, in their decision concerning this ultimate question of conscience."[11]

From his pessimistic postwar perspective of 1946 Hesse attempted a comprehensive summing-up of his politics of conscience in the Preface to *If the War Goes On: Reflections on War and Politics*:

> When I call my articles "political," it is always in quotes, for there is nothing political about them but the atmosphere in which they came into being. In all other respects they are the opposite of political, because in each one of these essays I strive to guide the reader not into the world theater with its political problems but into his innermost being, before the judgment seat of his very personal conscience. In this I am at odds with the political thinkers of all trends, and I shall always, incorrigibly, recognize in man, in the individual man and his soul, the existence of realms to which political impulses and forms do not extend. I am an individualist and I regard the Christian veneration for every human soul as what is best and most holy in Christianity. It may be that in this I partake of a world that is already half extinct, that we are witnessing the emergence of a collective man without individual soul, who will do away with the entire religious and individualistic tradition of mankind. To desire or fear such an eventuality is not my concern. (*War*, 5–6)

Because the ethics of *Eigensinn* served as the foundation of Hesse's reactions to the social and political upheavals of the twentieth century since his "first awakening" during World War I, his responses to the major political developments of his age have been surprisingly consistent: unlike many of his "colleagues and critics," he, the "utterly unpolitical man," has "not been capable of learning new lessons and rallying to a different flag every few years," but has "been sure of [his] judgment and offered a more than average resistance to mass psychoses and psychological infections of every kind" (*War*, 6–7). Thus in his view self-will is an effective antibody to those fanatical mass movements already prophetically invoked by Dostoevsky at the close of *Crime and Punishment*, which can madden whole societies.

Poised on his moral perch of *Eigensinn*, Hesse in practice found it easy enough to condemn the jingoistic extremes of German propaganda in the second half of World War I and again during the rise of Hitler. For instance, the hate mail he received from reactionary students after Germany's defeat in 1918 moved him to publish a polemic against that element of the German mentality that he most detested, "that smug, unself-reliant, strictly authoritarian . . . bourgeois [Bürger] faith, against which Goethe battled and protested so frequently, which broke Hölderlin, which Jean Paul ironized, and which Nietzsche denounced so furiously." Militaristic and mesmerized by Authority, this is a one-sided Germany that knows "only Kant, Schiller, Fichte, Wagner." Hesse did not want to dismantle this narrow pantheon of canonical figures enshrined in the Philistine imagination, but to expand it by putting Bach and Mozart next to Wagner, Goethe, Hölderlin, and Jean Paul next to Schiller, and Nietzsche and Schopenhauer next to Kant, as well as to internationalize it (compare the "European" ideal of Goethe and Nietzsche) by invoking the likes—an odd catalogue, to be sure—"of Jesus, Saint Francis, Dante, Shakespeare."[12]

Xenophobic nationalists proved an easy target, but it was more difficult for Hesse to assert the imperatives of self-will against the claims of the Marxists, particularly since, as we have seen, he held a certain amount of sympathy for the aims of left-wing revolutionaries. In private, at least, he could be brutally frank on this subject, as evident in a letter to Heinrich Wiegand, a socialist journalist and acquaintance to whom he admitted "deep antipathy to the middle-school cleverness and the shallow delusions of the Marxists," as well as distaste for the German socialists for putting the politics of the party above any genuine concern for the individual, which makes them enemies of "all spirit, all personality, all genuine fruitful forces in our people."[13] For the writer who could assert, "I can only take humanity seriously in the singular, as a personality [Persönlichkeit],"[14] the world-view of Marxists, no matter how worthy or progressive it might appear, was posited on a flattening out and assimilation of the individual into the crowd—hence a dehumanizing and inhuman ideal. He tried to phrase this in a diplomatic manner in his "Letter to a Communist," a set piece that he did not publish but sent out to correspondents as the need arose. It represents—in what strikes one as too much of a strategic concession, even considering the year is 1931—by far his most considered dialogue with the Left, for it grants at the outset: "I consider Communism not only as justified, but as a foregone conclusion . . . I believe with you, that the Marxist way will lead beyond a dying capitalism to the liberation of the proletariat, which is the path of the future, and that the world will travel it, whether it wants to or not."[15] After this concession, the rest of the letter develops why he cannot, as he puts it, "put my pen in the service of your Party" (295). Here his self-will joins with his view of art and artists as autonomous to reject any such demand:

> The poet is neither something more nor less than the minister [of state], the engineer, or the speaker of the people, but he is something entirely different from these. An axe is an axe, and one can split wood with it, or heads. But a watch or a barometer are here for different reasons, and if one wants to split wood or heads with them they go to pieces without any one gaining anything by it. (296–297)

Hesse also points out that Communism is not a movement above history, but is limited and fallible like any movement *in* history. Its claims to have *the* truth are false and overweening; its roots are all too squarely in the nineteenth century, "in the soil of the most arid and hobbyhorse hegemony of the understanding of a better-knowing, unimaginative, and loveless professorism"(296). Marx's "extremely one-sided and unelastic" conception of history and economics also comes from this barren world; worse yet, Marx the lover of literature fails to allow the arts the status of an essential human activity: "Karl Marx had a great deal of understanding of the poetry and the art of the past, and if at any point of his teaching he was perhaps not completely honest, then it was in the fact that despite his better knowledge he did not recognize the arts as an organ of humanity, but only as a piece of the 'ideological superstructure' " (297).

The Marxist critic may find it tempting to dismiss Hesse's views here as a belated version of *fin-de-siècle* aestheticism and nineteenth-century "art for art's sake," but Hesse's claim that the Communist order will prove a greater threat to literature and serious writers than "the age of the bourgeois" cannot be so easily dismissed. Hesse's more optimistic prognostication in this letter is that once humanity's material needs will have been satisfied by the New Order, it will become apparent that the mass man of the future will also have a soul and will want to satisfy spiritual needs—and so artists and poets will again have an important role to play. Hesse concludes his letter with a prophetic affirmation of art not as the instrument of a world-view or an ideology, but as its own instrumentality:

> With the right of those who conduct wars you [Communists] will probably kill this or that poet . . . but you will delude yourselves to your harm if you believe that a poet is an instrument which the currently ruling class can use at its convenience like a slave or a talent that can be bought. With this belief you would make a serious mistake and precisely the worthless ones would stick to you. But you will be able to recognize the genuine artists and poets . . . through their ungovernable urge for independence . . . they will not be for sale for bread and sugar and for high offices, and will prefer to let themselves be killed rather than letting themselves be used. In that you will be able to recognize them. (298)

Hesse's set piece to his Communist correspondents at the beginning of a decade when Marxism—and Fascism—were growing increasingly appealing to an idealistic yet disaffected generation coming of age, is his most politic statement about the role of the self-willed writer in an increasingly politicized world. His basic fear or anxiety, of course, was the growing threat to the traditional humanist concept of the individual posed by the mass movements of Right and Left. As he concluded in the troubled journal of 1933 about contemporary developments, the ideological apparatuses of Soviet Communism and of the Third Reich rely on similar methods.[16] The idolatrous and mindless cult of the great leader or *Führer* was for Hesse a manifestation of the general decline of culture as well as of the diminishment of *Eigensinn* and the evaporation of individual conscience in the modern world: "I confess that I have a downright hatred for that word so misused by German youth, 'Führer.' He who desires and needs a *Führer* is he who cannot think and be responsible for himself."[17]

The psychological dependence on an all-powerful *Führer* in the social realm presages the collapse of a humanistic culture posited on the respect of the rights of the individual, and Hesse saw that the political expression of this is the large-scale formation of ideologically

bonded masses whose long-range consequences are bound to be cat-
astrophic. His bleak résumé of this insight from the post–World War
II vantage of 1949 may serve as the conclusion to this survey of
Hesse's politics of conscience:

> In today's world there is . . . a different demand on people that
> is propagated by parties, nations, world-orders. It is the demand
> that man should completely renounce the idea that something
> personal and unique could be meant with him, that he . . . be-
> come a wheel in the machine, a little building stone. I wouldn't
> want to judge the moral worth of this demand; it has its heroic
> and splendid side. But I don't believe in it. Such a reducing of
> everything to the same denominator [*Gleichschalten*], no matter
> how well intentioned, runs counter to nature, and does not lead
> to peace and cheerfulness, but to fanaticism and war.[18]

For a lifelong humanist whose vision of self-will represents a distinctive version of Romantic individualism, such a *Gleichschalten* is tanta-
mount to the theological Death of Man. Since he sensed that such a
demise was probably inevitable—at least in the short run—it is no
wonder that at times he felt all the absurdity of being a little Don
Quixote tilting at such tremendous windmills.

A Child Possessed

So far I have considered Hesse's creed of *Eigensinn* in a largely positive light. However, Hesse's "favorite virtue" has—probably like all
virtues—its negative side as well. If the usual presumption is that we
choose our virtues but that our vices select us, in Hesse's case, self-
will has a vicious side insofar as it was not freely chosen, but has a
compelled, even demonic aspect to it. The rub is that Hesse possessed *Eigensinn*, but it also possessed him—as those closest to him,
like his parents and his wives, sometimes discovered to their grief.
His description of self-will as obedience to one's inner voice and his
sense of it as *amor fati* clearly suggest the compulsive and irrational
side of his chief good. Here there is a real consistency to Hesse, the
man and the writer, for his good and bad points are all of a piece.
Both aspects are implicit in the ambivalent connotation of the word,
in English as well as German, with the negative meaning being up-

permost: *Eigensinn*/self-will implies a stubborn and unyielding temperament, a headstrong nature, someone too persistent, inflexible, and fond of getting his own way, a personal eccentricity or bias pursued with a vengeance.

As a type of wilfulness sometimes raised to the pitch of a proud and vehement rebellion against all external authority, particularly family and school, it defines the emotional climate of Hesse's storm-and-stress childhood and adolescence, including the high or low points of his running away from the Maulbronn school, his enforced stay in an institution for epileptic and retarded children at Stetten (tagged with the diagnosis of "moral insanity"), his suicide threats and final dropping out of school to languish at home like an eagle with clipped wings, before settling into a menial apprenticeship in Perrot's clockwork shop. These youthful misadventures are captured in vivid and dramatic detail in the documentary volume edited after Hesse's death by his third wife, *Childhood and Youth Before 1900: Hermann Hesse in Letters and Life-Records 1877–1895*.[19] This engrossing collection of biographical material reads rather like a first-rate epistolary novel, one that conveys his adolescent identity crisis in a manner that makes his first major venture a decade later to deal with this material in fictional form (*Beneath the Wheel*, 1906) appear one-dimensional and impoverished by comparison: in this instance, the biographical *Wahrheit* (truth) of his life makes for better reading than its *Dichtung* (poetry). What *Childhood and Youth* offers with such a wealth of biographical documentation, and which is also manifest in the lively and poignant journals and letters of his mother, is the suffering and unhappiness Hesse brought upon himself and his family from his earliest years through his irrepressible self-will. He really was something of a demon child, possessed of an energy, vitality, imagination, and intelligence that in their ungovernable excesses became a source of affliction to the Hesse household, and that were thus not taken as a blessing, but as a defect or character weakness to be rooted out. Hesse experienced early the curse of genius, being an extraordinarily talented youngster whose gifts became the cause of the difficulties that nearly did him in.

It is important to stress that Hesse's mature *Eigensinn* concept is not principally or only a matter of intellectual influence or borrowing from sources as diverse as Socrates, Lao-Tzu, the Buddha, Luther,

Gandhi, Emerson, Nietzsche, Jung (all of whom helped in varying degrees in lending support to or confirming him in his beliefs), but is the conceptual equivalent—even rationalization—of a basic trait present in his personality from infancy on. Probably like most of us, Hesse "chose" his influences and role models to help him become what he already was potentially—a fact that helps to explain why the "Eastern" influence card (though a significant one) is sometimes overplayed by those who tend in any case to hold a rather simplistic view of the Gordian knot of literary-intellectual "influence." As Ninon Hesse observes in her epilogue to *Childhood and Youth*, "This documentation shows . . . how a very promising, highly gifted boy was tortured and nearly broken in the difficult period of his early development because of a false education and a communal atmosphere not suited to him—and how he worked himself out from under it through his own efforts to take his education into his own hands" (517). Hermann's tempestuous temperament refused during childhood to submit or conform itself to the system of expectations and demands that defined his role in the well-regulated and strictly Pietistic atmosphere of the Hesse household, which, like most nineteenth-century European middle-class families (no matter what the nation or ostensible religion) was informed by the ideal of paternal authority, the true deity of nineteenth-century domestic life. It is no accident that Freud at the turn of the century began to explode some of the favorite familial pieties of the age with his psychological parable of the Oedipus complex, and later of the primeval sons' rebellion against the tyrannical Ur-father at the dawn of human civilization. The Oedipal conflicts of the Freudian family romance are amply evident in Hesse's childhood and youth, and can readily be discerned in his fiction, as they can in D. H. Lawrence's, in regard to mother and father figures. Indeed, like Lawrence, Hesse was only able to achieve a precarious identification with the masculine spirit and paternal authority (*Geist*) in his later work.

The documentary chronicle of Hesse's childhood captures in graphic detail the protracted conflict of the self-willed boy with his familial and social environment, and the intermittent flare-ups that constitute its many crisis points. Pervasive in that childhood is what Rousseau celebrated as a major theme in his *Confessions* and elsewhere, and what Wordsworth revealed with such poetic splendor in the opening books of *The Prelude* as one of the normative elements of his early years, namely, that there is something wild, uncontrollable, and untrammeled in the child and its imagination that resists the molds of acculturation and the efforts of the grown-up world to socialize or domesticate it. In that regard Hesse's was an extremely Romantic childhood—which helps to explain the powerful love of or sense of being in intimate contact with the powers of nature, as an effective counter to the taming and constrictive reach of adult authority that can fall with such a heavy hand upon what Wordsworth calls "the first great gift! the vital soul" of young genius (*Prelude* 1, 1805 text, l. 161).

As the mediatrix between the passionate young Hermann and the intimidating figure of a father who appears to have been somewhat distant, stiff, and cold, and an even more remote, almost legendary scholar-sage of a maternal grandfather (dwelling mysteriously at the top of the big Calw house like a being from some other world), Marie Gundert Hesse had, as her journals reveal so vividly, a hard time of it. Powerfully attached in his emotional vehemence yet a perpetual trial to her, Hermann was obviously the *Sorgenkind* (problem child) among her six surviving children.[20] Even *in utero* Hermann seems to have proven a demanding customer. A month before his birth, she wrote, "I am having a difficult time now; many complaints, often great pain; unless it's twins, I can't comprehend it."[21] Here is her account of his birth: "On Monday, July 2 1877, after a difficult day, God in his grace gave us at six-thirty in the evening the fervently desired child, which right away is hungry, turns its bright blue eyes and head independently to the light; a splendid specimen of a healthy, vigorous boy" (MH, 160). Her summary characterization of her two-year-old son is revealing: "Little Hermann is developing very rapidly, immediately recognizes all pictures, be they of China, Africa, or India; is very clever and entertaining, but his self-will [*Eigensinn*] and obstinacy are downright extraordinary" (165).

Her jottings during the next few years show a similar admixture of anxiety about and love for this problem child, as can be seen from the following collation of vivid passages, which also exhibit Marie Hesse's considerable literary talent:

Little Hermann is indescribably lively and intelligent, yet suffers from a high degree of excitability. Adele is so much easier to raise and cheers my heart. (167)

Hermann is going to kindergarten; his excitable temperament is giving us much trouble. But then he is often so cute and so tender and dear, that he is very close to my heart. (170)

There's a remarkable struggling and battling within the boy. The day before yesterday I had to pray with him two extra times during the day that the dear Savior will still make him "terribly sweet." Immediately after this he beat and bit his patient little Adele, and when I spoke to him about it, he said, "Ha, then let God make me terribly sweet, I don't seem to have the knack for it!" True, I can recall similar feelings from my own childhood. (171–172)

[To her husband, Johannes] pray with me for little Hermann, and pray for me, that I gain the strength to raise him. It seems to me as if even my physical strength weren't sufficient; the lad has a life, a giant's strength, a mighty will, and really an amazing sort of understanding for his four years. Where will it lead? It really eats away at my life, this inner struggle against his high, tyrant's spirit, his impassioned raging and pushing . . . God has to take this proud will in hand, then something noble and splendid can come of it; but I shudder to think what a false or weak education could make of this passionate human being. (173–174)

Frequently we all have to be pagans and Africans, and he [Hermann] preaches to us as a missionary. If he didn't get so indescribably worked up, it would be truly a pleasure to be around him; he can constantly do something new, and never runs out of materials for all sorts of possible speeches; often one is amazed by this wealth of life always gushing forth. (174–175)

It's a good thing that we live as we do in the country and that Hermann can let off his excess energy in the meadow next to us. Yesterday I watched from the little worktable by the window how he rolled and threw himself about in the meadow, unbelievably wild, happy, and utterly alone; [he] danced, hopped, turned somersaults without interruption and without growing tired for over an hour like a frisky colt or little goat. Naturally his clothes look accordingly, but such physical exercise is the best thing for him, otherwise he gets into mischief, and then the complaints come from above and below and right and left: "Hermann has shoved my child! Hermann has broken a pane! Hermann is throwing stones at the neighbor children! Hermann is jumping far away!" and more like it. Only hearing someone mention his name outside makes me fear for what he may be up to again. Yes, he is simply terribly animated, quick, mobile and unfortunately does not obey. And then he can be so touchingly nice and sweet . . . (179)

Evening. Finally Hermann is sleeping, after I had to use the rod for his jumping out of bed. He lies there like a tired hero! It's amazing that the boy never slows down until the last waking moment; he is barely awake in the morning and everything excites him; and even if he has taken long walks and done who-knows-what, he always has energy to spare. (180)

Today I took real pleasure in the children, who played together so sweetly and quietly . . . Such peaceful hours are truly refreshing and allow me to hope that my wild imp is still capable of being tamed. (182)

Next to the mother's tender concern for her wild and wayward son, so audible in these excerpts, the father's reactions are much more considered and detached, even when confessing his inability to handle his six-year-old son:

As humiliating as it would be for us, I am seriously considering whether we shouldn't put him into an institution or a strange house. We are too weak, too nervous for him and our entire household not sufficiently disciplined and regular. He has gifts, it seems, for everything: he observes the moon and the clouds, fantasizes for long periods at the harmonium, draws quite wonderful pictures with pen and pencil, sings very nicely when he wants to, and is never at a loss for a rhyme. (*Youth*, 13)

Dr. Hermann Gundert counseled his daughter and her husband against the extreme solution of farming young Hermann out: "In my opinion you should prepare yourselves to expect and also to draw down many blessings from God with regard to him. You still couldn't hand him over to anyone who would care for him as much as you do. That is my opinion and I cannot write other than what is in my heart" (*Youth*, 13).

However, Johannes Hesse's way of dealing with his problem son was to keep him at bay emotionally, and where that proved impossible, to send him away from home during adolescence in a pattern that Hermann perceived as a series of cruel and unnecessary banishments that he resented deeply. Emotional closeness to the mother and the assurance that she would always be there to bail him out of trouble and to forgive and console him, no matter what the transgression, was offset by distance and estrangement from a father whose authority Hermann knew to be far greater than that of the mother, and who appeared primly uninvolved and morally superior and unbending even during episodes of reconciliation and forgiveness. This unfortunate—and not unusual—mother-father-son triangle reached its nadir during the adolescent crisis years following Hermann's traumatic episode of running away from Maulbronn after less than a year as a scholarship student, which resulted in his not returning, and effectively ended any hopes for a clerical-scholarly career according to the model of his father and maternal grandfather. His father even put him in the hands of a well-known faith-healer and exorcist, Pastor Christoph Blumhardt, a colleague and friend of the Hesses. The demon possessing Hermann, however, proved too much for the good clergyman, who capitulated melodramatically by sending summarily for Marie Hesse, for whom he put on quite a scene. She found her son "a prisoner, gloomy and disturbed . . . these were the most painful hours of my life—day and night—that I spent with him" (MH, 209). This man of the gospel delivered his bad news with un-Christian brutality: "Blumhardt, who seemed to have forgotten all sickness, spoke with terrible sharpness and severity, and thundered down at me only about evil and deviltry, so that my seeing and hearing went" (MH, 209). After this nightmarish episode, she took Hermann (on the advice of the minister acting as the proxy of paternal authority) to an institution for the mentally impaired, where, as she notes in her journal, his emotional and physical health showed considerable improvement, but where, as the impassioned letters of the fifteen-year-old Hermann reveal, he felt incarcerated and banished by his father.

His acerbic missives home crystallize a resentment and wounded pride through a language that (in style and tone) is far beyond anything we are accustomed to hearing from an adolescent. They have a cutting Byronic edge, a Luciferic flair of youthful rebellion informed by that perennial Romantic ethos, *non serviam*. The dreary Stetten institution was the grotesque crucible in which Hesse's *Eigensinn* was tested and found a ringing expression in a confessional language that has a real punch to it and that exhibits Hesse the nascent writer. Like all fledgling literary efforts of a Romantic sensibility, the grandiloquent pose of the *enfant terrible* has an (unintended) comic side to it as well. In any event, Hesse's ordeal at Stetten was formative of his self-will *as* a literary vocation, a positive experience that in the very process of negation enabled him to discover and give form to his identity as a writer. At Stetten, Hesse first found his voice; thus his resentment against his father, with all its conventional Oedipal overtones, was as fruitful for Hesse the future artist as was his passionate and ambivalent relationship to his mother. These extraordinary letters deserve to be quoted at some length:

> You see a better life after this wretched one, whereas I think about it quite differently and would therefore either throw this life away or get something out of it . . . Father [Papa] calls Stetten the "best" spot, because I am incarcerated there and you are well rid of me. O believe me, these cold explanations on my part are not what fill and move me; no, it is a sorrowful pain at the lost eternal spring etc., a homesickness, not for Calw, but for something true. But I see only illusion in living and striving, hoping and loving, only feeling—as Turgenev says, "haze, haze!" If I could have seen my present life several months ago, I would have taken it for an evil and impossible dream. This cold, half pedantic, half practical priest with his sermons, these uneducated guards, these sick with their repulsive faces and manners, etc., etc.; everything is hateful to my soul and as if made to order to show a young person how miserable life and everything that goes with it is. What didn't I always give for good music, good poetry! Here there is not a trace of any of that, only

the plainest and choicest bleak prose. It would be different had I grown up here. Like the newly emerged butterfly I could then rejoice in the sun. But I know the sun: lock the newly emerged butterfly in again! But wherefore these explanations, you are in Calw and not in Stetten, I am in Stetten and not in Calw. You breathe a different atmosphere; "Hermann in Stetten" is a stranger to you, is not your son . . . "My father couldn't use me and so sent me to Stetten," and that's that. Here I sit because I am not allowed to be elsewhere, and cry over myself while I laugh at the inspector . . . I will employ my last strength to show that I am not the machine that only needs to be wound up. I was forcibly put on the train, brought out here to Stetten; here I am and no longer disturb the world, because Stetten is beyond the world. For the rest I am my own master between these four walls; *I do not obey and will not obey.* (*Youth*, 260–261)

And now I ask you, only as a human being (because I permit myself, against your will and my fifteen years, to have an opinion): is it right to bring a young person who save for a small weakness of the nerves is pretty healthy to a "sanatorium for the *retarded and the epileptic*," to violently rob him of the faith in love and justice and thus also in God? (262–263)

Young Hermann's aggressive complaints against his parents and their religion are interlarded with passages of Rousseauistic self-pity and arch-Romantic longings for suicide: "You say I still have my entire life ahead of me. Granted, but youth is the foundation; at that time the heart is still receptive to good and bad. But alas, I forget that you are different people, without failings and flaws, like the statue, but also dead. Yes, you are authentic, true Pietists . . . and I—only a human being. I am an unhappy birth of nature; the germ of misfortune lies in myself" (264–265). Despite their melodramatic tone, these striking letters also reveal a considerable ironic and satiric gift, especially in his attack on the hypocrisy of bourgeois Christianity: "If you wish to write me, please not again [about] your Christ. He is being bruited about enough here. 'Christ and Love, God and Eternal Bliss' etc. etc. is inscribed in every spot, in every corner, and everything between is full of hate and enmity. I believe that if the spirit of the deceased 'Christ,' of the Jew Jesus, could see what he has brought about, he would weep" (265–266). This sounds rather like a nine-teenth-century Holden Caulfield (who imagines Christ vomiting in disgust at the spectacle of the Christmas show at Radio City).[22]

If in these outbursts Hesse's despair seems all-pervasive, the resentment against his father becomes explicit in a long sarcastic letter to him:

> Honored Sir:
>
> Because you are so noticeably ready to sacrifice yourself, might I perhaps ask you for 7 M[arks] or at once for the revolver. After you have brought me to despair you are surely ready to relieve me of it and yourself of me. Actually, I should have already croaked in June . . .
>
> "Father" is certainly an odd word, I don't seem to understand it. It must signify someone whom one can and does love straight from one's heart. How fond I would be of such a person! . . .
>
> Your relations with me are becoming ever more strained; I believe if I were a Pietist and not a human being, if I could change every quality and inclination within me into its opposite, I could harmonize with you. But I cannot and will not live thus any longer and if I commit a crime, you will be to blame as much as me, Herr Hesse, who have taken from me my joy in life. "Dear Hermann" has become another, a hater of the world, an orphan whose "parents" live.
>
> Don't write "Dear H." etc. any more; it is a dirty lie . . . I hope the catastrophe won't be long in coming. If only the anarchists were here!
>
> H. Hesse, Prisoner in the
Penitentiary at Stetten,
>
> where he is "not for punishment." I am beginning to wonder who is retarded in this affair. Moreover I would welcome it if you could come here occasionally. (268–269)

As the postscript to this letter shows, behind the turbulent self-assertion against the father is the naked desire to be close, to be loved. This most fundamental human trait is a strong constant in Hesse's personality, and one that counterpoises as much as it complicates his pronounced emphasis on self-will. Hesse's problem is of course a human given—the need for intimacy versus the need for independence, love versus freedom—but throughout his life it was exacerbated by the extraordinary *vitality* of these conflicting desires of the self. In the make-up of his introverted character the strong urge to be free and independent, which frequently (especially during childhood) took the form of resistance against or flight from the demands of others, came inevitably into conflict with the equally strong requirement to be loved and nurtured. And as the letters above suggest, sometimes the rebellious outbursts against his parents were simultaneously an attempt to provoke or bring on the love of these sorely tried parents.

The opposed drives of self-love taking the form of *Eigensinn*, on the one hand, and of being loved by others, on the other, constitute the distinctive psychic conflict of Hesse's childhood and maturity, and account as well for much of the thematic substance of his literary production. Put another way, what we find as the affective center of Hesse's personality and writings is the need to be or become oneself *and* the need to be accepted by a larger community; the strong ego wants both. Ninon Hesse has rightly concluded (with reference to the Maulbronn experience) that always the central theme in his fiction is "a breaking out of the community" (*Youth*, 519). The fact that Hesse himself placed such a rhetorical accent on the need to break away, and on the solitary, questing individual as the bearer of *Eigensinn*, however, should not blind us to the equally strong and basic need for human solidarity expressed in his life and art. One might call the former overt and the latter covert, but however one phrases it, the crux of his *Eigensinn* was that he wished to pursue a path of nonconformity, but feared its isolating and traumatic consequences— indeed, he experienced a good deal of discomfort and stress when they came his way at different crisis stages of his life, when his "outsider" status (as evident in *Steppenwolf*) became as much a curse as a blessing.[23]

His most effective way of balancing the claims of *Eigensinn* and community, of being himself and being accepted by others, was that of the artist whose works fulfill his self-expressive urges and at the same time earn the praise if not the love of a larger audience. For Hesse this was an ideal group of a few discriminating readers who could appreciate the substantial integrity of a career founded on the

values of psychic growth and self-making. Only with their coopera-
tion could he reconcile his obsession to be himself and his longing to
be accepted by others. Hesse may have made heavy rhetoric out of
his favorite virtue, but his literary practice exemplifies the truth of the
Wordsworthian sentiment that we live by admiration and by love.
Moreover, for Romantic and modern apostles of solitude and self-will
(from Rousseau and Blake to the likes of D. H. Lawrence in our century), the wished-for community is an ideal or imaginary one, projected into past and future, and traditionally expressed by the Romantic writer through versions of historical nostalgia or utopian
longing. The mature Hesse became enough of a realist or ironist to
submit these modes of wish fulfillment to the deconstructive lens of
criticism: after the Bolshevik version of utopia terminating in a "gulag
archipelago," and the fascist dream of the *Third Reich* in an extermi-
nation camp, this strikes one as a most salutary procedure.

Hesse had no problems elaborating his ideas about self-will on the
intellectual plane, but when he looked back on his childhood and
youth he was always rather hard-put to account for the trials and
difficulties occasioned by his headstrong temperament, and the root
causes of the proud *non serviam* within him. In his autobiographical
sketch, "Childhood of the Magician" (1923), he treated the matter
playfully and metaphorically with the explanatory fable of "the most
important and splendid" of "all the magic apparitions"—"the little
man":

> I do not know when I saw him for the first time; I think he was
> always there, that he came into the world with me. The little
> man was a tiny, gray, shadowy being, a spirit or goblin, angel or
> demon, who at times walked in front of me in my dreams as well
> as during my waking hours, and whom I had to obey, more than
> my father, more than my mother, more than reason, yes, often
> more than fear.[24]

As a self-will symbol, this figure is obviously a version of Socrates'
famous *daimon*, whom Hesse in one of his letters described as an "eu-
daimonion" or well-meaning spirit, the governing "center of gravity"
of the self that he also found exemplified in the personality of Goethe
as the center of the psyche that cannot be swayed by the outer world
and that guarantees the integrity of the individual.[25] Hesse's fabulous

"little man" is associated with the tasks of self-growth and may be interpreted in Jungian terms—as a version of the Shadow, and of the imperatives of individuation—as well as in Freudian terms: the goblin's commands are associated with disobedience against the father and with the unriddling of the tormenting "question of the difference between the sexes and the origin of children" (when it leads him to burst in upon Frau Anna, a pretty neighbor, who "was just in the act of undressing").[26]

In another autobiographical essay, "Life Story Briefly Told" (1925), Hesse acknowledges more prosaically, "I have always behaved rebelliously toward commandments of every sort, especially during my youth. All I needed was to hear 'thou shalt not' and everything in me rose up and I became obdurate." Here self-will as disobedience is also linked with the decision at age thirteen "that [he] wanted either to be a poet or nothing at all," a self-image that brought him increasingly into conflict with the expectations of his family and teachers. In this reprise of his life, the sexual aspect of his adolescent identity crisis goes unmentioned, and the nascent poet's difficulties are couched in vague Romantic tropes—he saw "nothing but abysses" between him and his goal. And the Maulbronn escapade and the string of misadventures subsequent to it are summarized in terms sufficiently unclear to indicate that the adult Hesse was at a loss to explain coherently to himself or others the nature of his youthful *crise de coeur* (a failure that is evident in his attempt to deal with this period in *Beneath the Wheel*):

> When I was thirteen years old and this conflict had just begun, my conduct in my parents' house as well as in school left so much to be desired that I was banished to a Latin school in another city. A year later I became a pupil in a theological seminary . . . when suddenly from inside me storms arose that led to flight from the monastery school, punishment by strict imprisonment, and dismissal from the seminary.
>
> Then for a while I struggled to advance my studies at a *Gymnasium*; however, the lock-up and expulsion were the end there too. After that, for three days I was a merchant's apprentice, ran away again for several days and nights, and to the great distress of my parents, disappeared. For a period of six months I was my

father's assistant; for a year and a half I was an employee in a mechanical workshop and tower-clock factory.

In short, for more than four years everything that was attempted with me went wrong; no school would keep me, in no course of instruction did I last long.[27]

As that epic case-book, *Childhood and Youth Before 1900*, his mother's journals and letters, and Hesse's own retrospective self-accounts all attest, he was something of a demon child who during and after these stormy years was unable to sort out the causes of his problems, other than adverting to his refractory self-will. In some ways he seems to have been a rebel in search of a motive, suffering from that well-known and objectless Romantic *malaise*, that primordial discontent with culture that from Rousseau onward is not so much the symptom of a diseased will as of a tremendous vitality and pristine hunger for the fullness of being, and that can assert itself against what it perceives as a stifling environment with anarchic, destructive vigor. From the later eighteenth century down to the neo-Romantic countercultures of youth, so virulent in the Western world in the sixties and the seventies, its protest has been as prone to take the form of some literal or psychological escape (running away from home, a flight into fantasy or drugs, and at worst, into madness or suicide) as actual, overt rebellion or defiance. A primary discontent originating in excessive energy and a surplus of the life-force, it can express itself in any number of destructive and creative ways on the level of personal behavior, and in a host of radically different world-views and ideological orientations, on the level of belief systems. In this regard, Hesse's adult stress on *Eigensinn*, the affective center of his values, represents the intellectual elaboration, or translation into a creed or philosophy of life, of the crucial experiences of his childhood and youth.

To round out this discussion of "The Sufferings of Young Hermann," I would like to introduce a concept from the psychologist Heinz Lichtenstein that Norman Holland has recently applied to the study of authors and texts—*identity theme*. In Lichtenstein's existential theory of personality, "man is the protean animal," endowed not with an invariable identity, but with "an '*identity theme*' . . . capable of variations that spell the difference between human creativity" and neurotic behavior. Rephrased in terms adduced earlier, the identity theme that Hesse was able to realize creatively through his writings is the psychic tension between *Eigensinn* and the wish to be part of a community, between the need to be himself and to be loved by others. There is yet a further aspect to Lichtenstein's theory that can aid our understanding of Hesse's self-concept, and do so by illuminating or interpreting it through his charged relationship with his mother. Lichtenstein posits that the "human infant in fact acquires an identity" because the mother "imprints" one on her offspring: "The mother does not convey a sense of identity to the infant but an *identity*: the child is the organ, the instrument for the fulfillment of the mother's unconscious needs." This psychological molding of the infant by the mother is not as inflexible as it may sound here, because the concept of identity theme allows for a nice balance between determinism and free will—the "theme" imprinted on the child, although irreversible, "is capable of variations," like a melody in music.[28]

The reason why Marie Hesse might have unconsciously endowed her inordinately gifted sprite of a son with the identity theme of *Eigensinn* is not hard to discover in her own life story, which is largely that of a highly intelligent and sensitive woman's consistent renunciation of what strikes one as a very strong self-will to the ideal of paternal authority and the demanding trinity of father, husband, and God. There were some tempestuous episodes in her youth, the most poignant, even heart-rending, of which was the sudden romance that developed between the fifteen-year-old Marie and a young Englishman, John Barns, when she was on a ship bound for India to join her missionary parents. She and Barns exchanged vows, but when he subsequently wrote to ask for her hand in marriage, he was summarily turned down by her father. She was never even informed of the proposal or given the letters that Barns was writing to her (only years later did she find out about all this). Here Freedman asks the crucial question: "Is this where Hermann Hesse's anguish began? On a deeper level than theology, the contradictions in the mother foreshadow those in the son."[29] Marie's response to the shipwreck of her adolescent love was a suppression of her own feelings, and a near-total submission to her parents. The resolution of the nervous crisis precipitated by her thwarted love for John Barns took, after an initial depression, the form of a conversion experience that in effect made a positive good out of her self-capitulation to her family and its religion. Her willpower was successfully turned against what she (now) perceived as her errant and worldly self. For the rest of her life her devout faith in her savior had to be supported by such a process of self-abnegation, one succinctly summarized toward the end of her life in a letter to her daughter Marulla:

> Dearest Marutschle! alas, the human heart is certainly wretched until it comes to rest in God . . . Jesus does his work; hold fast to that, and be glad to be worked and schooled by him, even if frequently the heart wants to cry out like a child that is being weaned from its mother. From my own youth I can speak of much heart-sorrow and dissatisfaction and inconstancy; the suffering of the world and the passionate nature of youth afflict us. Thus there is nothing to be done with our heart; let the Savior heal it. And it doesn't happen at once, but by stages of growth, through patient education and work. Yet He will accomplish it, that you can believe firmly. What often makes it more difficult for us is our halfheartedness. The more completely and undividedly we give ourselves to God and renounce what is properly ours, the more rapidly we shall find peace. He brings about the willing and the completion. We have to look toward Him, away from ourselves. Only in looking toward Him can we overcome the sin which sticks to us and which makes us slothful. Rejoice in Him, forget your self. (MH, 223)

For those endowed with little character or spunk, such a self-sacrifice is relatively easy, but for Marie Hesse it must have required an enormous, a brutal amount of self-discipline, as is vividly suggested in the metaphor of the crying weanling. Thus it should not surprise us that some of the significance of the very special relationship between Hesse and his mother—whose importance for his fiction Hesse's first biographer already more than hinted at[30]—may be located in Marie Hesse's unconscious transfer onto her favorite (and prodigal) son, by way of compensation and wish fulfillment, of the identity theme of an *Eigensinn* that in her own life was at first cruelly frustrated by others, and then consciously offered up by her for the greater glory of His will. Here her famous son's life story and his works become after a fashion the perfect negative, counterbalance, and complement to her own.

Moreover, in order to express creatively the burden of his identity theme, Hesse had to reject his mother's self-sacrifice, and to circumvent as well her conscious expectations of who and what he should be—which were of course largely an echo of the voice of paternal authority. In this way he may have been driven to hurt and frustrate her conscious hopes in order to fulfil her unwitting intentions. It may not be too implausible a notion that her unconscious desires might have included (by way of revenge against paternal authority) that of turning the son against the father, as in the Lawrencian model of "sons and lovers." At best, this might have been a small charge of unconscious motivation, for Marie Hesse was far too admirable and noble a woman to indulge in the psychological warfare of a Mrs. Morel. In any event, although Hesse acknowledged that his mother understood him better than anybody else,[31] and although he remained passionately attached to her image, from the vantages of his adult *Eigensinn* he could not approve of her life of extreme renunciation and self-sacrifice. As he wrote to his sister Adele in 1933, who was then editing the volume of Marie Hesse's letters and journals from which I have quoted extensively,

> All in all, when I try to see it objectively, her life does not appear to me "fortunate" and truly exemplary. E.g., in the case of grandfather Gundert I see a tranquillity and harmony, a clarified spirituality that irradiates everything else. But in the case of Mother I am on the contrary always moved and disturbed by her great passionateness, and I have never had the impression that she ever reached her true goal, namely, to extinguish her ardent and impassioned nature in the Savior. Precisely because I have inherited so much from her and suffer from the same dispositions, I do see in Mother's life a great and passionate approach to sanctity, but she did not become a saint.[32]

Ironically enough, this judgment by Hesse on his mother's life as not exemplary becomes in the longer perspective of time a self-judgment as well: if his mother's path of self-denial did not lead ultimately to harmony and sanctity, neither did her son's, which aspired to the same qualities on the opposite and singular path of self-will. These

were only distant ideals to which his life and art were forever looking, and which were sometimes provisionally glimpsed through the
rose-tinted binoculars of his fictional and hagiographic self-incarnations.

The Religion of Dissent

As suggested at the beginning of this chapter, Hesse's concept of *Eigensinn* also has a significant religious element to it. Although he re-
belled in early adolescence against the strict Pietism of his family—
indeed, the fifteen-year-old sought to provoke his parents by signing
one of his letters, "H. Hesse Nihilist" (*Youth*, 250)—he never rejected
the larger relevance of religion to his life. In fact, as discussed in the
previous chapter, he was torn as a confessional writer by the conflicting claims of artist versus saint as ideal self-images. In regard to theological and doctrinal positions, his religious outlook was so syn-
cretic—a quilt patched together from several of the leading world
faiths—as to preclude any systematic formulation or even dogma
other than that of *Eigensinn* itself. In the early stages of his career he
was able to admire the virulently anti-Christian Nietzsche as well as
the tender Saint Francis, and later the religio-philosophical traditions
of first India and later China became very important to him. What he
partly sought in all the religious and intellectual traditions and figures he admired was support and confirmation of his faith in self-
will, exemplary patterns of nonconformity in different ages and cultures.

   In its religious aspect as well, Hesse's *Eigensinn* stresses the inherent primacy of individual conscience. Yet despite its theological eclec-
ticism, Hesse's protest on behalf of the individual has a fundamentally Protestant character and represents the legacy of his missionary
forbears as this is assimilated in his adult thinking and writing. He
may have cast off their particular confession, Pietism, as too narrow
and provincial a vision of Christianity, but as he acknowledged in a
letter of 1930, the religious impulse is decisive for his life and his
works.[33] And in "Life Story Briefly Told," he points to what is sometimes overlooked by those too taken with the "Eastern" version of
Hesse:

> It was not by accident alone that I was born the son of pious
> Protestants; I am a Protestant by temperament and nature as
> well (to which my deep antipathy to the present Protestant de-
> nominations is no contradiction whatever). For the true Protes-
> tant is in opposition to his own church just as he is to every
> other, since his nature constrains him to affirm becoming above
> being. And in this sense Buddha, too, was certainly a Protes-
> tant.[34]

It is the Protestant and vigorously nonconformist, dissenting strain
in his work that makes for affinities between the German writer
Hesse and such English writers as Blake, Wordsworth (before his relapse into orthodoxy), and D. H. Lawrence, who come out of similar
backgrounds, and whose works have as much of a religious as a literary substance to them. Like them, Hesse conveys a post-Enlightenment sense of the self that is a secularized version of the Protestant
examination of the conscience. To be sure, his model of individuality
is also strongly influenced by the Goethean ideal of *Bildung* as the
harmonious cultivation of our faculties, and in a larger sense by the
German literature between 1750 and 1850 of which he was such an
avid student. But as he observes in the foreword to a planned edition
of German autobiographies (of which Goethe's is praised as the
greatest), even in those writings in which the Pietist-Protestant features are absent, "the German preoccupation with the course of one's
life, of self-examination and the drive to self-knowledge" are a
greater consequence of the Reformation, "just as all of the German
individualism of more recent times reveals this origin."[35]

The religious and moral context of this "self-examination" is for
Hesse what keeps it from turning into what some might impugn as
mere narcissism. One of his fondest beliefs was that the preoccupation with the self is not necessarily egotistical or merely self-indulgent, because the self is not synonymous with the ego, but is ultimately identical with the ontological ground of all being—a truth he
found exemplified in different ways in Eastern religion and in Jungian psychology. In a letter of 1920 he tried to explain the religious
significance of "the search for one's self" in his fiction to a skeptical
correspondent:

You assume that living from within our own selves is mere egoism. This appears so only to the European, who knows nothing
of the self. The "I" which the seeker means, and with which the
entire world of ideas beyond Europe . . . has been busy for three
thousand years, this "I" is not the single individual and how he
feels or appears to himself, but rather it is the innermost, essential core of every soul, which the Indian calls "atman" and which
is divine and eternal. He who discovers this "I," be it in the way
of Buddha or the Vedas or Lao-Tzu or Christ, is connected in his
innermost being with all, with God, and acts in harmony with
it.[36]

Hesse's affirmation of such a divine principle within the individual
remained constant throughout his adult life, as can be seen, for instance, in a letter penned more than two decades later in which he
distinguishes between two selves: the first is "our subjective, empirical, individual 'I'," which is governed by external circumstances; the
second is our secret, "high, holy 'I'," which is part of "God . . . the
whole, the un- and supra-personal."[37]

The elusive goal of Hesse's *Eigensinn* when considered in its religious aspect is that second and eternal self, affirmed (so he thought)
by all the major religions. Here his version of the Spiritual Way involves what Ziolkowski has discussed as "the triadic rhythm of humanization," and which is a version of what M. H. Abrams has explored in *Natural Supernaturalism* as a central feature of Romantic
thought, a secularized version of the Christian idea of the fall and the
coming of the millennium.[38] In the 1932 essay, "A Bit of Theology,"
Hesse outlines the stages of human development in categories that
are similar to the version of "natural supernaturalism" probably most
familiar to the English-speaking reader, Blake's Innocence, Experience, and their dialectic integration at a third and higher level:

The path of human development begins with innocence (paradise, childhood, the irresponsible first stage). From there it leads
to guilt, to the knowledge of good and evil, to the demand for
culture, for morality, for religions, for human ideals. For everyone who passes through this stage seriously and as a differentiated individual it ends unfailingly in disillusionment, that is,

with the insight that no perfect virtue, no complete obedience, no adequate service exists, that righteousness is unreachable, that consistent goodness is unattainable. Now this despair leads either to defeat or to a third realm of the spirit, to the experience of a condition beyond morality and law, an advance into grace and release to a new, higher kind of irresponsibility, or to put it briefly: to faith.[39]

Hesse grants the specifically European and Christian coloration of his mapping of these three stages, but insists that it is a generic human pattern expressed in symbolic forms by all the world religions, and given its highest theological form by Indian Brahmanism and by Buddhism. *Eigensinn* fits into this larger pattern as the signature of the second stage: in the first, man is still enveloped in the womb-like innocence of the group and has no individual identity, and in the third, self-will is preserved yet transcended—or to use that wonderful Hegelian term for dialectical synthesis, *aufgehoben*—into higher unity. As in the Jungian scheme of individuation, which is also grounded in Romantic thought, in Hesse's triadic rhythm the initial appearance of individuality is experienced as a misfortune, as a version of the fall—a transgression against and separation from the norms of the group—which is really a *felix culpa*.

Self-will, then, predominates in the stage of Experience, which is full of the thorns of doubt, confusion, despair, and bad faith. As Ziolkowski has astutely observed, Hesse *the writer* is primarily interested in this second stage, "for it is on the level of conflicts with reality that novelistic action can take place."[40] As Hesse explains, in practice the majority of humans remain fixed in the first stage, perpetual infants who never attain the threshold of humanity proper. Those (un)happy few who experience the fortunate fall and suffer the trials of the second stage cannot remain in it for the duration: they either end up fleeing back to Innocence (to Blake's Sleep of Beulah), or they struggle and suffer shipwreck in it—the traditional fate of many Romantic heroes—or they push on through to the third stage and overcome alienation and despair in a triumphant reconciliation of consciousness with nature and itself. For Hesse the third stage may actually be a composite of further stages of spiritual growth, whose guiding star is what Teilhard de Chardin in his famous phrase calls the Omega

Point, the merging of the human into the divine, of the *Mensch* into the *Übermensch*, "to Mahatma, to God, to the pure existence of spirit unencumbered by . . . matter."[41] Obviously the air up there gets rather rarefied: Hesse claims that all religions point to these higher gradations, but he admits that he has experienced nothing of their reality—unlike some of his fictional saints (Vasudeva and the Music Master) who actually merge into higher unity.

The third stage is also that of achieved spiritual community. Hence self-will, the particular virtue and problem of the second stage, is on the third reconfigured so that self-will qua individuality yields to the ideal of service to the whole. What one might call the prophetic or visionary element of Hesse's gospel of *Eigensinn* is the intuition of a radical individualism that does not lead in the end to isolation but to a reintegration with the greater unity of being. In fact, for Hesse there is no other way to achieve this unity than through the arduous path of self-will and the trials of the second stage: it is not possible to cross directly from the undifferentiated unity of Innocence to the dialectical synthesis of the third stage without passing through the needle's eye of *Eigensinn*. The religious upshot of Hesse's ideal of individuality is that only when we go the limit in finding ourselves are we able to gain the world.

It should be evident that Hesse's tripartite ranking of people according to the degree of individuation they have achieved amounts to an aristocracy of consciousness: the elect who push on to the second and the third stage are a diminishing minority next to the majority who, because they have never come of age, "never become fully human."[42] Hesse tried to resist the chief temptation inherent in Romantic concepts of a self-willed elite—contempt for ordinary humanity. Sometimes he even worked himself up into a Wordsworthian admiration of common folk, especially in his early fiction, where this accounts for some blatant lapses into bathos. Like many Romantics who know deep down the fundamental truth of man's spiritual *ine*-quality, who value the individual above the crowd, yet who nevertheless are committed to democracy and equality in the political sphere, Hesse had something of a problem. At least he was honest enough to acknowledge it on occasion. For instance, he observed in 1930 that

> One must not say this, and . . . it is forbidden from a human as well as from a democratic and a Christian viewpoint to call too much attention to the fact that people are unequal, that the genial ones give us more pleasure than the stupid, and that God's kingdom on earth would not be worth talking about without the aristocratic ones who are above the average. That these supra-normal ones have to pay for their plus with great suffering is another chapter altogether.[43]

Two years later he wrote to a Protestant theologian that what he finds most admirable in Jesus is his ability to love humanity, and confesses, "I find nearly nothing of this in myself; on the contrary, I often feel contempt for humanity." Lest this be taken as a passing fit of his Steppenwolf persona, let me point to a letter of two decades later in which he identifies the larger dilemma posed by his elitism: "I view the world as an artist and though I believe I think democratically, in my feelings I am nevertheless thoroughly aristocratic, which means to say that I can love every sort of quality, but the same is not true for quantity."[44]

Hesse's ideal (beginning with the *Demian* period) of a sort of clerisy of self-willed seekers also helps to explain his pedagogic intentions toward his young readers. As suggested earlier in this chapter, he may have found through his audience a sense of community that eluded him in actual life, an author-reader relationship that was further enhanced by his desire to function as a sort of Professor of *Eigensinn*. Only this need can help to account for the seriousness with which he took what in his later years became nearly a full-time job— the daily burden of keeping up a voluminous correspondence with his readers. There is something both poignant and absurd in Hesse's epistolary office, and in his sense of obligation in responding to those who wrote, even if he managed for the most part to avoid the newspaper-advice-column trap of dispensing specific solutions to personal problems. What Hesse's father observed of his adolescent son is still true of the famous author's transactions with his readers: "He writes remarkably many letters. Apparently his correspondence has to replace something else for him" (*Youth*, 477). Hesse was convinced that for some of his readers his books had "a very specific meaning and value . . . namely, that they find corroborated and clarified in them their own most important experiences, victories, and defeats. Their number is not large, but then neither is the number of people who have soul-experiences."[45] He summarized his epistolary office eloquently at the beginning of the 1930s when the political situation in Germany was directly threatening his most cherished ideal,

> I receive several thousand letters a year, all from people under twenty-five, and many of them also come to seek me out. Almost without exception these are talented but difficult youths, destined to an above-average measure of individuation, and confused by all the labelling of our standardized world. Some are pathological, some are so splendid, that my entire faith in the continued existence of the German spirit rests on them. To this minority of partly endangered but vital young spirits I am neither a minister nor a physician—for that I lack any authority and claim—but as far as my empathy reaches, I strengthen each one in what sets him apart from the norm, and seek to show him the meaning of it.

Hesse never thought much of large-scale schemes or programs to improve the world, but the teacher in him put his faith in the individual because, as he put it in 1956, "the individual is capable of being educated and improved; and my belief is and has ever been that it is always the small elite of good-willed, courageous people prepared for sacrifice who have preserved what is good and beautiful in the world."[46]

In this long chapter I have sought both to clarify and to document Hesse's root-concept of self-will by way of tracing its major branches in his life and his thought, including its central position in his politics of conscience, his troubled childhood and youth, and his religious outlook. The extensiveness of my treatment and the diversity of the perspectives I have brought to bear on this issue are warranted, I believe, by its significance as the identity theme of Hesse's life and as the personal myth projected in his writings—in short, as the master-key to his life and art that has not hitherto received the measure of critical attention it deserves.

It is of course possible to take a largely negative view of Hesse's "favorite virtue," and to construe his stress on it as an elaborate apology, a rationalization or cover for an enormous self-concern and a self-centered ego—in which case we would still have to admire the persistent artfulness with which the adult writer unfolds the idea of self-will as the pervasive defense mechanism of that massive ego. Leon Edel has concluded that the most difficult task of the biographer is to find "the figure under the carpet," which is "what people are really saying behind the faces they put on."[47] In our suspicious post-Freudian age the notion that on occasion we can credit the statements of authors about themselves and their works may sound unorthodox and naive, but I suggest that in Hesse's case we can take his concern with self-will at face value: here the figure in the carpet coincides with that under the carpet, the overt myth with the identity theme of his life. As I have tried to show in connection with his troubled childhood, Hesse's master myth does have a compulsive and irrational side, as a personality trait implicated in the dynamics of a family romance whose significance may have eluded him. But as an adult he accepted and lived out that myth in his writings, illustrating the fruitful paradox that at best we are capable of becoming what implicitly we already are. By our relative degree of success in this venture we are able to justify our lives to ourselves, wrote Hesse in 1949, with the biggest inner obstacle to the task of becoming ourselves being "that at bottom one wishes to be someone other than what one is; that one pursues models and ideals which one cannot and should not even attain." Judged by his own standards, Hesse succeeded as a writer in living out the inner myth of his being by expressing through his works the many faces of his self-will. That is why he was able in his later years to speak of his leading preoccupation with a wry self-irony that is a far cry from the more virulent inner-voice rhetoric of the World War I period: "I intend to die as a difficult individualist at whom people smile condescendingly."[48]

During the past two decades the glad tidings of the Death of Man—or at least the humanist version of him—have been announced in the influential language of post-structuralist demythologizing of the hidden metaphysical assumptions of writers and thinkers, one of which is the self-presence of the subject to itself. From such currently regnant critical perspectives, Hesse's expression earlier in our century of a Romantic humanism solidly grounded in a secularized Protestantism and in the German Romantic tradition from Goethe through Novalis and the *Frühromantiker* to Nietzsche, may appear hopelessly old-fashioned. Hesse certainly knew, as we have seen, that there was something quixotic about his unswerving faith in *Eigensinn*. But he also knew what we are sometimes prone to forget: the vagaries of history and intellectual fashions and the fact that (as the recent instance of the environmental movement ought to remind us) what may seem hopelessly passé to one age may strike the next as shiningly progressive and enlightened. In that sense, the age of Hesse's *Eigensinn* is perhaps not so much the past as the future.

CHAPTER IV

AUTOBIOGRAPHICAL

BEGINNINGS

What amazes me the most is the good success of my Peter. On the basis of that we are also getting married, and things are coming true in which I no longer dared believe.—Hesse letter of 1904

Romantic Apprenticeship

During 1894 and 1895 when Hesse, after the various academic failures and personal crises of early adolescence, toiled as a mechanic's helper in Perrot's tower-clock workshop in Calw, he devoted what spare time he had to "much serious reading."[1] While his manual work remained alien to him, he prepared himself for his true profession, writing, including the cultivation of a literary correspondence in which he could deliver the fruits of his reading and reflection. This self-described "lonely poetaster" touched in his letters—sometimes pretentiously but with a surprising self-assurance for a seventeen-year-old—on the state of modern German and European literature. And he was also reading the German Romantics, to whom he reacted at first largely negatively—"in general I don't like the Romantics, yet I love some individual ones"—dismissing Romanticism as "an already superseded viewpoint."[2] A few years later, however, when Hesse was employed as a bookdealer's apprentice, he was to reverse this negative evaluation, and to immerse himself in the literary and cultural milieu of German Romanticism. He had moved to the university town of Tübingen, and to work that brought him closer to his vocation, in 1895, and there his protracted study, especially of Goethe and Nietzsche, brought him back by the end of 1897 to an admiration verging on adulation of the same writers he had dismissed a few years earlier. As he acknowledged in a letter of July 26, 1898, "in my spare time I am almost exclusively occupied with serious study of the Romantics, and Novalis is especially important to me."[3]

What Hesse found in that by-then dim galaxy of German Romanticism—to most English-speaking readers hardly more than a list of unfamiliar names (in the letter of 1895 cited above Hesse mentions Eichendorff, Uhland, Brentano, the Schlegel brothers, Tieck, Hoffmann, and Lenau)—was an enchanting sense of the magic of the imagination within the flux of our ordinary experience. As he put it at the time,

> This Romanticism! All that is youthful and secret in the German heart is contained in it; all its superabundant force as well as all its disease, and above all a yearning for spiritual elevation, a youthful, genial speculation which our time is lacking altogether. The religion of art—that for me is the essence; it is the goal of Romanticism in its most naive as well as its most exquisite productions.[4]

In Tübingen and later in Basel (where he moved in 1899 to a better position in another bookstore) Hesse became the devoted literary apostle and epigone of this Romantic religion of art, but in a garb updated according to prevailing literary fashions. The bookstore clerk assumed the pose of a contemporary aesthete, indulging himself in moods of languid melancholy, languorous longing, and the nervous *frissons* of a belated Romantic whose sensibility is caught up in the rarefied atmosphere prevalent toward the close of the nineteenth century—of Chopin, Pater, Maeterlinck, Rossetti, the pre-Raphaelites and the aesthetic nineties. Hesse's first book, *Romantic Songs* (written 1897–1898, published 1899), whose printing costs he bore himself, signals with its title the provenance of his plaintive lyrical effusions. In it we find the same sense of mystery, loneliness, *Weltschmerz*, and longing for beauty as in the early Yeats, whose imagination was steeped in a similar literary tradition. But if the young Hesse's lyrics have the same musical charm as those of the Yeats of the nineties, they lack the suggestive power and hypnotic lure of such performances as "The Lake Isle of Innisfree" or "The Song of Wandering Aengus."

The Yeats parallel is instructive, because it reveals to what extent Hesse, working out of a similar literary context—late-nineteenth-century Romanticism—started off as an essentially weak and derivative talent. His lachrymose laments do not reach the level of a striking and representative utterance; the idiom remains a borrowed one, so that in reading through the bulk of these lyrics one grows tired of the repeated clichés of feeling. "Tomorrow I will be dead," promises the loquacious sufferer, but lives to sing for many more days of the same subject.⁵ These stylized and conventional neo-Romantic trifles also do not permit a deeper insight into Hesse's state of mind. As he wrote to his mother, "The 'Romantic Songs' already carry in their title an aesthetic and personal confession. I consider it the farewell to a period and believe that they do not permit any conclusions about my future poetic compositions."⁶ That Hesse was thus willing to write off his fledgling flights in print also shows his remarkable capacity for self-criticism, and for moving from weakness and disease toward strength and health.

Health, however, was not exactly around the corner. His second publication, *An Hour Behind Midnight* (written 1897–1898), continues his Romantic apprenticeship, but in the lyrical prose of six miscellaneous items ranging from impromptu fantasy ("Island Dream"), to medieval tale ("The Feast of the King"), invocation of his muse ("The Fever Muse"), monologue ("Conversation with a Mute"), and poetic reminiscence ("The Dream of the Ripe Corn Field"). If the language of this collection tends toward the consciously beautiful and precious, its title suggests an aesthete's dream world beyond space and time and the pressures of the mundane world—an inner realm of images presided over by the poet's "fever muse." Not surprisingly, the Narcissus motif recurs in different guises; more striking, however, and more revealing of Hesse's state of mind is the recurrence of the haunting and mysterious image of the mother.

In the aesthete's credo of *An Hour Behind Midnight* the mother myth that is an important element of much of Hesse's subsequent fiction is presented largely through Romantic stereotypes. In "Island Dream," the world-weary narrator, "a ship-wrecked dreamer," is driven by "disgust with life" to an island peopled by all the women he has ever admired, and whose beautiful queen, who knows him well, reminds him of his "distant mother."⁷ Associated with intimate consolation and advice, this cherished figure is an ethereal yet eroticized emblem of beauty, as well as a highly poeticized version of Marie Hesse in her son's imagination. She is also his "fever muse" with a pre-Raphaelite, Botticellian aspect, with "her pale, all-knowing gaze," who passes "ghostly-pale nights" with him that are full of "cruel vo-luptuousness."[8] In "Conversation With a Mute," the mother symbol is more directly associated with Marie Hesse's physical features: "Do you know what I mean when I say: my mother? You do not see from it her black hair and brown eyes." "To Frau Gertrud" shows the mother-muse figure as the guide to "the realm of eternal beauty," and as his guardian spirit. Hesse's praise of her eyes as "stars of beauty and truthfulness, full of kindness and severity, incorruptible, judging, improving, rewarding,"[9] is a beautiful tribute to his child-hood relationship with his gentle yet stern mother. And in "The Dream of the Ripe Corn Field," the mother myth is grounded in Ro-mantic nature: the field of corn becomes a charged metaphor of the innermost ground of his being, and of the childhood identified with his mother—from which the adult poet feels exiled. Yet what of the missing member in this fictional version of the family romance, the father? Only in "The Feast of the King" does the Oedipal triangle become apparent in the young minstrel-poet's near-successful seduc-tion of the beautiful queen in the very castle of the feasting king. Like another famous modern son and lover, D. H. Lawrence, Hesse would for the remainder of his literary career be working out the im-plications of such symbolic mother and father images.

Hesse's third book, *The Literary Remains of Hermann Lauscher* (1900), is still largely an assortment from the workshop of his Romantic ap-prenticeship, yet has more substance and range than the slight con-fections described above. The conventional framing device of Hesse as the editor of the papers of the deceased poet Lauscher ("Lis-tener"), characterized as "documents of the peculiar soul of a mod-ern aesthete and eccentric,"[10] helps to create some ironic distance be-tween Hesse and the melodramatic posturings of his hero. At *Lauscher*'s worst, Hesse is still trying to ride a magic carpet of beauti-ful language, as in the purple prose of "Sleepless Nights," another insomniac bout with his fever muse, replete with the stock-in-trade of a moribund romanticism—nightingale, snow-white castle, harp, midnight, fountain, the moon, and a passing reference, for good measure, to Rossetti (294–315). In the preface to a much later edition (1933), Hesse admits that he would have liked to delete or revise a number of passages in *Lauscher*, but felt that it was not permissible for him retroactively to falsify this portrait and performance of an earlier self.[11]

Lauscher's is still the religion of art, or as the ("self-torturing") "Journal of 1900" puts it, the belief "that this religion can bring one exaltations that do not take second place in purity and blessedness to those of the martyrs and saints" (321). Lauscher's aesthetic transports, however, are countered by his attraction to irony, and the desire "to dissolve [his] entirely thick-blooded manner and blow it into the blue sky as a pretty soap bubble" (323). Actually, Hesse-Lauscher is learning to transcend the limitations of a *fin de siècle* "art for art's sake" for a more thoroughgoing immersion in the world of the German Romantics (as opposed to their later imitators) that he had been studying for several years. As he put it with some defensiveness, "I know well enough that this is Romanticism . . . translated into a modern idiom. And why not?" (323). His most successful translation of the Romantic into the modern would have to wait until *Steppenwolf* two and a half decades later. In *Lauscher*, however, he begins to appreciate the value of witty self-deprecation as a means of personal and literary growth, and to tire of worn-out neo-Romantic affectations. As he exclaims sarcastically in the "Journal of 1900" of his pose as the suffering poet, "to the devil with it!" (335).

The most impressive item in the *Lauscher* collection is the "Lulu" outing, a delightful fusion of prosaic fact with exuberant fantasy in the manner of E.T.A. Hoffmann, to whom the piece is dedicated. Hesse imaginatively transforms a country outing with his Tübingen (student) friends—the so-called *"petit cénacle"* ("little literary society")—and their infatuation with Lulu, an innkeeper's pubescent niece, into a latter-day Romantic *Märchen*. As Freedman has commented, here "Hesse was bent on putting all his recent reading and romantic theorizing into practice."[12] The narrative's symbolic merging of the prosaic and the fantastic is presided over by an eccentric Hoffmannesque figure, the philosopher Drehdichum (Turnaround), whose name is apt, since every character and event in it, as so often in the German Romantic fairy tale, has a double meaning. Although Hoffmann is the major influence, the reader conversant with the German Romantics can find any number of other echoes and reminders, the most obvious of which is the association of Lulu with "the blue flower," Novalis's famous symbol (in the language of Hesse's

"Lulu") of "the united longing of all great souls" (273). More importantly, the lecture that Drehdichum delivers to the young students reflects Hesse's now-deepened appreciation of and tribute to the genuine spiritual dimension of Novalis and the *Frühromantiker*:

> Even today poets incline more than other people to the belief that there are certain eternal and beautiful forces lying half-asleep in earth's womb, the intuition of which lights up the enigmatic present like lightning in the night . . . Then too the highest and most eternal words of the great poets appear to me like the babbling of a dreamer who without knowing it is mumbling about the fleetingly glimpsed heights of an otherworldly realm with heavy lips. (269)

The student Ripplein's rejoinder, "very prettily said, Herr Drehdichum, but neither old nor new enough. This enthusiastic lesson was preached a hundred years ago by the so-called Romantics" (269), points to Hesse's ironic perspective in this tale that is at once a semiserious venture in Romantic writing and a critique of its inherent limitations. Hesse's tribute to the Romantics contains a realistic perception of their greatest defect, the estrangement from ordinary life. This valuation is explicit in the response of the simple Lulu, to whom it appears absurd that these young men "talked continually of beauty, youth, and roses, and built up colorful theater-walls of words all around them, while all the harsh truth of life passed them by without their knowledge" (280). Her debunking viewpoint is matched by Lauscher's own impression that he and his fellow infatuates were "altogether dream-figures of a fantasizing humorist" (281).

Another item in *Lauscher*, "My Childhood," is revealing because it does not fit the collection's predominant mood of stilted aestheticism. It was in fact written several years earlier (in 1895), and is a powerful reminiscence of selected childhood experiences up to roughly the age of fourteen.[13] Notable in this retrospect, particularly in its nostalgia for a lost relationship to nature, is an inherent or organic romanticism, as opposed to Lauscher's studied literary pose. Striking too in "My Childhood," particularly in view of the fact that the parent figures in his early fiction from *Camenzind* on are either signally distorted or omitted, is the richly modulated rendering of memories of his father and mother. In this vivid autobiographical memoir, Hesse fondly recollects his father taking him up to a mountain church to show him the Rhine valley below: "this earliest picture of my father is differentiated from all those that came later. His black beard touched my blond forehead, and his large bright eye rested on mine in a friendly manner" (223). Another powerful autobiographical reprise of the family romance is that of the child walking behind his parents through a cornfield on a summer evening. This epiphanic memory crystallizes the features of the pastoral and familial scene into a symbolic "spot of time" (to use Wordsworth's famous phrase):

> I see the very tall, lean figure of my father walking upright toward the setting sun with his head tilted back, carrying his felt hat in his left hand. My mother is leaning gently against him in her slow stride, smaller and more vigorous, with the white cloth around her shoulders. Between the now barely separated dark heads glows the blood-red sun. The outlines of their figures are firmly drawn and irradiated by golden light; at each side there is a rich, ripe field of corn. I do not know what day I thus walked behind my parents, but for me this sight has remained fresh and unforgettable. I know no living or painted picture that appears to me more splendid in line and color and that is more precious to me than these noble figures on the footpath between the rows of ripe corn, as they move toward the red glow which bathes them in an otherworldly radiance. (223)

After this remarkable rendering of the scene internalized in the boy's imagination, Hesse splits the family portrait, with the mother-image presented with a sensuous delicacy. She is recalled as the incomparable storyteller of his early childhood: "All that excessively rich world of a child's life has no sweeter and more sacred picture than that of the storytelling mother at whose knee a blond head with deeply-amazed eyes is nestled" (225). Here we encounter the unabashed rapture of Hesse's mother attachment: "I can still see you, my mother, slim, supple, and patient, with the beautiful head inclined toward me, with the incomparable brown eyes!" (225). Next to such maternal riches, the presence of the father begins to pale and, as he assumes the role of the punisher, to portend the conflicts of puberty: "though I used to oppose such chastisement from the hands of the beloved father with silent defiance, my little heart experienced them as unspeakably bitter, painful, and humiliating" (229). Later the impact of such paternal "beatings" came to seem less traumatic next to those regularly inflicted by cruel teachers, with the net result that the father was less feared after "a strict teacher's frequent beatings and detention" (332). The adolescent Hesse's conflicted relationship with his father—the tortured cycle of misbehavior, punishment, resentment, repentance, forgiveness, and renewed infractions—is exposed in "My Childhood" with a forthrightness rare in Hesse's early writings. Even rarer is its conclusion with a poignant exchange of tenderness between father and son. Again the human emotions are framed by an elevated and elevating natural prospect: on a silvery, moonlit night, Hermann and Johannes stand "on a wooded mountainside." In a poignant moment of silent communion, the father puts his arm around his son and recites a famous, melancholy lyric by Goethe. And ever after when Hesse came across this poem, it seemed "as if the words came from the mouth of my father leaning against me, as if I felt his arm placed around me, saw his broad, clear forehead, and heard his low voice" (239). In this experience of momentary closeness between father and son, we can recognize an early source of the later Hesse's cult of a paternal *Geist*.

Peter Camenzind

The muses favored the aspiring author of *Lauscher* in the form of a letter from the well-known publishing house of Samuel Fischer, who invited Hesse to submit a current manuscript. Spurred on by this recognition and encouragement, he finished the novel he was working on and sent it to Fischer: "it was immediately accepted. I had arrived."[14] After its appearance in 1903, Hesse was established in more ways than one, for the literary and commercial success of *Peter Camenzind* propelled him into literary prominence and allowed him not only to give up his job as a bookseller's clerk in order to devote himself henceforth to full-time writing, but also played an important role in his decision to get married.

As opposed to the earlier miscellany, Hesse's first novel is a sustained narrative that has a firmer grip on plot and character. Because in the long view of his career it is also a minor achievement, the contemporary reader may be hard put to account for its instant success.

Clearly part of its immediate popularity, as Freedman has summarized it, is its capitalizing on literary and cultural trends of the day,
including the German youth movement with its stress on hiking and
the outdoors, and its sentimental yet robust realism in the vein of
Gottfried Keller's popular *Seldwyla* narratives.[15] Then too, *Camenzind*'s prose is more earthy and open to the variety of life than that of
Lauscher's hothouse atmosphere. Ball goes so far as to call it a step
into life and the beginning of health,[16] a half-truth that ignores the
undertone of despair that pervades this sunny nature book, and that
becomes rather oppressive on a rereading. Yet with Camenzind,
Hesse successfully expanded his repertoire to give expression to
other areas of his experience and made a transition from the pallid
aestheticism of Lauscher to a more inclusive if still romanticized realism. As he noted at the time, "I have the feeling that when I write
prose an entirely different side of my being comes to voice that found
no expression in my lyrical poetry."[17]

   The Swiss Peter whom Hesse described as "my rather sour blend
of farm lad and poet"[18] is—despite lederhosen, yodeling, and the
mountain village of Nimikon—of course none other than Hesse himself. In *Peter Camenzind* we also encounter an inventory of themes
that are identifiably "Hessean" insofar as they define the world of his
mature fiction, and that here figure with varying degrees of autobiographical proximity, of confessional disclosure and disguise of the
author's actual experience: love of the outdoors, education, male
friendship, romantic love, hagiography, father-son conflicts, loss or
absence of the mother, depression and suicidal impulses, the outsider, attraction to the South and love of wine, the portrait of the
artist, critique of modern culture, and the search for the self. The
reason that *Camenzind* can come across as one-dimensional is because
of the sometimes mawkish treatment of these and related motifs. Obviously with some of these the young Hesse gets so much out of his
depth—Peter's attacks on modern city-life, for instance—as to become bombastic. Others, like his student days under the *patres* and
later at a university, are mere narrative props. Hesse in fact commits
some of the perennial blunders of neophyte writers, including the
preponderance of mere telling over showing (for example, Peter's
stay in Paris) and the introduction of characters who are either con-
veniently killed off (Richard) or simply left dangling.

What redeems *Camenzind* from being merely a charming period piece is the story's imaginative center, the coincidence of its major theme—the love of nature—with its only significant character, Peter. In the account of Peter's childhood and youth Hesse first found an adequate vehicle to transcribe his own powerful experience of nature and of natural scenery for a larger audience. The Rousseauistic bent of the novel was acknowledged by Hesse in 1951 when, in the long view of half a century, he concluded that his hero "seeks to get away from the ways of the world and of society, back to nature; he repeats in miniature the half courageous, half sentimental revolt of Rousseau, and on this road he becomes a poet."[19] It would be a serious mistake, however, to view Peter's attachment to nature merely as an imitation of Rousseau and the Romantics, for his feelings are cut from the cloth of his author's experience. Like that of the leading Romantics a century and more before him, Hesse's love of nature is organic and entirely sincere. If *Camenzind* reads, as Hans Jürg Lüthi has noted, like the confession of a pantheist, that is precisely what Hesse felt. Therefore Fritz Böttger's claim that the novel shows the belated recrudescence of "a nineteenth-century feeling for nature" seems substantially off the mark.[20]

In addition to the connection with Rousseau, to which Hesse lent his support, we might also mention a poet with whose sense of nature the early Hesse shows even closer affinities, though Hesse, like most German readers and critics, seems hardly to have known his name: Wordsworth. The opening paragraphs repeat in minor key some of the major concerns of the English Romantic poet in the opening of his verse autobiography, *The Prelude* (1805). The Hesse who recollects his childhood experience of nature through Peter Camenzind has the same sense of the mysterious, animating power in landscape that Wordsworth does. For both writers, the beginnings of individual consciousness merge into a myth of Romantic origins, of nature's mysterious, massive presence. Wordsworth records such numinous moments (often as frightening as joyful) in vivid detail in *The Prelude*'s early "spots of time," those visionary episodes when, as he writes, "the earth / And common face of Nature spake to me / Rememberable things" (1, ll. 614–616, 1805 text). In the shorthand of *Peter Camenzind*'s opening Hesse records a similar sensibility:

As a child I knew no names for the lake, mountains, and brooks where I grew up. My eyes beheld the broad, smooth, blue-green lake lying in the sun, glistening with tiny lights and wreathed by precipitous mountains whose highest crevices were filled with glazed snow and thin waterfalls, and at whose feet there sloped luminous meadows with orchards and huts and gray Alpine cattle. And on my poor little soul, still blank and calm and full of expectancy, the lake and mountain spirits etched their proud deeds. Rigid cliffs and scarred precipices spoke, in tones of awe and defiance, of the age that had given them birth.[21]

For both Wordsworth and Hesse, this primeval "language" of nature is as formative an early influence as parents and teachers. And for both, the Romantic myth of origins has strong suggestions of the mother world, of a powerful maternal presence that is both celebrated and mourned by the adult poet. Hesse continues the passage above by introducing elemental birth imagery ("they spoke of ancient days when the earth heaved and tossed and, in the moaning agony of birth, thrust mountain peaks and crests from the tortured womb"). In both *Peter Camenzind* and *The Prelude*, such protoplasmic, animized nature images are not merely conventional or decorative, but substantive metaphors of childhood experience persisting in the adult's consciousness as a dynamic source of preverbal, prerational feelings that are closely allied with the genesis of the writer's imagination.

Indeed, the Swiss peasant-poet is a sort of modern mini-Wordsworth, retiring in the prime of his life to spend the rest of his days rooted in the landscape of his early years: thus Nimikon becomes Peter's Grasmere, the Swiss mountains and lakes his equivalent of the English Lake District. Like Wordsworth, Peter sees himself as a combination of recluse, wanderer, and sage who has found his way back home from the alienating forces of the modern world through the connection with nature. Like Wordsworth, he faces the Romantic dilemma, "how I would find my way from a love of nature to love of mankind" (123), an issue that Wordsworth sought to resolve in Book 8 of *The Prelude* ("Love of Nature Leading to Love of Mankind"). Like Wordsworth, Peter-Hesse finds Franciscan spirituality attractive because of its veneration of the simple and the natural. Finally, Peter-

Hesse aspired, like Wordsworth, to write a major poem devoted to reconciling human consciousness and nature:

> As you know, it had been my hope to write a work of some length in which I intended to bring closer to people the grandiose and mute life of nature, that they might love it. I wanted to teach people to listen to the pulse of nature, to partake of the wholeness of life and not forget, under the pressure of their petty destinies, that we are not gods and have not created ourselves but are children of the earth, part of the cosmos. I wanted to remind them that night, rivers, oceans, drifting clouds, storms, like creatures of the poet's imagination and of our dreams, are symbols and bearers of our yearning that spread their wings between heaven and earth . . . But I also wanted to teach men to find the sources of joy and life in the love of nature. I wanted to preach the pleasure of looking at nature, of wandering in it, and of taking delight in the present. (145)

Peter keeps records and notes "to capture concrete, real things . . . light effects, winds, rain, rocks, plants, animals, the flight of birds, the shapes of waves and clouds, the color of the sea" (147), but unfortunately his long-projected work never materializes—in part because he realizes "that a work of such scope without human figures would be grotesque" (147). In any event, Peter's unachieved nature poem had already been realized, and with human figures in it to boot, in such masterpieces of Romantic autobiography as Rousseau's *Confessions* and *Reveries of a Solitary Walker*, Wordsworth's *Prelude*, Goethe's *Poetry and Truth*, and Thoreau's *Walden*, among others—and after these monumental works of nineteenth-century Romanticism, the young Hesse realized it once more at the beginning of our century with the miniature tribute of *Camenzind*'s fictional confession.

Next to the novel's treatment of nature, the only other theme invested with a significant emotional charge is the passionate friendship between Peter and the musician Richard. The Peter who asserts that "nothing is more delicious than an honest and forthright friendship between two men" (86) is so taken with Richard that he is jealous of his relationships with women. The episode in which the two friends bathe in the river, with Richard playing the Lorelei and looking "girlishly demure" (87) is colored by homoerotic sentiment, yet

Peter-Hesse refuses to acknowledge such feelings, presenting them instead as boyish playfulness. Even more idealized and sentimental is the friendship between Peter and the crippled Boppi, who become an odd couple when Peter has Boppi move in with him. Here Peter is trying to put into practice his Franciscan ideal of *caritas*, as well as his aspiration to translate the love of nature into the love of man. Despite Peter's painful condescension to Boppi, Hesse's portrait of the saintly cripple has a good deal of pathos to it, partly because of the nineteenth-century idea of the spiritualizing effects of suffering, which in Boppi's case are manifest in his beautiful singing.

If Peter is able to achieve an emotional bond with men, his relationship to women is impossibly sentimental. Like young Werther, a distant literary forbear, he prefers to be unhappily in love. Inherent as well in his Romantic attitude is the veneration of the mother: "For me, the love of women has been a purifying act of adoration . . . Owing to my mother's influence and my own indistinct premonitions, I venerated womankind as an alien race, beautiful and enigmatic, superior to men by virtue of beauty and constancy of character, a race which we must hold sacred" (31). Thus he has no wish to be noticed by the first object of his devotions, Rösi Girtanner, and the closest he comes to an amorous advance is to risk his neck by climbing a rock-face to pick alpine roses, which he deposits in the Girtanner hallway: "no one saw me and I never found out if Rösi received my greeting" (36). With the other women in his life he is at least able to establish friendly relations. His passion for the painter Erminia Aglietti, whom he admires as "a woman battling for her livelihood" (71), brings him to the edge of proposing, only to discover that she is unhappily in love with a married man. Erminia too harks back to the Romantic creed of suffering: "love isn't there to make us happy. I believe it exists to show us how much we can endure" (75). True to character, Peter temporizes long enough with his next amour, Elizabeth, to make sure she turns out to be engaged to someone else, after which he can again play the role of the unhappy lover. Not surprisingly, Peter's last prospect of passion, the Italian widow Signora Nardini, very much available and with her sights set squarely on Peter, does not prove very enticing to him: she is almost explicitly sexual and altogether too much a creature of this world and of the Southern sun. No wonder then that Peter is willing to let his repressed Northern desires expend themselves in *vino veritas*.

While Hesse's fictional version of his feelings about nature, friendship, and romantic love is largely autobiographical, his handling of parent images is marked by significant distortions and omissions. Peter's boorish peasant father is a selfish tippler whose physical appearance nevertheless shows some similarities with Johannes Hesse, particularly his "doleful, ailing expression" (21). The complex ambivalence of Hesse's childhood relationship to his father is reduced to "a strange rite of chastisement and atonement" (30), a beating administered every few weeks. At the close of the book, this relationship is in a sense reversed when Peter holds the keys of power in the household, including those of the paternal wine-cellar—possibly a bit of unconscious wish-fulfillment on Hesse's part. The brief account of Peter's mother also in part evokes the image of Marie Hesse: "My mother, who had been beautiful, retained only her firm, straight frame and lively, dark eyes" (20). Yet her role is minimized, which suggests that Hesse, while at least touching on the conflict with his father, no matter how crudely, was in *Camenzind* (save for the one notable exception below) not willing or able to deal with his powerful feelings about his mother. Here and in his next novel, the figure of the mother is largely erased, and the emotional charge attaching to the relationship is channeled into and expressed through the lyrical bonding with nature.

Moreover, in describing the death of Peter's mother, Hesse graphically alters the script of his biography, as Freedman has shown.[22] Marie Hesse died of a prolonged illness in 1902; during this time Hesse, although living relatively close by, did not come to visit, nor did he attend her funeral, but left his father and the rest of the family to fend for themselves in their bereavement. What might seem like flagrant callousness on his part was really his inability to deal with his powerful attachment to his mother. If Hesse distanced himself emotionally from the impact of her death in order to protect himself, his novel reverses the biographical situation by having Peter not only witness the event but announce it to the impercipient father who had slept through it. In this regard the episode of the death of Peter's mother is a confessional fiction not of what was, but in Hesse's (guilty?) retrospect, of what might or should have been. Revealing too in this narrative reversal of Hesse's actual behavior is the flare-up of Oedipal violence immediately following the father's realization of his wife's death, which allows the submerged family romance momentarily to surface:

> "She is dead," he said. "Did you know?"
> I nodded.
> "Then why did you let me go on sleeping? And no priest attended her. May you . . ." He uttered a grievous curse.
> At that point I felt an indefinable jab of pain in my head, as though a vein had burst. I stepped up to him, firmly grasped both his hands—his strength was a boy's compared to mine—and stared him in the face. I could not say anything, but he became still and timid. (41–42)

Significantly, this scene is preceded by that of Peter's farewell kiss to his dying mother, which in a sense completes in death the half-hidden Oedipal triangle of the novel: "At the very last moment—there was no light left in her eyes—I kissed my mother's wilted cool lips, for the first time in my life. The strange chill of this contact filled me with sudden dread" (41).

One of the leading concerns of the mature Hesse, the search for the self, is barely present in *Camenzind*. Peter does not experience the call of *Eigensinn*, and perhaps a good deal of the diffuse pessimism of the book is the larger consequence of such a lack. The theme of self-realization surfaces only in the most general and tentative form: "I had not lost sight of the goal of my dreams—some great fortune, a completion of myself. I had no idea what form it would take" (83). Having no idea of how to achieve positive self-definition, Peter opts in the end for a safe and sentimental solution. After Richard's accidental drowning, this "lost child" seeking to find "his way back home to his mother" (97) eventually rejects the most tempting solution in Hesse's fiction for getting back "home"—suicide—and returns instead to his native village to take care of his aging father. Such is his way of dealing with his "ghastly loneliness" and the "wide cleavage" between him and other people (101).

Thus the Hesse of *Camenzind*, who in his mid-twenties believes that you can go home again, glibly dismisses the problem of the outsider as the peculiar tic of the Camenzind clan. All Peter has to do to resolve his despair and restlessness is to recover and accept his family heritage, simply by rejecting everything that came after childhood—his elite education, career as a man of letters, and unhappy love affairs. O *sancta simplicitas*, to escape the crisis of adult selfhood by a flight back to childhood!

> I am glad that my clumsy pursuit of luck has led me back, against my will, to the old nook between lake and mountains where I started, and where the virtues and vices, especially the latter, are the normal, traditional ones. In the world outside I had forgotten what it was like at home and had come very near to regarding myself as some rare and remarkable bird. Now I saw once again that it was merely the spirit of Nimikon spooking about inside of me, unable to adjust to the customs of the rest of the world. Here in my village, no one thinks of me as out-of-the-ordinary. (197)

And so Hesse leaves Peter repatriated in his Swiss village, "in lederhosen and rolled-up sleeves . . . become completely native" (198) again. Obviously this outcome was grist to the mill of popular taste, but as Hesse came to see in the wake of psychoanalysis, the pastoral idyll of Peter back in the Eden of Nimikon gives Hesse's life and problems the lie. Ironically, it was a fiction Hesse himself was soon trying to live out, in somewhat modified form, in his Gaienhofen years.

Beneath the Wheel: Hesse's Past Redux

Hesse's composition of *Beneath the Wheel*, which appeared in 1906, coincides with the period of his courtship of and marriage to Maria Bernoulli (in August 1904), who was nine years his senior and who shared his mother's first name as well as some of her physical attributes. After Ball's and Freedman's biographies, there is no need to belabor the point that "Mia" was in some regards a mother-substitute for the twenty-seven-year-old author who had lost his own some two years earlier. From the start his marked misgivings about entering into matrimony—plus the fact that Mia, with her withdrawn and sensitive temperament was hardly the type to play "Maman" to his Rousseau—boded ill for the long-term success of this relationship.

Hesse's first marriage also betokens his attempt at *embourgeoisement* and the consolidation of his growing literary reputation in Germany. As he summarized this period from the ironic vantage-point of "Life Story Briefly Told" (1925):

> Thus, amid so many storms and sacrifices, my goal had now been reached: however impossible it may have appeared, I had become a poet and had, it would seem, won the long, stubborn battle with the world. The bitterness of my years of schooling and preparation, during which I had often been close to ruin, was now forgotten or laughed at . . . I had triumphed, and now if I did the silliest or most trivial thing it was thought charming, just as I was greatly charmed by myself. Now for the first time I realized the dreadful isolation, asceticism, and danger I had lived in year after year; the warm breeze of recognition did me good and I began to be a contented man.[23]

Hesse's sense of having "arrived" helps to define the frame of mind in which *Beneath the Wheel* was written: the suddenly successful novelist felt sufficiently secure to launch a polemical attack on the authoritarian and antiquated school system that had made the Maulbronn student suffer. Getting back at those who hurt us is part of the pleasure of confessional writing, and clearly the author of *Beneath the Wheel* relished pointing a critical finger at the whole pedagogic apparatus that had oppressed him not so many years ago. A further consideration that may have played into Hesse's decision to write a protest novel is that it allowed him, as in *Camenzind*, to link up with a type of fiction popular in Germany at this time, the so-called "school" literature centered on the conflict between talented student and repressive institution whose relevance to Hesse's novel Mark Boulby has demonstrated in some detail.[24] Finally, the self-righteous rhetoric of his attack on the school system permitted Hesse to avoid a deeper or more thoroughgoing confessional self-encounter by locating the source of his adolescent difficulties largely *outside* of himself. In that regard the novel is something of a confession *manqué*, with school, teachers, and parents—although in a sense guilty as charged—cast in the role of scapegoat for the adolescent Hesse's problems. As Hesse acknowledged nearly half a century later,

In the story and figure of little Giebenrath . . . I wanted to depict the crisis of those years of my development and free myself from the memory of them, and in order to make up for what I was lacking in mastery and maturity, I played somewhat the role of accuser and critic vis-à-vis those forces which defeat Giebenrath and which nearly did me in: school, theology, tradition, and authority.[25]

Despite the obvious parallels between Hesse's life and what happens in the novel—including the entry examination to and student life at Maulbronn, the sudden escape (which is credited to Heilner) and departure from the seminary, and the wearying apprenticeship in a mechanic's workshop—the narrative fails to make clear, as Ball already objected,[26] the fate of the scholarship student who places second in the examination only to fail dismally within a few short months. As I tried to show in the previous chapter, the fascinating biographical record that is *Childhood and Youth Before 1900* provides a richer and more revealing account of what actually went wrong with Hesse during and after the Maulbronn period. Even the confessional device so characteristic of Hesse, that of splitting himself into two or more characters, largely fails in *Beneath the Wheel* to sort out the complexity of his adolescent identity crisis. Hesse may have wished to liberate himself from a set of traumatic memories, but his two personas, Giebenrath the ambitious yet timid grind, and Hermann Heilner, the Romantic rebel, are stereotypical self-projections that between them fail to capture the gist of his problems at Maulbronn and after.

Hans Giebenrath is a young Hesse without the burden and blessing of self-will—and also without the powerful mother-attachment. The significance of the mother, already downplayed in *Camenzind*, is elided altogether in *Beneath the Wheel*. As for the figure of the father, he is presented in as reductive a form as in the previous novel, for Herr Giebenrath is a caricature of middle-class obeisance to the twin deities of respectability and authority. Utterly incapable of understanding his gifted son, this dull Philistine can only parrot the ambition handed to Hans by his teachers: "Agreed, you'll be a credit to the good name of the family? You'll obey your superiors?"[27] Lacking any positive self-concept, Hans internalizes these norms, and strains

to the limit of his abilities (thus the psychosomatic headaches) to attain them, without ever considering whether they are appropriate for
him. The only alternative vision of himself and his future is offered
by a potential father figure, the shoemaker Flaig, whose homiletic
strictures on the self-serving academic pressures that the pastor and
the principal have exerted on Hans fall on deaf ears. Presumably the
presence of an understanding mother could have made a world of
difference for Hans, but Hesse has chosen to radically alter the script
of his life.

Hans's only reprieve from this goal-obsessed masculine world of
school and teachers is nature, which, through the joys of fishing,
swimming, and sunbathing, is also a receding synecdoche of the
mother world. Yet even these simple pleasures are canceled when
the pastor and principal convince Hans of the necessity of sacrificing
his summer vacation to prepare for the rigors of Maulbronn. The late
nineteenth-century pedagogic ideal, which Hesse exposes with sententious irony through the principal's speech, is presented as the arid
force of acculturation blighting the child's vitality. Hesse's indictment
is in the vein of Romantic protests on behalf of the "natural" from
Rousseau and Wordsworth to Mark Twain (compare Huck Finn's
fear of being "sivilized") and beyond:

> In young beings there is something wild, ungovernable, uncul-
> tured which first has to be tamed. It is like a dangerous flame
> that has to be controlled or it will destroy. Natural man is unpre-
> dictable, opaque, dangerous, like a torrent cascading out of un-
> charted mountains. At the start, his soul is a jungle without
> paths or order. And, like a jungle, it must first be cleared of its
> growth and thwarted. Thus it is the school's task to subdue and
> control man with force and make him a useful member of soci-
> ety. (54)

Until he becomes friends with Heilner, Hans's resistance to this
"force" remains largely unconscious, and finds expression only
through neurotic symptoms and anxiety dreams, like that of having
to consume mountains of chocolate at the Stuttgart entrance examination. After he begins to attend to Heilner's tirades, Hans—at first
reluctantly—abandons his scholastic ambitions, which are later sacrificed altogether to the flames of passionate friendship with the ego-

tistical Heilner. If Hans is Hesse's vision of what could have happened to him without the resistance of *Eigensinn*, Heilner is Hesse's idealized image of his teenage self at its most self-willed and rebellious. Although the portrait of Heilner is not devoid of strongly critical touches, his very name ("Healer") suggests that he represents a therapeutic possibility for Hans's weak self. In Heilner's case as in Hesse's, the strong self is correlated with mother-love ("Before he had come to school he had been his mother's pet," 93). In this respect the Giebenrath-Heilner pairing is an early version of the Sinclair-Demian relationship. Unlike Demian, however, Heilner is an unstable and unreliable "healer" figure. Like Hesse, "a Black Forest boy from a good home" and "a poet and an aesthete" (74), he is a late-Romantic version of young genius always on the verge of running amok. The positive traits he embodies—independence of mind, a critical and courageous temperament, not to mention powerful erotic proclivities, passion, and pride—constantly burst forth to make him a threat to himself and others. He is also so self-centered that he uses Hans primarily as a sounding-board and as a source of consolation, never considering that the demands of such a friendship are in fact dragging Hans "beneath the [academic] wheel." Thus through the character of Heilner, Hesse is at once paying tribute to and confessing some of the negative aspects of his adolescent self, which included not only self-will but also "a pathological need to be pitied and fondled" (93).

As the bearer of Hessean *Eigensinn*, it is appropriate that Heilner should act out Hesse's escape and subsequent departure from Maulbronn. Having made this authorial decision, however, Hesse was hardly able to capture through Heilner the significance of the psychic implosion that is the Maulbronn episode in his life. Whatever else it may have been, Hesse's flight from the monastery school was the sudden impulse of a disturbed boy and not a concerted act of rebellion and defiance—and was clearly understood as such by the Maulbronn directorate, as evidenced by the letter of Headmaster Paulus to Johannes Hesse after Hermann's capture. Hesse's punishment of an eight-hour detention was quite mild, given the circumstances of his flight and the distress it caused at Maulbronn and in the Hesse household in Calw. Further, the headmaster's explanation of why it would not be desirable for Hermann to remain at the school shows an understanding of the boy's state of mind that sorts ill with Hesse's fictional caricature of the school authorities as vain and heartless pedants:

> During the investigation of his infraction it has come to light that he lacks to a high degree the ability to control himself and to confine his spirit and disposition within those limits which are necessary for his age and for a successful education in a seminary . . . He is too full of extravagant ideas and exaggerated feelings which he is only too inclined to give in to. Now if he communicates these to his fellow students, he will either—which has been the case so far—not be understood, and as a consequence and according to his own testimony, feel himself misunderstood, or—and this in due time would have to be feared—he will also draw others into the unnatural and unhealthy world of his thoughts and feelings.[28]

In the retouched portrait of *Beneath the Wheel*, the unruly poet on the lam is turned into something of a heroic figure, a Maulbronn *"cause célèbre* . . . looked back upon" by the rest of the students "as an eagle escaped from captivity" (132, 135). Thus failed escape is translated into proud defiance:

> The excitement was great at the monastery when the runaway was brought back. But he kept his head high and did not seem to regret his brilliant little jaunt. The authorities demanded that he throw himself on their mercy. He refused, and in front of the teachers' tribunal was neither timid nor subservient. They had wanted to keep him at the school but now his cup had run over. He was expelled in disgrace and in the evening he left with his father never to return. (134–135)

And so the headstrong Heilner exits the school and the text, becoming a legend within a fiction, and pointing all the way down the road to Hesse's last and by far greatest escapee, the Magister Ludi, who only breaks with his academic community after he has become its most illustrious embodiment: "He had vanished, and his physical appearance and his flight gradually became history and finally turned into legend" (136). This quasi apotheosis is qualified, however, by a vague sense of maturity not achieved, and of a future tempering of proud self-will through the school of hard knocks: "After many further brilliant escapades and misfortunes the passionate boy finally came into the strict discipline that a life of suffering can impose, and though he did not become a hero, he at least turned into a man" (136).

After Heilner's departure, Hans becomes a pathetic figure, making *Beneath the Wheel* the most pessimistic fiction of the self that Hesse ever wrote: much worse off than even Camenzind, Giebenrath is the only major Hessean alter-ego who never comes close to finding himself. Forced to choose between academic success and friendship, Hans, after some vacillation, commits himself unconditionally to the latter, only to lose both his friend and his standing at Maulbronn. The bitter irony is that he is destroyed for making a positively *human* choice. After Maulbronn, Hans is lost between two worlds, for he finds that he cannot return to an earlier stage of his life, nor is he able to move toward maturity. In taking his character into this depressing nether region Hesse also succumbs to the temptation of bathos:

> Why was he forced to work until late at night during the most sensitive and precarious period of his life? Why purposely alienated from his friends in grammar school? Why deprived of the needed rest and forbidden to go fishing? Why instilled with a shabby ambition? Why had they not even granted him his well-deserved vacation after the examination? Now the overworked little horse lay by the wayside, no longer of any use. (139)

While the demented condition of this "drowning soul" (138) is heavy-handedly blamed on the school authorities, the last third of the book adumbrates areas of experience that surely have as much or more to do with the adolescent Hesse's protracted *crise de coeur* as the exacting Maulbronn regimen. Just as the context of *Beneath the Wheel* fails to make clear why Hans the honor student fails so rapidly at Maulbronn, so too it does not adequately explain why he is devastated by his first sexual encounter. Here again the fiction seems to point beyond itself for the resolution of the problems it raises—to the author's hidden *vita*. Hans's sexual failure with Emma is particularly mystifying because one might expect that his earlier relationship with Heilner would, as is frequently the case with adolescent friendships between members of the same sex, serve as a bridge to heterosexual love. In fact, Heilner's earlier kiss, in its impact on Hans, is such a harbinger of romantic love (88). Further, Heilner has had a foretaste of the mysteries of sex, having been so bold as once to kiss his "sweetheart" (130). The timid Hans is so inflamed by this confidence that he "lay awake for more than an hour thinking of the kiss Heilner had given his sweetheart" (131).

Seen in this connection, the "nervous disorders" from which Hans suffers at Maulbronn, and which worsen to the point of a breakdown after Heilner's dismissal, appear to be related not primarily to academic pressures, but to the burgeoning sex drive that Hans is completely unprepared to handle, and which neither his father, teachers, nor the doctor who examines him (127) are able to identify. Thus Hans—as was probably Hesse—is overwhelmed by feelings he is incapable of understanding, and which are only suggested through vague dreams, images, and moods that disturb the boy: "It was wandering on alien grounds, or soft ground on which it was a comfort to walk, and it was breathing a strange air, an air full of lightness and a delicate, dreamlike pungency. Occasionally, instead of these images there would come a feeling—dark, warm, exciting—as though a gentle hand were gliding caressingly over his body" (128). Lost in a whirlwind of forces he cannot comprehend, Hans succumbs to depression and a paralysis of the will. Hence the appropriateness of the "drowning soul" metaphor (138) for his condition, which prepares us for the manner of his death (an event also foreshadowed in the earlier drowning of the student Hindu).

After his abortive return from Maulbronn, Hans seeks to recover a sense of security by regressing to childhood, ironically, just when the double pressures of young adulthood—sex and work—begin inexorably to act upon him. His attempt to escape into "an unreal second childhood" (150) is as desperate as it is short-lived, and another outlet that Hans discovers—suicidal fantasies—offers only temporary relief. It is in this emotionally impaired condition that he meets up with Flaig's sexually mature niece, Emma, who hails from Heilbronn (Healing Fountain) and who as the Eve figure of the conclusion presides at the apple-harvest festival ("She called out to every child that passed: Want an apple?" 169). The "sweet fear" Hans experiences when Emma flirts with him is, however, no healing balm to his anxiety but only another step in his downfall: "His small fragile ship had barely escaped a near disaster; now it entered a region of new storms and uncharted depths through which even the best-led adolescent cannot find a trustworthy guide. He must find his own way and be his own savior" (173). In the last sentence we can already hear a note of the *Demian* leitmotif, but Hans, unlike Sinclair, has no *daimon* to help him through these adolescent straits. In his fevered imagination, Emma becomes a charged erotic image of the eternal feminine:

> Often he would close his eyes and try to picture Emma to himself, how she had stood across from him at the [cider] press, how she let him drink from her beaker, how she had bent across the vat and come up blushing. He saw her hair, her figure in the tight blue dress, her throat and neck in the shadow of her dark curls, and all this filled him with desire and trembling. (174–175)

However, when Hans meets Emma in her garden, this Eve becomes a Harpy as Hans, in a dismal failure of masculinity, is scared off by her aggressive sexuality:

> He shied back trembling at once but the girl had seized his head, pressed her face to his and would not let go of his lips. He felt her mouth burn, he felt it press against his and cling to him as if she wanted to drain all life from him. A profound weakness overcame him; even before her lips let go of him, his trembling desire changed into deathly weariness and pain. (180)

Their second and final encounter merely reinforces this pattern in an anticlimax of romantic love as sheer exhaustion ("I feel so tired," 187).

Thus the Emma episode, which might have signified a fortunate fall and a healing experience for Hans, turns into yet another defeat. So too does his apprenticeship as a mechanic that, by introducing him to the rough-and-ready comradeship of the lower classes, might have also served as a potential resolution of his identity-crisis. The fatigue of Hans's sexual encounter with Emma carries over into his job—"he had liked the workshop itself, only he had become . . . so miserably tired" (198)—and the Sunday outing with his fellow workers is another failure of masculinity, for Hans is not up to the rigors of drinking and swaggering. His catastrophic lack of selfhood is also suggested in the ambiguous manner of his death, which does not represent a conscious choice, but something that happens to him, the passive victim weakened by his bout with alcohol: "No one knew how he came to be in the water. Perhaps he had lost his way and slipped . . . perhaps the sight of the beautiful water had attracted him and when he bent over the water the night and the pale moon had seemed so peaceful and restful that weariness and fear drove him with quiet inevitability into the shadow of death" (214).

His death by drowning, the quintessential Hessean fate plotted here with considerable bathos, represents the logical conclusion of Hans's passivity. Viewed in another light, it is also the final return to nature and the mother world that had been denied Hans, save for the foreshortened pleasures of swimming, fishing, and sunbathing. In view of the fact that Giebenrath's fate involved much more than the academic ambitions fostered by selfish teachers and an obtuse father, the narrative coda in which Flaig—surely Hesse's spokesman here—points an accusing finger at the principal and the pastor, rhetorically distorts the meaning of the life of the quondam honor student, and does so at the expense of the author's self-understanding:

> The shoemaker pointed after the frock coats disappearing through the churchyard gate.
> "There you see a couple of gentlemen," he said softly, "who helped to put him where he is now." (216)

CHAPTER V

DOMESTIC FICTIONS

It was the first refuge of my young marriage, the first legitimate workshop of my profession; here for the first time I had the feeling of permanence, and for that very reason occasionally a feeling of imprisonment, of being hemmed in by boundaries and obligations.—Hesse on his move to Gaienhofen

When Hesse married Maria Bernoulli in August 1904 and moved with her into a simple farmhouse in the out-of-the-way village of Gaienhofen overlooking the lower part of Lake Constance, he was consciously trying to live out the Romantic idyll of a picturesque retreat from the world. In this venture "Mia" had taken the lead, for she had scouted out "the village of Gaienhofen . . . and a vacant peasant house" while Hesse was back in Calw with his father and sister putting the finishing touches on *Beneath the Wheel*. The poetic "folk" ideal to which Mia aspired and which Hesse shared with her was "derived as much from Ruskin and Morris as from Tolstoy": "She was determined to live a simple, healthy life in the country, with a minimum of necessities; however, she laid great emphasis on living beautifully as well as simply."[1] Even at its best, however, Hesse's life at Gaienhofen wasn't exactly "poetic-idyllic," because the location was so "completely isolated and rural" that he had to do his own repairs on the old farmhouse, which lacked indoor plumbing, and had to row across the lake to buy groceries. As he put it in a letter to Stefan Zweig several months after his marriage, "Gaienhofen is a very small and pretty hamlet, has no railroad, no shops, no industry, not even a priest . . . other than my wife and my cat I have no company."[2] The primitive farmhouse soon proved inadequate to his and Mia's needs, especially once children were born, and thus the pastoral conceit pursued by Hesse and his wife included, by 1907, a new house built according to his specifications (with the help of a loan from his father-in-law) more on the scale of a modest estate than a peasant's dwelling.

What is more, behind the dream of Gaienhofen lurked the reality of a failing marriage and frequent attempts on Hesse's part to escape his domestication through extensive traveling (verging at times on impulsive vagabondage), the culmination of which was a trip to Indonesia with his painter-friend Hans Sturzenegger in the fall of 1911 almost immediately after the birth of his third son. After the initial charms of Gaienhofen and marriage had faded, Hesse felt increasingly burdened and hemmed in on the one hand by his responsibilities as the head of a family (which included tasks like regularly planting and maintaining a large garden and sawing and splitting firewood), and on the other hand, by his now-busy career as a man of letters whose contributions were sought by publishers and newspaper editors. At Gaienhofen as at no other period in his life, his literary workshop was pushed to its productive limits, and behind the façade of a simple country life and what Wordsworth celebrated as "wise passiveness" there was the reality of a too-busy writer with a literary reputation and a family to maintain. In addition to several collections of the bittersweet "Gerbersau" stories that were partly modeled on Gottfried Keller's sentimental-humorous brand of realism[3] and that made Hesse one of the more popular writers of his day, he produced a significant amount of poetry, lyrical nature descriptions and travelogues, book reviews and critical essays (some of which appeared in *März*, a liberal review of which he was a co-founder and an occasional contributor), as well as poetic biographies of Saint Francis and Boccaccio, and assorted legends. And granted that, as Mileck points out, "the brief narrative and not the novel characterizes Hesse's eight years at Gaienhofen,"[4] he also managed to complete three longer prose fictions: *Gertrude*, *Knulp*, and *Rosshalde*.

Because Hesse's prolific output in the decade between 1904 and the outbreak of World War I lacks a clear focus or a governing center, this phase of his career—despite his attempt to integrate life and art by rooting both in a domestic ideal and a countrified lifestyle—has a peculiarly miscellaneous and fragmented appearance from both a literary and a biographical viewpoint. If at Gaienhofen Hesse seems to have aspired to an unproblematic integration of his *Eigensinn* with the middle-class trinity of family, success, and respectability, his repeated polarization in the fiction of this prewar period of the outsider-wanderer-artist and the settled and smug bourgeois "insider" suggests the troubled realization that his attempt at *embourgeoisement* and his "success" may be inauthentic in terms of his inner needs and desires. Ironically, the Romantic fiction of Gaienhofen as the "refuge" of his young marriage turned out to be a trap as Hesse was increasingly unable to feel at home in and with what he had initially hoped would be his permanent home. By the time he was working on *Rosshalde* at the end of this decade of domestic—and domesticated—fiction, Hesse came to see that even his unhappy marriage, the focal point of this masterfully balanced family portrait, was only a special instance of a much larger malaise afflicting him—one only adumbrated in the explosive confession of *Demian*, and elaborated in his post–World War I writings.

Some Prewar Stories

Some of Hesse's Gaienhofen stories are minor masterpieces that adumbrate or touch upon issues that begin to obtrude themselves in major key and with a profoundly altered emphasis in his post–World War I fiction.[5] They are entertaining and minor precisely because they only move toward considering important moral and social questions without adequately framing or addressing them. Many of them are written in a neo-Romantic German prose of considerable charm and finesse that in its subtler nuances is almost impossible to render in English. As a stylist the Gaienhofen Hesse's major achievement may be his forging of a richly resonant, varied and musical, yet perfectly "natural" narrative idiom based on his study of the leading German writers between 1750 and 1850. Although it is easy for a professional Germanist to overlook Hesse's stylistic mastery because of his obvious models and the derivativeness of many of his themes,[6] a more just evaluation would have to acknowledge his genuine and refreshing Romanticism—particularly in his rendering of nature and landscape—above and beyond all the obvious "influences" and echoes of his favorite writers. As Walter Benjamin commented with reference to the first collection of Hesse's Gaienhofen stories, Hesse is able to render a landscape without animizing it, and yet make it a central as opposed to a merely decorative element; and he also has a way of seeing that "holds the middle between the contemplation of a mystic and the acuity of vision of an American."[7]

A persistent concern of many of the Gaienhofen stories is the relentless pressure of family and community on vulnerable individuals and how they deal or fail to deal with these forces. The deftness with which Hesse can blend character and situation with the natural scenery and the cycle of the seasons is manifest in the opening pages of "The Marble Works" (1904). Like the Lotte of Goethe's *Werther*, Helene Lampart, the beautiful daughter of the owner of the marble works, is torn between her betrothal to a mature, respectable, and successful man of this world (Gustav Becker, the manager of a large farm), and her attraction to the narrator, a student-aesthete basking in the freedom of a summer vacation. The carefully developed setting, "the cool wooded valley of the Sattelbach [brook]" (41) is suggestive of the world in which father and daughter have their emotional roots—a world of powerful elemental forces carefully managed by human will: "here blocks of marble were slowly and painstakingly sawed into slabs and disks, washed, and polished—clean, unhurried work that was a pleasure to watch" (41). It is part of the narrative's ambiguity only to hint at a quasi-incestuous attachment between the reclusive Lampart and the "tall, erect, dark-haired" daughter who "strangely resembled her father" (43). The image of a rigidly controlled domestic situation turns in the narrator's mind into the impression of the father's "unintentional tyrannical influence" over the daughter, whose "repressed . . . nature" and "vitality" will, so he suspects, break forth one day to result in "a deadly struggle between them" (44). At first the student's timid yet persistent attraction is rebuffed as Helene expresses a resigned acceptance of her role as the obedient daughter, but later she begins to respond to his wooing, at first by losing her composure and showing "an unmistakable sign" through her embarrassed shyness when he surprises her "among the tall dahlias in the garden" (50). Unlike in the mawkish encounters between Hans and Emma in *Beneath the Wheel*, here budding sexuality finds a more adequate expression even as Helene struggles against her impulses: "When we were in the doorway, she suddenly kissed me again with violent passion. And trembling so hard that I too was shaken, she said in a choked, hardly audible voice: 'Go, go! Do you hear, go now!' And when I was outside: 'Goodbye! Don't come back, don't come back. Goodbye!' " (55). Torn between the engagement authorized by her father and her growing attraction to the young student, Helene, instead of making the difficult choice of *Eigensinn*, opts instead for the perpetual Hessean escape—suicide by drowning. Even though character and situation are rapidly sketched in "The Marble Works," the story shows considerable finesse in its descriptive sequences, especially in the symbolic linking of natural scenery with human emotions.

"The Latin Scholar" (1906) turns on a similar if more sentimentally presented love triangle. The adolescent Karl Bauer, a student at a *Gymnasium* or elite secondary school (as Hesse had been in the year after his dismissal from Maulbronn) is infatuated with the pert Tina, a mature servant girl who pities but cannot love him, and who is on the lookout to marry a financially secure tradesman. Karl's self-pitying infatuation with Tina is reminiscent of the Hans-Emma relationship, except that next to the provocative but irresponsible Emma, Tina is a more caring and sexually less threatening figure. Unlike Helene Lampart, she is not torn by the choice between two suitors, but sensibly commits herself to an apprentice carpenter and treats Karl like a vulnerable younger brother. The melodramatic twist at the end of the story, through which the carpenter is almost killed in a fall, leaves Tina with the hard lot of marrying "a lifelong invalid and cripple" (96), an outcome by which Karl's "ache of lost love" is "reduced to absurdity" (96) next to the real sufferings of this working-class couple. In the moralizing conclusion, Karl's childish self-pity yields to a mature appreciation of how the power of love can triumph over "inexorable fate" (96).

In two other substantial Gerbersau stories, "Walter Kömpff" (1908) and "The Homecoming" (1909), Hesse's retrospective of late nineteenth-century German small-town life has a bitter irony and sarcasm reminiscent of George Eliot. The Wilhelmine values of Gerbersau (the fictional version of Hesse's native Calw) are rejected as smug, provincial, and life-denying—and if Hesse's satire is none too subtle, his control of narrative tone is quite effective. The unnamed narrator is evidently a member of the Gerbersau community very familiar with its ways, yet whose critical perspective also gives him a clear overview of its many flaws. In a sense he is the appropriate persona for the Gaienhofen Hesse, the successful author who lived uneasily as both an insider and an outsider in a middle-class world whose goals he simultaneously pursued and detested. The harsh social criticism of these stories does not aim at an open break with the values of the society described, but rather subverts them from within: the Gerbersau raconteur is one to the manor born who impugns its manners without wishing to leave the manor.

Probably the bleakest of the Gerbersau tales, "Walter Kömpff" is Hesse's pessimistic vision of the stifling of individuality by a cruel and callous society, and perhaps also reflects his fears, through Kömpff's mid-life crisis and subsequent breakdown, of the price exacted from the individual by the mind-forged manacles of such a world. The title character, who is descended from a long line of local merchants, is forced by his dying father—and against the wishes of the mother, who knows that he has no real affinity for it—to promise that he will carry on the Kömpff tradition. Though Walter has "the features and the build of the Kömpffs" (101), he has inherited his mother's dark eyes as well as her "soul" (106). The bond between Cornelia, the beautiful pastor's daughter who is a spiritual outsider in the crassly commercial world of Gerbersau, and her sensitive son is obviously grounded in Hesse's biography—except that the fate of Walter is a cautionary fiction of what might have happened to Hesse if he had not had the resistance of *Eigensinn*.

Despite the reservations of his mother, Walter serves out his merchant's apprenticeship and eventually takes over his father's business, only to find the "struggle for money . . . insufferably crude and cruel and dull." His resignation to a life of quiet desperation also suggests Hesse's domestic situation and mounting despair during the decade before the war: "A secret yearning, which he himself did not understand, for the freedom of a life that was its own clear meaning and satisfaction never left him, but it lost its intensity and came to resemble the faint sorrow with which, as he outgrows his youth, a man with deeper aspirations resigns himself to the inadequacy of life" (114). The only genuine element in Walter's life is his attachment to his mother, who can see that he "had not become a merchant; inwardly still a child, he merely played the role that had been forced on him" (116)—just as Hesse in a sense was merely playing the role of husband and father that he felt had been forced upon him. Significantly, it is only after his mother's sudden death that Walter is no longer able to maintain his false role, and succumbs to despair. In a belated and self-destructive rebellion against his inauthentic life, he gives away the goods he should be selling at a profit—a situation that leads the other merchants to protect themselves by having his store closed. To the Pietist shopkeeper under whom Walter had served his apprenticeship and who has come to help him in this crisis, Walter confesses, "all I know is that I was never a real merchant . . . Now I want to see if I can still make something of myself." His friend's commonsensical rejoinder carries a good deal of authority: "If you don't mind my speaking my mind, I believe it's too late . . . life is too short for such slow decisions" (128–129). Unable to make any positive identity choices, Walter finally cracks under the strain and becomes "the fool and laughing stock of the town" (135)—the scapegoat of its larger inhumanity. His grotesque foundering in despair and suicide (by hanging) is the consequence of his failure in early youth to attend to his inner voice, and his casting-off in middle age of a false role earlier forced on him by his father without having anything meaningful to put in its place. Kömpff's dilemma is the grotesquely simplified mirror image of Hesse's own at Gaienhofen—the inability to live according to his "true self" (111) because "he was profoundly attached to middle-class ways" (113). The greater significance of this moralizing parable typical of the Gerbersau Hesse is voiced by the narrator at the conclusion, where Kömpff becomes a potential Everyman, yet is polarized against the reassuring "we" of the narrative that connects the storyteller and his audience: "For a time the townspeople talked a good deal about his death. But few of them had any intimation of what his destiny had been. And few realized how close we all of us are to the darkness in whose shadow Walter Kömpff lost himself" (137).

"The Homecoming" also zeroes in on the moral shadows of Gerbersau, but only to dissolve them in the sunshine of renewed life and hope. If in "Walter Kömpff" the "outside" viewpoint of the mother had been nullified by the patriarchal mind-set of Gerbersau, in "The Homecoming" that mentality and its stifling values are successfully rejected by the main character. August Schlotterbeck, a prosperous businessman who has spent the better part of his adult life in different parts of the world and who is widowed in late middle age, is seized by an irresistible urge to return to "his own country and the town of Gerbersau" (159). He comes back unannounced to relish to the full the emotion of homecoming to "his native city, which he had

. . . transfigured by nostalgia and memory during his years abroad" (162). Its "charm," however, is soon dispelled when this citizen of the world cannot conform himself to the highly stratified bourgeois pecking order he had left behind so long ago. The first shock is a distant relative whose "thinly masked" greed fills him with "an invincible loathing" (168). Moreover, he is slowly forced to conclude that his hope that as a native son he can "in all essential respects easily fit into the life of the town" (170) is a fond illusion. Ironically, his flexible cosmopolitan outlook is perceived as a defect in Gerbersau, for—in Hesse's caricature of the social pretensions of small-town life—he is especially disliked by the "official circles, which formed the top of the social pyramid and set the tone, in the area between the chief magistrate and head postmaster" (170). With blunt irony the narrator plays off the enlightened viewpoint of the worldly outsider against Gerbersau's Philistine pieties: "He had learned to be polite in conversation with all sorts of people . . . but he had so far fallen away from his Gerbersau beginnings as to be quite unaware that in the center of Europe there are whole castes and social groups which regard it as crude to speak openly of death, eating and drinking, money and health" (171).

The full realization of Gerbersau's defective mores dawns on Schlotterbeck only when he moves next door to the attractive and recently widowed Frau Entriss. He discovers to his dismay that she has become the innocent victim of a slander campaign countenanced by the local officials in which her very virtues—economy, caring for a mentally disturbed sister-in-law, her quiet sufferance of her husband's philandering ways—have been blackened into vices. Not surprisingly, Schlotterbeck is drawn to this woman whose energies have been stifled by her community, and whose hidden vitality is suggested in the description of her luxuriously flowering garden. Fittingly, the tale ends with the widower effectively rescuing the defenseless and persecuted widow from the clutches of Gerbersau, with both looking forward to a married life together far away from the town to which he had come home with such high hopes. This unexpected outcome, however, is far from being a disappointment to this self-assured man, and the sarcastic tone of the conclusion finalizes the indictment of Gerbersau: "After a gentle kiss her betrothed sat her down in a chair and said gaily: 'Well, thank the Lord, that's that. But the house is being sold this fall, or do you absolutely insist on staying in this hole?' " (192).

Several other short pieces illuminate human life from a nonhuman perspective, again for critical purposes. In the powerful sketch, "The Wolf" (1907), three emaciated wolves are hunted down in the bitter cold of winter by angry Swiss peasants. Hesse's empathetic imagination seizes on the death of the third—"the youngest and most beautiful . . . a proud beast, strong and graceful" (99)—with vivid poignancy. After it drops on the Chasseral mountain with its gaze fixed on the "gigantic and blood-red" moon, the brute peasants fall on it with sticks and clubs. In the stark ending, Hesse contrasts the elemental dignity of nature with the casual brutality of man. What makes this brief narrative effective is its refusal to sentimentalize either the wolves—they are predators—or the peasants. The striking wolf image here is also the first harbinger of the full-blown symbol of the "Steppenwolf" of nearly two decades later.

That Hesse admired *Gulliver's Travels* will not surprise the reader of the more satiric prewar tales of which the beast-fable, "A Man by the Name of Ziegler" (1908), is a concentrated instance. Ziegler (whose name is a pun on *Ziegel* = brick) is a caricature of the modern mass-man who venerates "money" and "science" (151). His undoing comes when during a Sunday visit to the local museum he inadvertently swallows a pellet from a display case of medieval magic. When he proceeds to visit the zoo, he discovers to his dismay that he can now understand the language of the animals, whose comments on Yahoo-humanity are less than flattering: the caged creatures are "surprised that these ugly, stinking, undignified bipeds with the foppish disguises should be allowed to run around loose" (155). As in "The Wolf," man comes up absurdly short next to the "nobility and quiet, natural dignity" (156) of the animal world. This Swiftean spoof concludes with Ziegler, who has taken on the animals' contempt for this "degenerate, dissembling mob of bestial fops, who seemed to be an unbeautiful mixture of all animal species" (156), being trundled off to an asylum when he throws off his clothes to join a dignified elk in his cage.

The ironic contrast between the life of man and that of nature is developed in still another key in "The City" (1910), which charts the history of a city against the greater rhythms of nature. A pessimistic sendup of the modern idea of progress, it opens with an engineer's exclamation "now we're getting somewhere!" (193) at the laying of railroad tracks across the prairie; it culminates in the vision of a dead metropolis inhabited by a "brutish rabble" (197) of nomads sheltering amid the ruins. In a Wordsworthian reversion, nature has reclaimed what humanity has aggressively staked out; and the closing sentence sarcastically subverts the opening, as a woodpecker "hammering at a trunk" cries, "now we're getting somewhere" (198). With its vision of the larger life and death cycles of civilization, the story is an early twentieth-century period piece, especially in its "decadent" view of the flourishing of the arts in the final stages of a civilization.

Two stories written after Hesse's move to Bern shortly before the war suggest a break with his past and may be viewed as fault lines in the world of his fiction that presage the earthquake to come in the crisis of 1916. "The Cyclone" (1913) turns on the analogy between a summer storm and an embarrassed sexual encounter between a timid boy and a forward girl that is reminiscent of the Hans-Emma pairing of *Beneath the Wheel*. The cyclone becomes a metaphor for that adolescent nether world between childish innocence and guilty adolescent sexuality that the narrator sought to evade ("while my senses reeled with drunkenness, my heart resisted, struggling desperately against being taken by storm," 244). Indeed, the dramatic symbolism suggestive of the fall portends the later awakening of *Demian*, for the upshot of the cyclone's devastation is that the narrator cannot return to the landscape of innocence: "It seemed to me that I myself had been torn up with all my secret roots . . . a chasm had burst open between me and my childhood" (247).

"Robert Aghion" (1913) treats a similar sea-change in consciousness, but does so in a manner that is both richer and subtler. In its quiet way, this is a minor masterpiece in which Hesse's autobiographical stress on self-will is rendered in a veiled confession that polarizes his own sense of himself against the whole cultural and religious context of his missionary forbears. The story is loosely set in late eighteenth-century imperial India: Aghion, a Lancashire pastor's nephew "with good credentials but no private fortune" (201) is sent out as a missionary—on funds bequeathed, ironically, by a deceased merchant who had made his fortune in the India trade. Though Aghion's is a simple Christian faith, his real motive for going is his passion as a naturalist "for the colorful insect world" (201) of the East. He shares his author's love of butterflies, and thinks "with delight of the fabulous flowers, trees, birds, and butterflies there must be in those blessed climes" (203).

Because this young curate is nothing if not innocent, the conflict between the rigid moral demands of his religion and his attachment to the sensuous phenomenal world does not surface in his consciousness until he finds himself in India. Nor has he considered that as a missionary he must convert the native populace *from* something already in place *to* Christianity. Hence he is astonished when he beholds a Hindu temple and must acknowledge that "these half-naked people . . . were not creatures of a primitive paradise but possessed ideas and gods, arts and religions for several thousand years" (208). Unlike the overseer and business agent Bradley, in whose house he is quartered and for whom profit, Christianity, and imperialism are all of a piece, Aghion does not block out the cultural riches of India with European blinders of arrogance and racism. On the contrary, he struggles to learn Hindustani and to familiarize himself with the local meld of cultures, though at first he is quite confounded by the different religions he encounters, and by their degree of tolerance for each other (unlike in "the Christian countries of Europe," 215).

For the time being his missionary commitment takes a back seat to his realization that he can't teach the Indians unless he knows more about them. Ironically, without realizing it he is himself undergoing a sort of conversion, which takes an unexpected form when he takes shelter with a peasant family during a downpour and is instantly smitten with their adolescent daughter Naissa who, dark-haired and bare to the waist, is an exotic vision of paradise. That night Aghion has a symbolic dream of religious unity *and* sexual union: a Christian church and a Hindu temple stand next to each other, and as he preaches from the steps of the former to the assembled Hindus, the Christian god leaves the church and enters into the temple

> where with kindly gesture he received the homage of the white-clad Brahmans. Meanwhile the heathen gods with their trunks, ringlets, and slit eyes went into the church, where they found everything to their liking. Many of the devout folk followed them, and in the end gods and people were moving in pious

procession from church to temple and from temple to church;
gong and organ mingled fraternally, and dark, silent Indians offered up lotus blossoms on sober English-Christian altars. (222–
223)

Naissa also makes the crossing from temple to church, to stand before the missionary who "in a surge of delight . . . enfolded her in
his arms" (223). The ritual embrace between two religions, races, and
sexes already looks ahead to *Demian*'s merger of the "light" and
"dark" worlds.

Aghion's unconscious or dreaming self aspires to such an integration, yet his conscious or waking self is burdened by guilt and bad
faith at these revelations from within. Unable to sleep, he blunders
upon Bradley in bed with one of the female servants—a scene that in
fact reflects Aghion's libidinal desires—and self-righteously upbraids
him the next day only to be unceremoniously thrown out by the
overseer for his impertinence. This flare-up forces Aghion to admit
to himself "that though his coming to India had been a good and
wise decision he lacked the inner vocation and drive to be a missionary" (226). Unlike the middle-aged Walter Kömpff, however, he is
able to cast off a false role in order "to find suitable work" and "to
look upon India . . . as a promising haven and home" (226). In a
curious turn of events, the lapsed missionary takes a position as
"overseer of a nearby coffee plantation" (227). Is he on the road to
becoming a Bradley type?

The conclusion of this story takes still another surprising turn.
Aghion decides he will marry Naissa, but when he calls on her, she
receives him coldly. Then he experiences a tremendous shock as another "figure" emerges from the family's bamboo hut: "the form that
appeared in the door frame, crossed the threshold, and stood before
him was a second Naissa, a mirror image of the first" (230). It turns
out he had mistaken Naissa's sister for Naissa: "As the two girls
stood side by side, still barely distinguishable, the lover felt infinitely
cheated and lost. Two fawns could not have looked more alike, and
if in that moment he had been left free to choose one of them and
take her away with him and keep forever, he would not have known
which he loved" (231). With this tantalizing doubling or splitting of
the image Hesse may be suggesting that erotic infatuation is an op-

tical illusion: the conventional myth of romantic love is that we know the beloved—but where is fancy bred, in the eye or in the head? The upshot of Aghion's telling mistake is a sense of betrayal: "his love, which he had been so sure of only a few minutes past, had broken into two halves, just like the image of the girl, which had doubled so unexpectedly and eerily before his eyes" (231). Whereas his dream had signaled a larger integration of consciousness, the surprise ending implies that a union based merely on idealized lust is not a viable one. In "Robert Aghion" Hesse only glimpses the possibility of a reconciliation of conscious and unconscious desires that before his encounter with psychoanalysis he cannot implement or even frame coherently in his fiction.

Knulp

Of the three lyrical variations on a theme that make up the narrative of *Knulp* (1915), the middle piece ("My Recollection of Knulp") was written in 1907 at Gaienhofen; the first and the third ("Early Spring" and "The End") were completed in 1913 and 1914 respectively after Hesse's move to Bern. *Knulp* is one of Hesse's abidingly popular *German* fictions steeped in the folklore of traveling journeymen and peripatetic apprentices, and harks back to Eichendorff's legendary portrait of that lovable Romantic vagabond, the title character of *From the Life of Ne'er-Do-Well* (1826), a figure known to every reader in the German-speaking world.[8] Knulp, however, is no mere epigone of German folk romanticism, but an affecting confessional myth on Hesse's part—hence his fondness for this antihero whose conception is nothing if not sentimental. As Hesse wrote nearly half a century later, the figure of Knulp is inextricably linked in his imagination with his childhood memories of Calw, and "he belongs to those few of my things which above and beyond all development have always remained near and dear to me."[9]

Like Camenzind, Giebenrath, and Heilner, Knulp is another and still more sentimental reprise of Hesse's childhood; he is also, under the aegis of the "beautiful loser," a fantasy of escape from the double burden of unhappy domesticity and adulthood under which the prewar Hesse labored. The writer who conjured Knulp envied every tramp who passed his doorstep, and made frequent extended trips to flee from the discontents of married life. For instance, in 1909 he confided to a correspondent, "this year I was away for a full five months," and three years later he stated, "I myself will certainly always travel and wander a great deal, and the relationship with my family has for years limited itself more and more to my struggling to earn enough money for their maintenance."[10]

Knulp is an acceptable fiction of freedom for the Gaienhofen Hesse because it does not represent an open break with or affront to the values of the audience on whose approval the career of Hesse the popular writer depends. Though Knulp is a drifter, his vagabond's life is sanctioned by a long-standing folk tradition. As the ending makes clear, his role is partly that of the holy fool who serves as a literary safety valve to the humdrum pressures of bourgeois life. Unlike the later Klingsor and Goldmund, he is also a man of controlled impulses: for instance, his date with the young servant girl is chaste, and he does not yield to intoxication—indeed, he abandons the narrator of the middle story because of the latter's drinking. Knulp may have a wild animal's survival instinct and an intimate knowledge of the seasonal rhythms of nature (which are lyrically invoked in the settings of late winter/early spring, summer, and late fall/winter), but he is not threatening, like the Steppenwolf, or beyond the bourgeois pale, like the criminal Klein. His innocence and harmlessness, in short, are part of his appeal, for Knulp is a nineteenth-century Woody Guthrie sans protest.

Moreover, far from being an ordinary tramp, Knulp is a man of great gifts somehow never realized. No mere parasite though he disdains work, he has a punctilious regard for the amenities of social life, including refined table-manners, dress, and appearance. Like that of the artist, his role is "to participate in life as an onlooker and a listener."[11] He lives for the passing moment; his time is the ever-present *now*; the songs he composes are spontaneous and evanescent; the harmonica, as Boulby drily notes, is an apt symbol of his infantile temperament.[12] Practicing no trade, he is yet sufficiently proficient in many of them to pass for a member of the guild. Like the more substantial Goldmund, whose forerunner he in a sense is, Knulp is no man's minion, but the eternal child of Eros, at once infinitely gay and forever sad. And like his author's, Knulp's adult identity is rooted in an adolescent crisis. Knulp too had been a student in an elite school, a first-rate Latinist whose exercises were cribbed by the student who years later as a grownup doctor tries to nurse him in "The End." Unlike the Maulbronn Hesse, however, Knulp chose to fail out of Latin school because of his love for a tradesman's daughter who didn't want a student but a worker for her sweetheart. This episode turns into the greater disaster of his life when the girl he sacrificed his middle-class aspirations for betrays him, and thus propels him on his aimless wanderings.

Though Hesse provides only a few glimpses of Knulp's childhood and adolescence, the elegiac tone of the narrative suggests that the adult is only a remnant of the glory of his early years. In his hometown (again the mythic Gerbersau), "air and earth had lived in his dreams and wishes," and to Doctor Machold, who is now very much his social superior, Knulp had once been a "teacher and his bigger, more clever, admired friend."[13] The central symbol of Knulp's sentimental vagabondage and his exile from the paradise of childhood is that of the prodigal son, a parable whose note is struck lightly at the opening in his song of "the tired wanderer" who is "surely none other / Than the lost son," and in "The End" in the heavy pathos of Knulp's hallucinated colloquy with a loving Father-God who welcomes home his wayward son: "in my name you have wandered . . . in my name you have committed follies and have let yourself be mocked . . . you are my child and my brother and a part of me, and you have experienced and suffered nothing that I did not experience with you."[14] It is noteworthy that at the last moment Hesse transforms the father-son legend into his own distinctive mother myth: when the dying Knulp goes to sleep in the snow, he hears, like the dying Goldmund later, the call of the eternal feminine, as God's voice becomes the voice of different women he has loved, beginning with that of his mother.

Two Art Novels

Knulp the gifted vagabond remains naively fixed in the dream of childhood and nature, a mute inglorious folk figure who only occasionally bursts into spontaneous song. In *Gertrude* (1910) and *Rosshalde* (1914), however, Hesse's two major prose fictions before the war, romanticized nature almost disappears and the suffering and productive artist—a type much closer to Hesse's actual experience—moves into the foreground. And unlike the poet *manqué* of *Peter Camenzind*, these central characters are successful artists. With its stress on the alienated aesthete, and its correlation of creative achievement with personal unhappiness and a larger unfitness for ordinary life, Hesse's depiction of art and artists is still a merging of late Romantic and early modern motifs. Yet *Gertrude* and even more so *Rosshalde* are much more accomplished literary performances than *Peter Camenzind* and *Beneath the Wheel*, for they revolve around a single major theme and display a greater unity of design and narrative control than these earlier books. Hesse's presentation of the art theme by way of music and painting, those sister disciplines in which he had a life-long interest and some of whose practitioners he numbered among his friends (especially during the Gaienhofen period), allowed him to examine his personality and problems with a measure of self-detachment and objectivity.

Gertrude

When a hitherto sympathetic reviewer complained that *Gertrude* lacked the freshness of Hesse's previous novels, Hesse responded by contrasting its spare and disciplined style with the linguistic "enthusiasm" of *Camenzind*.[15] In subsequent years, however, he no longer thought highly of the book, and while the popular judgment has sided with this estimate, critical opinion is still divided on the question of its merits.[16] Granted the vogue of the *Künstlerroman* at the turn of the century, Hesse's portrait of the artist has a fundamental confessional integrity because he writes whereof he knows: his own experience as a poet and a "maker."

As is frequently the case in his fiction, Hesse here splits himself into two opposite yet complementary personas, the composer Kuhn and the opera singer Muoth. These names, variants of "daring" and "courage," may be partly ironic, as Field has suggested,[17] since Muoth commits suicide and Kuhn's attitude to life is nothing if not reticent. Yet these near-synonymous names also suggest a common ground, which is the shared assumptions about art and artists on which the friendship between the two is based: artists are misunderstood outsiders and sufferers ("a real artist has to be unhappy," asserts Muoth); their paths (according to Kuhn) are "strange and lonely"; they have a penchant for suicide and are consumed by "a continual desire, yearning, and dissatisfaction"; and they are capable of bursts of inspiration and transcendence through art, which lifts them momentarily yet triumphantly—and here we have a Schopenhauerian touch—above the dreariness of life and the brutality of "nature" and "fate."[18] Over and above these assumptions, which are Hesse's own, the contrast between Kuhn, the artist per se, and Muoth, whose art is in the performance of others' works, is developed in terms of Nietzsche's distinction between the Apollonian and the Dionysian: Kuhn's compositions are based on order, clarity, and restraint, whereas Muoth's performances and life are marked by a destructive urge to ecstatic self-abandonment and intoxication.

Kuhn, the narrator, recollects his past from the safe harbor of his success as a composer. The note of resignation and sacrifice is struck with the opening sentence. His one youthful indiscretion, the infatuation with a young flirt who at a sledding party dares him to plunge down a steep slope with her, results in his being crippled for life. The physical disability—here (like Baudelaire's "albatross") a symbol of the artist's impeded position vis à vis ordinary life—proves to be a blessing in disguise, for it frees Kuhn from the arena of love and marriage, and confirms him in his identity as a composer. Henceforth his fate is eros sublimated into *Kunst*. His first composition, a sonata, is a musical clarification of powerful emotions, an "almost glasslike brightness and transparency of feelings where . . . things were no longer labeled sorrow or happiness, but everything signified strength and sound creative release" from "the turmoil" of his "heightened sensibilities" (34). When Kuhn subsequently falls in love with Gertrude at a musical *soirée* at which she plays one of his compositions with him, his thoughts about her and about music merge into a momentary unity (94). Like many of Hesse's female characters, Gertrude is more symbol than person, for she is really Kuhn's muse, the "guiding star" (6) of his aspirations.[19] Since the basis of their relationship is aesthetic communion, it is evident from the start that their becoming lovers is not a viable option.

Muoth, whose greatest operatic triumphs are, appropriately enough, in Wagnerian roles, has sought the friendship of the timid and touchy Kuhn to relieve a loneliness described in terms that anticipate Harry Haller's ("he was as famished as a wolf from loneliness," 45).[20] This "demonic" (45) character is a later version of the adolescent Hermann Heilner; conversely, like Giebenrath, the shy Kuhn is attracted yet frightened by the passionate friend who, in sharp contrast to Kuhn's "resignation," is known for burning the candle at both ends and for abusing his mistresses. Afraid of being drawn into the Dionysian vortex of Muoth's passions, Kuhn nevertheless admits his attraction to "this moody, imperious man" (66). In vain he warns Gertrude against this *homme fatal* who "destroys everyone he is fond of" (115); and after Kuhn inevitably loses her to Muoth, he masters his suicidal despair and calmly resigns himself to an unhappiness whose depths are sounded when he secretly witnesses their wedding.

The marriage between Gertrude and Muoth turns out, predictably, to be a disaster, as she exhausts herself keeping his self-destructive temperament within reasonable bounds. While the particular circumstances of this marriage do not reflect Hesse's own, Hesse's larger characterization of its failure suggests his own domestic situation:

> None of us knew how terribly these two fine people suffered in secret. I do not think that they ever stopped loving each other, but deep down in their natures they did not belong to one another . . . they loved each other and yet were never quite close to each other, and while he saw himself cheated of all his hopes of finding peace and happiness through her, Gertrude realized, and suffered in this knowledge, that all her good intentions and efforts were in vain . . . Thus they both had their secret dreams and dearest wishes shattered. They could only remain together by making sacrifices and showing forbearance, and it was brave of them to do this. (208–209)

Hesse's treatment of Kuhn's life subsequent to his loss of Gertrude to Muoth has a revealing confessional aspect as well. A former professor of his diagnoses Kuhn's unhappiness as a modish affliction of sensitive people of the European upper classes: "It is related to moral insanity and can also be called individualism or imaginary loneliness" (154). (The term "moral insanity" is a not-so-oblique reference back to Hesse's adolescent crisis, since that is the clinical label he was then tagged with.) The remedy the professor recommends to this condition is the selfless love and service of others. Yet Kuhn's subsequent attempt to implement this ethic by devoting himself to his recently widowed mother strikes one not so much as applied *caritas* as yet another version of Hesse's family romance. In its fictional redistribution of various elements of Hesse's biography, the confessional burden of the novel is that of wish-fulfillment. Marie Hesse, as we have seen, died in 1902, after which Hesse maintained a rather distant relationship with his father. In *Gertrude*, however, this situation is reversed as Kuhn settles down with his widowed mother.

What is more, the novel reverses as well the mother's response to her son's identity as an artist: Marie Hesse had not approved of her son the published author, whose first three volumes appeared before her death. From her (and her husband's) strict religious viewpoint, the only legitimate role of literature was to praise the Lord. Thus she was shocked by the contents of his writings, and in a letter about *An Hour Behind Midnight* expostulated with him, "shun your fever muse as you would a snake; she it is who crept into paradise and who today would still like to poison thoroughly every paradise of love and poetry . . . O my child flee from her, hate her, she is impure and has no claim on you, for you belong to God . . . Pray for grand thoughts and a pure heart . . . Remain chaste!"[21] As Mileck points out in connection with this letter, "his mother's outspoken moral aversion hurt him deeply and infuriated him"[22]—yet, as is evident from his dedication of a volume of poems to her that appeared, ironically, shortly after her death, Hesse kept trying to win her approval of his path as a poet. Thus it is telling that in the Oedipal culmination of *Gertrude*, Kuhn's mother comes to approve of her son's profession, which earlier she and her husband had considered a frivolous occupation:

> My mother now became familiar with some of my music. She did not like every piece and withheld comment about most of them, but she saw and believed that it was not just a toy and a pastime but demanding work that was to be taken seriously. Above all, she was surprised to find that the musician's life, which she had considered very frivolous, was hardly less strenuous than the middle-class life that my late father had led. (186)[23]

Kuhn in a sense replaces his "respectable" father as he settles into a peaceable existence replete with the maternal comforts of "home": "I enjoyed hearing about the past and the family, and I no longer felt as if I did not belong" (186).

If the Muoth-Gertrude marriage mirrors some aspects of Hesse's unhappy relationship with Mia, Kuhn's quasi-idyllic ending in an Oedipal fantasy[24] and a regained middle-class respectability can stand as the confessional signature of Hesse's own aspirations toward *embourgeoisement* and domestic rootedness that define his Gaienhofen period. Yet just like his real-life marriage, this literary fantasy isn't finally fulfilling, as evident in the confirmed pessimism and the resigned acceptance of life's shortcomings in the final as in the opening chapter of *Gertrude*. Hesse speaking as Kuhn sounds as if his development has been arrested, and as if this mood of unhappy compromise and accommodation is to be his last word.

Rosshalde

Hesse's best book before *Demian* is a completely convincing and masterfully executed portrait of a middle-aged artist struggling in the toils of an unhappy marriage in order to make a clean break for renewed life and hope. The domestic dilemma suggested in the previous novel through the Gertrude-Muoth relationship is the substance of this lucid confessional fiction at whose center is the sinister family picture Veraguth is finally able to paint: "There were three life-sized figures: a man and a woman, each self-immersed and alien to the other, and between them, playing, a child, tranquilly happy and without suspicion of the cloud hanging over him."[25] Hesse conceived of the central issue of the book as "the overall problem of the 'artist's marriage', and the question whether the artist and thinker is in any case capable of marriage," but his principal focus, as his biographers have not been reluctant to point out, is his own troubled marriage. Hesse proceeds in the letter to his father quoted above to contrast the ending of his just-published novel with his own hopes for the future: "in it something is brought to a conclusion that I am hoping in my own life to be able to be done with in a different manner, and that is of great importance to me."[26] Yet despite Hesse's expressed wishes for a different outcome, *Rosshalde* is—like Veraguth's painting—a definite summing up of and farewell to his marriage several years before its actual dissolution.

Rosshalde is also the first stage of Hesse's decisive turning point as a man and a writer, the deceptive calm before the coming storm out of which he was to emerge a new author with a different style. But before plunging into that new stage during the crisis years of World War I, he wrote a book that is the culmination of his early dedication to a disciplined yet richly nuanced prose that he saw largely lacking in contemporary German literature. As he concluded in 1910, his cultivation of a carefully crafted style is "precisely that which seems to me to be the only deeper and more lasting value of my work" at a time when "not twenty of our famous poets write a clear and consciously controlled German."[27] In Hesse's astute assessment some three decades after he wrote it, he found in rereading *Rosshalde* that with it he had reached the formal high point of his literary art:

> I thought I would find a sort of refined *Kitsch*. But this was not the case. The book has held up well; there are only a very few sentences that I would delete or write differently today, and there are also a number of things in it that I couldn't do any more today . . . With this book I had attained that level of technique and craftsmanship that I am capable of and in which I have made no further advances. Nevertheless, it is appropriate that the war interrupted my development and instead of permitting me to become a master of good forms led me into a set of problems in the face of which the purely aesthetic was not able to maintain itself.[28]

Except for *The Glass Bead Game*, no other novel shows him such a "master of good forms," with such a pellucid and crisp style.

Rosshalde contains some curious permutations of the "poetry" and "truth" of Hesse's life. It culminates with Veraguth's decision to leave his wife and to accompany his friend Otto Burkhardt to India. Actually, Hesse wrote the book after his abortive trip to India with the painter Hans Sturzenegger in the autumn of 1911—and if Veraguth's is the conclusive step toward a new self, Hesse's disappointing journey to the East, which did not take him all the way to India and which resulted in an unhappy return to his family, represented the geographic displacement of an unresolved inner conflict. Hesse wrote the novel in a large and gloomy mansion on the outskirts of Bern, which had belonged to a recently deceased painter and friend of his, and for which he and Mia left the seclusion of Gaienhofen in the vain hope that a change in habitat could effect a change in their deadlocked relationship. A final and uncanny transposition of art and life is that the brain fever that claims the life of little Pierre in the novel almost took that of Hesse's third child, Martin, several months *after* he finished the book.

The central concern of *Rosshalde*, Veraguth's awakening from the "deep, potent hypnosis of resignation" (85) to a sense of "having recovered his health and his will" (155) is an attempt to embody in a single character the Apollonian/Dionysian split dramatized in *Gertrude* through Kuhn and Muoth. As the book opens, Johann Veraguth, a famous and financially successful painter, has lived for several years apart from his wife in the rooms he has added to his studio on the grounds of their estate. The only remaining "bond" between the estranged parents is their seven-year-old son who "alone did not recognize . . . this division of life and territories" (2), and who moves freely between the physically sundered realms of his father (studio) and his mother (mansion). Because the child's imagination does not accept this hostile separation of worlds, Pierre is "the sole lord and master of Rosshalde" (2). Hesse incorporates some deft symbolic touches here, including the mention of the boy's "proudest ambition," to repair, when he grows up, the manor house's "turret clock" whose strokes do not record the time correctly.

The family portrait includes an older son, the student Albert, who, unlike Pierre, is a party to the entrenched antagonisms between the parents. Now living away from Rosshalde, Albert had earlier turned on Veraguth to the point that the latter had to have his son sent away from home—an unexpected echo of the adolescent Hesse's conflict with his own father. The Oedipal tension that flares into emotional violence when Albert returns for a visit, includes Veraguth's angry reminder that his son had thrown knives at him (124). Unlike Pierre, who resembles his father, Albert is exclusively identified with his mother, and it is indicated that they will be companions, and give meaning to each other's lives, after Veraguth's departure. Suggestive also of Hesse's fictional filtering of memories of his childhood and family is Albert's telling observation, "isn't it strange, Mother, how the qualities of parents and grandparents, or a mixture of them, recur in children?" (115). If Pierre (the French meaning of whose name, *stone*, may be relevant as an archetypal image of psychic wholeness) embodies the vital unity of a child's imagination, his brother with his "pale forehead," "blond hair," glowing eyes, and "the full handsome mouth twisted with anger" (50) may be another glimpse of the adolescent mother's son that Hesse had been. Albert's attachment to his mother is strengthened by their love of music, but the compositions these two enjoy together strike Veraguth as "music for old people . . . with none of the Bacchic frenzy of the music he had loved beyond everything else in his youth" (86).

The missing Bacchic note is reintroduced into Veraguth's life with the visit of the friend of his youth, Otto Burkhardt, who has come with the secret aim of convincing Veraguth to accompany him back to his plantation in India for an extended visit. Otto's "presence" immediately brings into the tomb-like atmosphere of Rosshalde "a lighter, more cheerful, more childlike atmosphere" (25). The exotic appeal of Otto's invitation is not that of meditation and mysticism, but rather of a naive return to the senses. The photographs that Otto exhibits as "bait" offer a tantalizing view of "a radiant, multicolored paradise" (41) and coax into the open Veraguth's long-suppressed wish to make a new beginning. For the suffering painter, this "invitation au voyage" becomes an irresistible fantasy of escape:

> What bewitched him with images and roused his longing was not only the glitter of tropical seas and archipelagoes, or the color play of half-naked primitive peoples. More than that, it was the remoteness and quietness of a world where his sufferings and cares, his struggles and privations would pale, where his mind would cast off its hundred little burdens and a new atmosphere, pure and free from guilt and suffering, would envelop him. (42)

The detached yet sympathetic observer of the agonized impasse of his friend's marriage, Otto is also the fictional equivalent of that part of Hesse that was able to stand back and take stock of himself and his situation. A type of alter ego, Otto serves as a guide to lead Hesse qua Veraguth to a new understanding of his needs and problems, by getting him consciously to face up to "the loneliness and hopeless coldness that had descended on his . . . marriage and life" (58)—and to accept the sacrifices that his choice of a new life will entail, including the most difficult of all, leaving behind his beloved Pierre. Thus the façade of the Gaienhofen Hesse's resignation as a necessary accommodation with the inherent shortcomings of life is exploded by this Bern fiction that asserts, in the Romantic rhetoric of Otto, "anyone who hopes is happy . . . you don't even remember what life and joy are. You're contented, because you've given up hoping" (71). In the light of such affirmations—life, hope, becoming—Hesse's true state is revealed as the "abyss of inner loneliness and self-torment" (74), the only "refuge" from which was his "work" (66).

Veraguth's painful self-confrontation, with the help of Otto and a liberal complement of wine, breaks the impasse of his resigned despair and brings with it a burst of energy that shows up first in his painting through a new, unsentimental art of "pure reality" (102): "And so, in those days of inner anguish, Johann Veraguth, by a desperate effort, created one of his greatest and most beautiful works, the playing child between the bowed and sorrowful figures of his parents" (101–102). Focussed here in a symbolic picture, Hesse's larger family portrait in Rosshalde depicts his domestic situation in the decade before the war, even as it encodes Hesse's ironic judgment of his accomplishment and its meaning: "And when later, Veraguth's modest judgment to the contrary, some of his admirers numbered him among the truly great, it was largely because of this picture into which he had breathed all the anguish of his soul, though intending nothing more than a piece of perfect craftsmanship" (102). In Hesse's later writings, the incorporation of such sly passages in which the text mirrors and interprets not only its author but itself as well was to become a standard feature.

The denouement of Veraguth's departure from Rosshalde takes the form of one final crisis, the death of Pierre, which completes the symmetrical design of this formal masterpiece. On one level, the loss of the child who is the most precious link with his past and his marriage is the final sacrifice Veraguth has to make to gain his freedom. On another, the catastrophic illness of Pierre—the innocent victim who was unable to heal the rift between his parents—is the symbol of the collapse of that marriage. The failure of husband and wife to reach out to each other and to him is also reflected in Pierre's nightmare that marks the sudden onset of his meningitis, and in which "his mother and father . . . passed him and one another" without any sign of recognizing each other (123). Finally, the dying boy's face reflects back to Veraguth the grotesque reality of his marriage: "What remained was a pale, prematurely aged face, a gruesome mask with simplified features, in which nothing could be read but pain and disgust and profound horror" (187).

What is left to the author of *Rosshalde*, now in his mid-thirties, is a hard-won sense of artistic maturity, and a recognition of his position as an "outsider to whom it is not given to seize the cup of life and drain it," but who is a *spectator ab extra* in order "to participate with secret pride in the work of creation" (212). The chastened figure of Veraguth who at the conclusion knows that "the last shimmering lights of his youth and expectancy had been extinguished" (211) but who is full of determination to make the "bold, steep climb" to a "new life" beyond the nostalgias of his past is on the threshold of the profound changes from which Hesse was to emerge in several years with the message-from-the-depths of *Demian*.

CHAPTER VI

HESSE'S MARRIAGE OF

HEAVEN AND HELL

Without Contraries is no progression . . . From these contraries
spring what the religious call Good & Evil. Good is the passive
that obeys Reason. Evil is the active springing from Energy.
Good is Heaven. Evil is Hell.—William Blake, **The Marriage of**
Heaven and Hell

During the last period of our friendship he [Demian] had said that
we had been given a god to worship who represented only one ar-
bitrarily separated half of the world (it was the official, sanc-
tioned, luminous world), but that we ought to be able to worship
the whole world . . . And now Abraxas was the god who was both
god and devil.—Hermann Hesse, **Demian**

The *Demian* period (1914–1918) brought Hesse what in "Life Story
Briefly Told" he calls "the second great transformation of [his] life,"
one that forced him to a self-confrontation that exposed the compromise inherent in his literary success and *embourgeoisement*:

> One thing became clear at once: the benign content in which I
> had lived with the world had not only been bought at too high a
> price; it had been just as corrupt as the outer peace of the world.
> I had believed that through the long, hard battles of youth I had
> earned my place in the world and that I was now a poet. Mean-
> while success and prosperity had had their usual effect on me. I
> had become complacent and comfortable, and when I looked
> carefully the poet was hardly to be distinguished from a writer
> of cheap fiction. Things had gone too well with me.[1]

Such a self-judgment and subsequent self-transformation on the
threshold of middle age, when most individuals are getting more set
in their ways and consolidating their identities, does not come cheap.

For Hesse, it took a series of wrenching psychological and personal blows, culminating in his decision, in April 1916, to seek psychiatric help and to undergo the analysis that provided the cathartic context of his self-alteration. The serious illness of his son Martin in 1914, the sudden death of his father in March 1916, which triggered guilt and depression, the impasse of his increasingly unhappy marriage, and Mia's disturbed and disturbing state of mind (which finally exploded in her first psychotic episode in 1918 and which effectively ended Hesse's role as *pater familias*)—all of these are important ingredients in Hesse's "second great transformation." But perhaps the decisive factor or trigger of the second major crisis of his life was the dilemma posed by World War I, whose outbreak and initial phase elicited from him a hedging and ambiguous response.[2] The acute problem the war posed for Hesse the popular German author was a function of his need to be at once a solitary outsider *and* an admired insider—a conflict that had been largely glossed over in his rapid rise to literary prominence. As Freedman interprets it, Hesse's ambivalent response at the start of the war—"antiwar and patriotically German"—is rooted in "his continued childhood practice of wanting to be iconoclastic and approved at the same time."[3]

While deploring the wholesale perversion of traditional humanistic values by the war machine, Hesse still thought of himself as a German and even tried several times to volunteer for military service, but he also confessed, "I like being a patriot, but before that, a human being." At first he was still able to endorse naively "the moral values of the war" as an antidote to the corruptions of a complacent capitalism,[4] but he also publicly expressed his distaste for writers and intellectuals who before the war were "consciously at work on the supranational edifice of human culture and have now suddenly decided to carry the war into the realm of the spirit." Despite his solidarity with the German side ("I am the last man to forswear my country at a time like this") he tried to remind his readers of "the Goethean realm of the human spirit" and of an "international world of thought, of inner freedom, of intellectual conscience" over and above the military conflagration.[5] When these and other mild reservations led to a smear campaign against him by the German press he was stunned and psychologically ill-prepared to cope with having become a *bête noire* in Germany:

> In the press of my native land I was denounced as a traitor . . .
> The article containing the denunciation was printed by twenty
> papers in my country, and of all the friends I thought I had
> among newspaper men only two dared rise to my defense. Old
> friends informed me that they had been nurturing a viper in
> their bosoms and that those bosoms in future would throb only
> for Kaiser and Reich and not for a degenerate like me. Abusive
> letters from strangers came in stacks, and the book dealers gave
> me to understand that an author with such reprehensible views
> had ceased to exist as far as they were concerned.[6]

Hesse's dedicated and strenuous work during this stressful period at
the German consulate in Bern for the German Prisoners of War Welfare Organization (supplying German soldiers interned in France,
Russia, England, and Italy with reading materials, co-editing a newspaper for them, and founding a publishing house devoted to their
needs) represents his poignant effort to combine in an officially sanctioned role his patriotic impulses with his dedication to the Goethean
ideal of a supranational European culture.

Hesse's encounter with psychoanalysis in 1916 was more an emotional and cathartic than an intellectual experience. He appears to
have read in some of the leading figures of the movement as early as
1914 (Freud, Adler, Bleuler, Stekel),[7] but it was not until his sessions
with a young Jungian, Dr. Josef B. Lang, that psychoanalysis became
the inner revelation and emotional crucible from which emerged the
Eigensinn prophet of *Demian*. Between April 1916 and November
1917, Hesse had more than seventy sessions with the intense and
eccentric analyst who related to Hesse more as a friend and colleague
intimately involved in his inner life than as a doctor in a clinical setting. Aside from some bizarre metaphoric excerpts from Lang's diaries quoted in Hugo Ball's Hesse biography, we have little if any indication of the course of Hesse's analysis.[8] Presumably it involved a
Jungian exploration of his psyche and his past, particularly his childhood. The Jungian challenge and adventure of individuation as a
progressive realization of the Self, including those mysterious inner
entities, Shadow and Anima—all of which figure in the personal
myth of *Demian*—help to account for the sense of psychic urgency,
drama, enigma, and suspense that define Hesse's writings in the
years immediately following. Because Jung's basic concepts are in

some respects developed from the leading ideas of German Romantic poets and thinkers (from Novalis to Nietzsche), the inner world mapped by Jungian psychology is not the supervention of an entirely new or alien element in Hesse's thinking, but is in fact a confirmation and conceptual elaboration of some of his deepest beliefs and intuitions.

In his 1918 essay, "Artists and Psychoanalysis," Hesse credits the new psychoanalytical movement with three chief benefits for poets: it confirms the value of imagination and fiction; it makes it possible to establish a meaningful and permanent relationship to one's unconscious, and it requires "a truthfulness toward oneself to which we are not accustomed."[9] Hesse's pre-psychoanalytic interest in the unconscious is clearly evident in the dreams of some of his leading characters—for instance, Hans Giebenrath's nightmare of having to eat his way through a mountain of chocolate the night before his elite school entrance exam, or Robert Aghion's erotic dream of the mingling of "light" and "dark" realms that already, as we saw in the last chapter, looks ahead to *Demian*. What the sessions with Lang brought, however, was a programmed immersion in such an inner world, almost to the exclusion of outer reality. In "Life Story Briefly Told," Hesse speaks nearly a decade later of this venture, in a language poised between Romantic and psychoanalytic rhetoric, as "the journey through the hell of myself":

> I was wholly immersed in myself and my own fate, though at times with the feeling that the lot of mankind was involved as well. I found reflected in myself all the world's lust for war and murder, all its irresponsibility, all its gross self-indulgence, all its cowardice; I had to lose first my self-respect and then my self-contempt; I had no less task than to carry through to the end my scrutiny of chaos, with the now soaring, now sinking hope of rediscovering beyond chaos, nature and innocence. Every human being who has been awakened and really achieved consciousness has on one or more occasion walked this narrow path through the wilderness—to try to talk about it would be a fruitless effort.[10]

The prophetic correlation in this excerpt between his personal crisis and the "lot of mankind" has the unmistakable stamp of Jungian psychology, although it also has its roots in Hesse's admiration of the

Romantics, of Nietzsche's *amor fati*, and of the visionary strain in Dostoevsky.

The immediate impact of psychoanalysis on Hesse's view of himself, as we saw in Chapter II, was self-criticism and dissatisfaction with his works hitherto as falsifying confessions. From the new perspectives of 1916, his writings hadn't owned up to his life; they had been self-evasions or, as he put it sarcastically, "noble psalms" marked by an "unproductive homesickness for [his] youth." He had made his contribution to "German sentimentality," but now that the proverbial knife was stuck between his ribs, he had lost his taste for all that.[11] His fiction from *Camenzind* to *Gertrude* had denied the dark drives within him, with the result that he had fallen into a tired resignation. Now, after the crisis of the war and the failure of his marriage, his writings will compensate for his earlier euphemizing or repressing of the instincts: "I must above all examine and recognize all which I had earlier lied away or silenced, all that is instinctual, chaotic, wild . . . 'evil' within me."[12] Hesse's new outlook led him not only to a severe critique of his earlier writings as inauthentic autobiography, but to larger doubts for at least the next decade about the "literary" and belletristic aspect of literature. Art had to be subordinated to life, "formal perfection" to "authenticity of feeling." At times he seemed willing to stop being a writer[13] and to dismiss "the whole aesthetic impulse" as "a mistake." What are "beauty" and "harmony" of style, he asks, to one "running for his life between collapsing walls?" In this desperate mood, literature would have to yield to self-actualization: "I saw my task, or rather my way of salvation . . . simply in letting what little there was in me that was vital and strong live its life."[14]

Far from ceasing to write, however, in order to live more fully, Hesse felt a tremendous urgency to turn his new thoughts and experiences *into* literature, at first by way of the personal myth of *Demian* and of several fairy tales, a form he took up again under the impact of psychoanalysis.[15] Characteristic of Hesse's new confessional orientation is that the search for the self and the exploration of the unconscious lead the adult writer back to a series of symbolic encounters with the psychic polestar of his identity, the image of the Mother. This psychoanalytic journey, if considered from a Freudian viewpoint, shows Hesse in the grip of an unresolved Oedipus complex masked by Jungian archetypes—a possibility that cannot have been entirely lost on the writer who had read Freud, and who soon after his Jungian analysis (including later sessions with Jung) was consistently to praise Freud as the founder and leader of the psycho-analytic movement, as opposed to lukewarm and qualified expressions of admiration for Freud's rebellious disciple. Mileck concludes that for Hesse, "Jung's primacy seems to have been short-lived," and that "by the middle of 1918 Freud was again the master and Jung but one of his several outstanding students." In response to a query several decades later about his relationship to Jung, Hesse states that he first read him in 1916 and proceeds to the guarded acknowledge-ment, "I also read later books by Jung, but only until 1922 because thereafter analysis did not greatly interest me. I have always had respect for Jung, but his works did not make such strong impressions on me as did those of Freud."[16]

The issue of the Freudian versus the Jungian influences and elements in Hesse's fictional self-exploration under the aegis of psycho-analysis is a vexing one, because the differing perspectives of these analytic schools will yield substantially different interpretations of Hesse's writings. In my own view Hesse was too immediately caught up in the momentum of psychoanalysis to have any interest in sorting out "Freudian" from "Jungian" strands. Since one of Jung's students conducted the analysis and since the mythopoeic ideas and symbols of Jung were more congenial to the *poet* Hesse than Freud's hard-core rationalizing, the significance of Jungian psychology during these years can hardly be underestimated. Yet while it is not my purpose to attempt either a Freudian or a Jungian interpretation of Hesse, I do want to suggest that perhaps precisely because the Hesse of the *Demian* years was so caught up in Jungian ideas, a Freudian perspective on some of his writings at this time—and especially his treatment of the mother symbol—can provide a necessary critical counterbalance and corrective.

Several Mother *Märchen*

Though lacking the prophetic urgency of *Demian*, the symbolism of Hesse's Jungian *Märchen* is nearly as dense as that of the novel. In "The Difficult Path" (June 1916), which, as Mileck notes, "is the mythicized first stage of Hesse's analytical treatment,"[17] the inward journey is presented as the arduous ascent, under the watchful eye of a strict guide, of a distant mountain peak. The "terrible" trail that Hesse is forced to take leads from a sunny vale, the "beloved land-scape" of childhood, to the dizzying heights of individuation. The inertia of the old and the familiar hangs on the climber's feet "like a sphere"[18]—a metaphor that resembles the bird-egg emblem of *Demian*. When the narrator pushes through to the stony peak, he discovers in a tree a black bird with eyes as hard as crystal, singing of "eternity" (both *tree* and *bird* turn up repeatedly in Hesse's writings as symbols of the self). The bird soars off, the guide jumps, and the narrator, who follows suit, finds himself plunging through infinite spaces ("I fell, I jumped, I flew") in tortured ecstasy back down to— "the breast of the mother" (72–73: the German is ambiguous, because "die Brust der Mutter" can mean both "breast of the mother," and "breast of my mother").

"A Dream Sequence" (November 1916) is autobiography as a mael-strom of memories and images rising up from the unconscious. This rapid sequence of surreal transformations of erotic motifs, power fan-tasies, and ventures among the archetypes of the racial memory again culminates in an encounter with a mother figure who, unlike that of "The Difficult Path," is now identifiably Marie Hesse. Some of the phantasmagoric shifts anticipate *Steppenwolf*'s Magic Theater, and there is even a preview of Harry Haller in Hesse's cameo appearance as "a pale, gaunt musician with flickering eyes whose name was Hugo Wolf and who was on the point of going insane this evening" (83). Hesse's rapid collocation of dream fragments, too complex for simple summary, is replete with extensive Jungian imagery of the matriarchal stage of consciousness in which the child's relationship to the mother "is most vividly expressed in the 'prehuman' symbol where the Mother is the sea, a lake, or a river, and the child a fish swimming in the enveloping waters."[19] Clearly Hesse's symbolic ev-ocation of the primal rootedness of individual consciousness through a pervasive mother myth—including the recurrent imagery of a re-turn to the womb-source, the convertibility of "inner and outer" and of the human and the animal, the flight of the bird to the light and the fish to the sea, the identification of the self with the cosmos and with God ("We do not search for God anymore. We are God. We are the world"), and, finally, of everything with the Mother—reflects the Jungian cast of Hesse's psychoanalysis: "we create and are resurrected with our dreams. Our most beautiful dream is of the ocean, of the starbright night, and of the fish . . . and of the clear glad light—everything is our dream . . . voices resound, and every voice is the voice of the Mother" (78–79).

The concluding segment appears to correspond to the Jungian version of the onset of "self-consciousness . . . when feelings of transitoriness and mortality, impotence and isolation, now color the ego's picture of the uroboros, in absolute contrast to the original situation of contentment."[20] Afflicted by the fear of mortality—his teeth are falling out and a knee is rotting—Hesse struggles through "slime and loam" and laboriously climbs the steps leading to his mother's house, to be rewarded with a dramatic re-vision of his (now long-dead) parent:

> The gate stood open, and inside my mother in her grey dress was quietly and thoughtfully walking with a little basket on her arm. Oh, her dark, slightly greying hair in the small net! And the dress, the grey dress—had I then during all the many, many years entirely lost her picture, never really thought of her . . . ? There she was, there she stood and walked, only to be seen from behind, exactly as she had been, entirely clear and beautiful, nothing but love, nothing but the idea of love. (86)

At the end of this Jungian confession the uroboric paradise of childhood is no longer available to the adult dreamer, for his desperate cry to his mother goes unheeded—"there was a wall of glass between her and me"—as she disappears into "the garden" (87). Even the passing reference to Dickens (Hesse recalls that as a child he once found a list in her basket that included the reminder, "borrow a book by Dickens" (87), appears to be an oblique allusion to his own mother myth, since the best-known Dickens novel in the German-speaking countries, *David Copperfield*, is very much defined by David's sense of loss inherent in his loving recollection of early memories of his deceased mother.

If "A Dream Sequence" is Hesse's most striking Jungian inscription of the powerful mother archetype and the related sense that each of us is an "eternal Odysseus" laboring "deep within the shaft of our buried soul" (82), "Iris" (January 1918) is his most poetic and delicate mother *Märchen*. It follows the Romantic genre of internalized quest romance, and is clearly a psychoanalytically updated version of Heinrich von Ofterdingen's search for the blue flower (the title character of Novalis's famous *Bildungsroman*). The boy Anselm who is fascinated by the iris flowers in his mother's garden and the "bright path" leading "downward into the distant, blue secret of the calyx" (110) is the poetic image of Hermann, the mother-son miraculously at one with nature (compare "Childhood of the Magician"). The blue depths of the flower represent the "call of and key to creation," the mysterious way within "where every expectation would be fulfilled and every presentiment realized" (112, 113). The adult Anselm, who has lost his magical connection to childhood and his mother (with whom he quarrels and who later dies), subsequently falls in love with Iris, who is the poetic version of Maria Bernoulli (to whom, appropriately enough, this *Märchen* is dedicated):

> She was older than he would have wished in a wife . . . Most of all she liked to live in solitude and silence, surrounded by flowers, music, and perhaps a book; waited for someone to come to her, and let the world take its course. Sometimes she was so delicate and sensitive that any contact with what was alien to her easily hurt her and made her cry. Then again she beamed and glowed finely and quietly in her solitary happiness, and whoever saw this sensed how difficult it would be to give or mean something to this beautiful woman. (117)

Anselm, who has (like the later Goldmund) blocked out the mother-world, is drawn by her "wonderful name," which he associates with "deep, distant, important memories" that he is unable to identify. When he proposes to her, Iris—unlike Mia—sends him on a quest to discover what her name reminds him of. A latter-day Romantic searcher and perpetual wanderer lost in "the abysses of his memory" (124), he becomes, like Yeats's Wandering Aengus, so immersed in his quest that he loses all connection with the external world and its norms. He struggles in vain to recover a clear image of his mother in order to discover "what the name Iris signified to him" (124), but it is only after the death of Iris that he is able to dream again of his mother, whose voice merges with that of Iris, who—in a metaphoric transformation strikingly similar to the dream-painting sequence of *Demian*—becomes the voice of his inner self. Having restored the relationship to the trinity of childhood-mother-self, Anselm is finally able to experience the full significance of "Iris" when a flower in the frozen snow points him back to the mysterious focus of his early years. The symbolic climax of this sensuous confessional parable is Anselm's magical entry into the mother world through a cleft in a rock-face covered with moss. His symbolic descent into the mountain ("the bird in my breast sang clearly") becomes the path to "the blue mystery within" (128) synonymous with infancy and home: "It was Iris into whose heart he made his way, and it was the iris in the garden of his mother into whose blue calyx he stepped lightly" (128). While the intention of this haunting prose poem is to point to "the third stage of life to which Hesse began to look forward after his analytic treatment,"[21] the playful ambiguity of its mother myth is as open to a Freudian as to a Jungian interpretation. Indeed, it seems at times in these strange psychoanalytic fables as if Hesse is positively teasing the reader with such a double perspective.

Demian

Like Goethe's *Werther*, Hesse's novel emerged in a burst of confession. Written between September and October 1917, in the last stage of Hesse's treatment by Dr. Lang, it was not published until after the war. It appeared in spring 1919 under the name of the narrator, Emil Sinclair, and became for several years one of the most popular and influential books among German youth. Hesse's choice of a pseudonym (which he was forced to abandon in 1920 when his authorship was guessed by the critics) reflects his belief that through the crisis of the war he had emerged as a different writer, and it was also his way of resisting "the stupid role" of "the beloved writer of entertaining literature" that no longer suited him and that might put off a new generation "with the well-known name of an old uncle."

Though Hesse (like most Germans) seems never to have heard of Blake, *Demian* is his autobiographical marriage of heaven and hell in a late-Romantic, early modernist *Bildungsroman* strongly marked by the impact of Jungian analysis. As he wrote about the book a decade later, creative writing (*Dichtung*) is not a mere transcription of life, but a poeticizing of it (*ein Verdichten*),[22] and in *Demian* as in the psycho-analytic *Märchen*, Hesse's metaphorizing of his experience turns on the exploration of the unconscious through a pervasive mother myth. As a modern romance of the inner self and a fictional reworking of carefully selected aspects of Hesse's childhood and youth, *Demian* incorporates some basic features and tendencies of Jungian thought: the assumption that the individual is the primary reality, the portentous-prophetic language about the challenges and hazards of individuation, the amoral or neutral attitude to the "dark" suggestions of the self, the sense of the mysterious connections between the inner and the outer worlds (compare Jung's concept of "synchronicity"), the endorsement of creative activity as an instrument of self-realization (for example, the "positive function" of expressing "for example, in writing, painting, sculpture, musical composition" the suggestions sent by the anima[23]), the preoccupation with myth and religion transposed into psychic categories, the associative style of thinking and writing, and finally, some more bizarre aspects, like psychobiology (compare Pistorius's yoking, at the end of Chapter 5, of the vestigial air-bladder in fish with the "flying bladder" of dreams[24]). Jung himself was not shy about seizing on the Jungian element of *Demian*, as a 1919 letter to Hesse shows, in which he first compliments him ("your book hit me like the beam of a lighthouse on a stormy night"), then proceeds to an interpretation of the ending that doesn't seem to fit the plot: "the Great Mother is impregnated by the loneliness of him that seeks her. In the shell-burst she bears the 'old' man into death, and implants in the new the everlasting monad, the mystery of individuality. And when the renewed man reappears, the mother reappears too—in a woman of this earth." Jung concludes with the enigmatic suggestion that *Demian* is indebted to him for more than Hesse is willing to admit:

> I could tell you a little secret about Demian of which you became the witness, but whose meaning you have concealed from the reader and perhaps also from yourself. I could give you some very satisfying information about this, since I have long been a good friend of Demian's and he has recently initiated me into his private affairs—under the seal of deepest secrecy. But time will bear out these hints in a singular way.

I hope you will not think I am trying to make myself interesting by mystery-mongering; my *amor fati* is too sacred for that. I only wanted, out of gratitude, to send you a small token of my great respect for your fidelity and veracity, without which no man can have such apt intuitions. You may even be able to guess what passage in your book I mean.

The editor of Jung's letters suggests that the veiled reference is to Jung's "*Septem Sermones*, where the Gnostic figure of Abraxas plays a key role," and mentions that "the winged egg and Abraxas appear in a Gnostic mandala painted by Jung in 1916."[25]

In any event, the tone of this letter is of a piece with what Mileck has characterized as Jung's "presumptuousness" about his influence on Hesse,[26] which is evident in Jung's answer to an inquiry about their relationships: after noting that he met him in 1916, Jung mentions that Hesse had the benefit of the "considerable amount of knowledge concerning Gnosticism" that Jung had shared with Dr. Lang and that the latter "transmitted to Hesse. From this material he wrote *Demian*." Jung further claims that "the origins of *Siddhartha* and *Steppenwolf* . . . are—to a certain extent—the direct or indirect results of certain talks I had with Hesse. I'm unfortunately unable to say how much he was conscious of the hints and implications which I let him have."[27] The co-optive and condescending tone of this communication seems to justify Hesse's tart conclusion that "for analysts, a genuine relationship to art is unattainable: they lack the organ for it."[28]

Granted that *Demian* is significantly influenced by Hesse's protracted encounter with Jungian analysis, it is nevertheless true that the book resists any simple or consistent Jungian schematization of its basic ideas and symbols. Its leading characters, especially Demian and his mother, have obvious Jungian overtones, but not exclusively or unambiguously so: they are not paradigmatic fictional instances of psychological concepts, for *Demian* is not primarily a Jungian allegory, but a revised version, under the pressure of analysis, of Hesse's ongoing personal myth and fiction of the self. While the Jungian note is clearly the dominant one in the composition of *Demian*, the book is in fact a composite of various influences, or rather, confluences: of the conceptual world of the German Romantics and

of the tradition of dialectical thinking culminating in Hegel; of Nietzschean ideas, of Christian as well as Gnostic motifs and of assorted
other strands from Socrates to Dostoevsky, Bachofen,[29] and Freud.
Some of these "influences" make for strange bedfellows—Ziolkowski
has noted, for instance, how "Hesse creates a conscious stylistic tension by pitting Christian phraseology against Nietzschean
thought"[30]—and this matter is further complicated by the fact that
Hesse and some of his "influences" may share a common source or
tradition. In the case of Jung and Hesse, there is a shared literary and
cultural heritage that can be readily invoked to explain similar symbols and ideas without getting into the quagmire (or infinite regress)
of particular and demonstrable "influences."

Above and beyond the vexing question of Hesse's influences and
borrowings, the autobiographical message of *Demian* is as direct as its
symbolism is obscure: it is the creed of self-will proclaimed in a prophetic voice that gathers into itself echoes from Socrates and Jesus
down to Nietzsche and Jung, and that also has strong affinities with
the "inner light" tradition of Protestantism that in English literature
finds its greatest expression in the late eighteenth century in Blake's
prophetic books:

> An enlightened man has but one duty—to seek the way to him-
> self, to reach inner certainty . . . The realization that shook me
> profoundly . . . was . . . that I did not exist to write poems, to
> preach or to paint . . . All of that was incidental. Each man had
> only one genuine vocation—to find the way to himself. He might
> end up as a poet or a madman, as prophet or criminal—that was
> not his affair, ultimately it was of no concern. His task was to
> discover his own destiny . . . and live it out wholly and reso-
> lutely within himself. (107–108)

With its uncompromising gospel of the inner self forged in the crucible of psychoanalysis, *Demian* represents an autobiographical revolution in Hesse's career, and one that, for understandable reasons
(and especially in the U.S. in the wake of the Hesse wave of the
1960s), has received an extraordinary amount of attention from his
critics. As a writer, however, the "new" author of *Demian* is well below the level of formal and stylistic mastery Hesse had achieved in
his best work before the war, *Rosshalde*. *Demian* is a remarkable and

courageous book that breaks new ground as a consequence of probably the greatest crisis of Hesse's adult life, but it is also a "demonic" book whose author is as much controlled by as in control of his materials: too often its densely metaphoric and shrill confession comes across as a confused and confusing version of Hesse's disturbed state of mind during World War I.

Of its three major figures, only the narrator is a flesh-and-blood character, though from the perspective of the permissive late twentieth century, the summary of his student days as "a notorious and daring bar-crawler" (62) is very tame stuff. Next to it the proletarian masculinity of Kromer, even if largely undeveloped, offers a breath of vitality. The two other major figures of this triptych of Hesse's inner self, Demian and Frau Eva, are more symbols than characters. The former, a composite of Socratic *daimon*, Christian conscience, Jungian Shadow, and Nietzschean *Übermensch*, and the latter, the most revealing projection of Hesse's mother myth, exist on the magical threshold of the inner and outer worlds, whose fundamental convergence had become an article of faith to the Hesse drawing on his Romantic heritage as reinforced by Jung. This esoteric coincidence or identity is also the subject of his story "Inside and Outside" (1920), which turns on the (Goethean) slogan, "nothing is outside, nothing is inside, for that which is outside is inside," that Hesse also used as the epigraph of the 1919 essay, "The Brothers Karamazov, or the Decline of Europe."[31]

The basic conception of *Demian* is a prophetic and highly didactic late Romantic version of the providential pattern of the Christian fall and redemption internalized in the life of the narrator. In the opening chapter we witness Sinclair's fall from the paradise of childhood and innocence as a consequence of his lie (to impress a group of boys) about stealing apples from a garden. This symbolic episode, which is probably Hesse's conscious equivalent of the adolescent Augustine's robbing of the pear tree (*Confessions*, Book 2), shows how Sinclair's imagination is instrumental in his "fall" by driving a wedge of guilt, shame, and sin (13) between him and his family as he succumbs to the blackmail of his "evil" (11) Shadow, Kromer. Conversely, toward the end of the book this "Prodigal Son" beholds an apocalyptic vision of World War I as the beginning of the rebirth of a corrupt humanity. Seven of the eight chapter headings are references to the Bible, and the single non-Biblical one, "Beatrice," shows young Sinclair's attempt to turn *eros* into *agape*. Like Blake in his prophetic books, Hesse in *Demian* wields elements of the Biblical tradition to subvert Christian orthodoxies from a radical Protestant perspective. In his bold revaluation of scriptural figures—Cain, the Prodigal Son, the Unrepentant Thief at Golgotha—Hesse is at once drawing on and liberating himself from the Pietist teachings of his childhood, just as a much earlier and more famous autobiographer, Augustine, wielded the elements of his early education—the classical rhetoric of which he was such a brilliant student—in order to subvert the classical viewpoint for the sake of celebrating the Christian.

With *Demian*, Hesse seeks to present the stages of individuation in almost exclusively symbolic terms as a progressive integration of the "light" and "dark" realms of Sinclair's divided self (thus the punning appropriateness of his name: sin/clair) as a Blakean marriage of heaven and hell under the Gnostic sign of Abraxas (and his totem, the sparrow-hawk), whose esoteric function is "the uniting of godly and devilish elements" (78). In this figural autobiography the revaluation of values beyond the standard middle-class conceptions of good and evil takes the form of a confusing double movement through which external reality is internalized, and internal reality is externalized: that is, images appropriated from the outer world (Beatrice) become psychic stuff and metaphors of self, and inner images are transposed into the external world to function as figures in the plot (Demian and Frau Eva). While this double pattern includes a good deal of authorial sleight-of-hand, there is also an experimental daring in the manner in which Hesse deploys his symbols. The World War I years were, after all, those of a burgeoning *avant garde* and assorted modernisms, one of whose centers was Zürich, and their impact on *Demian* is clearly discernible in the book's more surreal dream sequences. In this connection it is also helpful to keep in mind the Romantic distinction between symbol and allegory, as updated by Jung in *Symbols of Transformation*, which Hesse had read, and which might well stand as the subtitle of *Demian*: "A symbol is an indefinite expression with many meanings, pointing to something not easily defined and therefore not fully known. But the sign always has a fixed meaning, because it is a conventional abbreviation for, or a commonly accepted indication of, something known."[32] *Demian's* signature of the self is symbolic in this way, invested with a numinous aura, pointing enigmatically to the unknown.

The imagery of this prophetic book is also fluid and dynamic, with constantly shifting boundaries and domains. Hesse's ambitious experiment with such kinematic and transformational sequences is a not always successful attempt to express the metamorphic processes of the self. Though the proliferating imagery of *Demian* defies schematization, some of the patterns are carefully developed through an experimental combination of musical and pictorial elements. Unlike the ironically voiced despair of T. S. Eliot's roughly contemporaneous *The Waste Land* (which also explores through obscure symbols the terms of a personal and a cultural crisis) the affirmative (and sometimes even manic) creed of *Demian* seems to be, "I can connect everything with everything." Caught up in its visionary momentum, Hesse seems to have believed that the book was not only a totalizing trope of his, but also of humanity's—or at least Europe's—psyche.

Three leading symbol sequences are those of the sparrow-hawk, Beatrice, and Frau Eva. The first, already adumbrated in the Prologue's assertion that "each man carries the vestiges of his birth—the slime and the eggshell of his primeval past" (4), is reintroduced in Chapter 2 when Demian points out the coat of arms (the sparrow-hawk) above the entrance of the Sinclair house (23), and is reinforced by his subsequent drawing of it in Chapter 3 (42). The bird-egg leitmotif is later internalized when Sinclair dreams that Demian has forced him to eat the coat of arms: "When I had swallowed it, I felt to my horror that the heraldic bird was coming to life inside me, had begun to swell up and devour me from within" (73–74). Thus the process of individuation and the onset of *Eigensinn* is experienced by the narrator as a symbolic pregnancy leading to the birth of a new self. When Sinclair re-externalizes this image by painting it, we have a fuller development of the central avian metaphor: "Now it represented a bird of prey with a proud aquiline sparrow-hawk's head, half its body stuck in some dark globe out of which it was struggling to free itself as though from a giant shell—all of this against a sky-blue background" (74). After mailing his "painted dream bird" to Demian, Sinclair receives the dramatic reply that relates the sparrow-hawk to the Gnostic deity who presides over this stage of Sinclair's development: "The bird fights its way out of the egg. The egg is the world. Who would be born must first destroy a world. The bird flies to God. That God's name is Abraxas" (76). The spiritual midwife of this difficult birth is Pistorius (a version of Hesse's analyst) who liberates Sinclair-Hesse from his old self by helping to deliver the new. As Sinclair puts it, their conversations (read psychoanalytic sessions) "helped me to form myself . . . to peel off layers of skin, to break eggshells, and after each blow I lifted up my head a little higher, a little more freely, until my yellow bird pushed its beautiful raptor's head out of the shattered shell of the terrestrial globe" (89–90).

If the greater sparrow-hawk pattern points to the future, the compact Beatrice sequence shows the adolescent Sinclair's futile attempt to escape the mounting pressures of individuation. His etherealized worship of the young woman whom he saw at a distance in a park is his second attempt to return (the first was after Demian had freed him from the clutches of Kromer) to the childhood world of purity and light. Yet the very name Sinclair chooses for this young woman is ambiguous, for it points as much to the "sin" as to the "clair" of his self, since she is clearly the raptly sensuous and highly eroticized devotee of Rossetti's famous painting, Beata Beatrix: "I gave her the name Beatrice, for even though I had not read Dante, I knew about Beatrice from an English painting of which I owned a reproduction. It showed a young pre-Raphaelite woman, long-limbed and slender, with long head and etherealized hands and features" (66). Far from checking his budding sex drive, Sinclair's Beatrice worship is a form of autoerotic fantasy that leads him right back to the "dark" self he had struggled to escape: the androgynous portrait he paints of her turns into a "mask, half male, half female," which he first recognizes as "Demian's face" and then as his "inner self," his "fate or . . . *dae-mon*" (70). Sinclair's attempted flight has gone full circle to another self-encounter, which Hesse describes, with iconic references to Novalis and Nietzsche, as fated (70).

The Frau Eva sequence that dominates the latter part of the book is introduced under the sign of Abraxas and explicitly related to the "sexual drive" (79) that Sinclair had sought to sublimate through his cult of Beatrice. More and more preoccupied by his inner world, Sinclair experiences a recurrent "fantasy" and "the most important and enduringly significant dream of [his] life," in which, returning to his father's house, he embraces under the aegis of the "heraldic bird"

above the entrance a figure who is at once his mother and Max Demian:

> This form drew me to itself and enveloped me in a deep, trem-
> ulous embrace: I felt a mixture of ecstasy and horror—the em-
> brace was at once an act of divine worship and a crime. Too
> many associations with my mother and friend commingled with
> this figure embracing me. Its embrace violated all sense of rev-
> erence, yet it was bliss. (79).

This "dark dream of love" with its double violation of ancient sexual
taboos that Sinclair is unable to "confess" (79) even to his friend and
guide Pistorius is *Demian*'s metaphorized burden of confession that
Hesse shares with his readers. His critics have been reluctant to face
the transparent Freudian suggestions of this mother myth, preferring
instead the "safe" Jungian interpretation of mother-son incest as a
symbol of rebirth. Thus Ziolkowski, while acknowledging the
"erotic-incestuous implications" and "the remarkable language of
double-entendre" of Frau Eva's exchanges with Sinclair, interprets
these, with the help of a long quotation from Jung, as the desire, "by
visionary paths to reenter the mother in order to be reborn again."
Such a view is defensible, given the metaphoric density and ambi-
guities of the text, but when a more recent critic rejects out of hand a
Freudian interpretation because Frau Eva "is not a libido object but
remains an . . . image of the divine,"[33] he can only do so by positively ignoring the ample evidence in Hesse's narrative that Frau Eva
is indeed—like Rousseau's beloved "Maman," Mrs. Warens—very
much a libido object: "There were moments when I sat beside her
and burned with sensual desire and kissed objects she had touched"
(127). Even if Sinclair's Oedipal desires are never fulfilled in fact, they
are consummated in his imagination: "I had dreams, too, in which
my union with her was consummated in new symbolic acts. She was
an ocean into which I streamed. She was a star and I another on my
way to her, circling round each other" (128). The transfer of Sinclair's
incestuous wishes from his own mother (whom he embraces in his
recurrent dream) to Frau Eva, Demian's mother and the Magna Mater, is a masking myth that does not change the basic situation.

Before ever meeting Frau Eva, Sinclair has already painted the
"half male, half female dream image of [his] *daemon*" (103) and

heaped it with lurid imprecations: "I questioned the painting, be-
rated it, made love to it, prayed to it; I called it mother, called it whore
and slut, called it beloved, called it Abraxas" (100). When Sinclair is
shown a photograph of Demian's mother, he has an ecstatic recognition in which again the internal and the external merge: "it was my
dream image! That was she, the tall, almost masculine woman who
resembled her son, with maternal traits . . . *daemon* and mother, fate
and beloved" (111). When the university student Sinclair meets up
again with Demian after a long interval, his introduction to Frau Eva
has all the earmarks of a homecoming to the Eternal Mother (the setting, a house in "a garden by the river," is Edenic, 116), and the
promise of an incestuous consummation. Under the symbolic aegis
of the sparrow-hawk painting that he had earlier sent Demian, Sinclair perceives Frau Eva as the (Hessean) trinity of mother, goddess,
and lover. The mythic aspect is heavily stressed ("Frau Eva! The
name fits her perfectly. She *is* like a universal mother!" 121), as she
obligingly invokes the book's symbol of the "new" self: "It is always
difficult to be born. You know the chick does not find it easy to break
his way out of the shell" (120).

The last part of *Demian* moves toward a sexual union between Frau
Eva and Sinclair, something she seems positively to encourage:

> At times I was dissatisfied with myself and tortured with desire:
> I believed I could no longer bear to have her near me without
> taking her into my arms. She sensed this . . . Once, when I had
> stayed away for several days and returned bewildered she took
> me aside and said: "You must not give way to desires which you
> don't believe in. I know what you desire. You should, however,
> either be capable of renouncing these desires or feel wholly jus-
> tified in having them. Once you are able to make your request in
> such a way that you will be quite certain of its fulfillment, then
> the fulfillment will come. (125–126)

However, Sinclair—like Hesse—vacillates between the sense of Frau
Eva as libido object and, as he puts it, "only a metaphor of my inner
self . . . whose purpose was to lead me more deeply into myself"
(127). Because the erotic fulfillment to which Sinclair aspires never
occurs, the apocalyptic ending of *Demian* is actually anticlimactic. In
a concluding episode that finally merges the Frau Eva and the spar-

row-hawk patterns, the momentum of incestuous wishes is diverted
by the outbreak of World War I. Sinclair's sudden vision of a cloud
formation as a "gigantic bird that tore itself free from the steel-blue
chaos of the stormy skies and flew off into the sky with a great beating of wings" (129) projects against the screen of the heavens the
death and rebirth symbolism of the self; and Sinclair's prophetic perception of Frau Eva as the muse of history is Hesse's portentous
myth of Europe in the throes of World War I:

> A huge city could be seen in the clouds out of which millions of
> people streamed in a host over a landscape. Into their midst
> stepped a mighty godlike figure, as huge as a mountain range,
> with sparkling stars in her hair, bearing the features of Frau Eva.
> The ranks of the people were swallowed up into her as into a
> giant cave and vanished from sight. The goddess cowered on the
> ground, the mark [of Cain = Demian's and now Sinclair's sign]
> luminous on her forehead. A dream seemed to hold sway over
> her: she closed her eyes and her countenance became twisted
> with pain. (139)

In short, Hesse has generalized his personal mother myth into an
archetypal vision of cosmic import.

Demian closes, as it opened, with only the reflecting figure of the
narrator who, himself injured in the war, receives in a field hospital
Frau Eva's farewell kiss from the lips of the dying Demian—an odd
consummation, that. The Narcissus motif that Boulby has identified
in the closing sentence[34] is appropriate because in a sense all the symbolic permutations of character and episode in the book are confessional self-projections on Hesse's part that are now reabsorbed, like
the figure of Demian, into Sinclair-Hesse's consciousness: "But sometimes when I find the key and climb deep into myself where the images of fate lie aslumber in the dark mirror, I need only bend over
that dark mirror to behold my image, now completely resembling
him, my brother, my master" (141).

The confessional imagination of *Demian* is a highly selective one,
excluding elements of Hesse's past treated in earlier works or dealing
with them in very different context, and incorporating aspects of inner and outer biography not hitherto explored. Thus the Maulbronn
crisis treated in *Beneath the Wheel* is not revisited, and the trauma of

adolescent sexuality, so mawkishly mishandled in the Hans-Emma relationship, is now paradigmatically framed through the "light" and "dark" worlds of *Demian*. If the biographical material taken up in *Beneath the Wheel* is largely excluded, the period at a *Gymnasium* subsequent to the Maulbronn crisis is touched on with the student "lowlife" scenes of the Beatrice chapter. Conversely, the issue of Hesse's unhappy marriage and the problems of the mature artist, the autobiographical substance, as we have seen, of *Gertrude* and *Rosshalde*, are absent in *Demian*'s seriated psychoanalytic review of Hesse's early life. Nature too, the lyrical synecdoche of the mother world in Hesse's early fiction, all but disappears, to be replaced by the mythic presence of Frau Eva. And the animus to the father so marked in the brief caricatures of *Camenzind* and *Beneath the Wheel* surfaces now in Sinclair's "recurring nightmare" of a "murderous assault" on his father, but with the shocking suggestion of Oedipal violence shifted to Sinclair's evil and torturing Shadow: "Kromer whetted a knife, put it in my hand; we stood behind some trees in the avenue and lay in wait for someone, I did not know whom. Yet when this someone approached and Kromer pinched my arm to let me know that this was the person I was to stab—it was my father" (28). In contrast, the figure of the mother who is frequently absent or whose autobiographical significance is disguised or elided in much of Hesse's earlier fiction is now elevated into a looming *magna mater* symbol with explicit incestuous suggestions. It is only fitting that Hesse's autobiographical reinscription of the Christian story of the fall should change Eve's role from that of the weak female who succumbs to temptation into that of a wise and powerful Frau Eva, a blissful homecoming to whom constitutes Hesse's vision of paradise regained in *Demian*.

Demian and "The Decline of Europe"

A troubling aspect of *Demian* is Hesse's prophetic linking of Sinclair's individual problems with the crisis of Europe on the eve of World War I: "The world wants to renew itself. There's a smell of death in the air. Nothing can be reborn without first dying" (131). The visionary imagination at work here is not that of a pacifist—quite to the contrary, for the mass destruction of the war is accepted as the necessary prelude to the renewal of a corrupt culture. As Demian explains, "war on a gigantic scale" is only the beginning of "the new world" (135) whose harbingers and hierophants are Demian, Frau Eva, Sinclair, and their circle, a Nietzschean group of the elect marked by the sign of Cain and "not separated from the majority of men by a boundary but simply by another mode of vision" (122). They subscribe to the Zarathustran premise that "humanity" is not something already achieved but only "a distant goal toward which all men were moving, whose image no one knew, whose laws were nowhere written down" (122). Hesse unfolds these heady ideas with considerable enthusiasm:

> Demian often said to me: "What will come is beyond imagining. The soul of Europe is a beast that has lain fettered for an infinitely long time. And when it's free, its first movements won't be the gentlest. But the means are unimportant if only the real needs of the soul—which has for so long been repeatedly stunted and anesthetized—come to light. Then our day will come, then we will be needed. Not as leaders and lawgivers . . . but rather as those who are willing, as men who are ready to go forth and stand prepared wherever fate may need them . . . That is why we are marked—as Cain was—to arouse fear and hatred and drive men out of a confining idyll into more dangerous reaches. (124)

One might well ask, what beast is slouching toward Bethlehem here to be born?

It is not surprising that some critics have expressed strong misgivings about such apocalyptic purple prose because it seems to align Hesse with a strain of irrational thinking that later helped to pave the way for Hitler and the Nazi ideology. Jeffrey Sammons has gone so far as to exclaim about the passage above, "I confess I have difficulty distinguishing this rhetoric from that of the early years of the SS into which the spirit of apocalyptic, elitist heroism eventually flowed,"[35] and Heinz Stolte, in a more balanced and probing critique, points to elements of Hesse's thinking that are politically dangerous because they link him with a "mental and emotional world" from which were later to emerge the founders and early supporters of National Socialism—a movement that Hesse, of course, was to find extremely distasteful when it reared its head in the 1930s. As Stolte observes,

Hesse's application of "individual psychology to the destiny of nations" in *Demian* is fraught with "dangerous consequences" because "a nation simply isn't an individual."[36] To this we should add that Hesse is far from alone in this tempting kind of analogizing and mythic thinking, for even the late Freud relies on it in *Civilization and Its Discontents* (1930) with the wholesale generalizing of the concepts of Eros and Thanatos—indeed, toward the close of his prophetic essay Freud speculates about the possibility of "communal neuroses" and "a psychopathology of cultural communities."[37]

Because Hesse's symbolic equation of individual and cultural crisis is entirely lacking in that playful sense of irony and critical detachment characteristic of his best writing—something, incidentally, that differentiates the tone of Hesse's marriage of heaven and hell from Blake's prophetic book, which is also a visionary satire—*Demian* is the most humorless and sententious novel he ever wrote. At times his tone is naively hectoring ("Always, you must think of these things in evolutionary, historical terms!" 124) or tinged with the arrogance of a Raskolnikov looking down his nose at lesser bipeds. In fact, Hesse-Demian can sound very much like Dostoevsky's fanatical student holding forth on the Special Individual's moral right to commit crimes for the greater good of humanity: "All men who have had an effect on the course of human history, all of them without exception, were capable and effective only because they were ready to accept the inevitable. It is true of Moses and Buddha, of Napoleon and Bismarck" (124).

We know that the prophetic and visionary strain of Dostoevsky became very important to Hesse during the *Demian* period, and provided him with yet another context for his apocalyptic perception of current events. His famous essays on Dostoevsky, written in 1919 and published in 1920 under the title *A Glance at Chaos*, provide a revealing gloss for the doomsday gospel of the latter part of *Demian*. For instance, in "Thoughts on *The Idiot*," Hesse characterizes Prince Myshkin as the embodiment of a "magical thinking" beyond good and evil that is rooted in the unconscious, of which "Dostoevsky's work . . . anticipates a highly developed psychology."[38] In Hesse's interpretation, "*The Idiot*, thought to its logical conclusion, leads to a matriarchy of the unconscious and annihilates culture" (91), for Myshkin's thinking is nothing less than "the acceptance of chaos" and a "return to the incoherent, to the unconscious, to the formless, to the animal and far beyond the animal to the beginning of all things" (92). This "return" from culture to nature, which Hesse sees as the road of the "future" and of "spiritual revaluation" (92) is the unfortunate transposition of his mother myth into a crude philosophy of history. The chilling aspect of his cyclic tropes of a dying Europe returning to the maternal ground of the unconscious in order to be reborn is that such a recommended recoil may not necessarily be one to an Edenic or even a Rousseauistic innocence, but—what is much more likely—to a brutish Hobbesian state of nature.

Thus the war that is welcomed as a necessary culture cleansing at the conclusion of *Demian* is interpreted in another of Hesse's Dostoevsky essays, "The Brothers Karamazov, or The Decline of Europe," in similar terms as Dostoevsky's " 'Asiatic' ideal" of "a return to the mother, to the sources, to the Faustian 'Mothers' " that "will lead like every earthly death to a new birth" (71). Like the Gnostic Abraxas-symbol of *Demian*, Dostoevsky's Karamazov-symbol of "Russian man" signifies the "primeval demiurge" in whom "good and evil, outer and inner, God and Satan are cheek and jowl" (73). Hesse's account of *The Brothers Karamazov* as a "mythic novel" (80) about the chaotic interim "before the old dying culture can be replaced by a new one . . . that anxious, dangerous, painful stage [when] man has to look anew into his soul, see once more the animal rising within, acknowledge anew the existence of primeval forces that are supramoral" (79) is an apt characterization of his own book of two years earlier. Yet his rhetorical advocacy in the Dostoevsky essays of a return to the dark promptings beyond good and evil of the collective unconscious is genuinely disturbing because it seems more uncritical and extreme than other such polemical-poetic programs by other major early twentieth-century writers—for instance, D. H. Lawrence's attempt to redress the extremes of "mental life" through a lyrical celebration of "blood consciousness" and erotic being.

For the reader caught up in—or put off by?—such momentous metaphors of cultural death and rebirth, it is easy to overlook the fact that for Hesse, ever the radical individualist, the endorsement of "the decline of Europe" is not a *sociopolitical program* or the call for a collective atavism, but primarily a psychic process enacted within a few individuals, a path "each one walks . . . alone, each by himself" (92). It is, in fact, "the way within" of Hesse's psychoanalysis, which led him to the prophetic birth and death tropes of *Demian* and the Dostoevsky essays. As he wrote in a letter of 1919, "What I call decline I see principally as birth. The 'decline of Europe' is a process which I experience within myself and which perhaps may be compared with the decline of antiquity: not a sudden collapse, but a slow, developing reorientation in the souls of people."[39] But when Hesse wrote these lines, he was already living in sunny Montagnola, and domesticating the prophetic energies that had overwhelmed him in the confessional explosion of *Demian*.

In the final analysis, *Demian* is, like Lawrence's *Women in Love* (completed in the same year, 1917), a World War I novel, though not one primarily *about* the war. (Like Hesse's, Lawrence's metaphoric journey into the self took "shape in the midst of a period of war."[40]) The German visionary who wrote in his Prologue that "each of us is able to interpret himself to himself alone" (4) could also have penned the sentiment of the English novelist's Foreword, "this novel pretends only to be a record of the profoundest experiences of the self." For both autobiographical novelists, what Lawrence calls "the period of crisis" of World War I had a massive impact on their fictional rendering of "the profoundest experiences of the self," which are linked with a prophetic vision of the greater life and death cycles of civilizations and with an obscure and mystifying symbolism of the unconscious that is perhaps as much an index of the disturbed temper of the times—its confused apocalyptic hopes and fears—as it is a record of the psychological fathoming of the "deep" self.

A Child's Soul

In *Demian* the figure of Sinclair's father remains almost entirely in the background save as an occasional object of Sinclair's resentment. In the novella *A Child's Soul* (written between December 1918 and February 1919, toward the end of Hesse's stay in Bern), however, the father-son conflict, which turns on an actual theft (as opposed to an imaginary one, that is, Sinclair's fib about the stolen apples), is the confessional focal point. And if in the novel the figure of Demian's mother is mythologized in a Jungian setting, in the novella that of the narrator's father is presented in the demystified context of Freudian family romance. Despite *A Child's Soul*'s graphic sexual symbolism, Hesse's treatment of both father and son is realistic and directly autobiographical and lacks altogether the persistent prophetic note of *Demian*. The fact that Hesse achieved a significant rapprochement with his father during the latter's final years, now recognizing some basic similarities between them,[41] must have helped him to a clearer understanding of his adolescent identity crisis.

Such a new in- or hindsight is reflected in this powerful sketch written less than three years after Johannes Hesse's death. The characterization of the father in *A Child's Soul* represents a tremendous advance over Hesse's earlier fictional portraits (in *Peter Camenzind* and *Beneath the Wheel*), so crudely distorted or simplified by an animus he was unable to fathom or unwilling to probe. Filial resentment is still very much a felt factor, but now Hesse's depiction of this relationship begins to do justice to the complex and painful situation documented in the composite biographical record, *Childhood and Youth Before 1900*. Hence *A Child's Soul* is a significant counterbalance and autobiographical coda to the pervasive mother myth of the *Demian* period, and one that already prefigures the later Hesse's movement toward the values of a paternal *Geist*.

At the opening of this tale we see the same self-division of the adolescent boy into "light" and "dark" halves that we saw in Sinclair, with the paternal world of "dignity and power"[42] juxtaposed to that of the instincts symbolized here in part by the working-class lout Oskar Weber, who is a less threatening version of the Kromer of *Demian*. Hesse's eleven-year-old is so troubled by this split that he has succumbed to a generalized *Angst*, suffering from "dread of punishment, dread of my own conscience, dread of stirrings in my own soul which I considered forbidden and criminal" (10). The single major episode unfolded in the narrative shows the son, who is in the grip of the "demon" self that resists the dictates of "father and judge" (10), seeking relief from his "guilty conscience" by going to see his father in his study: "With Mother it was easier and simpler to find comfort; but Father's comfort was more valuable. It meant peace with the judging conscience, reconciliation and a new covenant with the good powers" (11). In the description of his ascent to his father's rooms the big Hesse house in Calw becomes a metaphor of the psyche, as the quarters below, where mother and children are at home, is contrasted with the father's logocentric realm: "up here power and spirit dwelt; up here were the courthouse and temple" (10). When the boy discovers that his father is not home, the empty study, far from assuaging his *Angst*, tempts him to desecrate the paternal temple. In an almost too-transparent Oedipal impulse, he pockets pen nibs, needles, and toothpicks from the father's desk. The height of his violation of this inner sanctum is when he discovers (in an adjoining bedroom) an irresistible treasure secreted away in the drawer of a dresser: "I was looking into a wicker basket, of Indian or some other exotic origin, and there I saw something surprising, alluring: a whole round of pale, sugar-coated dried figs!" (14–15). As Boulby already noted of "the startlingly Freudian nature of the symbolism," the "selection of this particular fruit scarcely needs elucidation."[43]

The Oedipal nature of this theft is underscored by the son's subsequent fantasies of setting the house on fire and brutally murdering the father. Here we have a stark confessional glimpse of the disturbed fantasy world of the teenage Hesse who was fascinated by fire and fireworks. The narrator's resentment against paternal authority in which the images of Father and God merge, goes Rousseau's confrontation with the divine judge (in the opening of *The Confessions*) one better with an outraged *non serviam* that is also Hesse's not-so-fictional reprise of the institutionalized problem child tagged with the label of "moral insanity":

> And when I had been executed and was dead and came before the eternal Judge in heaven, I would by no means bow down and submit. Oh no, not though all the choirs of angels were gathered around him and he radiated pure holiness and dignity . . . I would not apologize and not humble myself, would not beg forgiveness, would not repent! If he asked me: "Did you do such and such?" I would cry out, "Yes, I did it, and more, and I was right to have done it and if I can I will do it again and again. I killed, I set fire to houses, because I enjoyed it and because I wanted to mock and anger you. Because I hate you and I spit at your feet, God. You have plagued me and hurt me, you have made laws nobody can keep, you have set grownups to make life a hell for us boys. (20)

The deeper conflict that was still suppressed in the failed confession of over a decade earlier now begins to burst forth rhetorically. In addition to the son's exultant sense of moral superiority already voiced through Sinclair ("I felt superior to my father! Momentarily I felt a certain sense of loathing for his ignorance," *Demian*, 15), there is now also the adolescent's indictment of an all-too-judgmental authority based on a secret appropriation of what he would also like to have: "But why then did my father have to keep such fig rings hidden in his chest of drawers?" (22).

In the denouement of this novella with not only Freudian but also Kafkaesque motifs, the power of an all-knowing parent asserts itself as the inevitable judgment against the son. After days of terrible guilt and anxiety about being found out, he is finally confronted when and where he least expects it—on Sunday as he is relaxing after his return from church. The father's silent and pained entry into his room is the signal that the "trial" has begun. The boy's pointless and palpable lies when he is interrogated only lead to further guilt and humiliation as these are methodically exposed by the forced calm of an all-too-just judge. The conclusion captures with stark force the sense of terror and dread inherent in childhood derelictions that as adults we are only too prone to forget. Ironically, the very self-control, judicial fairness and patience of the cultivated father are much more trying for the son than an act of parental brutality or blind injustice could be, for these would right the moral balance of power by for once putting the former in the wrong. His hapless lies exposed, the boy is reduced to a sullen silence by the demanding "why" of an inquisitorial parent (who might have benefited from the lesson of Wordsworth's "Anecdote for Fathers"):

> What playacting! What stupid, senseless torment! . . . He knew everything, of course! and he let me dance, let me perform my useless capers the way you let a captive mouse dance in its wire trap before you drown it. If he had hit me over the head with his cane right at the start, without asking me any questions at all! I would have preferred that to the calm and righteousness with which he caught me in my idiotic net of lies and slowly strangled me. (39–40)

Despite the exposé of his prosecuting father, the middle-aged Hesse presents a remarkably balanced and sympathetic portrait of the dilemmas of both parent and child in this unsentimental retrospect of a dismal failure of communication. Only now can the adult answer the question the eleven-year-old boy could not: he had stolen the figs out of his disappointment of not finding his father when he needed him, and he had rummaged among his father's things out of a desire to know something more intimate about this remote authority figure. Thus the theft is not only an Oedipal episode, but also the frustrated expression of his desire to be close to his father. While the narrator accepts this as the final interpretation, verbalizing now what he only knew then in his "unconscious" (41), it is highly unlikely that the author who earlier that year (1918) praised Freudian psychoanalysis for teaching us "to recognize, to examine, and to take seriously exactly those things that we have been most successful in repressing in ourselves"[44] was not aware of the Freudian symbolism of this revealing confessional father-son psychodrama. If the psychologist in Hesse incorporates the Oedipal aspect without explicitly commenting on it, the moralist in him sums up the larger tragedy of mutual incomprehension, misprision, and disappointment that was his adolescent relationship with Johannes Hesse: "Perhaps for the first time in my life I felt, almost to the verge of understanding and consciousness, how utterly two well-intentioned human beings can torment each other, and how in such a case all talk, all attempts at wisdom, all reason merely adds another dose of poison, creates new tortures, new wounds, new errors" (42). The probing psychological realism with which *A Child's Soul* renders the father-son conflict and the final impression of now-sympathetic authorial understanding with which the figure of the father is painfully yet fondly recollected, reveal Hesse's soul-searching revaluation of a biographical situation hitherto grossly distorted or glossed over in his autobiographical fiction.

CHAPTER VII

TICINO LEGENDS OF

SAINTS AND SINNERS

*I too must constantly struggle, now with the murderer, now with
the animal within me, but equally with the moralist and the wish
to attain harmony all too soon, with easy resignation, with the
escape into sheer kindness, noble-mindedness and purity. Both
have to be; without the animal and murderer in us we are cas-
trated angels without a proper life; and without the forever new
and supplicatory urge for purification, cleansing, and the worship
of the spiritual and the selfless we don't amount to much either.—
Hesse letter of ca. autumn 1919*

When in April 1919 Hesse put Bern and his marriage behind him to
settle in the southernmost, Italian-speaking canton of Switzerland,
the Ticino, he was belatedly acting out Veraguth's resolve at the end
of *Rosshalde* to begin a new life. It had taken the double impact of
personal and cultural crisis for Hesse to make a break with his past
and to set out for new regions, psychic and geographic. The movement south, as he describes it in the opening piece of *Wandering*
(1920, a collection of lyrical prose, poetry, and drawings that reflects
his eager embrace of his new surroundings), is the crossing of a
boundary that entails a harsh judgment of his past:

> I wanted to be something that I was not. I even wanted to be a
> poet and a middle-class person at the same time. I wanted to be
> an artist and a man of fantasy, but I also wanted to be a good
> man, a man at home. It all went on for a long time, till I knew
> that a man cannot be both and have both . . . I increased the
> world's guilt and anguish, by doing violence to myself, by not
> daring to walk toward my own salvation.[1]

In the very productive decade that followed, Hesse's fiction was to
be a daring experiment in modern autobiography, a further sounding

of "the way within" initiated in *Demian* two years earlier. Like Klein's, Hesse's flight to the south was exhilarating yet guilty, a definitive yet painful liberation from his middle-class existence as a man and a writer. Freedom also brought uncertainties: choosing where to live—the village of Montagnola, near Lugano, Hesse's safe harbor for the remainder of his life—was easier than the problem of how to make a living. His financial position was to remain precarious for years, as most of his disposable income went toward the support of his family, and as the earnings from his writings dwindled next to nothing due to the rising German inflation.

Though Hesse's new-found poverty sorted well with the monastic and reclusive self-image he cultivated during the early Montagnola years, it also forced him onto the reading and lecture circuit, and even to the expedient of selling handwritten and illustrated copies of selected stories and poems. And even so, without the generous support of friends and patrons, he might not have been able to keep afloat financially. These external constraints were troubling, yet about the central issue of his new life Hesse felt no hesitancy. His unwavering objective henceforth was the ideal of self-realization, even if for the remainder of his career his particular pursuit of "salvation" was marked by the conflict between his religious and his literary impulses. Hesse's inward journey in the wake of *Demian* still carries the imprint of psychoanalysis, but his style of thinking and writing moves progressively away from the portentous chiaroscuro of that prophetic book. In his Ticino legends he cultivated the image of the wanderer yet learned to be at home with himself. As he wrote to his sister Adele a few months after settling there, "in any event I have managed despite all worries . . . to live intensively again in my own way."[2] Intensive living translated into intensive writing, in a burst of confession that had indeed begun well before his move from Bern, but that peaked during the summer to make "the year 1919," as he noted in "Journal 1920–1921," the fullest, busiest, most prolific and blazing of [his] life."[3] The mid-career break with his past released a flood of pent-up energies, and initiated a new commitment to self-writing as the necessary center of his life. The amazing resurgence of Hesse's vitality during that memorable summer took other forms as well, however, as any reader of *Klein and Wagner* and *Klingsor's Last Summer* can readily guess: "I had hardly arrived in the Ticino when I began 'Klein and Wagner,' and hardly had I finished that when I wrote Klingsor, and besides that I covered day after day hundreds of sketch sheets; painted, and had active contact with many people; had two love affairs, sat for many nights in a grotto with wine—my candle burned at the same time at all ends."[4] One of his new creative activities, landscape painting, was both play and therapy. Freed from the pressures of "art" and of having to live up to a reputation, Hesse found through his charming post-impressionist aquarelles a means of expressing the light and childish side of his personality. A self-proclaimed amateur, he was able to jest about his avocation: "painting is marvelous; it makes one happier and more patient. Afterward one does not have black fingers as with writing, but red and blue ones."[5]

During his first year in Montagnola he was buoyed up by the knowledge that both his life and his work had undergone a "new beginning and upheaval." As he wrote in January 1920, the experience of psychoanalysis and the events of the time had completely altered his outlook and idiom. One consequence of this revolution—which he fears "will not delight his friends"—is that he "has worked ferociously this entire year nearly without a break."[6] Such is the literary consequence of an altered self-perception and an identity that, as he described it in "Self-Communion," was being "crystallized" anew. This brief but revealing essay (written in 1918 or 1919) evaluates the traumas of his recent past as conducive to renewal and rejuvenation, and concludes with the significant psychoanalytic comparison of his self to a lake, "whose deepest layers lay closed off, which led to suffering and the approach of death. But now what is above and below is busily intermingling, perhaps still imperfectly, perhaps still not actively enough—but in any event, it is flowing."[7] Water, which here on the threshold of his move to the Ticino is the image of psychic wholeness and the integration of conscious and unconscious, becomes in *Klein and Wagner* and *Siddhartha* the signifier of ontological plenitude and cosmic unity.

Psychoanalysis had broken up the stagnation by restoring the flow between the surface and the depths of Hesse's self; it had also made him take note of the myriad layers, currents, and shadings of light and dark of his inner world. To be sure, self-realization was more the goal than the product of his first Montagnola years,[8] and after the creative high of 1919 Hesse was to suffer repeated impasses, beginning with the prolonged depression of 1920, from which he sought relief through further psychoanalysis as well as an immersion in Eastern philosophy and religion. The release of energy Hesse experienced with his move to Montagnola, however, is that of a writer busily confronting his inner self who is continually amazed at what he discovers, and who now consciously owns up to the fact that his writing (*Dichtung*) is confession (*Bekenntnis*).⁹ As we saw in the last chapter, with *Demian* Hesse tried to come to terms with the overwhelming impact of new materials that had become available to him through psychoanalysis, and did so through an attempted synthesis of the "light" and "dark" elements of his psyche under the magical umbrella of the Abraxas symbol. In his subsequent fictional self-probings during the following decade, the obscure symbolism of *Demian* yields to a more immediate and tangible psychography that seeks to document the plenitude of the self through confessional personas in whose consciousness the polarities adumbrated in the personal myth of *Demian* are more convincingly and cogently projected. Despite startling differences of style, character, and setting, the leading self-reflectors of Hesse's early post–World War I fictions reveal more of his inner life and problems than anything he had written hitherto. In his powerful yet highly stylized Ticino legends of saints and sinners, the extremes of grace and guilt, enlightenment and despair, purity and corruption, *Angst* and bliss, dwell side-by-side in the same character.

The Psychomachia of *Klein and Wagner*

Hesse critics tend to agree that this novella that he wrote rapidly in the early part of his first Ticino summer is a brutally frank confession.¹⁰ A *tour de force* of Hesse's new style, *Klein and Wagner* resists "neat" interpretation because of its juggling of heterogeneous elements—psychoanalytic, religious, philosophical—that coexisted uneasily in its author's imagination.¹¹ The surface parallels between Hesse and Klein are transparent, especially the guilty flight from family and middle-class respectability into the freedom of an unsettled and precarious existence. Even the differences between author and protagonist only serve to underscore the transposition of life into art:

the crime of Klein (the bank employee who absconds with funds entrusted to him) correlates with Hesse's sense of guilt at breaking with bourgeois conventions in order to follow his inner urges—and the same is true of his sexual relationship with the demimondaine Teresina who, like Hermine in *Steppenwolf*, lives off middle-class society, yet has not lost the gift of passionate living and giving. The deeper convergence between Hesse and his character (in a tale that is, appropriately enough, full of mirror images) reveals that Hesse's new commitment to art as confession (*Kunst als Bekenntnis*) did indeed entail an unflinching examination of the psychopathology of his unpedestrian life.

From Klein's first glimpse of his "distorted face" ("a stranger's, a sad crazy mask")[12] in the train window, the story is a devastating résumé of Klein-Hesse's stifled individuality in marriage, and of a deep-seated resentment against his wife. Hesse's striking use of dreams here is almost too patly psychoanalytic as a revelation of suppressed impulses—for example, Klein's dream of taking charge of a car in which he is being driven, by wresting the steering wheel from the driver: "it was better to drive yourself even if it meant peril than always to be driven and directed by others" (50). The clue that the unknown driver was actually his wife is followed by Klein's admitting to himself his festering animus against her, which is in fact what led to his sudden flight. Klein's marital retrospect is Hesse's bitter recollection of his years in Gaienhofen and Bern: "He looked back . . . upon his whole marriage, and the distance traversed seemed to him a weary, dreary road on which a man toils alone through the dust bearing heavy burdens on his back" (51). His "long-forgotten yearning for the south" (52) may have its sources in German literature from Goethe to Thomas Mann, but it is also the married Hesse's nostalgia for the happy foot-journeys of his bachelor days through northern Italy and of his "never clearly formulated craving for escape and liberty from the serfdom and dust of his marriage" (52). Conversely, the mirror image of "the sad and anxious face of Klein the criminal" is a reflection of Hesse's guilt at having taken this "leap into space," as is the telling exclamation, "if his father had lived to see this!" (57).

Klein's flight is a more desperate and less successful version of Hesse's attempt at self-realization and a progressive purging of the bourgeois assumptions that had governed his married life. In order to understand himself, Klein has to face up to his repressed self and "evil shadow" (65) represented by the double reference of the name *Wagner*, who is both the schoolteacher Klein had read about in the papers "who had butchered his entire family in a horribly bloody way and then taken his own life" (and whose act Klein had self-righteously condemned just when "the obsessional idea of killing his family had first gripped him," 59) *and* the famous composer whose music he had loved in his youth but condemned as a husband and father "because youth and artistic enthusiasm and Wagner reminded him painfully of things he had lost, because he had let himself be married by a woman he did not love" (64). It is only when, in a revealing nightmare that anticipates *Steppenwolf*'s Magic Theater in its projection of unconscious impulses as dramatis personae, Klein enters "the theater called 'Wagner' " and recognizes it as "his own interior being," that he fathoms the full relevance of the name: "Wagner was himself—Wagner was the murderer and the hunted man within him, but Wagner was also the composer, the artist, the genius, the seducer, lover of life and of the senses, luxury—Wagner was the collective name for everything repressed, buried, scanted in the life of Friedrich Klein, the civil servant" (116).

This traumatic yet therapeutic dream is the psychoanalytic centerpiece of a psychomachia in which the divided self of Klein ("one visible, and one secret," 56) achieves a larger self-awareness. The wordplay of Hesse's conjunctive title (Klein = little, Wagner = *wagen* = to dare) appropriately signals the two sides of the protagonist's split personality. Yet Klein's dramatic mid-life change does not ultimately lead, like Hesse's own, to a viable identity and a productive life that integrates the two halves. His is a manic-depressive roller-coaster ride between the extremes of self-affirmation and despair that ends in the conventional Hessean escape, suicide. Unable to deal with his guilt and to sustain his positive moods, he fails to achieve that happiness which in a journal of 1918 Hesse defined as the ability to love, and whose precondition is self-love and acceptance.[13] Klein's peak experiences are those of a fleeting self-harmony when he can hear a "voice" which is that of "God" or of "his truest, innermost self" (76). It is this authentic self that leads him to the dancer Teresina, and to recognize in her, despite all the differences between them, the mirror image of genuine selfhood expressed through her art: "there is a resemblance between us; both of us here and now, at rare moments, do what is in us. Nothing is rarer" (94). If Klein's goal is authentic being, its negation and his particular demon is dread or *Angst*, a word Hesse invokes repeatedly for Klein's failure and despair and that may well include a conscious reference back to Kierkegaard, with whose writings Hesse had some familiarity, as manifest in a description (written in the same year as *Klein and Wagner*) that also fits his confessional persona: "how vain he is, how nervous, how suspicious, how full of *Angst* is this Kierkegaard, who said of himself that he is 'as caught up in his own reflection as a reflexive pronoun.' "[14] The *Angst* that preys on Klein is, like Kierkegaard's "dread," not a specific or identifiable fear of something, but a generalized and objectless anxiety. And like that of the founding father of existentialism, Hesse's characterization of *Angst* has a religious context that, though very different from Kierkegaard's version of Christianity, emerges as a major element at the conclusion of his novella. If the Kierkegaardian resonance of Klein's *Angst* suggests that Hesse's reading of the Danish theologian may have carried over into his characterization of Klein, his presentation of the extremes of suicidal "disgust, worry, and surfeit with life" (74) and its abrupt conversion into a resounding hymn of life at the conclusion carries the autobiographical seal of Hesse's experience.

That conclusion, which with its mystical aura is on the spiritual horizon of *Siddhartha*, is certainly not without its problems. The ecstatic finale of Klein's drowning has all the trappings of a religious revelation, for the despairing Klein becomes in death a visionary. Suicide as an apotheosis is a new turn in Hesse's fiction, and one with which he manages up to a point to make his attempted merger of not-so-commensurable elements work through an experimental and highly lyrical prose that resists analysis and disarms judgment. The epiphanic mode that marks the conclusion is already introduced earlier in the narrative (in the extended sequence in section three after Klein has met Teresina), when Hesse projects a Romantic-pantheist awareness of the immanence of the divine in ordinary reality that is quite similar to the ecstatic "sentiment of being" that Wordsworth celebrates in *The Prelude* (Book 2, l. 420, 1805 text). And Klein's realization "that life becomes meaningful precisely when we lose our grasp of all meanings" is a later, proto-existentialist version of Wordsworth's "wise passiveness" ("Expostulation and Reply"). Through parataxis of style and the rapid accumulation of impressions, Hesse struggles to get around the dilemma that "there were no words for this state," whose best indicator would not be language, but music:

> The wave passed through him like pain and like voluptuous delight. He trembled with sheer emotion. Life roared in him like surf. Everything was incomprehensible. He opened his eyes wide and saw: trees on a street, slivers of silver in the lake, a running dog, bicyclists—and everything was strange, like a fairy tale, and almost too beautiful. Everything looked as if it had come brand-new out of God's toy box. Everything existed for him alone, for Friedrich Klein, and he himself existed solely to feel this stream of wonder and pain and joy pouring through himself. There was beauty everywhere, in every rubbish heap by the wayside; there was deep suffering everywhere; God was everything. (99–100)

With this charged prose Hesse celebrates a sense of the fullness of being synonymous with the "grace" that has been taught "by all the sages of the entire world, Buddha and Schopenhauer, Jesus, the Greeks. There was only one wisdom, only one faith, only one philosophy: the knowledge that God is within us" (87). Yet the strongest support of Hesse's secularized and existential version of Klein's "revelation" is still the New Testament: " 'Unless you become as little children . . .' occurred to him, and he felt: I have become a child again, I have entered into the Kingdom of Heaven" (103). Hesse's celebration includes art, which "was nothing but regarding the world in a state of grace: illumination" (103). He is so bent on affirming a higher unity that he disregards the basic differences between the religious and philosophic traditions invoked in the canonical catalogue above, just as the novella as a whole seeks to overleap the tension of incommensurable ingredients with its passionate reaching after revelation—and it is perhaps this unreconstructed yearning for revelation that is *Klein and Wagner*'s most poignant and revealing autobiographical statement.

The dying Klein's epiphany certainly supports Hesse's later admis-

sion (in a letter of December 1930 to his sister), "despite all my rebel-
ling, I have nevertheless remained the missionary's son."¹⁵ Klein's
suicide as a "dropping into the maternal womb, into the arm of God"
(138) combines in a characteristic Hessean fashion aspects of the
mother and father worlds. The element of surprise is the drowning
Klein's realization, as he lets himself sink into the lake, that instead
of letting himself fall into death, "he could just as well have let himself fall into life" (138). His belated illumination—"wonderful
thought: a life without dread!" (119)—is a complete acceptance of
being *as* being: "Let yourself fall! Do not fight back! Die gladly! Live
gladly!" (119). The poetic notion of letting oneself "fall" may be
tinged with the Schopenhauerian renunciation of the Will (it is relevant that Klein had taken with him on his flight "a small volume of
Schopenhauer," 76) and with Oriental mysticism (which influenced
Schopenhauer's philosophy): "All life was a breath exhaled by God.
All dying was a breath inhaled by God. One who had learned not to
resist, to let himself fall, died easily, was born easily. One who resisted, who suffered dread, died hard, was born reluctantly" (118).
Yet despite Hesse's interest in Eastern philosophy, his notion of "falling" is not really synonymous with the Buddhist goal of Nirvana,
which in the "Journal 1920–1921" he defined as "the redeeming step
behind the *principium individuationis*, or, religiously expressed, the return of the individual to the world soul, to God." He finds this goal
questionable because "if God casts me out into the world to exist as
an individual, is it then my duty to return to the whole as quickly
and as easily as possible—or should I not, on the contrary, fulfil
God's will precisely by letting myself be borne along (in 'Klein and
Wagner' I called it 'letting oneself fall'), so that I expiate with him his
desire to forever split himself and live out his life through individual
beings?"¹⁶ In the light of this passage, Klein's insight seems closer to
modern Western, existentialist modes of thought—for instance, to
Heidegger's concept (in *Being and Time*) of *Geworfenheit* (Thrownness).

Klein's final vision of life as a "universal stream of forms" (143) is
an earlier version of the ubiquitous river symbol of *Siddhartha*. The
metaphysical claim, developed in major key in the novel, that time is
an illusion, is also briefly introduced in the novella, as is the idea of
music, here the signifier of a cosmic order beyond the reach of lan-

guage. Hesse's trope of a "dome of music, a cathedral of sound" in whose "midst sat God" (143) is meant to suggest the center toward which Klein is sinking, having been transformed even at the moment of his singing death into "a prophet and proclaimer" (144). For the writer whose actual life fell far short of such achieved concord, this cathedral of sound below the waves is the oddly mixed metaphor of psychic and ontological wholeness. Like Siddhartha's smiling apotheosis, Klein's "falling" death is the idealized self-projection of the Hesse who in the "Journal of 1920–1921" confesses that his "strongest and most tempting exemplary model" is that of the saint.[17]

Yet the sinner in Hesse is also acknowledged in *Klein and Wagner*'s confessional psychomachia, and perhaps nowhere more devastatingly than in the glimpse of Klein's troubled relationship with his wife. His long-festering resentment takes, in the "Wagner" nightmare, the grotesque form of phallic violence:

> He was seized by an overwhelming repugnance for this woman [who is both his wife and an innkeeper's wife with whom he has just had intercourse] and drove a knife into her abdomen. But another woman, like a mirror image of the first, attacked him from behind, drove sharp, powerful claws into his throat and tried to strangle him. (115)

With this stark glimpse of Klein's unconscious, Hesse generalizes the deadlocked relationship between two partners into a psychoanalytic vision of the battle of the sexes. The sexual violence that will crop up again in Harry Haller's stabbing of Hermine also has its counterpart in the last part of *Klein and Wagner*, when Klein resists his irrational impulse to stab the sleeping Teresina and opts instead for killing himself. If these fictional scenarios point up a real pathology, the moralist in Hesse, supported by the perspectives of his psychoanalysis, answers, "the less we shy away from those fantasies which make us into animals and criminals in our waking and our dreaming, the less is the danger that we will in reality and in deed succumb to these evils."[18]

To end this analysis on a somewhat different note, let me point out that *Klein and Wagner* also includes a more prosaic résumé of Hesse's married life: "He . . . realized, with sorrow, that he himself had remained a boy and a beginner in love, had become resigned in the course of a long, lukewarm marriage, was timid and yet without innocence, lustful yet full of guilt" (109). Hesse will make up for these inhibitions and repressions in his subsequent writings, which will reflect in heightened form his bold new style of living: Siddhartha, Harry Haller, and Goldmund all become happy adepts in the school of eros and succeed in varying degrees in conquering despair and discovering some meaning in their lives without having, like Klein, to kill themselves in order to do so.

Klingsor's Self-Portrait in an Expressionist Mirror

Like *Klein and Wagner*, this novella which was written toward the end of Hesse's first summer in Montagnola is a confessional virtuoso performance. It is his highly-stylized self-rendering in a poetic prose redolent of Expressionism, a movement that according to Freedman, Hesse had earlier ignored but was more receptive to when "in the postwar ferment it had become positively fashionable." Hesse rejected, as Field notes, "the extreme demands of Expressionists to throw out the old,"[19] yet the style of *Klingsor* shows the postwar Hesse's willingness to be innovative short of joining the *avant garde*, particularly since some of his assumptions in 1919 sorted well with those of the German Expressionists, including the animus against bourgeois society, the focus on the artist's creative powers, and on a use of words "as charged reservoirs of energy" in order "to bring forth the hidden metaphorical dimension of the poet's subjective vision."[20] From the vantage of the late twentieth century, Hesse's self-portrait in an Expressionist mirror may strike us as impossibly melodramatic:

> The little palette full of pure unmixed colors, intensely luminous, was his comfort, his tower, his arsenal, his prayer book, his cannon. From it he fired upon wicked death. Purple was denial of death, vermilion was mockery of decay. His arsenal was good; his brave troop stood lined up brilliantly, the rapid rounds from his cannon flashed.[21]

To appreciate *Klingsor's* autobiographical bravura one has to see how the metaphoric leaps of Hesse's startling prose are in fact modulated and controlled by a masterly touch. That he chose the form of the novella for this piece is fitting because it is above all a mood piece, a short but intense lyrical flight, "a pretty rocket."[22]

The Preface asserts that the work of Klingsor, who died at the age of forty-two (Hesse's age at the time of writing) will live on, as will "the legend of his life" (148); conversely, Klingsor's last is Hesse's first Ticino summer turned into a demonic prose poem of the artist that incorporates the polarities of sinner and saint under the aegis of Dionysian intoxication: Klingsor burns the candle at both ends in a desperate surge of living and working. Because these antinomies are momentarily merged in a single persona, there is for once no need for Hesse's characteristic confessional self-splitting. (This is not to deny that there is an obvious self-reference in a very secondary character, Hermann the Poet, who is in any case hardly more than a name.) Hesse also plays some intriguing biographical games, in the manner of the *roman à clef* (something that will peak in *The Journey to the East* a decade later) with the names of places and people dear to him that summer, including Louis the Cruel (the painter Louis Moilliet), the Armenian astrologer (his friend Josef Englert, who cast his horoscope), and the Queen of the Mountain (the young Ruth Wenger, who several years later became his second wife).

The fire imagery so prominent in the opening pages is well-chosen as the governing metaphor of Klingsor's climactic season, an orgiastic triad of the pleasures of wine, sex, and painting. Klingsor's rhapsodic and Nietzschean hunger for life has replaced the Schopenhauerian resignation and pessimism so pronounced in Hesse's earlier art novels: this painter's headlong experiment in intense living is not only fueled by his mid-life desire to make up for lost time, but by the omnipresent fear of death, the psychic equivalent, in this explosive tale, of Klein's *Angst*. The ecstatic sense of cosmic simultaneity that Klein achieves in death Klingsor wants to capture through a late summer binge in which Romantic intensity is translated into a searing metaphysical hunger for the fullness of being: "Why did time exist? Why always this idiotic succession of one thing after another, and not a roaring, surfeiting simultaneity?" (182). Klingsor's hunger expresses itself in an art that is open to "everything that is changing, filled with longing" (182). Fatefully conscious even in his flights of intoxication, this artist knows that his craving (of which eros is in a sense only the immediate instrumentality) brings him that much closer to the inevitability of a death invoked in the grotesqueries of one of the lyrics that intersperse the narrative:

Drunk, I sit at night in the windy wood,
Autumn has gnawed at the singing branches;
The grumbling innkeeper runs to the wine cellar
To fill my empty bottle.

Tomorrow, tomorrow pale death will slice
My red flesh with his humming scythe.
For a long time now that furious fiend
Has lain in wait for me.[23]

With the extremes of *Klingsor*'s style, Hesse succeeds in projecting a modern, revitalized Romanticism, something he will do even more effectively in the middle of the next decade in *Steppenwolf*. Indeed, much in this tale—like its name, which is a version of the poet Klingsohr in *Heinrich von Ofterdingen*—harks back to Romanticism, including the mixing of genres and the fragmentary structure, at the same time as it shows the impact of modernism. Thus the Romantic stress on the importance of art and artists is counterbalanced by a nihilistic sense of the futility of art in the modern world. In *Klingsor*, Hesse still presents this idea in the context of World War I and the decline of Europe, but does so less sententiously than in the earlier *Demian* and the Dostoevsky essays (which were in fact written later that fall). In "The Music of Decline" section, Klingsor claims modern art is suicidal and reflects the cultural and political "collapse" of Europe (190). The backdrop to Klingsor's drunken diatribe, the "mechanical music" of the whirling carousel (192) is the cacophonous swan song of a dying culture: half a decade later this music of decline will become the jazz rhythms of an Americanized Europe to which Harry Haller has such an ambivalent response.

Klingsor's Last Summer does not shy away from sentimentality, especially in its treatment of the painter's attitude to women. His lurid fantasy of having a host of females of all ages and types fighting over him is fit for the kitschy cover of a contemporary rock album, and his confession, "often I look at every woman like a cunning old libertine, and often like a little boy" (185) suggests that even after psychoanalysis Hesse's attitude to women had not escaped the Romantic stereotyping of his earlier writings.

The frenzied self-portrait that Klingsor achieves "at the end of that summer's . . . incredibly fervid, tempestuous period of work," and which is its "crowning glory" (211), is Hesse's pictorial parallel and self-reflexive metaphor for his writing of this novella. And Klingsor's compulsive self-observation in the mirror as he paints his masterpiece is of course the symbolic equivalent of the myriad self-mirroring of Hesse's Ticino fictions. In the self-conscious mirror of Klingsor's studied poses and posturings we witness the extremes of the fetishized self as *objet d'art*. The painter's impending death makes for an appropriate end, for such a radical self-reflexivity is in the end also self-devouring:

> In those madly intense days Klingsor lived like an ecstatic. Nights, he loaded himself with wine, and then would stand, candle in his hand, before the old mirror, study his face in the glass . . . One night he had a girl with him on the couch in the studio, and while he pressed her naked body against his he stared with reddened eyes over her shoulder into the mirror, saw beside her unbound hair his distorted face, full of lust and full of the abhorrence of lust. (213–214)

With its distorted and exaggerated Expressionist style, the *Klingsor* self-portrait also includes different possibilities for its interpretation "from a wide variety of viewpoints" (212). Surely the most relevant among those suggested by Hesse, the hermeneut of his own work, is that of "Klingsor . . . analyzed and interpreted by the artist himself with unsparing psychological insight—an enormous confession, a ruthless, crying, moving, terrifying peccavi" (212). For Hesse, this heightened self-portrait is also a symbolic vision of early twentieth-century European culture. His metaphoric correlation is couched in a hyperbolic language located somewhere between the prophetic voice of *Demian* and the satiric one of *Steppenwolf*, with a significant backhanded compliment to Nietzsche's autobiography:

> This is man, ecce homo, here is the weary, greedy, wild, child-like, and sophisticated man of our late age, dying European man who wants to die, overstrung by every longing, sick from every

vice, enraptured by knowledge of his doom, ready for any kind
of progress, ripe for any kind of retrogression, submitting to fate
and pain like the drug addict to his poison, lonely, hollowed-
out, age-old, at once Faust and Karamazov, beast and sage,
wholly exposed, wholly without ambition, wholly naked, filled
with childish dread of death and filled with weary readiness to
die. (213)

In his next major work, Hesse faced East, and uttered his autobiographical *ecce homo* in soothing meditative tones that present a striking lyrical counterpoint to *Klingsor*'s whirling rhetoric of individual
and cultural disintegration.

Siddhartha

Hesse began his "Indian legend"[24] in the winter of 1920; the writing
proceeded rapidly, and by spring, he was halfway through Part 2,
when he bogged down in the "By the River" chapter. For a time it
seemed that the book would be consigned to his collection of unfinished works, but after a painful hiatus of nearly two years, he tackled
it anew, and by May 1922 *Siddhartha* was finished. What had been the
obstacle? One explanation is that Hesse, like many artists, experienced a letdown after a spell of intensive work, for, as he laments in
the journal he kept to fill the void of *not* working on the novel, after
the sustained creative high of 1919, 1920 turned out to be "certainly
the most unproductive [year] of [his] life."[25] Another reason for the
prolonged cold spell is that in the second part of *Siddhartha*, Hesse
was reaching, as it were, beyond his confessional shadow: "My Indian poem proceeded splendidly so long as I composed what I had
experienced: the mood of the young Brahmin who seeks wisdom and
who torments and mortifies himself. But when I had come to the end
of Siddhartha the sufferer and ascetic, and wanted to write about Siddhartha the victor, the yea-sayer and master, I couldn't proceed any
further."[26]

His remedy to this dilemma was at once ingenious and simple: to
try and enter imaginatively into and make his own the states of mind
he wished to portray in his protagonist. He succeeded in this project
to the extent that he managed to bring to a conclusion his most pop-

ular "wisdom" book. Yet the catch in his presentation of Siddhartha the "yea-sayer" is that—as with nearly all attempts to formulate religious and spiritual truths—what is intended to be most edifying turns out to be inexpressible save through clichés. As a witty passage in his 1920–1921 journal reveals, Hesse was quite aware of what might be called the Polonius dilemma of proffering words of wisdom:

> There is nothing more difficult than being a father confessor or spiritual guide. When some poor person has told me his story, I can't at bottom say anything else except, "yes, that is sad, as sad as life frequently is, I know it, I too have experienced it. Seek to bear it, and if nothing at all helps, drink a bottle of wine, and if that doesn't help either, know that there is the possibility of putting a bullet in one's head." Instead of this I seek to produce my consolatory arguments and life-wisdoms, and even if I actually know a few truths, at the instant one utters them aloud and dispenses them as medicine for an actual and immediate sorrow, they are a bit theoretical and hollow, and suddenly one seems to oneself like a priest who seeks to console his people and at the same time has the wretched feeling that he is doing something mechanical.[27]

Hesse's attempt to experience in some measure the spiritual development he wished to portray in the last third of *Siddhartha* led him consciously to re-immerse himself in a world that had been one of the *donneés* of his childhood—Indian religion and culture, as it had been available to him through his missionary parents and his deeply learned, Sanskrit-speaking grandfather Gundert. In the essay "My Belief" (1930), Hesse reminds us that "my father, mother, and grandfather had not only a rich and fairly thorough knowledge of Hindu forms of belief but also a sympathy, though only half admitted, for those forms. I breathed and participated in spiritual Hinduism from childhood just as much as I did in Christianity."[28] Hesse's renewed study of "the Upanishads, the Bhagavad-Gita, and the discourses of the Buddha" in what Mileck calls "a profound spiritual experience"[29] was, however, not the only way out of the impasse of 1920–1921, for as he acknowledged, the Chinese spiritual tradition, chiefly in the form of Taoism, had a significant impact as well on the last part of *Siddhartha*. Finally, even if the novel's exotic setting and hagiographic style do not readily suggest it, psychoanalysis is also a powerful if invisible influence. Freedman has stressed the importance of Hesse's sessions with Jung in early 1921 in helping him to get out from under his literary paralysis, because these may have facilitated "the idea of interior space in which temporal strife is displaced by a transcendent vision."[30] And near the conclusion of his 1920–1921 journal, Hesse summarizes "the path of healing and development" that enabled him to complete *Siddhartha*: "next to the Asiatic teachings (Buddha, Vedanta, and Lao-Tzu)" it included as well "psychoanalysis . . . not as a therapeutic method . . . but as the essential element" of a new world view.[31]

If Hesse's turn to the East in *Siddhartha* is a natural extension of his childhood and his family background, it was also reinforced by the Orientalism in vogue at the time he began work on the novel, and which was due in part to the popular *Travel Diary of a Philosopher* (1919) by Count Keyserling, whom Hesse in a review of 1920 praised as "the first European scholar and philosopher who has really understood India."[32] In his own journey to India a decade earlier Hesse had failed, as he admitted to Romain Rolland in 1923, to get beyond "the charm of the exotic" and to enter into "the world of the Indian spirit"—in fact, the only item of his miscellany, *From India: Sketches of an Indian Journey* (1913), that he still considers valuable is "a curious little tale ['Robert Aghion'] which at that time (1911) gave me much pleasure."[33] In striking contrast to his earlier tourist-venture, Hesse's fictional journey to India in *Siddhartha* is an inward and spiritual one that largely eschews picturesque surface and exotic effects in order to explore the sinner-saint polarity within him through the geographic symbolism that Ziolkowski has definitively analyzed as "the landscape of the soul" and "the projection of inner development into the realm of space."[34]

Questions as to the extent and significance of the Oriental influence on this novel, and the related issue of the Indian (Hindu and Buddhist) versus the Chinese (Taoist) components, are difficult to answer, particularly since most Western critics (myself included) simply do not have the necessary expertise to address it authoritatively, and since scholars and critics with an Oriental expertise are understandably prone to overstating the case by taking a part for the whole.[35] In this regard Hesse's ample pronouncements over the years about his intentions in *Siddhartha* are not always helpful, for they can furnish, like the Bible, support for radically differing viewpoints and interpretations. Nevertheless, in my view the gist of these (when considered in the context of the novel) justifies the conclusion that even though the "Eastern" influence is important, the book as a whole expresses a fundamentally Western outlook. Indeed, I would suggest that one of the wonderful ironies of *Siddhartha*'s enthusiastic reception by the American counterculture and student generation of the 1960s is that in the guise of Eastern religion these young readers were taking in, unbeknownst to them, an essentially Western creed.

Perhaps a better way to address the complex matter of the Eastern versus the Western aspects of *Siddhartha* is to describe it as Hesse's mid-life examination of the foundation of his religious beliefs in an undogmatic formulation of his deepest intuitions that draws on three great spiritual traditions: the Christian, the Indian, and the Chinese. Here *Siddhartha* points to a core experience that resists neat or easy definition. Hesse's statement in 1958 that he sought in this book "to discover what all faiths and all forms of human devoutness have in common"[36] assumes a cross-cultural and transconfessional basis of religion, a premise consistent with the three-tiered scheme of humanization outlined in "My Belief" (discussed in the last part of Chapter III). The path of Siddhartha, which leads from the self-will of the second stage to the serene faith of the third, reflects Hesse's own struggles as much as his aspirations toward a higher harmony. Hesse's belief that there is a greater coherence to his career is evident in his insistence that—despite the palpable differences of style and setting—*Demian* and *Siddhartha* are "by no means contradictions, but segments of the same way": *Demian* "stresses the process of individuation, the development of the personality without which no higher life is possible," whereas *Siddhartha* is concerned with "the other side of our task and destiny . . . the overcoming of our personality and our being pervaded by God."[37]

The path of Siddhartha's self-realization—which, as Ziolkowski has shown, in some respects resembles that of *Demian*'s Sinclair[38]— indicates both Hesse's assimilation of as well as his critical self-distancing from the Indian element. As Hesse wrote to Stefan Zweig in a revealing statement, "it was only when . . . this Indian element began to be no longer important to me that it became possible for me to represent it, just as I am always able to represent only that which in actual life is taking leave of me and departing." Even if Hesse affirms that the Indian "garb" is more than a mere "costume,"[39] Siddhartha obviously bears his author's psychological features. His Sanskrit name, which is also the legendary one of the Buddha, means something like "he who has found the goal," and is ironically appropriate, for Siddhartha can only reach his goal by rejecting the Buddha's teaching of the Eightfold Path and by attending instead to the Buddha's living example of following the voice within, which in Hesse-Siddhartha's view is what brought Gotama his enlightenment under the Bo tree. Therefore it is not surprising that Hesse the perennial Protestant also characterized his book as "the expression of [his] *liberation* from Indian thought" because this "very European book, despite its milieu" takes the concept of individuality "much more seriously than any Asiatic teaching."[40]

Hesse's autobiographical meditation on the spiritual core of all religions can also be read as his further and belated attempt at a reconciliation with his father, an idea first developed by Ball, who notes that Hesse's new closeness to his father during the latter's last years turned into admiration and love after his death in 1916.[41] While Freedman qualifies Ball's terse conclusion that "in *Demian* the father is missing, in *Siddhartha* the mother" with the more balanced view that both aspects "seemed to exist side by side in Hesse's imagination as he settled into his Indian book,"[42] the new ascendancy of the father world is evident in *Siddhartha*'s series of guru and guide figures. While the novel by no means excludes the mother world, which is suggested by Kamala and the realm of the senses (Samsara), the unresolved father-son conflict of Hesse's youth is now transposed and spiritualized through a set of strategic rejections of father figures. With the possible exception of Siddhartha's confrontation with the head Samana, these are respectful partings-of-the-way without any of the overt resentment and even contempt that burden most of the father-son relationships in Hesse's writings up to *Siddhartha*. Now the legend of self-will is presented with a delicate but masterly touch: unlike Sinclair, who seeks repeatedly to flee back into the Eden of childhood and whose weak self continues to rely on strong guides, Siddhartha makes a definitive break at the beginning of the novel with the tradition of his family, and appreciates early in his quest that he must reject all gurus to find himself. That, incidentally, is why Govinda, Siddhartha's friend and early disciple who depends on mentors as a roadmap to salvation, is still searching at the end of the book. He may well represent, as Field has suggested, "passive Oriental acceptance,"[43] but he is also the type of the perpetual follower who can never find the proper rhythm of his own life.

In the stately modulations of its lyrical and liturgical prose *Siddhartha* develops with synoptic clarity the stages of its hero's spiritual development from the exemplary "Brahmin's son"[44] of the opening to the smiling saint of the conclusion. Hesse's paradigmatic patterning is everywhere evident: more so than any of his previous alter egos, Siddhartha—true to his name—achieves his goal; in his life's pilgrimage, the polarities of sinner/saint, mind/nature are symmetrically balanced and mediated by the unifying symbol of the river. Hesse's new maturity is also evident in the balance of objectivity and empathy with which both the roles of father and son are presented, and in the wry but pervasive humor that seems to have eluded most of his critics—this, after all, is a wisdom book in which even the River Mystical is known to laugh at an apprentice saint.

Surely the influential Augustinian model of conversion and the genre of the saint's life (with which Hesse was familiar because of his long-standing interest in the Middle Ages and Saint Francis, about whom he had written a poetic biography) must have helped him frame the hagiographic *vita* of Siddhartha.[45] Thus what sometimes seems in *Demian* like a series of chaotic transformations is unfolded in *Siddhartha* as a coherent progression. The earlier novel's "light" and "dark" worlds are now two landscapes separated by the river, and the hero's life is both a geographic and spiritual journey that culminates in an experienced unity of self and world. However, if Hesse's saint reaches the third level of humanization, his life is also characterized by the Romantic-existential sense, to borrow Kierkegaard's title, of "stages on life's way." The experience of "awakening," so important later in *The Glass Bead Game*, depends on a periodic self-renewal symbolized by the age-old trope of the snake shedding its skin (37). The informing dynamic of Siddhartha's life, "awakening," though marked by a feeling of utter aloneness and "icy despair" (41), differs from Klein's existential *Angst*, because it is a function of higher self-realization. It is a proleptic force, as Siddhartha realizes when at the end of Part 1 he decides *not* to return home to his father. Moreover, in this novel the diachronic succession of identity stages is countered by a synchronic perception of the atemporal totality of the self, which is in turn posited on the larger unity of the cosmos.

Siddhartha's "awakening" is already implicit in his dissatisfaction with the Brahminic faith of his forebears as a viable way "toward the Self, toward Atman" (6). His subsequent adolescent confrontation with his priestly father over his decision to join the wandering ascetics, the Samanas, is an ironic rescripting of the young Hesse's active and not-so-successful rebellion into a successful passive resistance (6–7). Unlike the adolescent Hesse, and like Demian, Siddhartha uses his uncanny self-control to master others. Thus the identity crisis of Hesse's youth is transformed into an amusing episode from which the son emerges victorious, but which also shows the figure of the father as compassionate and dignified. Siddhartha's subsequent rejection of the ascetic-Samana ideal as a "flight from the Self" that can be achieved with less trouble, as he explains to Govinda, by the ox-driver "asleep over his bowl of rice wine" (17), is his second step away from external authority figures and toward himself. Like his earlier departure from home, his parting with the Samanas turns on a sly assertion of his self-will, in a scene whose humor has a satiric edge when Siddhartha hypnotizes the head Samana and forces him into fawning acquiescence.

Siddhartha's subsequent encounter with the Buddha—who shares with him not only a name, but a similar *vita*—is the final exercise of his *Eigensinn* against the figure whom he recognizes instantly as the greatest of all teachers and saints ("Never had Siddhartha esteemed a man so much, never had he loved a man so much," 28). Yet he refuses to subscribe to Gotama's doctrine, raising instead, in this subtly comic encounter, objections to the Buddhist gospel of the Eightfold Path to Nirvana, because he knows now that the road to enlightenment simply cannot be taught: the one thing the Buddha's teachings do not contain, as Siddhartha points out like some forward sophomore, is the incommunicable secret of "what the Illustrious One himself experienced" in the hour of *his* illumination (34). The youthful critic then concludes his Protestant rebuff of the Buddha with the assertion that he must judge for himself, which earns him the well-deserved reprimand, "you speak cleverly, my friend. Be on your guard against too much cleverness" (35).

Siddhartha's "awakening" in the last section of Part 1 cuts specifically against the grain of the Buddha's teachings, for it is his entry into the maternal sphere of nature and the senses that marks the emergence of a radically this-worldly self. A psychoanalytic passage from the "Journal 1920–1921" throws some light on Siddhartha's sudden *volte face*: "All heroic demands and virtues are repressions . . . In fact, virtues, like talents, are a sort of dangerous if at times useful hypertrophy, like goose livers grown to abnormal size."[46] Like the later Goldmund's flight from the monastery, Siddhartha's transformation is one from the austerities of the father world to a life of pleasure whose focus is the courtesan Kamala. And like Klein's passionate transports after his meeting with Teresina, Siddhartha's "awakening" is the revelation, not of a transcendent meaning, but of one immanent in the everyday world. The lyrical meditation below may have an "Indian" cast, but its larger drift should be familiar to anyone acquainted with the epiphanic mode in English literature from Wordsworth to Joyce:

> He looked around him as if seeing the world for the first time. The world was beautiful, strange, and mysterious. Here was blue, here was yellow, here was green, sky and river, woods and mountains, all beautiful, all mysterious and enchanting, and in the midst of it, he, Siddhartha, the awakened one, on the way to himself. All this, all this yellow and blue, river and wood, passed for the first time across Siddhartha's eyes. It was no longer the magic of Mara, it was no more the veil of Maya, it was no longer meaningless and the chance diversities of the appearances of the world, despised by deep-thinking Brahmins, who scorned diversity, who sought unity. River was river, and if the One and Divine in Siddhartha secretly lived in blue and river, it was just the divine art and intention that there should be yellow and blue, there sky and wood—and here Siddhartha. Meaning and reality were not hidden somewhere behind things, they were in them, in all of them. (39–40)

Siddhartha's childlike and unreflective immersion in the world of the senses on the other side of the river brings him a sexual awakening through an encounter with a teacher that is just as stylized and replete with gentle humor as his earlier confrontations with male preceptors. The poem that earns him his first kiss from Kamala throws his earlier spirit-exercises into a wonderfully ironic light:

> Into her grove went the fair Kamala,
> At the entrance of the grove stood the brown Samana.
> As he saw the lotus flower,
> Deeply he bowed.
> Smiling, acknowledged Kamala,
> Better, thought the young Samana,
> To make sacrifices to the fair Kamala
> Than to offer sacrifices to the gods. (56)

It is characteristic of Hesse's light touch in this novel that the young man who has just abjured all teachers should now seek out a new mentor—but one who teaches not any dogma, but engages her new pupil in a protracted *practicum* in the *Kama Sutra*. And unlike many of Hesse's earlier protagonists who prove misfits in Cupid's school, from Giebenrath who almost falls down the cellar stairs at Emma's advances, to Sinclair's pallid cult of Beatrice, Siddhartha proves an apt student. In the fictions of his middle period Hesse may still stereotype sexual relationships through Romantic spectacles, but at least his confessional personas are now a far cry from the neurasthenic virgins of his early fiction—a fact that no doubt reflects his changed outlook and lifestyle after his move from Bern. Indeed, Hesse's request to a friend to return his copy of the *Kama Sutra*, because he "needed it very badly, as soon as possible"[47] may stand as a humorous footnote to the Kamala sequence in *Siddhartha*.

Siddhartha's immersion in worldly pleasures can be no more than a way station, for Hesse's aim is to show that, as he wrote in 1921, "the highest toward which humans can aspire" is the most advanced degree of "harmony within the individual soul." Hesse saw this issue in both religious and psychological terms, as evident in his gloss, "who achieves this harmony has at the same time what psychoanalysis would call the free disposability of the libido, and that of which the New Testament states, 'everything is yours'."[48] In *Siddhartha* this "harmony" is more effectively conceived than it was with the Abraxas symbol of *Demian*, as the dialectical integration of antitheti-

cal aspects of the self. Siddhartha has learned that the road of asceticism is a dead end; now he has to learn that the same holds true for
the contrary path of sense-indulgence. In the four segments from
"Kamala" to "By the River," Hesse the moralist demonstrates the old
lesson, preached from many a Christian pulpit, that the pursuit of
sense pleasure is in the end destructive of the very wonder and delight it first occasioned in us. Siddhartha has awakened to the innocent senses, only to lose himself in the headlong pursuit of hedonism
under the combined tutelage of Kamala (*kama* = love) and the merchant Kamaswami ("Master of this World" = materialism). What began in naive joy ends in "By the River" in suicidal disgust and surfeit
of the greedy round of pleasure. Siddhartha has succumbed to "the
soul sickness of the rich" (78) and has lost "the divine voice in his
own heart" (76)—something symbolized by his dream of the dead
songbird, whose actual release by Kamala is a metaphor of his renewed "awakening."

Having experienced the extremes of self-denial and self-gratifica-
tion—this noble spirit, after all, does nothing half-heartedly—and
discovered that each is a cul-de-sac, Siddhartha is ready for the
greater synthesis adumbrated in the third part of the novel. It should
not surprise us that the Hesse who in the "Journal 1920–1921" contrasted Augustine's religious with Rousseau's secular *Confessions*
should, in his depiction of Siddhartha's turn from the corrupt pleasures of the world (Samsara) to a saintly life (symbolized by Vasudeva,
the Ferryman), follow the well-known Augustinian model of a right-
angle turn from sin to salvation. In fact I may not be straining too far
if I discern a further parallel between Siddhartha's life and Augustine's: just as the young Augustine pursued false systems and practiced erroneous arts before finding the true faith—as a follower of the
Manicheans, as a professor of rhetoric, and as a student of neo-Pla-
tonic philosophy, all of which nevertheless contributed something
essential to the saint's final identity—so Siddhartha looked into three
different teachings (as Brahmin, Samana, and Buddhist) that proved
inappropriate to his needs but that were instrumental in shaping his
final outlook. In any event, after rejecting the suicidal impulse that
Klein succumbed to, Siddhartha experiences yet another "awakening" to a higher self. Now the metaphor is literalized as he wakes up
from a deep and healing sleep to a new awareness synonymous with

the basic message of Christianity: "he loved everything, he was full of joyous love towards everything he saw. And it seemed to him that was just why he was previously ill—because he could love nothing and nobody" (94). Cured of his self-hatred and despair, Siddhartha has become again "like a small child" (95) and is ready, like the dying Klein, to enter into the kingdom of heaven—or, to invoke the Chinese equivalent that is just as relevant to the last third of *Siddhartha*, into the mystery of the Tao.

Even a cursory examination of Taoist sayings will reveal basic similarities with the religious ideas of the last part of *Siddhartha*. We know that Hesse's interest in the Chinese tradition and particularly the figure of Lao-Tzu dates back to at least a decade earlier, when he characterized the *Tao Te Ching* as a "fashionable book" in Europe for the "past fifteen years."[49] His renewed interest in Taoism may have been stimulated by his father's pamphlet (published in 1914, the year before his death) on "Lao-Tzu as a Pre-Christian Witness to the Truth." In 1919 Hesse published in the first issue of *Vivos Voco* (a journal he co-edited for a short time after the war) "Tao: A Selection of the Sayings of Lao-Tzu" from a new translation of the *Tao Te Ching*.[50] Two years later he epitomized Lao-Tzu's Tao as "the quintessence of wisdom," and in 1922 he described *Siddhartha* as a work in "Indian garb that begins with Brahman and Buddha and ends with the Tao."[51] In the light of these avowals Hsia's conclusion that Vasudeva and the river are both versions of the Tao, and that, moreover, the former is also "a portrait of Lao-Tzu" seems plausible.[52] The impact of Taoist ideas on the latter portion of *Siddhartha* is most discernible through the imprint of Lao-Tzu's model of the wise man: the belief in the complementarity of opposites based on an underlying unity, the stress on a life of extreme simplicity, the heuristic use of humor and wit, the lack of a systematic doctrine, the ideal of nonaction (Wu Wei) and silence (which, like Wordsworth's "wise passiveness," is not mere passivity), the paradox that in striving too hard for enlightenment we are blinded, and the idea that wisdom cannot be formulated.

The central meditative emblem of *Siddhartha* is the most apt and natural image of the river. Siddhartha's devotion to it (when he joins Vasudeva as his fellow ferryman) is based on his discovery of the age-old paradox, "the water continually flowed and flowed and yet it was always there; it was always the same and yet every moment it was new. Who could understand, conceive this?" (102). Hesse's invocation of this long-standing trope (from Heraclitus and Confucius[53] to Wordsworth's *Prelude* and Thomas Wolfe's *Of Time and the River*) of flux and permanence, the temporal and the timeless, shows that he is capable of varying the expressive range of his favorite metaphors: water, which in his fiction typically functions as the token of the mother world, now signifies, as Ziolkowski has shown, "the natural synthesis" of "the familiar polarity of spirit and nature."[54] It is also to Hesse's credit that once he has demonstrated Siddhartha reaching the point, under Vasudeva's silent tutelage, of being able to hear the holy OM in the many voices of the river, he resists an easy "happy end," for Siddhartha must now suffer the trials he once imposed on his father when he left home to follow the Samanas.

Here there is a real autobiographical symmetry to the book's design, for if at the beginning Hesse identified with "the Brahmin's son" striking out on his own, in "The Son" (117) he identifies with the grief of Siddhartha the father—and by extension, with that of his own father—at the revolt of a headstrong child. With his depiction of "the festering wound" of Siddhartha's anxiety about his recently discovered and now prodigal son (left to him by the dying Kamala), Hesse shows suffering as a humanizing force (a "Western" and Romantic idea) as well as an instance of the cosmic rhythm of recurrence (a mystical and "Eastern" motif). We may read the poignant and ironic passage below as Hesse's confession of his belated reconciliation with a father with whom the middle-aged author is now able to sympathize:

> One day, when the wound [of his son's flight] was smarting terribly, Siddhartha rowed across the river, consumed by longing, and got out of the boat with the purpose of going to town to seek his son . . . The river was laughing clearly and merrily at the old ferryman. Siddhartha stood still; he bent over the water in order to hear better. He saw his face reflected in the quietly moving water, and there was something in this reflection that reminded him of something he had forgotten and when he reflected on it, he remembered. His face resembled that of another person, whom he had once known and loved and even feared. It resem-

bled the face of his father, the Brahmin. He remembered how once, as a youth, he had compelled his father to let him go and join the ascetics, how he had taken leave of him, how he had gone and never returned. Had not his father also suffered the same pain that he was now suffering for his son? Had not his father died long ago, alone, without having seen his son again? Did he not expect the same fate? Was it not a comedy, a strange and stupid thing, this repetition . . . of events in a fateful circle? (131–132)

When Siddhartha first crossed this river, Vasudeva had prophesied that "everything comes back" (49). Now, as Siddhartha experiences this with a perplexed resentment of which the old ferryman is the sympathetic onlooker, Siddhartha is suddenly rewarded with an intuition of the simultaneity of all being that Hesse seeks to render in a lyric-epiphanic prose that parallels Klein's final illumination, including the metaphoric conversion of water into music as a symbol of a higher unity beyond the reach of language:

He could no longer distinguish the different voices [of the river] . . . They all belonged to each other . . . They were all interwoven and interlocked, entwined in a thousand ways. And all the voices, all the goals, all the yearnings, all the sorrows, all the pleasures, all the good and evil, all of them together the world. All of them together was the stream of events, the music of life. (135–136)

The mystical note developed in Klein's ecstatic drowning is now further amplified in Siddhartha's spirit-hearing of "the great song of a thousand voices" merging into "one word: om—perfection" (136). In this religious experience of higher self-realization, Siddhartha's individual identity merges into cosmic unity: the metaphysical ground of self and world are one and the same; to reach the one is to touch the other. The icon of such a self-surrender, or *un*becoming—the problematic goal of Hesse's final phase—is already introduced here in Vasudeva's "going into the unity of all things" with a radiant smile and "a form full of light" (137) that we shall encounter again in the dying Music Master of *The Glass Bead Game* nearly two decades later.

Obviously the final hagiographic glimpses of Vasudeva and Siddhartha are at a far remove from the fractured reality of Hesse's actual life and experience, something implicit in the shift of the concluding "Govinda" section from the point of view of the enlightened saints to that of the forever-frustrated seeker.[55] After the metaphysical uplift of "OM," the reappearance of Siddhartha's old "shadow" and friend brings the novel back down to the second level of humanization and the world of unreconciled oppositions that is Hesse's true habitat. In addition to restoring the dialectical tension between faith and despair, salvation and seeking, the episode of the final encounter between Siddhartha and Govinda recaps the basic themes of the book: seeking precludes finding, loving the world is more important than understanding it, words fail to grasp the nature of reality. Yet Hesse is able to lighten these didactic concerns with the presence of humor, as the hapless Govinda, who earlier failed to recognize Siddhartha in the man of the world (when he guarded his sleep by the river) now fails again to recognize his friend in the saint. Govinda's need for a dogmatic faith typifies the hopeless quest of this mental traveler, for as Siddhartha teases him, "you do not see many things that are under your nose" (140).

Yet despite its ironic and light touches, the sermon of the concluding chapter cannot rise above the contradictions inherent in its logic, something that makes Hesse's most popular wisdom book a problematic achievement: it aspires to communicate wisdom even as it maintains that "wisdom is not communicable" (142); it seeks truth knowing full well that "a truth can be expressed and enveloped in words if it is one-sided" (143); it maintains that "time is not real" when the form of the novel, both as narrative and as print, is a mode of temporality. Moreover, the sentence about the unreality of time, already entertained by Klein, is reversible by the very law of the identity of opposites proclaimed in *Siddhartha* and elsewhere in Hesse ("in every truth the opposite is true," 143): *time, indeed, is most real*, a contrary sentence already vividly dramatized as the fear of death that fuels *Klingsor's Last Summer*, in many ways the stylistic and thematic counter-fiction to *Siddhartha*.

True, the concluding transformational sequence of the river, the parable of the stone, and Siddhartha's farewell kiss to Govinda is an impressive stylistic experiment in suggesting the greater unity of being. Asserting that time is not real, however, is ultimately only a verbal solution to the existential dilemma of our being irremediably in time, something Siddhartha had earlier recognized "by the river": "He had died and a new Siddhartha had awakened from his sleep. He also would grow old and die. Siddhartha was transitory, all forms were transitory" (100). To extrapolate from the perception of eternal transitoriness and flux (what Goethe in the title of a famous poem calls "Permanence in Change") that temporality is an illusion is not a logical move but requires a metaphysical leap of faith. Hesse was willing to take the plunge with a poetic prose that invokes cosmic plenitude and omnipresence through the rapid accumulation of myriad "flowing forms . . . of simultaneousness" in Siddhartha's "mask-like" smile of enlightenment (151). Seen in this light, the paean of presence of *Siddhartha*'s closing pages is Hesse's attempted escape, with an Eastern and metaphysical fiction, from the *ecce homo* of the *Klingsor* confession and the existential dilemma of our being in time and history that we Westerners have been painfully afflicted with since at least the eighteenth century and the rise of Romanticism.

CHAPTER VIII

LIVE(D) FANTASIES

I am living, insofar as I am living at all, in actual, vital romanticism and magic, and am frequently swimming again in the colorful depths of extraordinary, fantastic worlds of dreams and ideas. For me it is the only way to put up with life under the present circumstances . . . To what extent I will some day be able to communicate and turn into poetry my current glimpses of chaos and my inner experiences I do not know; it seems almost impossible.—Hesse letter of January 1926

The 1920s—that classic period of modernist art—is also the most troubled and productive decade of Hesse's life, during which personal and cultural crises again coincided as they had done during the *Demian* period, but with a far different result as Hesse probed the fault lines of his psyche and his age with a disconcerting frankness and a caustic humor that are a far cry from *Demian*'s muffled symbolism and rhetoric. What followed in the years after the completion (during spring 1922) of *Siddhartha* was a veritable confessional explosion, including two autobiographical sketches, *A Guest at the Spa* (written 1923, published 1924) and *Journey to Nuremberg* (written 1925, published 1926), that frame Hesse's personal problems and his despair with modern life in comic-grotesque terms; and two major novels—*Steppenwolf* (written 1926, published 1927) plus the related *Crisis* verse diary, and *Narcissus and Goldmund* (written 1927–1928, published 1930)—which explore Hesse's divided self in very different settings. During this *decas mirabilis* his creative fires burned with a sustained brilliance that peaked during the middle years (1924–1927) in a mid-life crisis with an intemperate interlude of dangerous living that turned on the aging writer's erotic self-renewal and the belated gratification of too-long-pent-up instincts in the face of inevitable physical decline and the specter of old age. "It is not good to learn of the intimacies of great men," Hesse noted in 1926 with reference to a biography of Tolstoy,[1] yet the author of *Steppenwolf* had the courage or nerve to live out the most private and shocking intimacies of his life in the bizarre transformations of this most autobiographical of fictions. In the magic confessional mirror of the mid-1920s Hesse finally arrived at the questionable result professed but never achieved by the prototype and progenitor of the modern confessional tradition, Rousseau: a full, frank, and unflattering self-revelation.

Hesse's life and art, early and late, are rife with multiple self-divisions, but his writings of the 1920s are marked more than ever by the acute clash, to use Yeats's term, of fundamental antinomies—intellect and instinct, art and life, youth and age, male and female, despair and hope, time and timelessness, outsider and bourgeois—that he struggled to shape into coherent contrapuntal patterns. The desideratum of self-harmony is expressed at the end of *A Guest at the Spa* with the extended and highly appropriate simile of musical counterpoint:

> If I were a composer, I could without difficulty write a melody for two voices, a melody that would consist of two lines, of two rows of tunes and notes that correspond with one another, complement one another, fight with one another, limit one another, but in any case at every instant, at every point in the sequence, have a most profound interrelationship and reciprocal effect. And anyone who can read music could read off my double melody and always see and hear with every tone its counter-tone, its brother, its enemy, its opposite. Now it is just this . . . double line, that I would like to express in my own medium, in words, and I work myself to the bone trying and do not succeed . . . I would like to find expression for duality . . . to write chapters and sentences where melody and counter-melody are always simultaneously present, where unity stands beside every multiplicity, seriousness beside every joke. For me, life consists simply in this, the fluctuation between two poles.

Hesse's struggle "to force the two poles of life together"[2] became more psychologically strained and formally resourceful precisely in proportion to the energy with which his conflicted self pulled him in opposite directions. The confessional counterpointing of his writings of the 1920s does not gloss over or harmonize away the substantial contradictions and ambivalences of his life, but aims rather to represent them with graphic clarity and honesty. If Hesse's tacit hope is to achieve psychic mediation through literary confession, that hope is checked by the insight that whatever self-integration can be attained through self-writing must be the result of an open confrontation with the root and branches of one's problems, and that a writer's identity crisis can only be resolved by being lived *and* represented in its extremity. Thus the Hesse of the mid-1920s radical "art as confession" stance was not willing to leap beyond the clash of polarities into the *sancta simplicitas* of *Siddhartha's* culminating apotheosis.

Hesse's *Piktor* Fable

The double melody of Hesse's life and art during this decade included the impact of two strongly contrasting women, the singing student Ruth Wenger and the archeologist Ninon Dolbin (née Ausländer), his second and third wives respectively. Whereas the latter helped to calm the troubled waters of Hesse's psyche in the last third of the decade, the former contributed significantly to the emotional turmoil of the Steppenwolf "incarnation." The mature, self-sacrificing, and diplomatic Ninon managed to bring a measure of serenity and security after she joined him in Montagnola in 1927 (they were married in November 1931); the ill-sorted relationship with the immature, moody, and demanding Ruth appears to have brought Hesse the intoxication of a mid-life sexual renewal through a woman half his age, followed by the trauma of mutual misunderstanding and misplaced expectations that spelled the (almost immediate) failure of his second marriage.

Hesse had met the Wengers during his first Ticino summer (1919); they lived in nearby Carona, and he felt drawn, for different reasons, to both the mother and her twenty-two-year-old daughter. Lisa Wenger, herself a writer, seems to have encouraged this May–September *liaison* between Hesse and Ruth from the start, flattered by the friendship and the attentions to her daughter of the famous writer, with whom she cultivated a maternal and advisory tone. The poetically heightened account in *Klingsor's Last Summer* of a visit to "the Queen of the Mountains" vividly captures Ruth's appeal for Hesse: "Suddenly the Queen of the Mountains stood there; a slender lissome flower, body straight and pliant, all in red, burning flames, image of youth."[3] Klingsor's desire to paint her has a phallic immediacy: "He knew at once that he would paint her, not realistically, but the ray within her that had struck him . . . youth, Redness, Blondness, Amazon." Keenly aware of the age differential between them, Klingsor wryly rejects the possibility of a more immediate involvement: "If only I were ten years younger . . . this girl could have me, capture me, wind me around her finger." Afraid of the demands that this young "Amazon" might make on him, Hesse-Klingsor translates her appeal into fuel for art: "For you the love that Klingsor has to give away between a day full of work and a night full of red wine is not enough. All the better, then, my eye will drink you down . . . and know you when you have long since faded within me."

Hesse didn't follow Klingsor's advice, though his ambivalence remained—passionate attraction versus the fear of not being up to the demands of such a pairing, not to mention his strong need for solitude and independence. He and Ruth became more intimately acquainted a year later, but at what point their relationship became a sexual one is not indicated by the biographers. It certainly appears to have been that by 1922, when he lovingly produced several handwritten and colorfully illustrated copies of the erotic fable, *Piktor's Metamorphoses*, which in the beautiful version of Easter 1923 (chosen for the Insel facsimile edition) is explicitly dedicated to Ruth on a title page adorned with two striking eggs and followed by a full-page drawing of archetypal images of complementarity, including traditional male and female genital symbols (a line between two points, an inverted V with a point at the base).[4] According to Volker Michels, the first stage of Hesse's involvement with Ruth Wenger came in 1920 when Hesse was unable to proceed with the second part of *Siddhartha*, and *Piktor's Metamorphoses* is Hesse's balancing of accounts and token of gratitude for their first year together.[5]

This highly symbolic and personal confessional fantasy (which Hesse for understandable reasons chose not to publish) playfully inscribes the psychic script of his life since his settling in Montagnola in the context of a central juxtaposition of fixity-isolation-barrenness versus metamorphosis-relationship-creativity. No sooner has Piktor entered "paradise" than he encounters portents of duality—a tree "which was at one and the same time man and woman" and another, "the tree of life . . . that was both sun and moon" (29). A bird answers his childish question about "where happiness dwells" by first naming and then demonstrating the richness of life by successively transforming itself before Piktor's eyes into a flower, a butterfly, and a crystal. Worried about missing his chance at happiness, Piktor succumbs to the sinister advice of a snake curling "on the branch of a dead tree" to make his choice before "it is too late" (31). His fall into a paralyzing stasis is his choice to become a tree, "because trees seemed to him to be so full of peace, power, and dignity" (31). At first he is pleased with his new form, though he realizes that in this Eden "most creatures transformed themselves very frequently, that, indeed, everything swam in a magic stream of perpetual metamorphosis" (32)—a statement reminiscent of the protracted transformational sequence (the kiss and the parable of the stone) of the last part of *Siddhartha*. When Piktor-the-Tree realizes that he is no longer immersed in the stream of becoming, he begins to despair and age. As Mileck has pointed out, this *Märchen* is symbolic of Hesse's choice of a new life in the Ticino[6]: what was at first bracing and invigorating, his tree-like independence and solitude, became in the end too limiting and oppressive. In Hesse's life as in this autobiographical parable, what puts him back in touch with the magic stream of becoming is "a young girl" who fills him—like many a stultified, middle-aged male suddenly confronted by a nubile vision of youth—with "a great longing, a desire for happiness such as he had never yet experienced" (32–33). The perceptive maiden responds with vibrant sympathy to the solitary tree's silent longing: from a realistic viewpoint, her response, limited largely to pity, already spells trouble for a long-term relationship. Unlike Hesse's drawn-out affair with Ruth, this *Märchen* has a happy end, because the sympathetic girl is able (with the help of a magic carbuncle, of course) to transform herself into a tree in response to Piktor's "burning desire for union": "[she] grew as a strong branch from his trunk, grew rapidly up to him" (34). United with the female—who, it should be noted, has come to embrace him on *his* terms—and merged again with the stream of life, Piktor feels alive and whole again, open to endless possibilities of change: "He became deer and fish, became human and snake, cloud and bird. But in each shape he was complete, was a pair, had sun and moon, had man and woman within himself, streamed as a double stream through the world, stood as a twin star in the heavens" (35).

Thus in this playfully metaphoric vision of psychic self-integration the female is instrumental in reconnecting the barren and isolated male with all the richness and multiplicity of the phenomenal world. Hesse here takes the Romantic madonna off her pedestal and refashions her into an erotic symbol of self-renewal. The Piktor who loudly chants at the close of this wish-fulfillment fantasia, "Piktoria, Viktoria" (35) to his female savior and (in the Blakean sense) emanation, dwells in a magic realm where the "two poles" and the "dual voices of life's melody" envisioned at the conclusion of *A Guest at the Spa* have been achieved in a sexual embrace that joyfully reflects Hesse's early relationship with Ruth. Not surprisingly, this wonderful dream of a wedding of opposites that Hesse celebrated in *Piktor's Metamorphoses* was to turn into a nightmare when this troubled middle-aged author half-heartedly tried to turn autobiographical fantasy into biographical reality several years later by marrying a difficult and equally troubled young woman half his age.

Living/Writing on the Horizon of the Steppenwolf

The conflict between Hesse's poetic self-image as an aging and alienated outsider versus his need for contact with others is fundamental to his life and writings for the better part of the 1920s. While the "Steppenwolf" legend was incubated in his imagination for several years before the composition of the novel in mid-decade, the crisis that precipitated the metamorphosis of Hermann Hesse into Harry Haller was the virtual collapse of his second marriage less than three months after he had entered into it—with much trepidation and "sheer terror,"[7] like a condemned man going to the scaffold. The nuptials took place in Basel in early January 1924; by the end of March, after a series of (partly psychosomatic?) illnesses, Hesse retreated south to his mountain hermitage to lick his wounds. An attempt the following winter to make a go of the relationship with Ruth led to new lows of despair and the promise of suicide that later found its way into *Steppenwolf*:

> For fourteen days I've been back again in the Ticino, after my attempt at life in Basel turned out a fiasco . . . For a while I was pretty desperate and didn't want to live any more. But then I found a way out. I decided that in two years, on my fiftieth birthday, I would have the right to hang myself, in case I still wished to do so—and now everything that I found so difficult to bear has taken on a new aspect, since in the worst case it can only last for two more years.[8]

The fiasco of his second marriage was the most acute setback, but there were other disappointments and disasters as well, which accumulated to the point of the grotesque and which contributed to Hesse's mood of fate turning on him with a vengeance: his exhausting editorial work of over seven months on an anthology of German Romantic writers was nullified when the publishers suddenly backed out of the contract; in May 1925, Ruth, who had been ill during the winter when Hesse was still in Basel, was diagnosed as suffering from tuberculosis and had to be hospitalized; worse yet, a month later a further burden descended suddenly on the shaken Hesse when his first wife suffered another breakdown as a consequence of her older brother committing suicide and her younger brother going mad, leaving Hesse with the task of handling Mia's finances and finding new homes for two of his three sons. Clearly the desperate complaints of his letters are substantially grounded in these biographical *données*: "For seven years now I have been living beyond the human world, without family, without any real community, and confronting nearly every day the problem of suicide."[9]

Not only is his conviction of being the perpetual outsider aggravated in a protracted mid-life crisis, but also his sense of his literary vocation is shaken to its foundation and takes on a bitterly questionable aspect. As we saw in the last chapter, the joys of landscape painting after his move to the Ticino had served as a happy escape from the unwelcome demands of being a well-known man of letters. Now, perhaps in part under the impact of an *avant garde* that had been active in the previous decade in various European cities, including Zürich, where his friend Hugo Ball had been a founding father of the Dadaists, Hesse bridled against the bourgeois system of expectations and rewards that defines the role of the successful writer in our commercial culture. Hesse's various self-divisions now include that of the poet and the producer of remunerative print parting ways—though, ironically, *Steppenwolf* would prove to do moderately well in the literary marketplace. More acutely than ever, Hesse faced the dilemma of being no longer sure of his vocation, his audience, and his subject matter, or even the worth of literature (his own, of course, included) in an increasingly commercialized age of irresponsible and ephemeral print.

In *Journey to Nuremberg*, the farcical record of a reluctant reading tour of November 1926 whose literary stations of the cross included Ulm, Augsburg, Nuremberg, and Munich, he tries to focus with satiric wit the dissonance—the comedy of mutual misprision and misplaced expectations—between the modern writer and the general public. Confronted with the performance pressure of the reading circuit, he toys again with the idea of "escaping from literature" entirely and making his "living at the more appealing trade of painter."[10] With mawkish levity Hesse seeks to exorcise the discomfort inherent in his role as *Literat* (man of letters) and bourgeois shaman, one that he maintains even as he attacks it. To be thus an author, a name product on the publicity exchange, is to be in a false position, craving anonymity in the place of a fetishized celebrity:

> not to be known, not to be a sacrifice to the idiotic cult of personality, not to have to live in that filthy, lying, suffocating air of public life! Oh, I had often attempted to withdraw from this fraud and had been forced to recognize each time that the world is inexorable, that what it wants from the poet is not poems and thoughts but his address and personality, to honor him, then kick him out, to adorn and then undress him, to enjoy and then spit at him the way a naughty girl behaves with her doll. (185)

The same Hesse who confesses that as a youth he had lusted after and found early fame[11] now regrets "that incomprehensible youthful delusion" he gave in to by "turning a talent into a profession" (185).

Hesse's frustration with his dubious position as a professional writer, however, also serves as a stimulus to his writing and becomes part of the confessional texture of the *Steppenwolf* years. In fact, his literary self-questioning is heuristic insofar as it helps to propel him to the radical confessional aesthetics of the mid-1920s. Since he can-

not discern in contemporary German literature anything more than
an ephemeral and transitional period, and since the original writer
cannot now retreat into mere imitation of the "fossilized model" of
the greater past (whose "last great period" is that of the Romantics),
Hesse champions instead the "worth of a transitional literature . . .
become problematic and uncertain, in its conscientious expression of
its own shortcomings and the shortcomings of its time with the greatest possible candor" (204). Hesse's particular solution to the modernists' dilemma of a fragmented and meaningless world, the accent on
autobiography, is crucial, for art as confession will be his narrow
bridge from the old to the new: "I know that the value of what we
people of today write cannot lie in the possibility of a form emerging
valid for our time and for a long while to come, a style, a classicism,
but rather that we in our distress have no refuge except that of the
greatest possible candor" (204–205). The distressed author of *Journey
to Nuremberg*, which harks back to the Romantic-ironic modes of
Hesse's favorite German writers in order to confront the challenge of
modernity, unfurls the self-consciously *non*literary banner of "candor" and authenticity (*Aufrichtigkeit*) but is as yet unable to envision
an answerable style or idiom, though Nietzsche and psychoanalysis
seem to provide precarious indicators:

> For even if we prepared for the greatest candor to the point of
> self-surrender—where could we find the means of expressing it?
> Our literary language will not provide it nor will the language of
> the schools, our handwriting has long since become fixed. Iso-
> lated, desperate books like Nietzsche's *Ecce Homo* seem to reveal
> a path, but in the end they reveal far more clearly that there is
> no path. Psychoanalysis appeared to offer us aid and it has
> brought advances, but as yet no author, either psychoanalyst or
> writer trained in analysis, has freed this kind of psychology from
> its armor of too narrow, too dogmatic, much too vain academi-
> cism. (205)[12]

With these sentiments *Journey to Nuremberg* is the obvious prolegomenon to *Steppenwolf*, whose symbolism and style are a Hessean hybrid of Nietzsche and psychoanalysis.

The emergence of the "candid" confessional style of *Steppenwolf*
was protracted, painful, and replete with manic swings from wild

bravado to extreme despair. Hesse's reply to Stefan Zweig about the recently published *Crisis* poems sums up his larger "problem" as

> not merely that of the man who is beginning to age and who must taste the difficult years around fifty, but even more the problem of the author whose profession has become questionable and nearly impossible, because he has lost its foundation and meaning . . . For the time being, I don't know any other way out of this and the incredible and increasing difficulty of producing (every word is torture) other than the attempt to articulate precisely this need, that is, to write confessions, a part of which are those poems. [13]

In the two books that came after *Steppenwolf*, Hesse was able to reticulate autobiography back into a confessional fantasy less acute and more disguised because distanced in time and space (the Middle Ages, the "East"), but before such a renewed self-masking was possible, he had to implement to the full his program of art as confession. As he put it sarcastically in a letter of October 14, 1926, "I abandoned the aesthetic ambition years ago and don't write poetry (*Dichtung*), but only confession, just as someone who is drowning or has been poisoned is not concerned with the cut of his hair or the modulation of his voice, but simply screams out." [14]

Autobiography as auto-therapy, as a way of spelling out and resolving an identity crisis, is very much part of Hesse's radical confessional poetics of the mid-1920s. His writings now not only mirror his life, because writing itself becomes a survival issue, an intense manner of living and of experiencing himself that can momentarily anneal the distinction between *vita* and text. The therapeutic aspect of Hesse's modernist confessional program also indicates the continuing impact of psychoanalysis, including the taxing sessions with Jung in the winter of 1921, and later, of the daily meetings with Dr. Lang (now more Hesse's friend than analyst) during the time Hesse was most caught up in *Steppenwolf's* phantasmagoric swirl. [15] Insofar as it is even possible to maintain a conceptual distinction between life and writing during these years, there is an odd reversal of the usual relationship between the two, for in one respect art now seems to seize the initiative from life, as Hesse seeks out certain kinds of experiences—those revolving around the night life, demimonde sequences of *Crisis* and the novel—in order to be able to exploit these as the materials of his art, and in writing about them, *live* them yet more fully in his imagination. If this is a dizzying confessional circle, it is not of the reader's making, for it is the author who now turns back upon himself in increasingly indistinguishable and accelerating loops of living/writing/living/writing.

The visionary and self-refracting hermeneutic of *Steppenwolf*'s Magic Theater is only the culmination of Hesse's contrapuntal self-multiplication through mirror images and double perspectives in his writings of the 1920s. At the start of the *Steppenwolf* period such metaphoric double images are played off against each other with ironic wit, as in the "Piktor-Viktoria" of his *Märchen* for Ruth. In what is probably the earliest version of the Steppenwolf persona in the 1922 fragment, "From the Journal of One Who Has Been Derailed," the unnamed diarist is a prototype of Harry Haller: one side of him lives for the moment—"I, an aging man, squander my days and hours like a student"—the other side—"the second one in" him, a "busy historiographer"—seeks to transcribe the experiences of the fleeting moment: "he requires and thirsts for the future, he calls passionately for continuity and connection, and seeks hour after hour to nail down the evanescent whirl of life, to note, frame, and hang it on the wall of eternity." This rowdy fragment offers no resolution of the tension between living and writing, yet in the very act of recording it, a part of Hesse, a tertiary self, as it were, is able to rise above the current psychomachia—"there I stood for several minutes outside myself and observed me"—and to achieve a larger view that looks forward to and even beyond the *Steppenwolf* mask: "For some moments I observed my 'I', my current incarnation, a used-up instrument, which will not serve me much longer, and I called to myself, 'put an end to yourself, mannikin, you belong to the old iron!' "[16]

This self-subverting conclusion is a bridge to the extended autobiographical essay of two years later, *A Guest at the Spa*, where Hesse invokes the metaphor of musical counterpoint, as we have seen, to reconcile the various self-divisions presented through a humor ranging from the quaint to the grotesque. From the outset the author who stresses "the great antinomies" and "the secret of . . . bipolarity" (AW, 72), uses his self-flagellating wit to satirize his pathetic double, Hesse the bourgeois spa guest. The spectacle of the Romantic-Nietzschean outsider, "the old solitary" to whom "the life of the herd and the hotel is profoundly obnoxious" (78), seeking refuge and letting himself be pampered in the lap of a luxury hotel is sufficiently absurd to do away with the last vestiges of self-respect. Who is this Hesse, anyway, who is willing to yield himself up to the clinical categories of the psychiatrists, and his psychosomatic ills—so he labels them—mild sciatica and the gout, to the clutches of spa doctors specializing in the fashionable afflictions of the well-to-do? A not very admirable man, obviously, who is both exorcising his self-hatred and achieving a new if unflattering vision of himself in what Freedman has rightly called "his funniest and in some ways the most penetrating of his various fictional and semi-fictional autobiographies."[17]

Before Hesse can move toward a renewed self-integration, the inner split into lone wolf and bourgeois herd animal has to be pushed to its limit in the self-exposé of his caustic wit. The wolf image has to be strengthened as the totem of his unacculturated and asocial self, which turns against middle-class values as well as the world of *Geist* or "spirit" that "is immortal and boring": "At this moment I reject it; by no means do I see the spirit as eternal life but as eternal death, as what is congealed, fruitless, shapeless, and can only regain shape by surrendering its immortality" (92). The *Guest*'s wolf symbol points to the matriarchy of the unconscious, and to the repressed instincts also suggested by the "two young martens in a wire cage" (on display in the hotel lobby) whose "clear animal eyes" are portents of "God" and of "the primeval world, still instinct and nature" (111–112). The spa guest's Lawrencian perception of these "two beautiful, noble creatures" as "potent" images of authenticity is polarized against his "dull disgust with [modern] life," whose objective correlative is the sham resort world of "picture postcards . . . concerts . . . the gambling hall" (112).

Just as Hesse reinforces the guest's sense of what is abiding and real, so he intensifies his comic vision of middle-class complacency through the satiric portrait of the "Dutchman," the noisy businessman in the adjoining room whose laughter, "lusty good health . . . prosperous appearance," (116) and "biological and social superiority" (120) grate more and more on his frail nerves. Hesse's demonizing of everything he detests about the European middle classes—and, need it be said? his own middle-class self—has a Flaubertian gusto if not subtlety, for the flatulent denizen of Room 64, with his revolting optimism, cheerfulness, "health and normality," his "dignified deportment and fat wallet" (117), is a lineal descendant of that arch-Philistine of the previous century, Monsieur Homais. Perhaps because he feels guilty about the ferocity of his attack, Hesse suddenly lapses into sentimentality by converting the guest's homicidal fantasy ("to seize the Dutchman, choke him or shoot him dead and survive as victor over his brutal, undiscerning vitality," 123) into nothing less than Christian love—an unconvincing mood swing that suddenly returns us to the gospel of *Siddhartha*, including the consoling sense of unity ("I believe in nothing in the world so deeply . . . as unity, the conviction that everything in the whole world forms a divine whole," 121). This religious affirmation, however, does not correspond to the reality of the divided self and the multiple resentments and frustrations that are the substance of *A Guest at the Spa*: before Hesse can forgive if not forget the Dutchman and affirm the principle of love through his recognition of "*tat tvam asi* (that art thou)" as the Hindu version of the Christian love ethic, "love your neighbor, for he is yourself!" (162), his ill will has to be vented, and the strengthened "wolf" self has to bare its fangs at the detestable double of the irrepressible Dutchman.

Like the fragment of 1922, *A Guest at the Spa* also deploys an observing persona detached from the ordinary self. But unlike that of the earlier fragment, the guest's "hovering" self is symbolically developed, through the wolf motif, as the image of a *recovered* self "keeping watch on Hesse" and "his fellow guests eating in boredom." This "recently . . . lost" and now recuperated identity is that of "the old somewhat antisocial hermit and lone wolf Hesse, the old wanderer and poet" (148). Through the spectacles of Romantic irony, Hesse manages to catch a glimpse of his divided self and its cultural milieu in "an instant by no means horrible and tragic but simply enormously funny":

> The spa guest Hesse was just lifting his glass, simply out of boredom . . . when the union of the two I's took place, the eating and the observing I, and all at once I had to put the glass down, for I was shaken from inside by the sudden explosion of an immense desire to laugh, a quite childlike merriment, a sudden in-

sight into the infinite absurdity of this whole situation. For an instant I saw mirrored in this image of the hall full of sick, cheerless, spoiled, and lethargic people . . . our whole civilized life, a life without strong impulse, running compulsively along fixed tracks, joyless, without connection with God or with the clouds in the sky. (149)

To be sure, humor, "the old mediator between the ideal and the real" and "a crystal that grows only in enduring pain," as Hesse was to write two years later in *Journey to Nuremberg* (AW, 206, 178), is only one kind of mediation of the divided self. Humor, the perspective of "the eternal Self in us" as it "examines the mortal 'I' and its leaps and grimaces" (206), enables us to recognize and to bear the fragmentation and incoherence of our experience without being destroyed by this recognition. As Hesse realized in *Steppenwolf*, laughter is only a provisional solution, a sort of compromise with reality and the status quo without losing sight of the ideal. Though the Immortals are the first to chortle at the human comedy, for Hesse the higher path to "the oneness . . . behind all multiplicity" (164) lies in the mystery of music, a spirit-journey that his novel of life's middle passage, *Steppenwolf*, will attempt, but which in *Guest*, that prelude and piquant foretaste, is only intimated through the metaphor of musical counterpoint, "the dual voices of life's melody" (169).

The Making of *Steppenwolf*

During the 1920s Hesse was not only the poet-recluse of Montagnola—the image he liked to project—but also very much a connoisseur of the mixed blessings of city life. For the winters of 1923–1924 and 1924–1925 he lived in Basel; thereafter, until 1932, he wintered in Zürich, an experience reflected in what Freedman has analyzed as the "symbolic city" of *Steppenwolf*, "the only work by Hesse in which the entire action takes place in a contemporary metropolis."[18] The steppe which that lone wolf, Harry Haller, haunts is a cityscape; its hotels, bars, cafés, lecture and concert halls, and rain-slicked streets were frequented by Hesse himself. The book was written on location; the experiences on which it is based were not recollected in tranquillity but almost immediately reworked in his imagination and transferred onto paper.

The extraordinary degree to which Harry Haller corresponds to Hermann Hesse has been repeatedly stressed, most recently by Mileck in his summary of the numerous parallels between author and protagonist, from their respective backgrounds, childhoods, ages, and physiognomies to their psychological make-ups, social relations, proclivities, and prejudices. "Haller," asserts Mileck, "was clearly heir to Hesse in all but name," and *Steppenwolf* is "not only the most novel but also the most autobiographical of Hesse's many stories."[19] Yet his most autobiographical fiction is also his most fantastic, a harrowing exploration of his teeming inner world without succumbing to the demons within. From it Hesse emerges with his book triumphantly in hand, one whose ironic perspectives and experimental style make this by far his most spectacular fiction of the self. Formal inventiveness and originality of style have sometimes been denied to Hesse by those willing to dismiss him as a sentimental neo-Romantic, yet Thomas Mann legitimated this novel's modernist credentials with his assertion in 1948, "and need it be stated that, as an experimental novel, *Steppenwolf* is no less daring than *Ulysses* or *The Counterfeiters*?"[20] When Hesse was on the verge of finishing the book he spoke of it with untypical elation as "very daring and fantastic" and later repeatedly stressed its musical structure: "What no one has noted hitherto, including no critic, is the form of this composition, a new form, which is by no means (as many believe) fragmentary, but proportionally built like a sonata or a fugue." Five years after its writing Hesse still invoked the musical parallel to point out that in *Steppenwolf* he had attained the highest degree of form possible for him, and added the revealing gloss that the book's "serenity . . . has its sources . . . in a degree of despair" unknown to his correspondent.[21]

The idea of musical composition, so important to Hesse during the twenties, was instrumental in helping him to shape some very elusive inner experiences and states of mind into a tangible if still mystifying narrative. Here Ziolkowski's probing analysis of the novel as "a sonata in prose" is very helpful in clarifying its underlying structure,[22] and if there is a problem with Ziolkowski's exposition, it is that the parallel between musical and literary form has to break down at some point, because, to put the matter baldly, a sonata in prose is ultimately not a sonata. Thus in addition to the musical analogy, we might consider one also provided by Hesse when he compliments his friend Hugo Ball for having captured the inner meaning of his life in the biography commissioned by Hesse's publisher for the occasion of his fiftieth birthday. Reading Ball's book presented the author of *Steppenwolf* with yet another mirror image of himself, but one, as evident from the striking dream he shares with Ball, that reveals a second self more real than the mere biographical subject: "Last night I dreamed in connection with your book: I saw myself sitting, not in the mirror, but really myself as a second living figure, more living than myself, but an inner restraint kept me from looking at myself directly, that would have been sinful; I only squinted for a moment through the crack of my eyelids and saw the living Hesse sitting there." If this frank communication suggests an instinctive taboo against autobiography as self-love, its compliment to Ball, which every aspiring biographer should take to heart, privileges the *legend* of his life over the mere biographical record: "I see only now how well you have written, not the banal history, but the legend of this life, how you have found the magic formulas. Even there, where you are actually in error, i.e., where you assume false dates, you are still right and hit the nail on the head."[23] The biographer Ball had the rare discernment to grasp the legend of his subject's life, to find the magic equations to express its inner meaning: is this not an account as well of the confessional imagination at work in Hesse's novel, the poetry of whose "magic formulas" and distorting mirrors is a more meaningful adumbration of the truth of Hesse's life and experience during the mid-1920s than a strictly factual and biographically accurate and verifiable self-account could ever be?

Steppenwolf was written in a sustained burst of hard work at the end of 1926—"for the last six weeks I have worked like mad day and night, and have finished my new book," wrote Hesse in January 1927[24]—but the larger creative process of which the novel and the associated *Crisis* poems are the product had preoccupied him for at least two years. According to Freedman, "the idea of the novel took concrete shape" almost a year earlier in February 1926, "even as the events that make up the novel's plot actually occurred."[25] Hesse's desperate plunge at this time into an urban night life of bars, jazz, dancing, and worldly women was his attempt to deal with his mounting depression and sense of alienation after the failure of his second marriage. He was quite aware of the absurdity of this venture to overcome his inhibitions by immersing himself in the destructive element of the metropolitan demimonde, but his willingness to hazard such a change is also the clue to his ability to grow as a writer—as May Sarton has recently reminded us, in order to be able to write, the poet "must remain open and vulnerable."[26]

Hesse's sense of the gulf between himself and the modern world had in any event grown so acute that only an extreme solution seemed to offer any hope. Though he insisted in his letters, sometimes with morbid humor, that he was "a hopeless outsider," he maintained at the same time that the "neurosis" of a "spiritual person" is a symptom of the ills of the age.[27] Those whom the gods wish to damn, grant them their wishes, says the adage, and Hesse now found that his lifelong aspiration to independence and solitude had become his doom. His sense of isolation reaches a grotesque extreme—in what must surely be one of the strangest experiences recorded by *any* writer—when he attends a "Hermann Hesse Evening organized by an art association" without being recognized by anyone there. He had come across an announcement of the event in a newspaper, and proceeded to attend, only to find himself turned off by the spectacle of his earlier poems recited by "prettily dressed ladies." For Hesse this is really a traumatic encounter with an earlier self that entails a harsh self-judgment:

> I paid a mark and was given a program, and after . . . some time, the festivities began. There I heard a series of compositions which I had written in my younger years. At the time I wrote these I still had the inclinations and ideals of youth, and was concerned more with enthusiasm and idealism than with honesty.

In this absurd episode, he felt utterly cut off from his public image, his very author-ity annulled: "Even at this literary evening entertainment, where in a sense I should have been able to function as an expert and specialist, I noticed again that isolation which destined me to be a recluse."[28]

How can a literary eremite become a man of the world, a potential suicide a bon vivant, a greying, middle-aged neurotic writer an urban

Don Juan? Despite the raised eyebrows of respectable friends, colleagues, and admirers, Hesse had the courage of his mid-life foolish-
ness. His belated course of dissipation seemed to work, after a fashion, as the ecstatic epigraph of this chapter attests. He was
swimming, so at least he felt in exultant moments, in "actual, living
romanticism and magic" next to which the languid neo-Romantic
poses of his early writings were but a pale nineteenth-century
shadow. He was acting out the Nietzschean injunction to live dan-
gerously, though on a realistic level the way to the playground of the
liberated libido involved something as mundane and bourgeois as
taking a series of dance lessons and buying a phonograph in order to
practice in his room those sexy American jazz steps of the Roaring
Twenties—the Boston, the one-step, the foxtrot, the shimmy. The
salutary effects of his climacteric high jinks during the winter and
spring of 1926 are evident in a letter written that February: "It didn't
come about without much alcohol . . . but recently I do have the feeling that I will be able to go on somehow and that life will be possible
for me again."[29]

The culminating point of this frenzied interlude in Hesse's life as
well as in *Steppenwolf* is the adventure of attending a great masked
ball. Held at the Hotel Baur au Lac by the Zürich Artists' Association,
this entertainment to which he went with a group of friends opened
a new world to him, as he acknowledged the next day in a thank-
you note with a delightful pun: "I've been a proper *Foxtrottel* [*Trot-
tel* = slang for "fool"] that I plagued myself for thirty years with the
problems of humanity without knowing what a masked ball is."[30] According to the memoir of the sculptor Hermann Hubacher, Hesse arrived with a "sweet-sour" and skeptical expression, "until a charming *pierrette* . . . sat down on his knee . . . and lo and behold, our
friend was 'parti pour la gloire'." Hubacher's witty account shows
how closely Hesse's experience at the ball corresponds to Haller's before the latter's psychedelic adventures in the Magic Theater:

> The great dance hall was darkened, and in its middle, above us,
> hovered and revolved a globe covered with hundreds of small
> mirrors that cast its light like small shards of lightning over the
> dancing pairs. The orchestra played the latest hits; everybody
> hummed along . . . it was a crazy whirl. Paper snakes shot

through the air and sent their colorful signals from table to table, from pair to pair. But where is Hesse? Has he run away? Morning was already approaching when we all sank down in fatigue into the chairs at our table, and Bacchus alone spoke. Look, there comes Hesse in the most carefree of moods, fresher than all of us he leaps up on the table and dances a one-step for us so that the glasses tinkle. Then he writes . . . a verse on the no longer stiff front of my shirt, and Schoeck [a composer who had set some of Hesse's poems to music] puts the notes next to it. Never have I borne home the front of my shirt more proudly.[31]

Hesse's cavorting in early 1926—drinking, partying, and quick infatuations with various women—was both a resource and a stimulus for his writing. Indeed, he was at work on the earliest version of *Steppenwolf*, the *Crisis* poems that emerged more or less pell-mell under the immediate pressure of his experience. Some of these were published in a journal that November under the title, *The Steppenwolf: Excerpts from a Diary in Verse*, and the complete set was issued as a separate volume in a limited edition in 1928.[32] It was only after writing these poems that Hesse decided to do a "prose Steppenwolf," into which he still wanted to incorporate the poems, contrary to the plans of his publisher, who was only able to keep them out of *Steppenwolf* by guaranteeing their separate publication. In light of Hesse's original plan there are good grounds for including the poems with the novel, perhaps in the form of an appendix, for like the Editor's Preface, the Treatise on the Steppenwolf, and Haller's Records, they provide an important perspective on Hesse's *Steppenwolf* incarnation.

The *Crisis* cycle (which in the 1928 edition contains forty-five poems) is the kaleidoscopic confession of a man of fifty caught up in the "well-known tragicomedy," as Hesse puts it in his Epilogue, of being torn between the world of the mind and that of the senses. That conflict is of course quintessentially Hessean, but in the context of his mid-life crisis Hesse tries in these poems to take to the limit his art-as-confession poetics of the 1920s, of which his Epilogue is the most concise statement and apology. Because his earlier writings had played up the spiritual at the expense of the sensual, *Crisis*—like the experiences on which the poems are based—is a still more radical stab at what he had pursued in most of his writings since his move to the Ticino:

> Now that with advancing years the writing of pretty things as such no longer gives me pleasure and that only a certain belated but passionate love of self-knowledge and honesty can impel me to write, I had to move into the light of consciousness and to represent this hitherto suppressed half of my life. I did not find this easy, for it is more pleasant and flattering to show the world one's noble and spiritual side, than the one at the expense of which the sublimation has been effected. Thus indeed many of my friends have told me in no uncertain terms that my new ventures in life as well as literature are irresponsible derailments and that the author of *Siddhartha* owes to himself a dignified attitude. I think differently about this, or rather, the issue here is not that of opinions and attitudes, but of necessities. One can't subscribe to the ideal of honesty and always show only the pleasant and significant side of one's being. (161)

With the possible exception of the two items that did find their way into the novel ("Steppenwolf" and "The Immortals"), *Crisis* does not add up to major poetry, though Hesse's grotesque self-portrait in verse has a biting wit (for example, "Hermann the Booze-Hound to John the Baptist") that can take the form of bawdy doggerel reminiscent of Goethe's Mephisto: "What use is fame's laurel wreath / If no apples hang beneath? / What use is the prettiest tail / If I can't wag it without fail?" (182). Torn between youth and age, animality and spirituality, inebriated cynicism and devout hope, the confessor of these risqué lyrics burns the candle at both ends, like Klingsor, expecting to be consumed in the flame and arise from his ashes with a new identity. With his cacophonous *carpe diem* songs, Hesse the tippler is both a belated Don Juan, a prodigal son returning to the Eternal Mother, a lover, a killer (as in *Klein and Wagner* and *Steppenwolf* there is the fantasy of killing the object of his love), and a potential suicide. Highly stylized even in their ribaldry, these poems are written to and for the moment, flares that light up Hesse's deranged state of mind with lurid flashes. Because in the fragmentary and shorthand notation of *Crisis*, Hesse touches on most of the major themes and motifs of *Steppenwolf*, this verse diary may in retrospect be considered a trial run and final approach to the novel—though at the time Hesse was tossing them off, late at night and under the influence of whisky and cognac, he certainly did not consider them in any such light.[33]

The Magic Mirrors

In a perspectival mode that makes this novel a veritable hall of mirrors, *Steppenwolf* presents a wide spectrum of autobiographical fact and fantasy—from the intensely subjective and uncritical to the extremely ironic and detached—that calls into question, revises, and extends the author's self-understanding. The biographical background of Hesse's mid-life crisis is briefly summarized in Haller's self-pitying reflections after he has finished reading the mysterious "Treatise on the Steppenwolf": his mention of the loss of "profession . . . livelihood" and public "esteem" points back to the crisis of the previous decade—the consequences of Hesse's speaking out against the war and the collapse of his "family life . . . when [his] wife, whose mind was disordered, drove [him] from house and home" and when "love and confidence had changed of a sudden to hate and deadly enmity." Hesse then alludes to the *Siddhartha* phase of his "new life" in the Ticino "inspired by the asceticism of the intellect" and whose "mold too was broken" in "a whirl of travel . . . fresh sufferings . . . and fresh guilt,"[34] an oblique account at best of his more recent problems, including the failure of his relationship with Ruth Wenger. The tone of Hesse's edited résumé here is naively self-serving:

> Looked at with the bourgeois eye, my life had been a continuous descent from one shattering to the next that left me more and more remote at every step from all that was normal, permissible and healthful. The passing years had stripped me of my calling, my family, my home. I stood outside all social circles, alone, beloved by none, mistrusted by many, in unceasing and bitter conflict with public opinion and morality; and though I lived in a bourgeois setting, I was all the same an utter stranger to this world in all I thought and felt. Religion, country, family, state, all lost their value and meant nothing to me any more. (78)

This is Haller's—and up to a point, Hesse's—melodramatic low point, for he does not want to accept the Treatise's recommendation of a renewed self-encounter, which in his despair he dismisses as a perpetual "destroying of the self, in order to renew the self" (79). Harry Haller wants the easy way out: "Let suicide be as stupid, cowardly, shabby as you please, call it an infamous and ignominious escape; still, any escape . . . from this treadmill of suffering was the only thing to wish for" (79). Hesse, however, will not permit Haller such a self-evasion, for he offers him—and himself—the heuristic and therapeutic challenge of the Steppenwolf Treatise, the Socratic imperative modernized, to "look deeply into the chaos of his own soul and plumb its depths" (64). Here as elsewhere in the novel Hesse's irony works to undermine Harry's sentimental self-presentation as the lonely outsider, doing all good, yet suffering all ill. Far from privileging this idealized self-image, Hesse's text subverts it in the mode of an ironic autobiography whose most fantastic episodes nevertheless serve the author's progressive *dis*illusionment.

Thus rather than acceding to the personal and literary temptation of a belated suicide as the resolution of his problems, Hesse writes his way out of and beyond the Steppenwolf crisis by achieving a more substantive and less flattering self-knowledge. If this book is surely his most sensational and courageous confession, its most notable formal and autobiographical feature is its deployment of multiple perspectives on and reflections of the self. Despite his Nietzschean rhetoric and his reliance on certain conventions of Romantic narrative (including elements of the *Märchen*,[35] and the framing device, as in Goethe's *Werther*, of a fictitious editor), Hesse's crafty manipulation of his readers' expectations and responses through the multiplication of magical mirror images of the same subject makes *Steppenwolf* a masterpiece of modern autobiography.

The three major perspectives around which the novel is constructed—the Editor's Preface, Haller's Records, and the Steppenwolf Treatise—make up the composite and myriad mimesis of Hermann Hesse. Each of these, especially Haller's Records, involves a series of rapidly shifting subperspectives and sequences yet represents a distinct narrative viewpoint; and each is intervolved with and mirrored in the other two. Thus, to cite one striking example, the Editor's account of Haller's ablutions in his landlady's vestibule before the auracaria plants as "the very essence of bourgeois cleanliness" reappears in Haller's Records (as the soothing icon of middle-class respectability) and is reintroduced in the Steppenwolf Treatise

in terms of the larger question of Haller's "relation to the bourgeoisie" (as his "attraction to those quiet and respectable homes with tidy
gardens, irreproachable staircases and . . . modest air of order and
comfort," 57–58).

Hesse's complex and pervasive deployment of mirror images in
Steppenwolf allows him to open up his self-image to a far-reaching
reflection and to aim at a result sometimes regarded as beyond the
reach of the autobiographer: a viewpoint genuinely different from his
own. Two of these mirrors, that of the Editor and the Treatise, represent Hesse's narrative attempt to get outside of himself by seeing
himself as others see him. Conversely, with the third, Haller's Records, he strives for a more subjective and uncritical self-reflection that
in the end coincides, paradoxically, with the other two.[36] For the autobiographer as well as for the historian, perspectivism can lead to
relativism and nihilism, that is, to a proliferation of equally valid—
and hence invalid—viewpoints. While Hesse's perspectival self-mirroring in *Steppenwolf* seems to call into question the traditional psychological notion of personal identity as a function of memory from
Locke to Erikson, Hesse's aim is not to refract and fragment the self
out of existence, but rather to explode the fiction of an identity sim-
plex, or simply unified, in order to work toward a more representative and inclusive sense of personal identity as a complex unity-in-
multeity. The aim of his perspectival and perspicacious self-understanding in this novel is to destabilize or *derange* a "normal" and
much-too-limited conception of identity in order to arrive at a truer
arrangement, a more substantial mimesis, including of course that of
the unconscious. Hence the subheading of Haller's Records, "For
Madmen Only" (29), is triumphantly ironic, because in *Steppenwolf*
madness—an idea vulgarized by the pop psychologists of the 1960s—
is the signifier of a higher sanity next to which the conventional fiction of normality and of a simple or fixed identity is highly questionable. The literal translation of the subtitle (it appears at several points
in the book) is "for the deranged only" ("Nur für Verrückte"),[37] a
refrain that clearly points back to the 1922 fragment, "Journal of One
Who Has Been Derailed"—and that, as we saw, initiates the peculiar
playing with perspectives so characteristic of the *Steppenwolf* period.

Right from the start of the novel there is something playful and
humorous in Hesse's manipulation of different viewpoints, a childish

yet sophisticated delight at the juggling of heterogeneous aspects of his self that is everywhere evident in the ironic texture of his style, and whose positive metaphor is surely the "building up of the personality" chess game Haller witnesses in the Magic Theater. Hesse's humor counterbalances the more serious and shocking elements of this novel, including the prophetic critique of Germany preparing for a second world war after having just recently lost the first, and Harry's grotesque fantasy of murdering Hermine. Unlike in *Demian*, where Hesse seems more under the compulsion than in control of his inner demons, in *Steppenwolf* he presides over these as the accomplished impresario of his unconscious.

Hesse's sly wit is already evident in his Editor's solemn introduction, which prepares his "mainstream" audience for the strange revelations to come. The Editor, a near parody of middle-class conventionality, is Hesse's crafty device for manipulating his readers. On the one hand the Editor represents the bourgeois norms from which Haller thinks he has increasingly strayed in his professed status as an outsider, but on the other hand he is, like the Dutchman in *A Guest at the Spa*, not only Harry's opposite but also a satiric version of the middle-class self Harry is in the end forced to own up to—one whose first reaction to finding the lovely Maria naked in his bed is "that [his] landlady would give [him] notice when she knew of it" (156). Because the fictional framing of the bizarre through the conventional works effectively to neutralize the readers' defenses, Hesse's Editor is an artful bridge to Haller's "deranged" records: to the extent that Hesse's audience can identify with his Editor, it is seduced into a sympathetic understanding if not acceptance of Haller. Hence the Preface allows Hesse to emphasize both the Editor's virtues and limitations ("I am not he, and I live my own life, a narrow, middle-class life, but a solid one, filled with duties," 23), and, by implication, those of his audience, as well as Haller's unusual strengths and weaknesses.

Admittedly the Editor's objective stance is more pretended than real, for the deck is stacked by Hesse in Haller's favor. The opening is in fact a preambular interpretation or hermeneutical exercise in which the author presents his novel as a Goethean merger of poetry and truth:

> It was not in my power to verify the truth of the experiences related in Haller's manuscript. I have no doubt that they are for the most part fictitious, not, however, in the sense of arbitrary invention. They are rather the deeply lived spiritual events which he has attempted to express by giving them the form of tangible experiences. (22)

This passage again displays the persistent tendency of Hesse's later fiction to inscribe within the text a "reading" of itself. As evident in the Editor's pronouncement below, the work has become self-reflexive, and with respect to its audience, self-justifying as well:

> I should hesitate to share them [Haller's records] with others if I saw in them nothing but the pathological fancies of a single and isolated case of a diseased temperament. But I see . . . them as a document of the times, for Haller's sickness of the soul . . . is not the eccentricity of a single individual, but . . . the neurosis of that generation to which Haller belongs, a sickness, it seems, that by no means attacks the weak and worthless only but, rather, precisely those who are strongest in spirit and richest in gifts. (24)

Thus the bourgeois Editor has discerned the larger meaning of Haller's suffering, and arrived at a Nietzschean appreciation of the subject of his labors as an instance of the "widespread sickness of our times" and as a type of latter-day, middle-aged German Hamlet "whose fate it is to live the whole riddle of human destiny heightened to the pitch of personal torture, a personal hell" (25).

Haller's narrative plunges us into the suicidal legend of "the homeless Steppenwolf, the solitary, the hater of life's petty conventions" (32) whose discontent with the "spiritual blindness" (35) of his age is occasionally relieved by fleeting glimpses of "a divine and golden track" (34). This recurrent metaphor points to the realm of the Immortals that is synonymous with the human imagination and where abide the imperishable works of art and the monuments of unaging intellect: the artist's heaven or Byzantium of *Steppenwolf* is as musical (Mozart, Bach) at it is literary (Novalis, Goethe, Nietzsche).

Such poetic phrases as "the eternal, . . . Mozart, and the stars" and "the golden trail" (41) signal Hesse's powerful nostalgia for a traditional European humanism that has all but expired in the urban culture of the early twentieth century. Significantly the fateful summons to the Magic Theater and the Immortals comes to Haller in "one of the quietest and oldest quarters of the town" in the form of an electric sign above "a pretty doorway with a Gothic arch" (36). Gothic arch and neon billboard, Bach fugues, Mozart sonatas and the "raw and savage gaiety" (43) of modern jazz—these make for the incongruous concatenation of classic and modern, past and present among which Harry has lost his bearings, but whose meaning is not necessarily, as he is to apprehend, that of a sheer disjunction or rupture. Mozart and the jazz musician Pablo can play side by side, or even become each other, as Harry will discover in the Magic Theater. On the level of plot, the figure of the golden track is literalized as Harry is led by the advertisement for the Magic Theater to the "Treatise on the Steppenwolf. Not For Everybody" (45–46). The "everybody" (*jedermann* = everyman) too is partly ironic, since Harry will discover in the Treatise that far from being unique, he belongs to a type, and then in the Magic Theater, that he indeed is an Everyman. To foster the illusion that the Treatise is a sort of cheap pamphlet sold at fairs, Hesse had it printed in the first edition in different type and on paper of a different color—a typographical ploy that also draws attention to it as a graphically different view of Haller.

Hesse claimed that the novel is "built around the intermezzo of the Treatise as strictly and as firmly as a sonata."[38] The scientific and objective tone of this "intermezzo," which is developed in striking counterpoint to Haller's extreme subjectivity, cauterizes the wound of his self-consciousness even as it confers the stamp of official recognition upon it. Although its language tends to the primly professorial, Harry devours it with "engrossing interest" (46) because he recognizes it as a fateful interpretation of his deepest problems by some unknown author(s). A type of probing case study (including review, diagnosis, and prognosis), it can be read, as Ziolkowski has suggested, "as the work of the Immortals themselves,"[39] though joint authorship by a panel of (unusually literate) social scientists would serve just as well. The Treatise describes itself aptly as a "fragment" of Harry's "inner biography" (64), and Harry himself considers it a portrait "painted with the air of lofty impartiality by one who stood outside and who knew more and yet less of me than I did myself"

(76)—a shift through which "inner" and "outer" images of his self are for the moment oddly equated. The Treatise is in fact the thematic center of the novel, serving as the psychological profile of Haller, as well as a précis of the major ideas around which the increasingly fantastic episodes of the plot are structured: insofar as the Treatise takes up and greatly extends the interpretive task of the Editor's Preface, it becomes in fact a critical treatise on *Steppenwolf*.

The ideas developed discursively in it are far from original, but the manner of their presentation shows a clarity and control characteristic of Hesse's later work. Opening with a provisional definition of Haller as a "dual and divided nature" (50), an oversimplification it will soon explode, the Treatise relates this divided self (man versus wolf) to the categories of the suicide and the artist in an analysis of the creative personality that is still on the horizon of Romantic concepts of genius, but which has considerable validity in the context of the literary modernism of the 1920s. The Treatise next proceeds to account for Harry's troubled social relations in terms of a dialectic of outsider and bourgeois, with humor postulated as the mediating principle. Even though they despise it, "most intellectuals and most artists" are unable to break with the world of middle-class values. Through humor, however, they manage to reach an accommodation with it, for humor, the "third kingdom . . . an imaginary and yet sovereign world" (62) allows them to live in the bourgeois world without being fully of it. As an instrument of self-knowledge, humor correlates with the mirrors of the Magic Theater that, as the Treatise informs Harry, still await him. The glass of humor in which Harry will learn to see a new self also throws into relief the false pathos of his simplistic fiction of the divided self, for what the Treatise posits and what the Magic Theater will dramatize is, to paraphrase Shakespeare, that all of the self is a stage, with a cast "not of two" (Faust's "two souls") but "of a hundred or a thousand selves" (66). The Treatise also prepares Harry and the reader for the Magic Theater with its interpretation of "the drama" as offering "the greatest possibilities of representing the self as a manifold entity", that is, of the heroes of Indian epics as "not individuals, but whole reels of individualities" (68), and of a modern work like Goethe's *Faust* as a multiple psychomachia.

The concluding portion of the Treatise inscribes Hesse's psychobiography back into a Romantic plot of humanization. In Zarathus-tran language it informs us that

> Man is not by any means of fixed and enduring form . . . He is much more an experiment and a transition. He is nothing else but the narrow and perilous bridge between nature and spirit. His innermost destiny drives him on to the spirit and to God. His innermost longing draws him back to nature, the mother. Between the two forces his life hangs tremulous and irresolute. (70)

Here Hesse's favorite polarity—Nature versus Spirit—is doubly grounded: on a biographical level it is obviously rooted in his child-hood experience of his parents, and on a linguistic and philosophical level it resonates with the cultural typecasting inherent in the Ger-man words, *Natur* and *Geist*. Relying on a Romantic mythography in its clinical categories, the Treatise demystifies the legendary self-im-age of the novel's title, because Harry's desire to "turn back again and become wholly wolf" (72) is sentimental in Schiller's sense:

> There is, in fact, no way back either to the wolf or to the child. From the very start there is no innocence and no singleness. Every created thing, even the simplest, is already guilty, already multiple. It has been thrown into the muddy stream of being and may never more swim back again to its source. The way to in-nocence, to the uncreated and to God leads on . . . not back to the wolf or to the child, but ever further into sin, ever deeper into human life (73).

With a final pointer to the Magic Theater, the Treatise informs Harry that suicide will not be a viable solution, something that can be found only in accepting the momentum of individuation and the painful expansion of the individual soul "until it is able once more to embrace the All"—which is also the perpetual spirit-journey of higher humanity, "the road that Buddha and every great man has gone" (73). The final recommendation of the Treatise is smiling at "this Steppenwolf" (75). Laughing one's way to enlightenment is the psychologized wisdom of this dissertation, a lesson that extends the theory of humor adumbrated in *A Guest at the Spa* and *Journey to Nu-remberg*. The totemic self-image privileged earlier in *Guest* to counter-

act the hypertrophy of the bourgeois ego symbolized in the Dutchman is now, however, ironized out of existence with the ideal of "the
thousand flowers of his [Harry's] soul" (75).

With its pathetic image of the aging wolf in a wintry landscape, the
"Steppenwolf" poem frames the return to the action, just as the contrasting poem, "The Immortals," later sets the tone for the Magic
Theater sequence. Harry's refusal of the Treatise's advice to risk "a
new incarnation" (79) leads him unwittingly to a series of fated self-
encounters, beginning with his attack on the sentimental Goethe portrait cherished by the wife of the young professor who has invited
him to dinner. Harry's outrage with all that is inauthentic in the modern world finds a satisfying target in "this empty and self-satisfied
presentation of the aged Goethe" (91) qua "magnate of poetry" (93)
that is—though Harry is not able to see this yet—no more false or
kitschy than the "Steppenwolf" poem's central metaphor. What
Harry will discover only later is that the sickly sweet Goethe icon is
the double of his own sentimental self-image:

> He himself, the old Harry, had been just such a bourgeois ideal-
> ization as Goethe, a spiritual champion whose all-too-noble gaze
> shone with the unction of elevated thought and humanity, until
> he was almost overcome by his own nobleness of mind! The
> devil! Now, at last, this fine picture stood badly in need of re-
> pairs! The ideal Herr Haller had been lamentably dismantled!
> (149)

Harry's disastrous evening with the professor is also a satiric demonstration of his uneasy relations with the bourgeoisie (just ex-
pounded in the Treatise), and his outburst against the professor as a
right-wing anti-Semite (whose views are contributing to the coming
of another war) allows Hesse to vent some of his own outrage.

The most important mirror of Harry's mounting self-knowledge is
of course Hermine. In some respects she (Anima) fits neatly, like Pablo (Shadow) into a Jungian scheme of individuation. But *Steppenwolf*
is more than a Jungian romance, and Hermine's character is, despite
some conventional associations, convincingly complex. Admittedly
she harks back to nineteenth-century stereotypes—the Romantic ma-
donna-sophia figure, the noble prostitute (she even has a touch of
the religious mania of Dostoevsky's Sonya), the loving sister. Even

such a listing suggests her symbolic multivalence, but what it does not explain is the successful mystification that Hesse—like John Fowles with some of his intriguing heroines—accomplishes with Hermine. She is simply everything that a woman can ever be to a man: mother, lover, sister, friend, confidante, guide, listener. Hermine is at once Hesse-Haller's opposite and double, as suggested by her name, which is the female version of Hesse's own (Hermann). Like Kamala and Teresina, she is accomplished in the worldly arts of living and the pleasures of the senses; she has mastered the dance of life into which she will initiate Harry by teaching him modern jazz steps, and by sending Maria as her teaching assistant. Yet as "the magic mirror" (124) of Harry's innermost feelings, she is also at home in the world of thought and the soul. A liminal being, she points to Harry's past as well as to his future; she stands on the threshold of the temporal and the timeless. An appropriately androgynous figure, she combines the experiences of both sexes: she reminds Harry of "Herman, his boyhood friend, the enthusiast, the poet" (143) in whose costume she will charm Harry in the "Hermine in Hell" episode of the masked ball, yet it is also intimated that she is the lover of both Maria and Pablo.

First and foremost, however, Hermine is the Eternal Feminine as Mother, for she takes the suicidal Harry firmly in hand, scolds him like a wayward son, and sets him on the right path, from death back to life. (In this sense, she is as much a Freudian eros as a Jungian anima figure.) Like *Demian*, *Steppenwolf* too enacts a movement toward a sexual union with the female mentor that is in the end frustrated. Yet the mother myth implicit in the Harry-Hermine relationship is less obtrusive and more convincing on the level of character and plot than that explicitly present in Sinclair's attraction to Frau Eva. Both Hesse and his work have matured, and the symbolism of Hermine is more substantially grounded in his adult experience, as a compensatory metaphor for the failure of two marriages, and in a larger sense, for all the love and sympathy he had always sought in women but apparently never found in real life.

Hesse also gives to Hermine the most comforting message of *Steppenwolf*, the transcendence implied by the "golden track" metaphor: those individuals who have *that within* (to cite Hamlet's famous phrase) which can find no proper outlet in this one-dimensional world—those with "a dimension too many" (172)—may appear to be doomed to alienation, yet they are nevertheless metaphysically centered and "true." Here the visionary Hesse boldly valorizes imagination over "reality," and inner over outer:

> "Time and the world, money and power belong to the small people and the shallow people. To the rest, the real humans belongs nothing. Nothing but death."
> "Nothing else?"
> "Yes, eternity." (174)

One can dismiss this as wishful thinking and otherworldliness—as one can Christianity and Platonism, two Western traditions on which Hesse's poetic idea of "home" draws heavily. *Steppenwolf*'s heaven is a nondenominational one made up of "the image of every true act, the strength of every true feeling" (174); unlike Plato's realm of Ideas, Hesse's "eternity" is not purely intellectual but something that corresponds to our innermost aspirations, the hypothetical place where our metaphysical hunger (*Sehnsucht*) is stilled: "Ah, Harry, we have to stumble through so much dirt and humbug before we reach home! And we have no one to guide us. Our only guide is our homesickness" (175).

Hermine's metaphor of "home" carries the powerful charge of an unreconstructed Romanticism, yet the characterization of the Immortals is remarkably *un*emotional. Indeed, it is paradoxical that Hermine, the harbinger of eros, should point to the hard and cool wisdom of the Immortals, which is primarily logocentric. For instance, the Goethe of Harry's marvelous dream is an immor(t)al prankster and ironist for whom "eternity is a mere moment, just long enough for a joke" (111) and who has one foot in the world of the senses but the other in the timeless reaches of empty space. Goethe's "roguish leer" (110) and his tempting Harry with the "diminutive effigy of a woman's leg" reveal Harry's ambivalence about sex, for he is torn "between desire and dread" (symbolized in the dream by the leg being also a scorpion, 112). Yet if this surreal Goethe has, like the historical one, his erotic side, as a representative of the Immortals his principal allegiance is to the ghostly world of mind (*Geist*), as evident in the poem in which the Immortals identify themselves with the "eternal being" of the "ether's star-translumined ice" (178). Their "cool and star-bright . . . laughter," however, is very remote indeed from human life, for their serene humor has been purchased at the cost of cosmic indifference. Their ironic objectivity is exemplary but inhuman, and their humor, like the infinite negativity of Romantic irony attacked by Hegel more than a century before *Steppenwolf*, is more life denying than affirming. Like the Castalians of whom they are already an adumbration, these Immortals do have their limitations.

Montaigne's sentence, "each man bears the entire form of man's estate,"[40] might be written above the entrance of the Magic Theater, which with its surrealistic transformations takes Harry Haller beyond the Romantic sense of personal uniqueness proclaimed at the opening of Rousseau's *Confessions* to an oneiric vision of the teeming plenitude of his inner world. The Magic Theater is also a modernist fun house in which the three major narrative viewpoints (Editor, Treatise, Haller's Records) are confounded in an internalized *theatrum mundi* of mirror images upon mirror images. The stage director and presiding magus of this performance is Pablo, who initiates Harry into its magical merging of inner and outer with the help of hallucinogenic drugs with which Hesse apparently had some familiarity.[41] The "merry peal of laughter . . . made of crystal and ice" (197), the leitmotif of the Magic Theater, identifies Pablo as one of the Immortals, whose introduction to this "little entertainment" ("for madmen only," 198) helps to orient both Hesse's protagonist and his readers:

> Only within yourself exists that other reality for which you long. I can give you nothing that has not already its being within you. I can throw open to you no picture gallery but your own soul. All I can give you is the opportunity, the impulse, the key. I can help you to make your own world visible. That is all. (199–200)

The final prerequisite for entering this "visionary world" (200) is the test of humor, which Harry passes when he is able to laugh to pieces the sentimental wolf/man (double) image that appears in Pablo's "pocket mirror."

What Harry—the Hessean psychonaut par excellence—discovers in the Magic Theater is the hidden, repressed, or undeveloped areas of his emotional life. Hesse's self-writing now also includes self-persiflage: the page-long menu for the entertainment at hand, beginning with "MUTABOR: TRANSFORMATION INTO ANY ANIMAL OR PLANT YOU PLEASE" and ending with "GUIDANCE IN THE BUILDING UP OF THE PERSONALITY, SUCCESS GUARANTEED" (217), is a marvelous sendup of some of his favorite themes. Nor does this confessional spoofing pull its punches, for the absurd vision of Brahms and Wagner "who drearily led a large following of some ten thousand men in black"—all supernumerary notes in these composers' "thick orchestration" (234–235)—is turned against Hesse's own career as a too-prolific man of letters: "I was now thoroughly miserable. I saw myself as a dead-weary pilgrim, dragging myself across the desert of the other world, laden with the many superfluous books I had written, and all the articles and essays; followed by the army of compositors who had had the type to set up, by the army of readers who had it all to swallow" (235–236).

The different episodes of the Magic Theater capitalize on a type of confessional exposé of the unconscious Hesse first employed in the Wagner dream or "theater" (*Klein and Wagner*). Thus in the absurd "Great Hunt in Automobiles" the aggressive charge beneath Hesse's ideal of nonviolence surfaces, as Harry and his friend Gustav, a professor of theology, become road warriors in the conflagration between man and machines that has at long last broken out. Freud's Thanatos seems to run the show here, though Eros is also in evidence when Harry is smitten with the pretty secretary of the attorney general whom they have taken prisoner. The libidinal agenda of Harry's unconscious is more fully explored in the "All Girls Are Yours" segment, in which he returns to his past and makes good on a number of "wishes, dreams, and possibilities that had once had no other life than [his] own imagination": "I was living a bit of myself only—a bit that in actual life and being had not been expressed to a tenth or a thousandth part, and I was living it to the full" (229). Two other episodes are dramatic variations of themes introduced earlier in the novel: "the building up of the personality" chess game is an existential metaphor of the self as a complex set of constituent elements capable of continual rearrangement (a point initially made, as we saw, in the Treatise). Conversely, the "Marvelous Training of the Steppenwolf" circus act is a theater-of-the-absurd version of Harry's self-serving myth of his division into man and wolf, with each half by turns (sadistically) dominating and being (masochistically) dominated by the other.

When Harry emerges from this illuminating set of self-encounters, he is ready for the momentous union with Hermine to which the second half of *Steppenwolf* has been steadily tending. A marriage between them would certainly make for a tidily packaged happy ending, something that Hesse wisely refuses, opting instead for an anticlimactic, problematic, and provisional one. When Harry emerges from the cinematic "All Girls Are Yours" wish-fulfillment fantasy he feels "ripe for Hermine" (231), only to find himself on the "How One Kills for Love" set, knife in hand, leering back at himself in "a gigantic mirror" as a large wolf. In search of Hermine, he meets up with Mozart, who after ridiculing his writings in doggerel rhymes ("rotten plagiarisms ill gotten," 236), hurls him through the "rarefied and glacial atmosphere" of interstellar space. Searching for *eros*, that is, he is thrown for a loop by *logos*. After the "thousand souls" therapy of the Treatise and the Magic Theater, Harry is right back to his old self-division and despair. Thus when he finally does meet up with Hermine, his eager anticipation has already turned into a blend of *Angst* and cynicism ("a strange marriage it was to be . . . bah, the devil!" 238), and his violent reaction to the unexpected sight that meets his eyes is in keeping with his relapse:

> What I saw was a simple and beautiful picture. On a rug on the floor lay two naked figures, the beautiful Hermine and the beautiful Pablo, side by side in a sleep of deep exhaustion after love's play. Beautiful, beautiful figures, lovely pictures, wonderful bodies. Beneath Hermine's left breast was a fresh round mark . . . a love bite of Pablo's beautiful, gleaming teeth. There, where the mark was, I plunged in my knife to the hilt. The blood welled out over her white and delicate skin. (238)

Although the stabbing of Hermine is imaginary, being only a "picture" in his mind, the violence of the impulse is real enough. Klein's temptation to murder the sleeping Teresina and the *Crisis* persona's confession of having stabbed to death his beloved Erika Maria Ruth[42] (the last two names match those of Hesse's first and second wives) are vividly realized in this bloody nightmare. A hidden complex of erotic and aggressive desires is brought up into consciousness and spelled out, a homicidal fantasy that may be the symbolic equivalent of both Hesse's guilt and resentment at the failure of his two marriages. Something like this is surely the confessional burden of this disturbing episode, and those critics who disclaim any wrongdoing on Haller's part because the killing is "only imaginary" or symbolic argue more like zealous defense attorneys ("my client is not guilty because he killed only in his imagination, and an imaginary person to boot") than psychologists.[43] Yet the interpretation of the murder as "only" imaginary belies the deep structure of *Steppenwolf*'s confessional imagination, and also runs counter to Hesse's repeated emphasis on the close and "magical" connection between inner and outer.

Like that of the Magister Ludi, the death of Hermine has proved something of a conundrum for Hesse critics, and the wide range of divergent interpretations of this episode points to the fact that it is symbolically overdetermined (in Freud's sense). The more positive readings tend to see the murder as a metaphor of Harry's self-realization. Two German critics, for instance, interpret the episode as Harry's leavetaking of Hermine, and Mileck too speaks of "Hermine's mock murder" as "Haller's absorption of his externalized *daimon*."[44] Conversely, the more negative readings have emphasized the obviously destructive character of the act as revealing Harry's jealousy and his fall back into his bourgeois self. Some have further extended this negative evaluation to show that Harry is really killing off a part of himself, or committing an act of "self-mutilation." More recently a Jungian analyst has interpreted Hermine's death as Harry's assault on his anima through his destructive intellect, which puts him "into the Judas category," save that here "the betrayer has really betrayed himself." This analyst concludes with an insight that also applies to the writings of Hesse's final phase, that "it remains a dangerous psychological situation when . . . the positive feminine is slain, when Logos stands alone."[45]

I have ventured on this excursion into Hesse criticism to demonstrate the wide range of possible interpretations of Hermine's death and to suggest that Harry's symbolically overdetermined final act in the Magic Theater invites such different readings, from a positive self-integration to psychological suicide. In what is at once an autobiographical self-exposure and a confessional fantasy, Hesse reveals that a fundamental psychic conflict—instinct versus intellect, *eros* versus *logos*—is far from resolved for him. Despite his best efforts and the unprecedented daring, honesty, and thoroughness of his fictional self-analysis, a basic polarity of his life and his art has not been harmonized. Had Hesse achieved this goal through the writing of *Steppenwolf*, the project of his ongoing autobiography would be at an end, and there would have been no need to proceed to the three major fictions still to come. In sum, the conflict between masculine and feminine, father and mother, nature and spirit is left unfinished at the conclusion of *Steppenwolf*, a fiction that reflects accurately enough Hesse's position on his life's journey.

To return from Hesse's life to his book, Harry's assault on Hermine may be construed as a temporary failure or setback in his quest for a fuller self-realization. It is a relapse, by way of violence, into his earlier self, when he knows or should know better who and what he has become, but it is not a definitive defeat or downfall. Mozart's ironic lecture to Harry that classical music heard on a cheap radio is representative of the relationship between "the ideal and the real" (243) is not merely a retreat into a sterile Platonism, as some critics have intimated, but rather a way of keeping the door open to continuing growth, whose precondition is not succumbing to despair. And the sentence handed down for Harry's violation of the Magic Theater, the gallows humor of his mock execution—being laughed out of court by a chorus of Immortals—makes light of his recent failure of self-understanding in the Magic Theater by using humor as a way of assuring that Harry will not be borne down by his faux pas, or turn it into a self-fulfilling prophecy. In the mode of Romantic irony, Hesse both under-stands and stands behind and above his novel and its characters: when Mozart-Pablo picks up the body of Hermine, "who at once shrank in his fingers to the dimensions of a toy figure and put her in the very same waistcoat pocket from which he had taken a cigarette" (248), Hesse reminds us of the artificiality of art, of the fact that his book is *only* a fictional construct. The writer's self is always more than the fiction of the self, which is here wryly deconstructed with the notion that both life and art are, like music, an unending game with infinite combinations, to be played again and yet again.

On the verge of the legendary age of fifty, Harry Haller and Hermann Hesse keep the road open to continuing growth and creativity, despite all the shortcomings and multiple disappointments of the recent past: "One day I would be better at the game. One day I would learn how to laugh. Pablo was waiting for me, and Mozart too" (248). No, Hesse has not achieved the elusive goal of a harmonious self, but at least the "Steppenwolf" crisis is over; it has been lived through and written out, and therefore this spectacular "incarnation" is no longer necessary or functional. To paraphrase the book's concluding sentence, Narcissus and Goldmund were waiting for him, and Leo and the Magister Ludi, too.

Narcissus and Goldmund

Begun in the spring of 1927 and completed toward the end of 1928, *Narcissus and Goldmund* appeared in 1930. Thus there is no real hiatus between *Steppenwolf* and this new novel that addresses in a calmer and notably more schematized fashion the issue of the divided self so sensationally voiced through Harry Haller. Hesse observed in a letter of 1932 that the "problem" of Goldmund had already been on his mind during the writing of *Steppenwolf*,[46] and that there is a close connection between the two books is evident in the fact that the career of Goldmund is prefigured in the "All Girls Are Yours" fantasy of the Magic Theater. Presumably the presence of Ninon in Montagnola during the spring and summer of 1927 played its part in Hesse's new and erotically charged portrait of the artist.[47]

Hesse's pseudo-medieval tale of the friendship between the libidinal sculptor and the intellectual monk is deceptively easy to read yet hides a problematic that makes this book difficult to grasp and even more difficult to characterize—a fact that may help to explain the sharply divergent critical opinions on its quality.[48] Mileck has drawn attention to the fact that "from its inception, the story was to be Goldmund's,"[49] and the conjunctive title Hesse finally chose is something of a misnomer that may itself be an index of some of the deeper identity problems he struggled with in the book. The failure of the narrative to support the equation of its copulative title may help to account for the "tragic undertone" and the "dark doubts" that Boulby has discerned in it.[50] This failure is evident in the double negation of the ending: that is, Goldmund's inability to achieve the statue of the archetypal Eve-Mother figure that has haunted his imagination, and the critical question of the dying Goldmund that burns into Narcissus "like fire": "But how will you die when your time comes, Narcissus, since you have no mother? Without a mother, one cannot love. Without a mother, one cannot die."[51]

These concluding references to *loving* and *dying* point to the contrapuntal confessional imagination at work in this late Romantic and not always successful hybrid of *Bildungsroman*, novel of ideas, and unabashed picaresque tale. Love and death are continually paired in it, as the symbols of the maternal source and mystery of life: "The mother of life [Eve] could be called love or desire; she could also be called death, grave, or decay . . . She was the source of bliss as well as of death; eternally she gave birth and eternally she killed" (168). Like *Demian* with its Frau Eva archetype, *Narcissus and Goldmund* projects the unresolved polarities of Hesse's experience through a personal (mother) myth as "a fusion of the greatest contrasts of the world, those that cannot be otherwise combined . . . birth and death, tenderness and cruelty, life and destruction" (183). It is fitting that Goldmund, the childlike artist caught up in the vision of the Eternal Mother, should be privileged with tantalizing glimpses of the cosmic coincidence of opposites. Early in his vagabond's life he discovers that the expression on a woman's face distorted by the pain of giving birth is "little different from those he had seen in other women's faces during the moment of love's ecstasy" (128). As his artistic vocation matures, he comes to perceive the enigmatic Eve figure as the source and goal of the impulses that govern his life, as well as an instinctive force that can be tender and loving but also rapacious and brutal. Goldmund, the child of eros, experiences both poles, from gentle lovemaking to the violent impulses that lead him to kill his fellow vagabond Viktor (in self-defense) and the stranger who tried to rape one of his mistresses—not to mention his determination to escape from prison and an impending execution by murdering the confessor who turns out to be Narcissus.

The recapitulatory references to life and death in the concluding paragraphs sort well with the image of fire in the final sentence of the novel. In *Narcissus and Goldmund*, fire is the symbol of both the creative and the destructive side of life: it is the comforting torch that illuminates the scene of the peasant woman giving birth (128), but it

is also the incendiary torch that lights up the skies of the plague sequence: "In one town, Goldmund watched with grim heart while the
entire ghetto was burned, house after house, with the howling mob
standing around, driving screaming fugitives back into the fire with
swords and clubs" (219). What is more, fire is also an apt metaphor
of Goldmund's restless life, and of the artist's libido or creative eros
that transforms raw life into the sublime forms of art.

Dying: more than any of his other books, this one is pervaded by
the consciousness of death and the felt pressures of mutability and
mortality. These are most vividly portrayed in the plague chapters
whose stark descriptions hark back to a literary and folk tradition of
the ravages of the Black Death from the Middle Ages down to the
nineteenth century and Manzoni's *The Betrothed*. Alongside his
highly personal symbol of "the universal mother . . . with Medusa
eyes," Hesse draws on traditional images of death, including the autumnal "song of the mowing scythe" (202). The grotesque iconogra-
phy of mortality that Goldmund encounters in a cloister is something
Hesse may himself have witnessed on one of his youthful foot-journeys through northern Italy:

> A dance of death had been painted on a wall: pale bony death,
> dancing people out of life, king and bishop, abbot and earl,
> knight, doctor, peasant, lansquenet—everyone he took along
> with him, while skeleton musicians played on hollow bones.
> Goldmund's curious eye drank in the painting. An unknown
> colleague had applied the lesson he too had learned from the
> Black Death, and was screaming the bitter lesson of the inevita-
> ble end shrilly into everyone's ear. (220)

Though impressed by this traditional Christian *sic transit*, Goldmund
prefers to think of death not as "a judge or hangman, a stern father,"
but a mother or mistress whose "call was a mating call, its touch a
shudder of love" (221). For Goldmund death is doubly seductive, because, as so often in Hesse, it is a homecoming to and recovery of
the metaphysical ground of being. But in what is the more pessimistic vision or confession of an aging author, death is also a release
from the perpetual incompleteness and incoherence of life. This
novel contains Hesse's bleakest evaluation of the "duality" of "all
existence," and the either/or dilemma posed by "the split [that] ran

through . . . creation" that "had not turned out right or was incomplete" (246–247). The failure of life to achieve its promise or to sustain meaning is evoked through a rhetoric of transience that is a strange admixture of the nihilistic and the consoling in its suggestion that "nothing lasted, not even our suffering." Goldmund realizes this larger insubstantiality of life when he returns after the end of the plague to the city of Master Niklaus, only to find his master dead, his workshop closed, and his once beautiful and haughty daughter Lisbeth a deformed and bitter hag (233).

Such pessimistic reflections are of course grounded in Hesse's biography, including his fears of aging and mortality (he turned fifty in July 1927), in the trauma of his friend and biographer Hugo Ball's agonized death of stomach cancer earlier that spring, and finally, in his larger evaluation of his own life as botched. Beset by various physical complaints (sciatica, gout, inflamed tear ducts), Hesse thought of himself at this time as prematurely aged—Freedman points to a note to Ball's widow in which he presents "himself as an old man, sliding visibly toward death." And there is also that despairing epistle cited by Boulby in which Hesse confesses that he has failed to achieve "a real, personal, intensive life":

> I have become a writer, but I have not become a human being. I have reached a partial goal, but not the main one. I have failed . . . My writing is personal, intensive, for myself often a source of joy, but my life is not, my life is nothing else but readiness to work; and the sacrifices which I bring by living in extreme loneliness, etc., I have been bringing in fact for a long time no longer for my life, but only for my writing. The value and intensity of my life lies in the times when I am poetically productive, therefore precisely those times when I am giving expression to the inadequacy and despair of my life.[52]

Deflected from the immediacy of living, he has been forced into the aporia of writing. But in this very diminishment there is also something precious that is affirmed in the letter above, and even more so in *Narcissus and Goldmund*, as his, the artist's, true mission and meaning: as we saw in Chapter II, for the true writer, writing *is* life.

Narcissus and Goldmund develops its double theme of life and death in the context of Hesse's adult experience as a poet and writer as well as of the parental pressures that burdened his early years, and does so in a manner that makes this novel his autobiographical defense of poetry and *apologia pro vita sua*. It is only in the context of the later Hesse's sense of life's limitations that this novel assumes its rightful place as his central act of autobiographical self-justification and as his most balanced and mature portrait of the artist. It may well be true that all creative writing serves the writer's desire for immortality, but certainly autobiographical writing seems to be the literary equivalent of the biological instinct of survival and self-preservation. Here *Narcissus and Goldmund*, a book about the fear of death but even more so about the creative effort to redeem life from the dance of death, is doubly autobiographical, for it seeks artistic self-preservation even as it reflects on the efficacy of such a project. Much less overtly confessional than *Steppenwolf* in terms of biographical correspondences and parallels, Hesse's final novel of the 1920s is a paradigmatic redaction of the tensions between art and life, *eros* and *logos*, that help to define his outlook and literary career.

Hesse's meditation on the meaning and value of art is developed through the divergent lives of his title characters in what is in some ways an updated confessional version of the old quarrel (going back to the Greeks) between the poets and the philosophers. In his role as Goldmund's mentor and analyst, Narcissus appears initially as the supremely self-assured and strong character: by restoring his troubled friend's "lost" memories of his mother, he puts him in touch with his true but repressed self, thus propelling him out of the monastery and into the world of eros and the senses in which he will realize himself as an artist. By the end of the story, however, this situation has been effectively reversed, and this despite the fact that Goldmund is by then already dying. In the larger schematization of the novel, Narcissus is in every sense a secondary and subsidiary character next to his charge and admirer, the *seemingly* weak and labile Goldmund. Yet the assignment of a lesser role to Narcissus is not simply a regrettable structural flaw, because as an autobiographical text the novel dramatizes through Goldmund the for-now ascendant side of Hesse's conflicted self.

While in the concluding perspective of the book the austere values that sustain Narcissus are revealed as questionable, the portrait of the ascetic intellectual that Hesse paints is full of genuine admiration and may also be something of a composite tribute. Narcissus may well have a touch of the analyst who first put Hesse in touch with his deeper self and the world of the Mother, and even more so of Hugo Ball, perhaps his most important friend of the 1920s whose cool and keen intellect Hesse much admired.[53] But the most substantial and poignant tribute is surely signaled by the statue of Saint John, Goldmund's first masterpiece that he models after his intellectual friend. Curiously enough, Narcissus' name matches that of the statue when Goldmund meets up with him again (as his confessor in prison): "Since the day I took my vows, my name has been John" (259). By a telling coincidence, the German version, *Johannes*, is also the name of Hesse's father.

If Mariabronn is a thinly disguised version of Maulbronn, the opening chapters set in the monastery represent yet another fictional version of Hesse's adolescent identity crisis: like Hesse, Goldmund is placed with the *patres* in violation of his true nature by a stern father; like Hesse, only more wrenchingly so, Goldmund is cut off from the world of his mother; like Hesse, Goldmund too escapes the confines of the monastery in violation of his father's plans in order to embark on a very different—and at first certainly wayward, but ultimately productive—career. At least as important as these similarities, however, arc the differences, because if Goldmund resembles the adolescent Hesse, Narcissus is the model student Hesse should have been in order to fulfill the expectations of his parents. As his name suggests, Narcissus qua *Johannes* may be an idealized vision of the understanding father (as friend and mentor) that Hesse wishes he might have had—one who instead of forcing him into an adolescent pedagogic straight jacket would have shown sympathetic understanding and fostered his self-will, even if it led in directions diametrically opposed to those of parental hopes and plans. Such a wishful revision of the past constitutes, to be sure, an implicit critique of Johannes Hesse, but it is as much a loving tribute to what was best and most admirable about that much-maligned and now belatedly honored figure of a father. And the extended dialogues between Narcissus and Goldmund in the last third of the book—so different in their friendly dialectic from the stormy relations between the young Hesse and his father—may betoken the later Hesse's continuing revaluation of and reconciliation with that parental image that began nearly a decade earlier in *A Child's Soul* and was carried a stage further in *Siddhartha*.

Despite the polarity inherent in their radically differing characters and lives, what gives Narcissus and Goldmund a common ground is their goal to immortalize or preserve life—an intuition Goldmund first has upon completing his statue of St. John:

> He thought that fear of death was perhaps the root of all art, perhaps also of all things of the mind. We fear death, we shudder at life's instability, we grieve to see the flowers wilt again and again, and the leaves fall, and in our hearts we know that we, too, are transitory and will soon disappear. When artists create pictures and thinkers search for laws and formulate thoughts, it is in order to salvage something from the great dance of death, to make something that lasts longer than we do. (155)

Through the idea of art and intellect serving ultimately the same purpose, the earlier dichotomy of the "Journal 1920–1921" between the artist and the saint (discussed in Chapter II) seems provisionally resolved. There is still some tension between them, but at least the aspirations of monk and sculptor are equated: they are both instrumentalities of Mind (*Geist*). This notion is elaborated by Narcissus in his extended conversations with his friend with a rather-too-neat thesis about the relative equivalence of *ideas* and *images* as the respective vehicles of thinker and artist: both ideas (philosophy) and images (art) serve "the creative mind" that is "at the center of the endless and meaningless dance of fleshly existence" (270).

The fact that these theoretical elaborations serve retroactively to justify and validate Goldmund not only in Narcissus' but in his own eyes suggests the fictional compensation of Hesse's literary and worldly career as valuable and worthy of approval by his devoutly religious and unworldly parents: "It seemed to Goldmund that his life had been given a meaning. For a moment it was as though he were looking down on it from above, clearly seeing its three big steps: his dependence on Narcissus and his awakening; then the period of freedom and wandering; and now the return, the reflection, the beginning of maturity and harvest" (270). In this recasting of the parable of the prodigal son, the creative "harvest" that Goldmund begins to realize is one achieved within the precincts and under the sanction of Narcissus' monastic order. Through a return to the father world after his erotic immersion in maternal nature's seasonal cycles of birth and death, Goldmund completes his first major new work, which earns him the awed admiration and respect of the "arrogant" mentor who had looked down on art and artists:

> Only now do I realize how many paths there are to knowledge and that the path of the mind is not the only one and perhaps not even the best one. It is my way, of course; and I'll stay on it. But I see that you, on the opposite road, on the road of the senses, have seized the secret of being just as deeply and can express it in a much more lively fashion than most thinkers are able to do. (290)

In these revealing passages in which Hesse has his father speak as it were from the other side of the grave, we have the son's self-affirmation and validation vis-à-vis the parental pressures that nearly broke him during adolescence, as well as the mature Hesse's apology for and defense of his career as a creative writer. In the concluding movement of *Narcissus and Goldmund*, the justification of the artist's life includes the attempt not only to reconcile the different values of Johannes (as Narcissus) and Hermann Hesse (as Goldmund), but also to mediate the opposed claims of *eros* and *logos* in and through the work itself. The account of Goldmund's plans for his first major project at Mariabronn, with its spiraling movement from "the world" to "the Word of God," is also emblematic of Hesse's conception of his ascending path as a writer: "The lower part, the stairs, growing out of a sturdy oak trunk and winding around it, was to represent creation, images of nature and of the simple life of the patriarchs and the prophets. The upper part, the parapet, would bear the pictures of the four apostles" (283). This ascent, however, is not unproblematic, for if Goldmund's identity as an artist wins the approval of Narcissus, the world of Narcissus does not gain the unqualified admiration of Goldmund. And if there is a basic "asymmetry" in the novel's presentation of the title characters,[54] its autobiographical significance is that in an ironic role reversal Narcissus' self-assurance is "shaken" to its core by Goldmund's art:

Smiling and sad, Narcissus remembered all the times since their early youth when he had guided and taught his friend. Gratefully his friend had accepted, always admitting Narcissus' superiority and guidance. And then, quietly, he had fashioned his works, born of the tempest and suffering of his ragged life: no words, no instructions, no explanations, no warnings, but authentic, heightened life. How poor he himself was by comparison, with his knowledge, his cloister discipline, his dialectics! (299)

The persuasive *apologia* of *Narcissus and Goldmund*, which incorporates the experience of more than two decades of active literary production, is Hesse's most representative portrait of the artist. It rises above the one-sidedness of such earlier portraits as those of the Apollonian and Dionysian painters, the resigned formalist Veraguth (*Rosshalde*) and the reveller Klingsor (*Klingsor's Last Summer*), or the crippling withdrawal from life of the composer Kuhn (*Gertrude*) and the misanthropy of the nature poet Peter Camenzind. With its assimilation of both Nietzschean and Freudian ideas, Hesse's presentation of the creative process has a distinctively modern cast. Hesse felt on his pulses that art, as his hero puts it unabashedly, is born of sensuality (307). What the libidinal artist cannot fully possess in life he recreates in his work: "again and again" (236) Goldmund draws the defiant young Rebekka who refused his sexual advances during the plague; later he lovingly carves the statue of Lydia as a madonna figure: "And as Lydia's figure gradually came toward him out of the wood, as he draped the strict folds of her dress over her knees, a deep, painful joy overtook him, a nostalgic falling in love with the image, with the beautiful shy girl figure, with his memory of that time" (294). In thus commemorating the images of these lovely young women, Goldmund is doing the Freudian work of sublimated libido and wish-fulfillment, yet he is also engaged in the Nietzschean task of conferring value and meaning, "to halt the gracefully drifting nonsense of life with his mind and transform it into sense" (193): as the author of *The Birth of Tragedy* affirmed, existence can only be justified as an aesthetic phenomenon.

Because Hesse transfers to Goldmund the gist of his own experience as a poet (*Dichter*), it is appropriate that the view of the creative process in *Narcissus and Goldmund* has a strong experiential or empirical component. As he pointed out in a letter written the same year that he began his new novel, "the poet does not live by conjuring pretty things for his readers, but rather by showing and interpreting through the magic of the word his own being and experience, be it pretty or ugly, good or evil."[55] Though he may not be aware of it at the time, Goldmund-the-lover is in fact doing the necessary field work for Goldmund-the-artist, sowing the passionate seeds for his later artistic harvest. That Hesse, despite the short-lived sexual escapades of his Steppenwolf incarnation, never actually lived out Goldmund's erotic *vita* is immaterial, because as he confessed in another letter, "Like Goldmund, I have a naively sensuous relationship to woman, and like Goldmund, I would love boundlessly, if only an inborn as well as acquired respect for the souls of my fellow humans (that is, women) and a culturally conditioned shame about a mindless self-abandon to the senses did not hold me back." In the same epistle Hesse formulates his conception of the creative process with a striking analogy between the artist and the honeybee, the "purpose of whose existence is to repeatedly deposit the extract of its experience in honeycombs, the filling of which is thus honeybee-happiness and honeybee-fate."[56]

This experiential "honeybee" aesthetic merges readily into the commemorative view of art, as is evident, for instance, in Goldmund's aesthetic perception of Lydia even at the height of his frustrated passion for her:

> These instants during which he thought he recognized the basic forms and laws that constituted her being, her soul as well as her body, had more than once roused in Goldmund the desire to retain something of this form and to re-create it. On a few sheets of paper that he kept most secret, he had made several attempts to draw from memory the outline of her head . . . the line of her eyebrows, her hand, her knee. (117)

Later these fleeting urges jell into a vocation when Goldmund happens upon a true work of art, "the inexpressibly beautiful" madonna of Master Niklaus, "a statue that spoke to him so strongly and attracted him so much that he . . . looked at it with reverence and deep emotion" (146). Goldmund's epiphanic experience of the call of art is his timely if largely unconscious response to the cumulative momentum of death in which his vagabond's existence has been caught up, and which now leads him to serve a genuine master and to create his apprentice's masterpiece, the statue of Narcissus as Saint John. When after this triumph Goldmund refuses the tempting offer of Master Niklaus (to settle down and become his partner and son-in-law), because he knows that for now he has exhausted his experience and touched the limits of his technical expertise, Hesse in effect recapitulates the old split within himself between the artist/outsider and the successful bourgeois. The parting-of-the-ways between Master Niklaus and Goldmund reverberates with autobiographical significance: whereas Goldmund, on the one hand, is Hesse's vision of the artist as Romantic purist who will work only when inspired (and all of whose considerable technical skills are subordinated to that end), Master Niklaus, on the other hand, who is also capable of the inspired masterpiece, but who more typically yokes his talent to the drudgery of an unending series of well-remunerated and competently executed commissions, is a version of Hesse the prolific man of letters who had compromised his artistic integrity.

After his return to his vagabond's career, which reaches its grotesque low point in a world devastated by the Black Death, Goldmund experiences a second call or rededication to the life of the artist in what is now a more conscious response to the dance of death. This time too the call comes through the encounter with a masterwork—a group of stone statues in a church—that conveys to him a powerful consolation reminiscent of that of Keats's most famous ode:

> Now, returning from a world full of images, his soul marked by the scars and tracks of violent adventures and experiences . . . he was suddenly touched with extraordinary power by these strict, ancient figures. Reverently he stood before the venerable images, in which the heart of long-past days continued to live on, in which, still after centuries, the fears and delights of long-since-vanished generations, frozen to stone, offered resistance to the passage of time. (226)

Like Keats's Grecian urn, Hesse's "silent symbols of human life" hold a soothing message that is teased out by the meditating poet: "Strict and deaf they stood there in their narrow niches, inaccessible to any request or question. And yet they were an infinite consolation, a triumphant victory over death and despair . . . in their dignity and beauty, surviving one dying generation of men after another" (227). It is only after this Keatsian moment that Goldmund, full of "the horror of his wasted" life (226), is ready for the mature harvest that will be his in the monastery.

In its larger reflection on art and artists, however, *Narcissus and Goldmund* is ultimately still a work of unresolved tensions, for its strongly experiential aesthetic is countered by what turns out to be an equally powerful idealist creed. Hesse thinks of the work of the artist, as we have seen, as the extract and correlative of his experience, yet at the same time he suggests that the aesthetic impulse is an innate element of Goldmund's identity long before it can be tested or shaped through experience. Thus while still a student at Mariabronn, Goldmund is already fascinated by the medieval art around him: "It seemed a valuable, intimate secret to him that, outside of nature with its plants and creatures, there existed a second, silent, man-made nature: these men, beasts, plants of stone and wood" (36). Like Hans Giebenrath at Maulbronn, Goldmund lives in a "dream world more than in the real one" (59), something that already presages his later vocation even as it points to his nascent sexuality: "Once he dreamed that he was tall and adult . . . that he had clay in front of him and was modeling clay figures, like a child: a small horse, a bull, a tiny man, a tiny woman. The modeling amused him and he gave the animals and men ridiculously large genitals; it seemed wonderfully witty to him in his dream" (59). With this revealing dream of Goldmund as maker, Hesse explores what had been glossed over in the failed autobiography of *Beneath the Wheel*, namely, the simultaneous emergence and intimate interplay between the libidinal and the artistic in the adolescent boy's imagination. These fundamentally connected drives are inborn yet emerge only later as conscious goals after Narcissus has propelled Goldmund on the road to self-realization—one that first takes him beyond and in the end brings him back to the monastery. In the concluding clarification attempted through the dialectic exchanges between the two friends, the earlier empirical view of art is now overwritten by an idealist aesthetic: Narcissus claims "that art is more than salvaging something mortal from death" or "merely [the making of] faithful copies of a specific person who once lived and whose shapes or colors the artist has preserved." And Goldmund (Hesse?) assents to this redefinition of his libidinal career: "You are right . . . The basic image of a good work of art is not a real figure of flesh and blood; it is mind. It is an image that has its home in the artist's soul. In me, too, Narcissus, such images are alive, which I hope to express one day and show to you" (269).

This remarkable rhetorical shift toward an idealist view of art in a sense corresponds to Hesse's attempt to reconcile the conflicting claims of mother and father worlds dramatized throughout the narrative. In the final formulation of Narcissus, both his intellectual and Goldmund's artistic labors are posited as equally valid approaches to "mind" (*Geist*), the central ground of and clue to the mystery of being: "In you this mind is not that of a thinker but that of an artist. But it is mind, and it is the mind that will show you the way out of the blurred confusion of the world of the senses, out of the eternal see-saw between lust and despair" (270). Whereas Goldmund, and so it seems, Hesse, are content for the moment with this neat resolution, the "see-saw" ending of the novel—which shows Goldmund once more breaking out of Mariabronn to seek new adventures and, ironically, to find his death—invalidates the larger mind-synthesis postulated in Narcissus' speech. The dying Goldmund's return to Mariabronn is not an act of contrition that countermands the spirit of his departure, particularly since, as we have seen, his dying words to his erstwhile mentor are a devastating indictment of the latter's narrow values. Thus the sought-for integration of mother and father realms, of *eros* and *logos*, emerges mostly as a belated exercise in wishful thinking on Hesse's part. Far from being the ultimate mediating principle, *Geist*/mind remains, as so often in Hesse, primarily the attribute of the logocentric thinking personified in Narcissus—a truth supported by the conclusion, where the mother world emerges as the supreme reality and fulfillment, and where the *vita* of the wandering mother's son is valorized over that of the motherless and unsexed intellectual. As it was for Knulp, an earlier and more sentimental version of the errant artist, so for Goldmund death is a blissful return to the maternal source: "I hope death will be a great happiness, a happiness as great as that of . . . fulfilled love. I cannot give up the thought that instead of death with a scythe, it will be my mother who will come to take me back to her" (308). In the confessional imagination of *Narcissus and Goldmund*, this maternal ground is primary or prior in both an ontogenetic and an ontological sense. The very name of the monastery alludes to this valuation, and puts into ironic perspective its logocentric outlook: *Mariabronn* = Mary's Fountain is the true source of life, and in Goldmund's dying fantasy, also its final repository. Seen in this light, the Magna Mater myth that pervades this novel is a powerful recapitulation of something presented already a decade earlier in *Demian*'s Frau Eva archetype.

With its powerful portrait of the artist, Hesse's *apologia pro vita sua* in *Narcissus and Goldmund* in effect reinscribes in a more schematic manner the basic conflicts of his life and art. The failure of its author, however, to achieve a greater synthesis of the conflicting tendencies within him through self-writing does not mean that this highly readable book that tells a truth greater or other than Hesse had intended—Narcissus *or* Goldmund?—is an artistic failure. If Hesse does not move beyond the impasse of the problematic conclusion of *Steppenwolf*, the conflicts of the divided self are nevertheless formulated in a lively and lucid manner that makes this work a masterfully constructed bridge between Hesse's autobiographical fiction of the 1920s and that of his final phase culminating with *The Glass Bead Game*. As his most paradigmatic overview of the perennial tensions of his life and art, this novel can be taken as a way station on Hesse's ascending path that looks back, through Goldmund, to a series of earlier self-incarnations, and ahead, through Narcissus, to the patristic mentality of the journeyers to the East and the Castalian hierarchy. The winds of Hesse's past and future waft through its open windows; its walls are decorated with poetic images of the mother and father world, of artist and intellectual, maker and thinker, locked in a stylized dialectical struggle.

CHAPTER IX
HOME TO THE
UN-BECOMING SELF

*The task, desire, and duty of youth is that of becoming; the task
of the mature individual is the yielding up of one's self, or, as the
German mystics used to call it, of "un-becoming."—Hermann
Hesse, 1933*

*If it [The Glass Bead Game] turns out as planned, then it will
be my last major work and will give complete expression to the
final phase of my inner existence which began with* **The Journey
to the East.***—Hermann Hesse, 1936*

Very great is that sublime work of old age, **The Glass Bead
Game,** *fed by all the sources of human culture, Western and Eastern.—Thomas Mann, 1947*

The Glass Bead Game *accompanied me for twelve years and
was to me more than a book. May it also help some of its readers.—Hermann Hesse*

The threshold of Hesse's final phase is 1931, the year he finished *The
Journey to the East,* formalized his relationship with Ninon through
marriage, and moved into the spacious house (built for him according to his specifications by his friends and patrons, Hans and Elsie
Bodmer) that was to be his picturesque hermitage until his death in
1962. His aspiration in the 1930s, however, toward a life of ordered
serenity and clarified wisdom—which made him the resident sage of
Montagnola and which also informs his last and greatest novel—is
not without its underlying problems and tensions. Presided over by
Ninon, the *"pater familias"* and manager of their new life,[1] the Casa
Hesse became his refuge and tower against the corruptions of the
contemporary world and the blood-dimmed tide being loosed by the
inexorable rise of Hitler. After the Nazis came to power, it also became a way station for a series of famous and not-so-famous refugees

from the new order, including Thomas Mann, Stefan Zweig, Bertolt Brecht, and Peter Weiss. Hesse's meditative cultivation (literal and symbolic) of his garden was less than idyllic, for the political nightmare across the border disturbed and touched him and Ninon too nearly for that, including the mounting fear and uncertainty during the war about the fate of her Jewish relatives in Eastern Europe.

Then too the relationship with Ninon, the emotional anchor and mainstay of Hesse's later years, was not without its difficulties, for while he was willing to depend on her ministrations, he was not always able to give of or share himself: if he counted on her to keep their domestic life on an even keel, he also insisted on his right to keep his emotions and the life of his imagination to himself, as evident in a revealing note (written in the same year as their marriage) in which he pleads with her not to "despair" because he had been unable to respond to her questions the day before: "I need a space within myself where I am completely alone, where no one and nothing may enter. Your questions endanger this space. . . . On several occasions recently you have disturbed the tempo of my soul. Yesterday too this was the case." He concludes this strange apology by begging her not to pry into "the zone of dreams and poetry" of his soul: "In this matter I can only ask for your trust and patience."[2]

Clearly there were times (as earlier at Gaienhofen during his first marriage) when his domestic retreat seemed more like a gilded cage, and when the thrice-married and aging author felt a belated nostalgia for the footloose wanderings of his bachelor days. Caught up in the routine of his "too-well-off and comfortable life," including the pressure of the daily mail "to play the ever-busy and famous man," Hesse in the early part of the new decade found attractive the legend of "the old Tolstoy" who ran away from home "in the moment before his death" in order to regain with his "last breath the feeling of the open road, freedom, air, and space."[3]

Does this sentiment already presage the Magister Ludi's abdication?

The Journey to the East

It is tempting for even the devoted Hesse reader to dismiss *Journey to the East* (written 1930–1931, published 1932) as a trifling confessional conundrum. All of Hesse's writings are of course intensely personal, but of his leading fictions, this is surely his most private. Unlike much of his earlier work that reaches out to as wide an audience as possible, this esoteric book seems to exclude all but a small circle of knowing insiders, something implicit in his acknowledgment, "I have sometimes asked myself if I wasn't a little all-too-personal . . . and put into it too many things that are entirely private."[4] Some critics have agreed, finding this, in the words of one of its detractors, perhaps the weakest of his published works.[5] While many of the playful allusions of Hesse's autobiography à clef are fairly obvious, like that of the princess Fatima (of *Thousand and One Nights*) who as the romantic object of the narrator's quest is linked with "Ninon, known as 'the foreigner' "[6] (a pun on Ninon's maiden name, Ausländer), others require more specialized literary or biographical information: for example, the "magic circle" (31) of characters at the feast given by "Max and Tilli, the lords of the castle" (29)—Hesse's friends and sometime hosts, the Wassmers—which includes Longus the stargazer (Dr. Lang), Othmar who plays Mozart on the piano (Hesse's composer friend Othmar Schoeck), Louis the Terrible who speaks Spanish with Puss-in-Boots (Hesse's painter friend Louis Moilliet), Archivarius Lindhorst (of E.T.A. Hoffmann's "The Golden Flower Pot"), Heinrich von Ofterdingen (the hero of Novalis's novel), and Anselm (of Hesse's earlier *Märchen*) still "in search of the purple iris of his childhood" (24). Other references are more or less decipherable to the literary and biographical detective: for example, the Order's archive entry on Fatima (94), "princ. orient. 2 noct. mill. 983 hort. delic. 07," the second half of which "probably pertains to the. . . . *Hortus Deliciarum*, a twelfth-century illustrated manual of instruction for nuns,"[7] or the entry to the narrator's file (109), "Chattorum r. gest. xc civ. Calv. infid. 49," whose Latin alludes to Hesse the citizen of Calw who fell away from the Order at the age of forty-nine,[8] or even the association of Leo with rope [he wears shoes with "soles of plaited rope" (68) and lives on the "Seilergraben" (59), that is, Ropemaker's Lane], which according to Ziolkowski points to the ropemaker Oknos who in Bachofen's *Grave Symbolism of the Ancients* is "the symbol of the highest level of human existence."[9] Finally, some references seem wilful exercises in extreme mystification, like the Order's archive card on Leo ("Cave! Archiepisc. xix. Diacon. D. vii. cornu Ammon. 6 Cave!," 93).

Confronted with such recondite allusions, the puzzled reader may well ask, what is the point of these autobiographical games, and for whom, if anyone other than the author himself, was this book written? Perhaps one way to answer such objections is to point out that far from being necessary to an understanding of Hesse's basic ideas and themes in *The Journey to the East*, the network of cryptic allusions is a literary feint or camouflaging device. Clearly on one level many of the teasing literary and biographical references are ironic arabesques with which Hesse indulges his long-standing penchant for autobiography as self-disguise and fantastic costuming—indeed, even the narrator, H. H., involves something of a trick perspective, being at once close to yet ironically distanced from his author. Yet on another level the hide-and-seek tactics of this ambiguous narrative are not merely Hesse's overindulgence in a favorite idiosyncracy, but also a considered choice that aligns the novel with the writings of many of his famous modernist contemporaries in their desire to consciously render their works difficult and even inaccessible to a large and commercially manipulated reading public.

Here the book's very excesses signal the later Hesse's elitist and aristocratic outlook inherent in his need to withdraw himself and his work from the glare of literary publicity and the fate of being "famous" and "popular." More consciously than before, he targeted his fiction at a "future psychocracy," to borrow that odd coinage from the beginning of *Journey to the East*,[10] and wrote for a small group of discriminating readers who could appreciate the deeper meaning of his ongoing autobiography behind the literary roadblocks he put up to keep out the uninvited. *Fit audience let me find, though few*, could be the slogan of Hesse's final phase, for he was convinced that the sensational success, for different reasons and with different groups of readers, of *Steppenwolf* and *Narcissus and Goldmund* had been based on a radical misprision of their meaning and message. Thus in 1930 he characterized the appeal of *Narcissus and Goldmund* to the middle-class German reader as that of an escapist fantasy that allows him *not* to think about "his life, his business, his wars," and in the 1941 postscript to the Swiss edition of *Steppenwolf* he described the novel as the most consistently and vehemently misunderstood of his works.[11]

Because of this, his writings of the 1930s target their audience through acts of exclusion: as he asserted two years after the publication of *Journey to the East*, "the more shallow . . . the life of the German and the European mind becomes the more it becomes necessary for the few genuine poets to withdraw into a secret language and to confine themselves and their impact to a very small circle."[12] We can, of course, fault his later works for their failure to address a larger audience—so long as we realize that Hesse aimed precisely at such a result, beginning with this novel, of which he observed that it was intended for "a very few" and "completely sealed off from the masses" because, as he put it, "I am seeking to withdraw my books more and more from mass circulation and 'success'."[13]

Though its arcane puzzles and disguises may put off the reader, Hesse thought of the book as among his most important, grouping it with *Demian*, *Siddhartha*, and *Steppenwolf* as a "life-saving" fiction.[14] In part this is due to the fact that it was written to come to terms with yet another crisis, the postpartum depression following the completion of *Narcissus and Goldmund* that, as Mileck notes, brought into the open once more Hesse's residual despair of the previous decade at the futility of living and writing in the modern world. On finishing *Journey to the East* he insisted rather defensively that it was meant "not at all as a pretty plaything . . . but very much as a confession, even an appeal to tendencies which run counter to those of the present time," and that far from being "a flight" from "today," it was in fact a "battle unto death."[15] Like most of his other leading confessions, Hesse's new novel is both the expression and clarification of an inner struggle, but on a new level and with modified means that make this a symbolic prolegomenon to *The Glass Bead Game*. The poles of Hesse's doubt and affirmation, despair and hope are now farther apart than ever, and while one extreme of *Journey to the East* sounds a pervasive pessimism about the possibilities of self-writing that aligns it with the bleak vision of a late modernist confession like Beckett's *Company* (1980), the other extreme plays with the imaginative possibilities of life as aesthetic patterning in a mode that looks ahead to Nabokov's *Speak, Memory*.

As an agonized dialectic of hope and despair, Hesse's *Journey* employs one of the hoariest of tropes for human life, yet it presents us with an *interrupted* narrative about a *failed* journey that submits the issue of the very possibility of autobiography to a skeptical reflection. The motifs of rupture, interruption, and incompletion are prominent in the book because it is in some sense a problematizing narrative about the feasibility of autobiographical narrative, and thus touches in a new key on Hesse's dilemma as a subjective writer, already voiced in the lament of the "Journal 1920–1921," that a dozen or more separate diaries aren't enough to document the teeming plenitude of the soul. What a decade earlier, however, had appeared as an embarrassment of experiential riches overwhelming the diarist is now seen as the writer's impotence or inability to present his life-experience in narratable form.

His narrator, we recall, set out to write a concise history of the unsuccessful journey to the East of which he had been a fellow traveler, an expedition that had lost its meaning and center with the sudden disappearance of the ever-pleasant and devoted servant Leo "in the middle of the dangerous gorge of Morbio Inferiore" (37), a spot near "the Italian border" (38) whose name Hesse must have chosen for its metaphoric value (self-doubt, failure). When H. H. comes to describe the nadir of their trek, his belief in the ability of narrative to capture the reality of the past also vanishes, and he is left with a Kafkaesque sense of futility: "But through what expedient is it possible to tell the story of the journey to the East? I do not know. Already this first endeavor, this attempt begun with the best intentions, leads me into the boundless and the incomprehensible" (46). The narrator's shifting metaphors themselves point to the instability of his narrative: he discovers that "instead of a fabric" he holds "a bundle of a thousand knotted threads," and that he lacks a "center" around which the "wheel" might revolve (47–48). His very self proves to be a blank, a nonreflecting "mirror" that is "nothing but the uppermost surface of a glass plane" (48). The result is "a dreadful doubt" about the practicability of autobiography: "This doubt does not only ask the question, 'Is your story capable of being told?' It also asks the question, 'Was it possible to experience it?' " (49). In his paralysis at the end of Section 2, H. H. is not at a far remove from the "crawling and falling self" of Beckett's *Company*, but unlike Beckett's speaker, Hesse's cannot even entertain the possibility of "devising figments to temper his nothingness."[16] With his sense of radical alienation from his own experience and the past, Hesse's narrator has succumbed through the

Morbio Inferiore episode to a more-than-Cartesian doubt about the possibility of autobiographical narrative without for the moment having any confessional equivalent of a saving *cogito*.

The resolution of his impasse comes through the sheer instrumentality of his will, which is also—despite the ironic gap between Hermann Hesse and H. H.—the gist of the existential self-saving act of *The Journey to the East*. Trapped in the symbolic straits of Morbio, H. H. seeks out an old friend who has produced a much acclaimed history of World War I, and who admits that he also found it initially impossible to narrate the events that he had experienced at first hand. His dilemma was that on the one hand only those readers who had lived through the war would be able to understand his account, and that on the other hand he was struggling against the nemesis of all efforts to recover the past: the need to forget, which, so he claims, is only second to the hunger for experience. And though this historian does not mention it, still another obstacle to giving a coherent account of the past is the infinite multiplicity of possible perspectives on it, as H. H. later discovers to his horror when he reads, in the archives of the Order, several fundamentally differing accounts of the Morbio episode by other participants of the journey. What turns out to be his naive literalism about his (misunderstood) past is shattered by a Nietzschean perspectivism that Harry Haller had already encountered in the mirrors of the Magic Theater: "A shudder went through me. . . . How awry, altered and distorted everything and everyone was in these mirrors, how mockingly and unattainably did the face of truth hide itself behind all these reports, counter-reports and legends! What was still truth? What was still credible?" (115–116).

It is only in the mode of such a probing and skeptical self-reflection that the autobiography of Hesse's final phase can be elaborated in a fiction that forms the biographical contingencies of his life into an autobiographical legend, and truth into poetry. The impetus H. H. receives from his historian friend is rooted in the latter's conclusion that "I either had to write the book or be reduced to despair; it was the only means of saving me from nothingness, chaos and suicide" (57)—or, to translate the narrator's dilemma into his author's, the confessional parable that is *Journey to the East* is also a life-preserving act of will arising from the extremities of doubt and despair. Admittedly this solution—which both Hesse and his narrator accept—is self-centered and ignores their audience, just as the historian Lukas in writing his account of World War I did not permit himself "to think at all of any other reader but" himself, "or at the most, here and there of another close war comrade" (58). When H. H. takes up again his interrupted chronicle of the journey that fell apart at Morbio, he is no longer concerned with the larger account of an abandoned expedition, but only with the personal goal (like his friend with his war book) "of saving [his] life by giving it meaning again" (62). His new self-knowledge is reflected in his frank avowal that far from serving "a noble cause," his "laborious task" is an act of "egoism" (61–62).

The affirmative rhetoric of *Journey to the East* that counters its morbid crisis of self-doubt turns on the idea of the League of Journeyers as an eternal aspiration of the human spirit. True, the journeyer H. H., whose twelve-year retrospect generally parallels Hesse's career since his departure from Bern for the Ticino in 1919,[17] has failed miserably. The "journey" itself, however, is the signifier of a set of eternal values above and beyond the flux of history that in the two preceding novels had been suggested through Narcissus and the Immortals respectively, and that we will encounter again as the Castalian ideal of the Glass Bead Game players. Hesse alerts us to the brittle metaphoricity of his title (*Die Morgenlandfahrt*) as a voyage to what already and always *is*, with the resonating pun on *Morgen*: because it means both *morning* and *tomorrow*, it suggests both past and future, dawn and sunset, life's beginning and end. As in the Romantic myth of Wordsworth's "Intimations of Immortality" ode, the morning/East of Hesse's poetic autobiography harks back to the dream, radiance, and freshness that is our "innocent" childhood in the first stage of humanization, but it also implies the "third realm of the spirit," that of grace and faith.[18] Like the speaker of Wordsworth's ode who is burdened with a sense of loss and grief, H. H. too is weighed down by the disillusionment and despair of the second stage. However, the moral darkness of this stage—and here is where Hesse parts ways with such modernist apostles of abject despair as Beckett—is only a test or trial of the spirit, as H. H. discovers when he has met up again with Leo and receives the sentence of the Order for his multiple derelictions. H. H.'s mounting suffering helped him break through the apparent cul-de-sac of the second stage, as Leo, now resplendent as Primate of the Order and speaking in the "cool" and "clear" voice of the Immortals, points out in a sentence that fuses psychoanalytic and religious thinking: "as soon as suffering becomes acute enough, one goes forward" (106). The irony of the Order's sentencing of H. H.'s unwitting apostasy is, like the assembled Immortals' laughter at Harry Haller's failure of the test of the Magic Theater, a heuristic device that propels him toward the third level:

> Brother H. was led to despair in his test, and despair is the result of each earnest attempt to understand and vindicate human life. Despair is the result of each earnest attempt to go through life with virtue, justice and understanding and to fulfil their requirements. Children live on one side of despair, the awakened on the other side. Defendant H. is no longer a child and is not yet fully awakened. He is still in the midst of despair. He will overcome it and thereby go through his second novitiate. We welcome him anew into the League. (106)[19]

It is admittedly a strange paradox that by far the most personal and private of Hesse's novels should point so insistently to an impersonal and eternal set of values. Yet another symbolic version of his struggle through the dark night of the soul, this book presents the opening movement of Hesse's final phase as his mature recommitment to a higher faith from which he had repeatedly lapsed during the psychic lows of the 1920s. Like that of *Steppenwolf*, the autobiographical hermeneutic of *Journey to the East* sets up an ironic distance between author and narrator, only to dissolve it in the latter's recognition of his multiple failures. Whereas H. H. thought that he was the last surviving member of a moribund League, he discovers that it "is as completely stable and mighty as ever," only he had lost touch with it because he turned, without even knowing it, into "a traitor" and "deserter" (99). Far from being a dereliction of duty, Leo's disappearance at Morbio is now revealed as the League's test of the journeyers' faltering dedication. As Leo informs H. H. with a powerful phrase when the latter is finally able to re-establish contact with him, "I am still on the journey, sir, I still belong to the League" (73).

Thus the autobiographical question posed in the relationship between Leo and H. H. is that of loyalty versus apostasy, commitment to versus defection from an ideal, an issue that in a different context will also be central in *The Glass Bead Game*. And the theme of loyalty and apostasy is inextricably linked here, as it will be in the *vita* of the Magister Ludi, with that of service: Leo is the saintly and pristine image of an unswerving and Quixote-like commitment to an elusive ideal, and precisely because he is its most devoted and humble servant, he is also the hidden master of the League. Conversely, H. H. is the obtuse defector who in some ways is even more reprehensible than the young acolyte who near the beginning of the journey, in a fit of pique he later regrets, "renounced his vows and relapsed into disbelief" (17). In his condemnation of the journeyers' "intermingling of life and poetry" (18–19) and his succumbing to worldly common sense and skepticism, this passionate young defector stands for the dilemma of all those who have experienced glimpses of the third stage but have fallen back into the shallow rationalism of the second. With its typology of such failures (which is also Hesse's retrospective self-judgment), the autobiographical legend of *The Journey to the East* again resembles the myth of Wordsworth's famous ode:

> A similar thing has already happened to many other people; great and famous men have shared the same fate as this young man. Once in their youth the light shone for them; they saw the light and followed the star, but then came reason and the mockery of the world; then came faint-heartedness and apparent failure; then came weariness and disillusionment, and so they . . . became blind again. (22)

Just as H. H. is something of a caricature of the weak and despairing side of his author, so Leo is Hesse's alter ego exalted to the level of sainthood, a serene sage who, like Siddhartha, Vasudeva, and the Music Master, has attained the third level of humanization where the innocence of our first childhood is integrated with a higher faith. Appropriately enough, the heavily metaphoric ending of *Journey to the East* shows a proleptic movement from the second to the third level by means of which the weak H. H. is transformed into the ideal or "Leonine" Hessean self. Through a quasi-religious wish-fulfillment ritual Hesse demonstrates that for him autobiographical self-understanding is not static introspection but a dynamic self-grasping that implies further growth. Thus when H. H. finally consults his own file in the League archives, he discovers two figurines "made from wood or wax" (116) joined at the back. As he examines these strange idols under the light of the candles that came with them, he sees the inner substance of the "unpleasantly weak and half real" (117) figure (which represents him) melting and merging into the other (which represents Leo): "I perceived that my image was in the process of adding to and flowing into Leo's, nourishing and strengthening it. It seemed that, in time, all the substance from one image would flow into the other and only one would remain: Leo. He must grow, I must disappear" (118).[20]

The symbolic burden of this metamorphic sequence, which in a striking fashion combines two of Hesse's favorite metaphors of the self (mirroring and flowing), is that the desired "strong" self conjured in the act of writing—"the other" (*das andre*) of the passage above, a pun on Leo's last name, Andreas—must absorb the weak identity of H. H. Earlier the narrator had noted the curious fact that the characters created by writers are "without exception . . . more beautiful, happier and certainly finer and more real than the poets and creators themselves," who next to them seem "only half real, only half there" (33). Here at the conclusion H. H. recalls this phenomenon, for it obviously applies to his own, or rather, to his author's situation: the "only half alive" (33) biographical figure of Hermann Hesse will be supplemented by the much more "real" presence of his metaphoric and fictional self-incarnation. The alchemical transubstantiation of the ending with which Hesse envisions a supernumerary self, his other (*das andre/Andreas*), seems to confirm Avrom Fleishman's recent emphasis on "the inescapable alteration in the act of writing autobiography." In arguing against the deconstructive view of "this transformation of self into text" as "the autobiographer's self-destruction," Fleishman prefers to stress the autobiographer's "self-creation."[21] In the esoteric *Journey to the East*, Hesse is writing autobiographical fiction as a lifesaving type of symbolic self-creation, and does so because he knows that autobiographical narrative qua first-person biography unmediated by "poetry" is virtually impossible. Yet the later Hesse also knows that such symbolic self-creations have their limits: the figure into which H. H.'s substance flows is, after all, not Hesse, but, like Hermine and Pablo at the end of *Steppenwolf*, only a figurine—thus a fictional figment, a mere plaything and toy.

On its affirmative side *Journey to the East* is also a prolegomenon to

The Glass Bead Game that struggles to push beyond Hesse's self-es-trangement through a celebration of the perennial sources of his imagination in the hope of achieving some sort of integration with a larger community of belief. The homecoming, however, to a supra-personal ideal envisioned in this neo-Romantic quest romance is one, curiously enough, to a home built largely out of materials of Hesse's own making. His whimsically assorted and eccentric company of journeyers—famous artists, philosophers, as well as characters from his writings, and lovers, friends, and patrons of his—does not cor-respond to any existing faith or movement. The journey itself is a Hessean hobbyhorse that cuts across space and time, and the narra-tive happily explodes the geographic frame of its title, for as H. H. informs us, "our goal was not only the East, or rather the East was not only a country and something geographical, but it was the home and youth of the soul, it was everywhere and nowhere, it was the union of all times" (27). In their ability to "exchange outward and inward easily, to move Time and Space about like scenes in a thea-ter" (28), the League brothers are arch-Hessean magicians.

If theirs appears to be the metaphysical realm of simultaneity for which the later Hesse still has an unreconstructed yearning—and which indeed is suggested in a different key by the infinite holdings of the Order's archives—what is nevertheless largely absent from *Journey to the East* is the world of the Mother and eros that had played such an important role in Hesse's writings up through *Narcissus and Goldmund*. Presumably the middle-aged author had exhausted the li-bidinal side of his imagination through the "all girls are yours" career of Goldmund, and his last two novels explore the logocentric men-tality of Narcissus.[22] There are still residual touches of eros in the depiction of Leo (his youthful and vigorous appearance, his associa-tion with creaturely life, including dogs and birds, and his ability to whistle spontaneously and beautifully), and the libidinal aspect of the narrator's quest is also acknowledged (in a rather fetishistic way) when he consults the archive's file on the princess Fatima and discov-ers her "miniature portrait" wrapped in a silk cloth whose scent is redolent of the romantic dreams of his youth (94).

The Journey to the East could be described as a critical litmus test for the discerning Hesse reader, for it is a difficult and consciously self-disguising confessional parable almost entirely lacking in the popular appeal of his better-known fictions. Like all of his major books it looks before and after: back to the see-saw motion of the previous decade between hope and despair, and ahead to Hesse's final incarnation as Magister Ludi. Some of its leading ideas, themes, and strategies will be taken up and developed in a very different context in *The Glass Bead Game*, including the absorption of the individual in an intellectual fraternity of the elect, the ideal of mastery as dedicated service (and the related dilemma of those who break with the rules of the order), the exclusion of eros and the feminine by a masculine hierarchy, the playful view of life (as Leo exclaims to the desperate H. H., "that is just what life is when it is beautiful and happy—a game!" 72), and, finally, the use of narrative perspectives ironically distanced from a hidden and ever-elusive author.

The Riddling "Bird" of Montagnola

In 1935 Hesse wrote, "The Glass Bead Game . . . is the mental world in which I have been living for at least three years or more; this way of thinking slowly developed within me in connection with the myth of the Journey to the East, and frequently I live in it as if it were a genuine myth and not my own invention."[23] The *Märchen* "Bird" ("Vogel," 1932), which Hesse wrote around the time he was beginning to be preoccupied by his dream of Castalia, might serve as a caution to all aspiring interpreters of *The Glass Bead Game*, for in it, as Mileck observes, "he fantasized his relationship with his readers and particularly his critics."[24] Despite all the research, reports, and dissertations extant about him, "Vogel of Montagsdorf" (read Hesse of Montagnola), is an elusive old bird indeed, for "no other creature is able to appear and disappear with such lightning speed and almost always at the moment when one least expects it." When the ministry of culture offers a reward for him, dead or alive, a local villager, Schalaster, who has come to know his ways manages to sneak up on and shoot the unperturbed Vogel at point-blank range. But when Schalaster searches for Vogel's remains in the grass, "he couldn't find a single one of his feathers."[25]

The Glass Bead Game is Hesse's last major and unquestionably his greatest book, but also the one that has caused the most difficulties for even his best critics, who sometimes verge on suggesting that it is all but uninterpretable.[26] This crowning achievement of his career, which Hesse in one of his earliest references to it calls a "very complicated work,"[27] is maddeningly allusive and devilishly esoteric. Some of its strongest readers, while granting its status as a masterpiece, have found it to be marked by what appear to be basic defects and contradictions. For instance: Hans Mayer sees the prefatory Latin motto as conflicting with the depiction of Castalia, and asks the probing question, "should Castalia be founded if at the same time its questionability is being demonstrated?"[28] Ziolkowski detects a structural flaw inherent in Hesse's changing attitude toward Castalia during his writing of the book; and Boulby observes that it is "internally inconsistent" and that the "fiction" of the Castalian narrator "is certainly lost from time to time."[29] A number of commentators have also complained of the *Glass Bead Game*'s style as too abstract and dry, and Freedman has gone so far as to write of the world of the novel as "an arid, intellectual [one] whose harmonies remained theoretical and whose characters were puppets." A German critic in a largely sympathetic essay of 1971 criticized the book's lack of "concreteness," adding that "it is for long stretches a novel about music," and a more recent discussant describes Hesse's narrator as "hiding his identity behind a smokescreen of empty verbosity."[30] While most of these critics are aware of the fact that the interpretive difficulties posed by *The Glass Bead Game* are closely related to the later Hesse's pervasive irony, we can readily imagine the "Bird" of Montagnola laughing at them/us from behind his plumage as they/we take dead aim at his book. In the manner of one master relishing the performance of another, Thomas Mann already noted in 1947 the element of parody, persiflage, and self-disguise in Hesse's device of the scholarly biographer.[31] *The Glass Bead Game* is indeed itself a magisterial and dazzlingly intricate Glass Bead Game, and part of its author's game plan seems to be to toy with his readers, to intrigue, baffle, and even miscue them.

Take for example the matter of the influence of Hegel, which Hesse appears to signal with a strategically placed mention in the text: as a student at Waldzell, Knecht read "the German philosophers . . . among whom Hegel exerted by far the strongest attraction upon him."[32] The philosopher's version of *Geist* seems to have some affinities with Hesse's Bead Game, in which, to quote Oskar Seidlin, "the

Spirit has—to use a Hegelian term—come to itself." While the range of critical opinion on the putative influence of Hegel and on what Boulby calls "the puzzling quasi-Hegelian perspectives of the book"[33] is considerable, Hesse himself seems to minimize the significance of the Hegel reference in his text in a late letter correcting Hans Mayer's conclusion that *The Glass Bead Game* is the work of a man who has read his Hegel intensively and carefully. Hesse offers the humble disclaimer that, with the exception of the Greeks, he has never liked the majority of Western philosophers and that he has read so little Hegel as to be ashamed of it.[34] Hence the appearance of the philosopher's name in the novel seems to be the sort of clue that turns out to be a miscue but that if looked at yet again may be significant after all.

The later Hesse's confessional irony includes an intricate hide-and-seek with his audience, so that Plinio Designori's characterization of the Magister Ludi after his death appears even more appropriate as a wry Hessean self-description—and one in keeping with the "Bird" parable: "I see more and more plainly that his power was based on magic and, I must add, on a streak of roguishness. He was an arch-rogue, far more than his underlings realized, full of playfulness, wit, slyness, delighting in magician's tricks, in guises, in surprising disappearances and appearances" (299). More so than even *Steppenwolf* or *The Journey to the East*, this fiction is an extraordinary blend of the tongue-in-cheek and high seriousness, of the teasingly recondite and of plain-speaking in deadly earnest.

In a letter of November 1936 Hesse remarks that he has come to consider the first fifty-five years of his life as a preparation for *The Journey to the East* and "for the work which is to follow it and on which I have been quietly at work for almost five years."[35] Though he may be right in seeing all of his writings as a progression toward this new novel, none of his earlier books suggest such a massive and cerebral culmination of his literary career. True, Hesse's final fiction of the self still carries the signature of his perennial polarities and dualisms—the individual versus the community, the temporal versus the timeless, the aesthetic versus the religious, masculine versus feminine, mind versus nature—but these are clarified if not resolved with a serenely calm and confident mastery. The final loop of the ascending spiral of Hesse's life and art, *The Glass Bead Game*, enters Prospero's charmed circle of wisdom and power where the eternal human questions are not answered, only seen in a new and radiant light. As Boulby has put it with simple eloquence, the novel is "a luminous revisualization of the patterns of a lifetime's dreams."[36] As the wisdom book of Hesse's later years, it is also a *totalizing* work, for it seeks to integrate the many facets of Hesse's complex personality within a broad spectrum of cultural and religious traditions and values that Hesse the pilgrim soul had explored and assimilated in his reading, thinking, and living over more than four decades. To play with the metaphor of his title, each one of the myriad beads of Hesse's final game is a reflection of the microcosm, the man and writer, as well as of the greater macrocosm of the human mind and culture. What Peter Suhrkamp, the later Hesse's publisher and friend, identified as "the object of all the efforts of Hermann Hesse," was achieved by him most adequately in *The Glass Bead Game*: "an anthropology, a picture of humanity."[37]

It is the older Hesse's desire to look beyond the concerns of the individual, to the greater world of history and culture, that accounts for his stress on impersonality and "un-becoming" (*Entwerden*). Comments like that recorded by his son Bruno in 1952, "the highest is not personality; above it stands the supra-personal,"[38] reflect the changed emphasis of his *Alterswerk*, which does not overlook or deny the subjective reality of the individual—to the contrary—but which now locates all higher achievements in the actions of richly endowed and highly evolved personalities like Joseph Knecht who embody a representative and exemplary human value by virtue of which the personal merges into the suprapersonal. Or, as Pater Jacobus put it with his historicizing wisdom, "great men are . . . the raisins in the cake of world history" (151). It is in this regard that Knecht's departure from Castalia, as we shall see, is both an act of genuine self-will and a gesture of service and commitment to the greater community. Indeed, as the author of *The Glass Bead Game* seems to intimate, on a deeper level, the true needs of the individual and the community coincide.

The Long Making of *The Glass Bead Game*

In a well-known letter of 1955 to the critic Rudolf Pannwitz, Hesse explains that the germ of his novel was the idea of "reincarnation as a means of expressing the stable within the flowing" and the greater continuity of the life of the mind: "One day several years before I attempted to commit anything to paper there came to me the vision of an individual but supratemporal biography: I thought of an individual who experiences in several reincarnations the great epochs of human history. What has remained of this original intention is . . . the series of Knecht's biographies, the three historical and the Castalian." He adds that between "the first conception" and "the actual beginning of work on the book" he had to accomplish two other tasks—which is probably a reference to *Narcissus and Goldmund* and *Journey to the East*.

Mileck's inference (on the basis of this letter) that *The Glass Bead Game* had "its shadowy beginning in early 1927"[39] is supported by the vision of the Immortals in *Steppenwolf* (1927), particularly of Goethe, who from the mid-1920s on became increasingly a symbol for Hesse of a higher type of impersonal wisdom. In "Goethe and Bettina" (1924) he speaks of the "tendency of the old Goethe" to escape "from the confines of an almost overcultivated personality" into the "suprapersonal, the anonymous" through what is a process of both dying (*sterben*) and growing (*wachsen*).[40] If this description anticipates the transformation of H. H. into Leo at the close of *Journey to the East*, it is because Hesse's perception of Goethe as "a secretive old man who is in the process of progressively depersonalizing himself and disappearing altogether into anonymity" (190) is closely correlated with the ideal self-image to which the works of his final phase aspire. A 1932 essay, "Gratitude to Goethe," calls attention to the esoteric wisdom of the late Goethe: "He is timeless, because all wisdom is timeless. He is impersonal, because all wisdom transcends the person" (152). What is more, the later Hesse's identification of the later Goethe with the archetype of the sage makes for a significant link with the novel's vision of the exemplary individual as a servant of *Geist*: Goethe's wisdom, which "breathes a common air with the wisdom of India, China, Greece . . . is no longer will or intellect, but . . . devoutness, desire to serve: Tao" (152). The cultural traditions invoked here also enter into the novel, particularly that of China, and therefore it is not surprising that the Hesse who professes "a special love for the classical Chinese authors" should be "pleased to discover" in the author of the *West-Eastern Divan* "a Chinese face as well" (153).

As is evident from an outline of circa 1931 or 1932, Hesse's plans for a series of reincarnations changed considerably from his first conception to the final product. His early plans call for "X" (the name Knecht does not yet appear) to be born five times, and only two of these lives (the first, "Rainmaker with Mothers," and the fifth, "future . . . highest culture: Bead Game in many categories, encompasses music, history, space, *mathematics*") correspond to the novel as we know it. It is revealing that in this early blueprint Hesse already envisions the intellectual community of the Bead Game players subject to the forces of history and the outside world: "those who are suffering and without culture . . . smash everything (and rightly so); they hate the Bead Game players and consider them ridiculous."[41]

We do not know by what steps and stages Hesse's initial notion of several biographies of a single individual in different periods of history was modified to focus principally on the fifth, that is, the Castalian, life of this early outline—and with it, the eventual relegation of the other biographies to an appendix as the conjectural autobiographies of the Castalian Knecht. As Hesse explains in the letter to Pannwitz, however, the "poison gas" that "emanated from the speeches of Hitler and his ministers" was "the pressure of the moment" that strongly influenced the book's emerging shape and vision: "Two things mattered to me: to build up a mental space, a refuge and fortress, in which I could live in spite of the poisoning of the whole world; and . . . to express the resistance of the spirit against the barbaric forces and if possible to strengthen my friends over in Germany in their determination to resist and endure." His growing need to render Castalia "undeniably visible" as "the realm of the spirit and the soul" was also his act of inner resistance to the evil unleashed in Germany: "thus my work turned into a utopia, the picture was projected into the future, the terrible present was banished into a past that has been weathered." Hesse's way of resisting was not that of the revolutionary, the politician, or the terrorist, but that of the poet: "In the midst of these dangers and threats to the psychic and mental existence of a poet of the German language I reached for the lifesaving means of all artists, production."[42]

Probably the crudest (and still not uncommon) misunderstanding of *The Glass Bead Game* is to view it merely as Hesse's retreat into the proverbial ivory tower in order to escape the pressing issues of his time. As Martin Pfeifer has emphasized, Hesse's writing of this book was his way of making his despair at the political corruptness of his age productive by meeting its deeper demands head-on.[43] *The Glass Bead Game* is a visionary engagement with these, an act of mental and spiritual warfare in Blake's sense. To study the conception and slow emergence of the novel is to see how much it is a spirited response to the decade in which it was written, and to what extent Hesse's visionary autobiography of the 1930s—the "personal" element—is also the symbolic autobiography of his age—the "suprapersonal" element.

Hesse's explanation in the 1955 letter to Pannwitz comes nearly a decade and half after the *Glass Bead Game*'s completion, yet the general tenor of his comments on the book during the years he was at work on it is consistent with his later summary and thus indicates that we are not overhearing an aged author's unreliable and self-serving memories. This is an important matter because some have not forgiven Hesse for not openly attacking the Third Reich and aligning himself with the leftist program of the German émigré circles. It is indeed one of the bitter ironies of Hesse's life that once again, as during World War I, he was a man caught in the middle: at the very time when his book reviews were no longer welcome inside Germany and when he went out of his way in a series of contributions to a Swedish journal (March 1935–September 1936) to praise German authors blacklisted by the Nazis (including Kafka, Bloch, and Zweig), he was being maligned simultaneously in the German press by a Nazi critic for betraying German literature (because he had been corrupted by the "influence" of "the Jew Freud and his psychoanalysis"), and by the émigré *Paris Daily* (January 19, 1936) for being a Nazi sympathizer![44] Though the smear campaign against Hesse inside the Reich was eventually stopped on orders of the Ministry of Propaganda, his writings did not enjoy official favor in what Hesse in a 1933 journal already referred to as "the Reich of the loudspeakers."[45] Many of his earlier (and politically non-threatening) works were permitted to appear well into World War II, and it was not until 1943 that, as Freedman notes, "Hesse's books were actually prohibited" inside Germany.[46]

Hesse's choice not to break openly with the Nazi régime by declaring, like Mann, his solidarity with the émigré opposition, is based— in addition to his lifelong refusal to commit himself (as we saw in Chapter III) to a particular political organization or platform—on his increasingly problematic status as a German writer living outside Germany. A resident of Switzerland since 1912 (and Swiss citizen since 1923), Hesse had felt estranged from *political* Germany since World War I. Culturally, however, he was willy-nilly a German-language author who, though opposed like Goethe and Nietzsche before him to German nationalism, knew that his audience (unlike that of a Mann or a Brecht) was primarily if not exclusively German. Therefore he did not wish to force the hands of the Nazis and foreclose the possibility of his writings appearing inside Hitler's Germany. In the case of a writer whose livelihood depends on the sale of his books, financial motives can of course never be ruled out, yet it is clear that Hesse's decision was not financial—in any event, his German earnings diminished to a trickle during the Nazi period—but moral: he was motivated by a sense of responsibility and commitment toward his readers that is also evident in the massive correspondence with the many who sought his counsel and solace, and which took up more and more of his time and energies during the second half of his life. Albeit he knew that his true audience was only "a small circle of outsiders," as he acknowledged in the journal of 1933 (195), his relationship with it was precious to him, a sacred office or trust like that of the Magister Ludi. As long as his writings remained accessible in Germany he could continue to exert his literary and pedagogic ministry, to nurture and guide, encourage and admonish that core constituency of readers who had not yet succumbed to the distortion of thinking and "the mass psychosis" (191) of National Socialism. Hesse's fond hope that *The Glass Bead Game* would be able to appear inside Germany was shattered when the authorities refused Suhrkamp permission to publish the book when he submitted it to them in 1942. After Suhrkamp (whose efforts on behalf of the book may have contributed to his being finally arrested by the Gestapo and taken away to a concentration camp) returned the manuscript in person, Hesse arranged for its publication in Switzerland, where it appeared at the end of 1943. Yet he felt deeply frustrated because, as he wrote to a friend, his work would not be available for its intended circle of readers.[47]

That Hesse's refusal to publicly denounce the National Socialist régime was based on his desire to keep open his line of access to his readers, something that would be endangered or terminated by giving in, as he wrote to Mann in 1935, "to the pleasure of an occasional outburst of rage,"[48] and was not a matter of moral timidity, indifference, or worse on his part, is amply evident in the whole context of his thinking and writing during the 1930s, of which *The Glass Bead Game* is the *summa*. The early years of the new decade are particularly decisive for his emerging vision of Castalia as a counterpoise to the Third Reich: Hitler was named Chancellor in January 1933 and in August 1934 was overwhelmingly confirmed *Führer* in a national plebiscite. The first political refugees began arriving at the Casa Hesse on their way to permanent exile in the spring of 1933, including Mann and Brecht. Hesse's journal leaves no doubt about his clear-eyed assessment of "the entire mentality of the Third Reich" as "evil and infernal" (185). There he concludes that the Nazis have learned from the Bolsheviks "a new method of power and control of the masses" that represents above all a break with "the Christian conventions" (187). He also grants that, "considered from a rational viewpoint," the Soviet ideology is less crude than "the blood and race blather" of the Nazis. Though no admirer of "this Marxism and its thin rationality," he knows that in order to rival Communist propaganda, the Nazis "would have to have something more than the swastika and the blue eyes" (188). What Hesse finds most disturbing is the mounting hysteria in Germany, for behind "the swastika and the fanatical pogrom mood of the Reich" he senses "powers that cannot be refuted by reason" (188), something evident in many of the letters he receives, written "as if in the highest stage of fever, exactly like the letters of August 1914, burning . . . intoxicated hate songs" (195).

As Hesse wrestled in the privacy of his conscience with the unfolding nightmare in Germany, his vision of Castalia began to take shape. The 1933 journal already mentions three different versions of the opening section of his book, the "Introduction" to the Glass Bead Game. The first of these appears to have been written by the spring of 1932; the second was finished in July, and the third was drafted either in summer 1932 or the beginning of 1933.[49] Hesse notes in his journal that this most recent version will have to be redone, because "the spiritual condition of Germany is foretold there with such exactitude that it sounds like a parody of current events that has just been written" (184). The earlier drafts touched too directly on current political developments in Germany to ever be publishable there, particularly the third, which included a transparently satirical reference to Hitler with its account of "a leader of youth, conspirator and adventurer by the name of Litzke who for ten years was considered as 'the secret emperor' of Germany" and who perpetrated the legend of "the green blood." In Hesse's parody of the Nazis' Aryan myth, this mystical green blood was the "holy stigmata" of the nation's elite who could trace the purity of their descent for at least thirty generations: "No one dared to contradict this legend in public, for one was accustomed to terror and knew that one risked one's life if one attracted the ill will of the fanatical youth."[50] By summer 1933 Hesse realized that his satiric digs did not give his introduction the necessary "distance between Knecht's world and that of today" ("Journal of 1933," 184). The fourth and final version (May–June 1934) unfolds its critique of the first half of the twentieth century—the age of the *feuilleton*—without such specific animadversions to the Third Reich.

The rise of fascism also reinforced the older Hesse's turn, already in full progress in *Journey to the East*, as we have seen, to the logocentric values of Narcissus, and away from nature and the world of the senses in which the libidinal artist Goldmund has the roots of his being. A significant way station in Hesse's conception of Castalia as the clerical order of *Geist* is the poem "Reflection," written in November 1933 (the German title, "Besinnung," has no precise English equivalent, for it also means something like "self-recollection"). This "confession," as he put it, "in which I have sought to represent with the greatest accuracy possible the foundation of my present belief," is a crystallization, under the pressure of the historical moment, of the outlook of his final phase:

> Divine and eternal is the spirit.
> Our way leads toward him whose
> Image and instrument we are.
> Our innermost yearning is to become
> Like him, to shine in his light.

But we are created earth-bound and mortal,
Dull sloth weighs us creatures down.
Tenderly, and even with a mother's warmth,
Nature harbors us, earth gives us suck,
Cradle and grave bed us down;
Yet nature does not satisfy us,
Her maternal magic is pierced by
The father spirit's eternal spark that
Turns the child into the man,
Extinguishes innocence and spurs us on
To conflict and to conscience.
Thus between mother and father,
Between body and spirit,
The fragile child of creation vacillates,
A trembling human soul, capable of suffering
As no other creature, and capable of the highest:
Faithful, hopeful love.
His path is difficult; sin and death, his food.
Often he is lost in the dark, often
He would prefer never to have been born.
But his yearning radiates forever above him,
His fate is the light of the spirit.
And we sense that he, the endangered,
Is loved by the eternal with an extraordinary
Love. And for that reason love is possible
For us erring brothers even in division;
And not judgment and hatred,
But patient love,
Yes, loving patience
Brings us nearer to the blessed goal.[51]

Hesse's perennial mother-father myth is poetically recast here in terms of the three-stage scheme of "A Bit of Theology" of two years earlier, as the spark of *Geist* propels us from the maternal embrace of nature and our first innocence, to the second stage or moral struggle and despair, to the enlightenment of the third. In contrast to the racial and totalitarian myth of the Third Reich, Hesse's religious vision of the third kingdom is informed by the monistic premise "that beneath the division in race, color, language, and culture there lies a unity, that there are not various peoples and minds but only One Humanity, One Spirit."[52]

Hesse acknowledged with a suggestive phrase that "Reflection" was his "return to the faith of the fathers." That his attempt thus to formulate the essence of his faith in mid-decade is a response to the official Nazi ideology is indicated by his use of the terms *logocentric* and *biocentric* in a letter of 1935: "You assume correctly that the poem ["Reflection"] is based on a transformation, namely, a beginning recollection [*Besinnung*] of my heritage, which is Christian. But the need to formulate it arose from the current struggle concerning 'biocentric' and 'logocentric' outlooks, and I clearly wanted to commit myself to the 'logocentric'. "[53]

Hesse's logocentric counterpole to the Nazis' biocentric (Aryan) myth, the world of the Bead Game players, also turns on the concept of an elite, but one, as Knecht points out, based on "the old Castalian principle of selection of the best" (215). In contrast to the fascist concept of an absolute *Führer* elite that mystically embodies the will of the people, the Castalian ideal of aristocracy, as Knecht reminds the province's authorities in his circular letter (330), is not a function of blood and descent, but of qualities of mind and spirit. Moreover, the Castalian pursuit of intellectual excellence is informed by the idea of "the inner unity of all the cultural efforts of humanity . . . which has found perfect expression in the Bead Game" (213). As an intellectual aristocracy, Hesse's Castalians resemble Plato's philosopher-kings— Plato, the born aristocrat, notes Knecht, was also "the founder of a sort of Castalia" (330)—but Hesse's priestly caste is not there to tyrannize over society, like the Nazis, or even to rule over it in an enlightened manner for its own good, like Plato's philosophers, but to *serve* it by educating its young and by maintaining its intellectual and moral integrity through a strict dedication to truth. Hesse's contrasting of the Castalian cult of service to the mind with the excesses of "the late Feuilletonistic age" is his veiled attack on Hitler's régime, and, in a larger sense, on the aggressive insistence of modern nationalisms that "Mind itself must serve politics or the military. Just as the church bells were being melted down for cannons, as hapless schoolboys were drawn on to fill the ranks of the decimated troops, so Mind itself was to be harnessed and consumed as one of the materials of war" (331).

Like the Orwell of "Politics and the English Language" (1946), Hesse is centrally concerned with the betrayal of standards of truthfulness and morality for political and ideological ends, which can only result in the decline of culture and the debasement of language into propaganda. Through Knecht's summary of the Castalian code, Hesse voices his trenchant critique of those German intellectuals and writers who have, for whatever reasons, sold out or given in to a corrupt state:

> He would be a coward who withdrew from the challenges, sacrifices, and dangers his people had to endure. But he would be no less a coward and traitor who betrayed the principles of the life of the mind to material interests—who, for example, left the decision on the product of two times two to the rulers. It is treason to sacrifice love of truth, intellectual honesty, loyalty to the laws and methods of the mind, to any other interests, including those of one's country. Whenever propaganda and the conflict of interests threatens to devalue, distort, and do violence to the arts, and to everything else that is organic and highly cultivated, then it is our duty to resist and save the truth, or rather the striving for the truth, since that is the supreme article in our creed. The scholar who knowingly speaks, writes, or teaches falsehood, who knowingly supports lies and deceptions . . . no matter how things may seem at the given moment, does his people a grave disservice. He corrupts its air and soil, its food and drink; he poisons its thinking and laws, and he gives aid and comfort to all the hostile, evil forces that threaten the nation with annihilation. (332)

Like Shakespeare and Swift in their darker moments, Hesse came to perceive from the example of Hitler's Germany (whose minister of propaganda, after all, was the intellectual Goebbels) how the corruption of the mind is the ultimate evil: "The mind of man is beneficent and noble only when it obeys truth. As soon as it betrays truth, as soon as it ceases to revere truth, as soon as it sells out, it becomes intensely diabolical. Then it becomes far worse than instinctual bestiality, which always retains something of the innocence of nature"

(332). In the blunt satire of the third draft of the "Introduction" to the Bead Game a similar notion of the betrayal or prostitution of intellectual standards was expressed less effectively than in Knecht's Orwellian pronouncements above: one Professor Schwentchen, whose "specialty was not philology, but the science of tennis," provided academic support for Litzke's (Hitler's) legend of "the green blood" by writing a tome with the same title in which he "cited Zoroaster and Manu, borrowed words from the Sanskrit, the Sumerian, the Greek," though ignorant of these languages, and was rewarded by being promoted to the peak of the academic ladder—where a special professorship had to be created for him because in the glow of national celebrity he had forgotten how to play tennis.

When we consider the complex conception and genesis of *The Glass Bead Game* under the pressure of the historical moment, it should not surprise us that the book, which had already been on Hesse's mind in the late 1920s and of which he wrote one or more outlines and several drafts of an introduction in the early 1930s, should have been something rather different from what he set out to write by the time he finished it in April 1942. That the crowning achievement of a long literary career that preoccupied its author for fifteen-odd years should have at its base a fixed and unchanging conception unswervingly adhered to and executed without major alterations—like some static geometric design or an architectural blueprint—is surely an impossibility that only someone altogether deficient in an understanding of the creative process and the workings of the imagination could expect or demand. While Ziolkowski's thesis that Hesse's focus in the novel shifted from an aesthetic to an existential one may be questionable in light of early manuscript material not available to him, as Boulby and Field have asserted, Ziolkowski's larger emphasis on Hesse's changing conception and perspectives is certainly supported by the cumulative record of Hesse's writing of *The Glass Bead Game*.[54]

Once Hesse had finished the book, he was naturally inclined to seeing it as a unified whole, but as he acknowledged in a letter to Siegfried Unseld, his "perspectives changed slightly several times during its composition": "at the beginning, I was chiefly, in fact almost entirely, concerned with rendering Castalia visible, the scholars' state, the ideal secular monastery . . . an idea or wish-image which has existed since at least the Platonic academy." Subsequently he concentrated on embodying "the inner reality of Castalia" through "a dominating person, a spiritual hero"; and finally, after Knecht had moved to the center of his fiction, Hesse's focus shifted once more to depicting Knecht not primarily as "the ideal Castalian, of which there are many," but as an exemplary figure "who cannot be satisfied for the duration with Castalia and a perfection that is cut off from the world."[55] If these "slight" shifts in outlook are not as slight as Hesse would like to think, we must remember that he not only wrote *The Glass Bead Game*; he lived it for a number of years, and his three-stage résumé above demonstrates his evolving conception of his Castalian dream from a quasi-utopian ideal to a less-than-perfect cultural organism in need of renewal and reform. Indeed, his protracted vision of the pedagogic province culminates in the self-criticism inherent in the revolutionary act of submitting to the play of critical reflection, and defecting from, his model society. This, as one recent critic has convincingly argued, is "the explosive force of a criticism which in turn criticizes itself."[56]

What we know of the chronology of the book's composition[57] can be summarized as follows: Hesse wrote the appended biographies first, beginning with "The Rainmaker," which is roughly contemporaneous with the third version of the "Introduction" to the Bead Game (1933), and which was published separately in May 1934. Subsequently he immersed himself for the better part of 1934 in historical and musical studies for what has come to be known as the Fourth Life, set in eighteenth-century Swabia, where Knecht is both a student of the leading Pietist figures of the age and a passionate devotee of music. Though by far the most ambitious, substantial and promising of the non-Castalian biographies, it exists only as a long fragment in two redactions. Hesse claims he abandoned this tale (in October 1934) because the poetic element was being overwhelmed by a wealth of historical information,[58] but perhaps another reason was that, as we shall see, it began to conflict with the basic values of Castalia. Knecht's second life, "The Father Confessor," cannot be precisely dated, but it was sent out for publication at the end of May 1936; the third, or "Indian," biography was probably written last and was also submitted to the *Neue Rundschau* in April 1937 (where all three lives appeared). Only after the completion of these earlier incarnations did Hesse settle down to Knecht's Castalian career, which was chronicled by long fits and starts, and mostly in the same sequence as it appears in the book, between January 1938 and April 1942.[59] For considerable intervals the manuscript lay untouched in Hesse's desk drawer, and when he did get back to work, the writing often proceeded with agonizing slowness—he laments that the last twenty pages took him nearly a year to finish! As for Knecht's poems, all but "Stages" (May 1941), as Mileck notes, "were in print even before Hesse had finished the first chapter of Knecht's life."[60]

There are a number of reasons that account for Hesse's slow progress on what he liked to refer to as his *Alterswerk*. In moments of self-doubt he sometimes wondered if it was a matter of flagging or failing powers due to the onset of old age. As for real causes, there was, first of all, the complexity of his conception and the (aforementioned) problem of a shifting focus. Sometimes, indeed, his project promised to turn into a modern version of one of those impossibly vast and hugely ambitious Romantic superfragments, like Coleridge's (never-achieved) *Opus maximum* (a logocentric synthesis of the major branches of human knowledge that itself would have been a sort of Glass Bead Game), or Wordsworth's unfinished epic, *The Recluse*. As Hesse confided to Thomas Mann when he was immersed in research for the eighteenth-century life, his plan for the book was beginning to swell into that of "a multivolume work, even a library, and the more attractive and complete the fantasy, the further it recedes from the possibility of ever being realized."[61] Second, there was the felt trauma of Nazi Germany in the form of refugees who came to stay with Hesse and Ninon (including her sister), as well as the anxiety about the fate of relatives and friends, especially those of Ninon, living in Germany or German-occupied territories. Third, there were the time-consuming and frequently futile efforts on behalf of the refugees: Hesse noted in 1938 that at the same desk at which *The Glass Bead Game* was being written the affairs of "many refugees and émigrés were being taken care of day after day,"[62] including appeals and petitions to various authorities and bureaucrats in Switzerland, Austria, and elsewhere about matters like official papers and exit and entry visas for those seeking to leave the Third Reich. In 1931 he had already complained of the age's "leaden weight of inhumanity" as inhibiting his creative energies, and by 1938 he felt "the misery of the refugees" so acutely that he began to doubt whether he had the inner strength to finish his book. As he wrote in a poignant moment of despair, "perhaps the genuine experience (and conscious realization) of the horrors of our time is more important today than all productive activity." The seer's curse of "living in the midst of the blindness" of his age "with open eyes" took its emotional toll. In *Steppenwolf* he had already prophesied the coming of another world war, and by 1934 he was more gloomily certain than ever that "we shall soon have wars again, great wars, and take the death struggle a little further."[63]

A final and perhaps surprising reason for Hesse's slow progress on *The Glass Bead Game* is that in some sense he did not really want to finish it, for he was reluctant to put his Castalian dream behind him. Writing the book was his spiritual resistance to the evils besetting his world, but also his fortress or refuge from them—or to adapt another of his graphic metaphors, a gas mask that allowed him to breathe in an atmosphere poisoned by the Nazis.[64] When he finally finished the novel, he was sorry to have to take leave of Joseph Knecht who had been, as he confided to a correspondent, "for twelve years [his] companion and frequently [his] cover against actuality." Even in its early stages he described his "fiction of a dated future" as that of "a spiritual culture . . . which it will be worthwhile to live in and to serve."[65] And because it was an ideal "anchored" in the past via the earlier lives of Knecht but primarily and most substantially projected into the future, it is not surprising that with some regularity Hesse described his Castalian dream as "utopian": in 1934 it is "at once a utopia and a retrospect"; in 1937 it is "a sort of utopia"; and in the final phase of writing Hesse still epitomized his book with the same phrase. Only after its completion did he begin to qualify the utopian characterization, as evident from his reply to one of the earliest critics of *The Glass Bead Game*, Robert Faesi, to whom he sums up "Castalia, my utopia" as "not an ideal to be considered forever valid, but a possible world aware of its relativity."[66] In any event, those readers who are tempted to view Castalia as Hesse's utopia pure and simple should be reminded that he tends to use the (already ambiguous) term in a fairly vague and ill-defined context. An examination of his repeated use of the words "utopia" and "utopian" suggests that his meaning does not necessarily contradict Knecht's later critique and departure from Castalia, because Hesse is denoting (1) a possible, that is, hypothetical and future world, and (2) not one necessarily without flaws or beyond any need for change, but rather one obviously vastly better than and preferable to the contemporary one in which Hesse is writing—and in that respect, certainly "utopian." In other words, Hesse's use of the concept, like his book, must be viewed in the historical setting of its production.

That *The Glass Bead Game* is not just the book that Hesse wrote but the substance of the life of his imagination during the 1930s—as much mental process as product—is strikingly evident in the hexameter longpoem, "Hours in the Garden" (1936), in which he describes the reclusive ritual he practices while gardening, an activity that has both its esoteric and its practical side: he builds a fire at which he burns a mixture of wood, earth, and plant matter, all of which is then sifted, with the resulting residue of ash added to the best garden beds. For Hesse the gardener, his contemplative vigil at the fire is symbolic of the alchemical "process of purification":

> To me . . . fire signifies
> (Beyond much else that it signifies)
> A chemical-symbolic cult
> In the service of the deity,
> A transformation of multiplicity back into unity.
> And I participate in it
> As a priest and a servant,
> I complete and am completed,
> Convert wood and plant to ash
>
> ———
>
> And repeatedly I take within
> Myself through meditation
> The self-same purgatory steps
> Back from the many to the one
> Devoted to the contemplation of the divine.[67]

It is of course easy enough to lampoon such a poetic self-image, as *Der Spiegel* did in the late 1950s when it put the well-known picture of Hesse the gardener with his straw hat and his ironic smile (a photograph he liked to call "The Rainmaker") on its cover and titled its *feuilleton* essay on the last-surviving German Nobel laureate, "Hermann Hesse in the Vegetable Garden." This German equivalent of

Time or *Newsweek* offered a disparaging portrait of the quaint poet who relishes the small pleasures of gardening and who knows the language of redbreasts and holds dialogues with almond trees and cats, yet who has no significant relationship to "the international concert of world literature" and who has "refused all his life to give clear and direct opinions on current political problems."[68] True, in the poem (above) that furnished the magazine with matter for its depreciation, Hesse included an ironic disclaimer about his account of his garden ritual and his turning into "parables" his "childlike enjoyment in solitary dreaming" as being, like "all [his] writings, only a confession" (120–121). "Hours in the Garden," however, also indicates the seriousness of Hesse's thought-exercises as he "squats like a Chinese, a straw hat shading his eyes," for he is caught up, as he puts it, in

> A game of ideas which I have already
> Been pursuing for years
> Called the Glass Bead Game,
> A pretty invention
> Whose scaffolding is music
> And whose ground is meditation.
> The Master to whom I owe this beautiful
> Imagination is Joseph Knecht. (122, 124)

When Blake wrote, "The Child's Toys & the Old Man's Reasons / Are the Fruits of the Two seasons" ("Auguries of Innocence"), he meant to trivialize neither children's games nor the reasoning of the elderly, but to point to the larger reality of the imagination that contains both poles of the human life cycle. And when Hesse calls the intensely concentrated activity of his mind in the process of meditation and reflection a "game," a play of ideas (*Gedankenspiel*), he points to the serene synthesis of humor and seriousness of his final phase, a refined playfulness that may appear insignificant and trivial to the merely insignificant and trivial-minded. The esoteric thought-experiment that is the Glass Bead Game and *The Glass Bead Game* may involve a withdrawal from the world, but it is far from being a will-o'-the-wisp escape from the questions posed by and in that world. To the Hesse undertaking the strenuous spirit-exercise and exertion that is his last major book, the process and the product may have been the refuge of a "purified atmosphere" from the horrors of the Third Reich, but it was also a celebration of the best human possibilities and powers within himself, a cherishing of higher cultural values now threatened with annihilation, and a devout wish "to confront chaos with the mind and pass on to those who will come after us the belief in the spirit, both as creator and logos."[69]

In the midst of a dark time when too many of his former country-men and women lost or sold their faith or uncritically embraced a new and diabolic one, Hesse preserved and strengthened his, made the exercise of the spirit that is The Glass Bead Game his personal and timely affirmation of the suprapersonal and the timeless, and wrote his final fiction of the self to pass the torch of his faith to suc-ceeding generations. As he put it simply in January 1935, "I am in the middle of this work whose goal it is, in the midst of terror, to support clean thinking in a minority and if possible to save it from the worst and carry it across to another epoch."[70] *The Glass Bead Game* is not a utopian work in any strict or narrow sense so much as it is a work that, in the passionate instrumentality of its hope, is interested in and oriented toward a better and more human future.

Knecht's Non-Castalian Lives

The Glass Bead Game, so its author stressed, is not a work of philoso-phy, but only one of the literary imagination (*Dichtung*). Yet what he also called his "Platonic dream"[71] is a novel of ideas that in its reflec-tion on the problematic role of mind in human history and culture is concerned with some broadly philosophic issues. In fact, all four non-Castalian lives ("The Rainmaker," "The Father Confessor," "The Indian Life," and the unfinished eighteenth-century life) are varia-tions on the basic theme of service to the Mind (*Dienst am Geist*). And not surprisingly, the student-teacher relationship, which represents the oldest and most traditionally human way of transmitting the cul-tural heritage from one generation to the next, is central to all of Knecht's incarnations. Moreover, as preludes to Knecht's Castalian career, the appended biographies develop significant parallels and contrasts with that career.

Hesse's narrator describes the annual "Life" or "fictitious auto-biography set in any period of the past" (99) required of all elite stu-

dents during their period of postgraduate or "free" study as "creations of wishful thinking and exalted self-portraits" in which "they
portrayed their dream and their ideal" (100). If this is clearly an account of Hesse's own confessional procedure in scripting all of
Knecht's lives as well as a clever ploy that allows for the inclusion of
the earlier biographies *as* the Magister Ludi's writings, the narrator's
further assertion, "we regard them [the appended lives] as possibly
the most valuable part of our book" (101), must be taken with a grain
of salt. Here a tongue-in-cheek author is probably poking fun at his
narrator's solemn deference to his subject, for while the non-Castalian lives are far from negligible, they are clearly not as important or
"valuable" as the Castalian one.

The first of these, "The Rainmaker," provides, as an anthropologi-
cal recasting of Hesse's mother myth, an intriguing (and for some
reason, consistently ignored) interpretive clue to *The Glass Bead Game*.
The shorthand notation of the early outline (ca. 1931), "Rainmaker
with Mothers?"[72] is developed at the beginning of the story: "It was
many thousands of years ago, when women ruled. In tribe and family, mothers and grandmothers were revered and obeyed. Much
more was made of the birth of a girl than a boy" (314). The young
Knecht who serves as the apprentice of Turu, the Rainmaker, and
who in turn passes the art on to his own son Turu (in a pattern of
recurrence that is central to the overall conception of the novel) lives
in a primitive stone-age village ruled by "a tribal mother . . . an ancestress . . . whom everyone revered and feared as if she were a
queen" (413). This matriarchal society makes for a striking contrast
with the community of the Bead Game players, whose cult of Mind
is strictly a masculine affair: indeed, in going from the world of the
archetypal "ancestress" several thousand years in the past to that of
the Magister Ludi several hundred years in the future, we take a one-
hundred-and-eighty-degree turn from the realm of the Mothers to
that of the Fathers. Hesse's depiction of the Rainmaker's "Mother"
culture probably owes something to the Swiss anthropologist J. J.
Bachofen, whose *The Law of the Mother* (*Das Mutterrecht*, 1861), which
he had studied two decades earlier, argues that "the dominant role
of the mother . . . was a phenomenon common to all primitive societies and that this role was inseparably linked to religious beliefs that

established the secular primacy of woman on the basis of a cult of a female deity."[73]

It is important to note, however, that the early matriarchy of Hesse's tale already contains the beginnings of a masculine cult of Mind as an esoteric craft passed on from Master to acolyte. Before the boy Knecht can gain Turu's confidence and become his official assistant and appointed successor, he has to woo him and to undergo a long period of probation. What he must acquire through a blend of primitive inductive reasoning and intuition is a knowledge of the rhythms of nature that will enable him to determine the schedule of annual planting and harvesting on which the survival of the tribe depends:

> A great heritage of traditions and experience, the sum total of man's knowledge of nature at that era, had to be administered, employed, and even more, passed on. A vast and dense system of experiences, observations, instincts, and habits of investigation was slowly and hazily laid bare to the boy. Scarcely any of it was put into concepts; virtually all of it had to be grasped, learned, tested with the senses. (422)

Hesse the heir of the Romantics emphasizes that though the Rainmaker has "no culture and no arts" as we know these, "the world of his imagination" is "no poorer on that account" for he is surrounded by "inexhaustible mysteries" (420). Here the narrative explicitly rejects crude notions of human progress, for if modern science has eliminated the superstitious fear that governs the lives of these primitives, it has fallen into a hubris and an alienation of which they know as yet nothing:

> No doubt they were really seeking the same ends as the science and technology of later centuries, dominance over nature and control over her laws; but they went about it in an entirely different way. They did not stand off from nature and try to penetrate into her secrets by violence. They were never opposed and hostile to nature, but always a part of her and reverently devoted to her. (428)

Because the master-apprentice relationship is centered in the conveyance of a sacred tradition from one generation to the next accord-

ing to laws of spiritual as opposed to genetic heredity, it is only for-
tuitous that Knecht's appointed successor should also be his
biological child. The miracle of spiritual paternity consistently invoked in all of Knecht's lives is that of the "call" (*Berufung*) or vocation. This core experience shared by Master and student is to serve
(hence the significance of the name *Knecht* = Servant) the mystery of
Mind that—and here we seem to come up against the undeniably
Hegelian side of Hesse's vision—is always and already there:

> For all these ways of comprehending the world through the
> mind no doubt lay within [Knecht] . . . still in the germ, but es-
> sential to his nature . . . And if we were to go . . . several thou-
> sands of years further back into the past, wherever we found
> man we would still find . . . the mind of man, that Mind which
> has no beginning and always has contained everything that it
> later produces. (435)

The germ of Mind that is already present at the dawn of human life
develops only much later into the consciously articulated idea and
belief systems that are the arts and sciences, all the way to the abstract extremes attained in the exalted introspection of the Bead
Game. Hence Hesse's view of the instrumental role of Mind appears
to be an evolutionary and historical one in which *Geist* achieves, in
Hegelian terms, ever higher stages of conscious self-realization.[74]

"Of all that is suspect I find philosophizing about history the most
suspect," wrote Hesse in 1940.[75] Yet despite his rhetorical rejection of
such philosophizing under the acknowledged impact of Jacob Burckhardt, whose hostility (in his posthumously published *Reflections on
World History*, 1905) to Hegel's interpretation of history as the grand
progress of the rational Spirit Hesse clearly took to heart, his scripting of Knecht's lives from the Rainmaker to the Magister Ludi is quite
compatible with Hegelian thinking. Or it is so at least up to a point,
for where Hesse parts ways with the progressive and dialectic interpretation of history of both Hegel and his (revisionary) student Marx
is in his refusal to envision a final stage or end point (the Absolute
Knowledge of Hegel's *Phenomenology of Mind* as the spirit having
achieved full philosophical self-realization; Marx's vision of achieved
communism as the final overcoming of alienation). Instead, Hesse
seems to opt for a modified cyclic view that combines, as it were, the

circle with the spiral in an unending dialectic. The gist of this view, which is never presented discursively in *The Glass Bead Game*, but only implicit in the larger plot of Knecht's lives, is that the powerful cult of Mind that culminates in the symbolic language of the Bead Game is not the zenith of culture, but rather a too-limited mentality in need of renewal by what has been progressively excluded: the vital energies embodied in the primeval Ancestress, "thousands of years ago, when women ruled." The Castalian world of the Fathers, in other words, needs to turn back to the counterpole that is the world of the Mothers.

Such an overarching Nature/Mother–Mind/Father paradigm inherent in Knecht's millennial spirit-journey must be understood as inscribed, like Hesse's ongoing fictional autobiography, under the sign of the spiral and not that of the closed circle: far from being a regression back to the dark beginnings of human culture, the turn to the "Mothers" is the recovery at an advanced level of what has been lost in the course of cultural development, but without sacrificing the gains made in or through that development. The author of the logocentric *Glass Bead Game* by no means desires a return to the life of the primitives, but celebrates the values of Mind and rational consciousness even as he envisions them ultimately as endangered by a progressive divorce from their grounding in nature and the unconscious as by an atavistic throwback to mindless savagery.

Already in the matriarchal culture of "The Rainmaker," which is still in intimate contact with the mysterious forces of nature, the lines of spiritual transmission from one generation to the next have been ritualized in the master-apprentice relationship. The carefully developed scene of Knecht's initiation by the Rainmaker Turu is the model of all the subsequent teacher-student relationships in Knecht's biographies, and, as Hilde Cohn observed nearly four decades ago, contains a number of important parallels with the novel's concluding scene between the Magister Ludi and Tito Designori ("the early morning . . . a projecting piece of rock . . . the physical sensation of the cold felt by the boy, the solitude of the extraordinary hour shared with the master, and, above all, the solemn mood of the unique occasion").[76] Such similarities focus the larger coherence of Knecht's lives as based on a mystery into which both the Rainmaker's assistant and Tito are initiated by their respective magisters. Indeed, the "inner voice" (424) that Knecht hears on his initiation by Turu is analogous to the impact of the Magister Ludi's death on Tito:

> For a moment it seemed to him that the mind could grasp everything . . . This first inkling of the great mysteries . . . came to the young man in the coolness of the forest as night moved toward morning and he crouched on the rock above the multitude of whispering treetops. It came to him, touched him like a ghostly hand. He could not speak of it, not then and never in his whole life, but he could not help thinking of it many times. In all his further learning and experiencing, the intensity of this hour was present in his mind. (423–424)

If this powerful experience confirms the youth in his identity and his calling, it is also Hesse's version of the Romantic sense of cosmic unity, a "presentiment of wholeness, the feeling of connections and relations"—in Knecht's case, a radical intuition that he will "be able to grasp the whole world . . . and to discern, in every part and sign, every other part" (424).

Young Knecht's initiation into the cult of *Geist* is therefore also a movement toward the center—the esoteric goal of the Glass Bead Game—and the quintessential experience of "awakening" that will mark the major episodes of the Magister Ludi's life. A crucial difference, however, is that the novice Rainmaker cannot consciously realize his feelings *as* thoughts, the way the Magister Ludi—and Hesse—can in the luminous abstractions of the novel:

> All this was experienced and preserved by Knecht . . . as his admission into a league and a cult, into a humble but honorable relationship to the Unnamable, the cosmic mystery. This and many other similar experiences could not be put into thoughts, let alone words. Even more remote from his way of thinking, even more impossible than any other thought, would have been words such as this: "Is it only I alone who have created this experience, or is it objective reality?" (425)

In the infancy of the human race as in the magic realm of childhood invoked by the Romantics, the great divide between inner and outer, subject and object has not yet cast its shadow.

The Glass Bead Game's ideal of service includes the necessity of self-sacrifice to the point of laying down one's life if circumstances should require it. Turu is only threatened by this dire fate that Knecht, having become Rainmaker in his turn, must suffer when his magic refuses to prevail against a prolonged drought that threatens the survival of his community. When a hostile nature refuses to yield to his powers, the community's faith in his office is compromised, something that can only be restored by his becoming the willing scapegoat of its mounting resentment and fear. In the earlier crisis of a spectacular meteorite shower of several hours' duration[77] that had driven the terrified villagers to the brink of "madness, fury, and self-destructiveness" (444), Knecht had only been able to maintain public order through the master-stroke of converting the rising hysteria into a ritual of dancing and chanting. His *sang froid* had managed to transform a chaotic scene into an "orderly chorus of the multitude," in a restorative process in which music played a crucial role. In this second crisis, however, Knecht can only appease the forces of chaos and ensure that his apprentice and son will be able to carry on after him, and thus maintain unbroken the succession of Mind, by offering up his life.

It should also be noted that with the motif of Knecht's ritual murder Hesse introduces the issue of human evil. This is focused through the character Maro, who had earlier sought to be Knecht's assistant but had eventually been rejected by him because Knecht saw that he was one of those "highly talented" but unprincipled who wish "to rule without being able to serve" (439) and who only strive "for power and advantage over others" (438). In the symbolic character of Maro we again have the gist of Hesse's idea that the truly evil are those who have corrupted their higher powers and put them in the service of their basest impulses. The evil student who now heads the chorus of drummers and who actively incites the group's paranoia and resentment against Knecht is also Hesse's psychological profile of a Hitler-type of demagogue. Knecht, however, defeats his enemy by offering himself as a victim before this is demanded of him, and by nominating Maro as his executioner. In his public humiliation of Maro, who is unable to perform the bloody deed demanded of him, Knecht reveals the cowardice behind the cunning of his enemy and affirms the triumph of mind even at the moment of his sacrificial death.

The two other Lives appended as the writings of the Castalian Knecht are slighter performances and not as significantly related to the central biography of the novel as is "The Rainmaker." "The Father Confessor" is set in fifth-century Egypt and contrasts the personalities and careers of two Christian desert hermits who, in order to make "up for the pleasure-seeking, brutality, and sensuality of many past and future ages" (455), practice an ascetic "*ars moriendi*" far removed from the Rainmaker's nature lore. In the outlook of these Patristic penitents we see a later stage of culture in which "Mind" has separated itself from and is carrying on a heroic struggle against our lower nature. Thus their self-mortification is in the service of a higher humanity of which their office as confessors and soul-healers is the exemplary and applied instance. Joseph Famulus [a Latin version of *Knecht*], the younger of the two, has excelled in the art of gentle listening as his way of absolving sinners, whereas Dion Pugil, as his name ("Boxer") implies, is known as "a great judge" and "chastiser" who "ordered marriages, compelled enemies to make up, and enjoyed the authority of a bishop" (457). If, as Field claims, "the two hermits represent the *vita contemplativa* and the *vita activa* respectively," this contrast may include an allusion to those legendary Chinese opposites that have been identified as important influences on *The Glass Bead Game*, Lao Tzu, with his quiet mysticism, and Confucius, with his stress on ethical action in the world.[78] In fact the latter, like Dion Pugil, was famous for his robust strength.

The themes of defection and spiritual paternity are brought together in "The Father Confessor" when both Famulus and Pugil, unbeknownst to each other, succumb to self-doubt and despair. Having fallen victim to the occupational hazard of those whose lives are dedicated to service, each decides to seek out the other for comfort and guidance: as we know from the legends of Confucius and Lao-Tzu, such antithetical spirits attract one another. The ironic upshot of their encounter is that each is reconfirmed in his calling through service to the other. Famulus, who confesses first, is taken by Pugil to his hermitage and becomes his assistant, and at the end of Pugil's life, his declared "son" (482) and successor. Only before his death does Pugil admit to Famulus that he too had abandoned his office and was en route to confess to Famulus when the latter, as it were, beat Pugil to the punch: "The more I put myself into his place, the sorrier I was for Joseph, and the more it seemed to me that God had sent him to me so that I might understand and cure him, and in so doing cure myself" (482). Like Hesse's other saints, Pugil departs this life with a "radiant smile" (483). It is noteworthy that the temporary defection of the two men from their religious offices presents a partial parallel with the Knecht who at the start of his tenure as Magister Ludi decides that he will give up his office if he should ever grow weary of it.[79] The crucial difference between the two confessors and the Magister Ludi, however, is that the former seek to abandon their calling because of a crisis of doubt, whereas the departure of the latter is the active fulfillment of his life's meaning.

"The Indian Life" has some nice poetic touches and also makes for a considerable contrast in setting and emphasis with "The Rainmaker" and "The Father Confessor." It can be read as the late Hesse's final fictional tribute to the world of Indian spirituality that had meant much to him at an earlier stage of his life before the impact of the Chinese philosophical tradition began to displace it. The tale of Dasa (the Sanskrit variant of *Knecht*), the rajah's son and foundling child who is raised by shepherds, is cut from the timeless cloth of fairy tale and legend. The worldly life of pleasure and passion that he leads as a young man—he marries the beautiful Pravati, only to lose her to his half-brother, the rajah Nala, whom he murders, to become a hunted criminal—presents a striking contrast to the lives of the other Knechts, whose dedication to the values of the mind takes the form of an active commitment to serving their fellow humans.

The concluding sentence of "The Indian Life" ("he never again left the forest," 520) signals the Hindu, and in its attenuated version, the Buddhist, note of this Eastern version of a strictly passive *vita contemplativa*. Like his other namesakes, young Dasa receives the spirit-call from a master, the solitary yogi deep in meditation in the forest who makes Dasa sense "the presence of divinity" (487) through "the complete dedication of his service" (488). After his libidinal plunge into a worldly life that ends with his killing of his brother, Dasa returns to the forest only to suffer from unquenched desire for Pravati. His master then teaches him an unforgettable lesson about Maya, or the world of appearances. (This episode, incidentally, is also a marvelous trick played by Hesse on his readers.) Sent by the yogi to fetch water at a spring, Dasa encounters Pravati, from whom he learns that he, the cast-out foundling and criminal, has been sought everywhere as the new rajah. Dasa eagerly plunges back into a life of pleasure and power whose epitome is the sexual bond with Pravati, the female temptress and symbol of worldly illusions. Dasa, however, suddenly awakes from the bitter end of this life (his son murdered by, and he and his estranged wife prisoners of, his arch-enemy) only to find that he is still standing by the spring to which he had gone at the yogi's behest. This is Hesse's exotic version of *we are such stuff as dreams are made on*, and of the "revolving [Samsara] wheel" of creaturely life (519) from which Dasa gladly "awakens" to a yogi's life of "discipline and service" to "a realm beyond pictures and stories" (520). Hesse may have found this Indian version of the mind's total withdrawal from the world an attractive fantasy, but in the final analysis this is also his tale of the road not taken.

The unfinished eighteenth-century life, which is much longer than any of the appended narratives, deserves at least equal consideration with the others, because this very revealing tale provides some significant counter-perspectives on Knecht's Castalia. Hesse's decision to set one of his conjectural autobiographies in the Protestant-Pietist world of eighteenth-century Swabia takes him close—perhaps too close—to his cultural and personal roots, and represents his last attempt to deal with that powerful constellation of family, religion, education, and budding artistic vocation that defines the tensions of his early years and that already at the start of his literary career had frustrated his essay in autobiographical self-understanding in *Beneath the Wheel*.

Now, some three decades later, he makes some important changes in the fictionalized landscape of his youth: unlike Giebenrath, and like the Castalian Knecht, the Swabian Knecht is a first-rate student who passes with ease through a succession of church-run schools on his way to a clerical career. Unlike Giebenrath, he is not troubled by the sexual demons of puberty: presumably the sexagenarian Hesse had no further interest in such long-forgotten traumas. A basic conflict of Hesse's life since early adolescence, however, emerges with new clarity, for this Knecht is torn by the aesthetic and the religious impulses within him, between his goal to become "a priest, a servant of God" and that "to make music, to learn how to play the organ . . . to serve art."[80] Like the other Knechts, he also experiences a powerful call, which comes when at the age of seven he is the unwitting witness of the head of his religious community, "the honored and rather feared preacher, the man of God, the father of all" (114), wrestling in the privacy of his chamber with his conscience and his God. While the "symbolic force" (110) of this moment propels him toward the priesthood, his love of music, nurtured by both profane and sacred song, is also very much a part of his childhood and begins during his student years to rival and finally to overshadow his clerical vocation. The longer of the two fragments (of nearly eighty pages) ends with Knecht having completed his theological studies at Tübingen, but Hesse's outline for the remainder of his life indicates that he later resigns his priestly office to become "a quiet organist" (179). It should be apparent from this summary that the Swabian Knecht's turn from the priesthood to a simpler and more fulfilling way of life that does not deny but rather extends to other areas his desire to serve presents something of a parallel to the Magister Ludi's resignation of his office to become a tutor.[81] As a church organist he will, like Hesse the writer, be able to give both religion and art their due.

A very surprising feature indeed of the eighteenth-century biography is its inversion, in the depiction of Knecht's parents, of Hesse's usual association of the male with Mind and the female with Nature. In some regards this marriage is like that of Mr. and Mrs. Morel in Lawrence's *Sons and Lovers*, for it involves the same set of symbolic contrasts, but without any of the overt Oedipal stresses of Lawrence's family romance. Like the coal miner Morel, Knecht's father has the roots of his being in the subterranean life of nature, while his mother embodies, like Mrs. Morel, the ego drives of will and consciousness that propel her son away from the father's world of instinct toward the mother's sphere of mind. This juxtaposition of "dark" and "light" realms goes back as far as the conflicts of young Giebenrath and Sinclair, but now it is the father who is symbolically associated with the life force: he is the "fountain-maker" responsible for the community's water supply, a job that includes making sure that the wooden pipes carrying the water from the springs in the forest to town are in good repair. His is a solitary occupation, for like Lawrence's Mellors (another keeper of the life force), he spends much time alone in the woods, is sparing of speech, and rather out of place in his home. He likes folk tunes, which he plays on "a small wooden flute" (105), an instrument that turns up again at a crucial juncture in the Castalian Knecht's life. His wife, who comes from a more cultivated and clerical family, is like her husband a devotee of music, but unlike him, she inclines to church hymns. Thus music is the common ground of this marriage of opposites, which however is not harmonious, because the wife's attempt to spiritualize her husband has succeeded only in part: occasionally he goes off on a discreet drinking spree to give "vent to the remainder of his drives and instincts which cannot be disciplined" (107).

Hesse's sketch of this difficult marriage in no way corresponds to the relationship between his parents, but it does provide a suitable backdrop against which to dramatize his protagonist's conflicted musical and religious drives. Moreover, this family portrait shows that for once he was capable of departing from his male and female stereotyping, and to present a father who has his being in Hesse's "mother" world, and vice versa. If the pressure Knecht's mother puts on him to enter "the thoroughly masculine and timeless world" (127) of the church may reflect Marie Hesse's ambitions for her favorite offspring, Hesse's characterization of a mother who champions the values of the father world is very different from the matriarchal Ancestress of "The Rainmaker" and the corrupt temptress Pravati of "The Indian Life." That Hesse's treatment of Knecht's parents here does not quite fit into the *Glass Bead Game*'s model of a masculine cult of Mind may be one reason why he left what is surely the most ambitious and promising of the non-Castalian lives unfinished. Only in the light of the (later) Magister Ludi's departure from Castalia does Hesse's inversion of male and female images begin to make sense as a sort of symmetrical complement or early counterpoint to the one-sided value-system of the Bead Game players. Indeed, there is one more explicit and startling counter-perspective on the later Castalian mentality in the Fourth Life of 1934, which I will only mention now and discuss later in connection with the narrator's "Introduction" to the Bead Game: the subversive evaluation of the meaning of "classic" works of art.

Introductory Matter to *The Glass Bead Game*

The Glass Bead Game is ringed by concentric circles of Hessean mystification: first comes the choke-pear title (*The Glass Bead Game: A Ten-*

THE UN-BECOMING SELF 281

tative Sketch of the Life of Magister Ludi Joseph Knecht Together with Knecht's Posthumous Writings Edited by Hermann Hesse), then the dedication ("to the Journeyers to the East"), the table of contents, and finally, the pedantic heading of the opening chapter ("The Glass Bead Game: A General Introduction to Its History for the Layman") followed by a Latin citation and "Joseph Knecht's holograph translation." The cumulative impact of all this on the reader might be summarized as, "ye who enter here, be prepared to find it tough going." The book's blend of the tongue-in-cheek with high seriousness is epitomized by the prefatory citation, whose Albertus Secundus is none other than Hesse, who had two friends render his German version (1932) into medieval Latin, and repaid them by encoding their last names (Schall = Clangor, and Feinhals = Collof.). Yet implicit in this hoax of a fictive scholarly quotation is the whole visionary dynamic of hope that is *The Glass Bead Game*, summed up in the paradox that "non-existent things" (objects of reflection and imagination) can be brought "a step closer to existence and the possibility of being born" only if "serious and conscientious men treat them as existing things" (2).

The citation's playful paradox also signals an important if problematic element of this novel's reflection on being and becoming, namely, a Platonizing tendency that exists side by side with the historical (and historicizing) account of the pedagogic province. Such a double perspective informs the narrative right from the start, beginning with the "Introduction," which insists on the one hand that the Bead Game, "like every great idea . . . has no real beginning" (7), but on the other hand, presents Castalia as a historical development of and reaction to the twentieth century—with a series of significant antecedents from Pythagoras and Plato to the scholastic philosophers, Leibniz, and Hegel. The Castalian narrator underscores the transcendent and metaphysical character of the Castalian ideal with his description of the Bead Game as a symbolic and "highly developed secret language" based on mathematics and music that constitutes "the *unio mystica* of all the separate members of the *Universitas Litterarum*" (28). Yet at the same time his summary of the game's synthesis of all the arts and sciences as a type of "worship" without "any theology of its own" (31) identifies Castalia as the late product of an aging culture whose "epitome and quintessence" is the "cheerful serenity" of the period of classical music "between 1500 and 1800" (33–34).

Writing some six centuries after the end of that efflorescence and in the full (Spenglerian) awareness that "the youth and creative period of our culture was over" and that "old age and twilight had set in" (15), the narrator acknowledges Castalia's cultural belatedness and its fundamentally uncreative character. Its very devotion to the cultural riches of the past is a function of its renunciation of "trying to vie creatively with those generations" (18). Already in the "Introduction" the Castalians are implicitly (post)modern midgets parasitically perched on the shoulders of classical giants, sustained by the creative energies of a past to which they cannot add anything but a finer and fuller appreciation in their "uncreative, epigonic, but reverent fashion" (18). Nor is it possible to arrest the narrator's historical retrospective at the time he is writing (circa 2400 A.D.), for by the logic of temporal implication his narrative points, not to the timeless center of the Bead Game, but to a Castalian future that will become progressively more uncreative and epigonic the further it is removed in time from the classical peak of European civilization. In sum, even before we read his biography of the Magister Ludi or encounter the spirited attacks of Plinio Designori and Pater Jacobus, it follows from the narrator's historical overview that Castalia is caught up in a type of cultural entropy, of which his very style (with its stance of pseudo-objectivity, exaggerated deference to his subject, and general sense of belatedness and inferiority) is itself the linguistic correlative. The only possible way to halt if not reverse the protracted process of decline is for the Castalians to cease being strictly Castalian, that is, to open up, like Knecht, to the call of life, to become creative again, to combine *logos* with *eros*. (Since the Magister Ludi of this sanctioned biography did precisely this not only in the last stage of his life but also in his youth through the nonsanctioned activity of writing poetry, and since this official biography includes his poems as well as a series of devastating critiques of the Castalian mentality, the narrator's chronicle of Knecht and Castalia might be seen as something of a Trojan horse—or as the tool of Hesse's irony.)

Perhaps another way to put this matter of the double perspective inherent in the "Introduction" is to distinguish between the Castalian ideal and Castalia as a human reality and a cultural institution. It is important to keep in mind that Hesse is not attempting a meta-physical description of *Geist*, but only of a particular human approach to it. Like the hierarchy of the Catholic church (an analogy fairly consistently maintained throughout the book), that of the pedagogic province serves and celebrates a transcendent principle, but is far from being identical with it. As a cultural establishment it is prone, despite its high aims, to the historic shortcomings of human institutions. Only in the Castalian equivalent of the papal high mass that is the Magister Ludi's annual celebration of the Bead Game does the exercise of Castalian spirituality, as Knecht emphasizes to his students, point toward the metaphysical "center" on which it is founded. But in so doing, Castalia also points beyond itself as a historical entity, and in fact, transcends itself at the moment of its most adequate self-realization: such is the gist of Hesse's nontheological (and quasi-Hegelian) theology.

The negative implications of the narrator's introductory sketch of Castalia also create an appropriate background against which to project the Magister Ludi's unusual life. The vital impulses that inform it ultimately run counter to the Castalian view of culture as a closed pantheon to which no new works can now be added—a tradition with no more room for individual talent—but only, in extremely rare instances, new signs for works and ideas from the past that have not yet been taken up into the language of the Bead Game. Unlike Knecht, the Castalians are the opposite of Harold Bloom's strong poets contending with their literary forbears for mastery and independence. In a higher sense they can never come of age because, like Swift's rational horses, they are moral eunuchs, forever cut off from the passional sources of life, of which the great works of art are the sublimates in the human imagination. So long as they remain mere Castalians, lacking Knecht's capacity to change and grow, they are doomed to the second-hand existence of vicariously living off the creative accomplishments of earlier ages. Their cult of the past threatens to become a *rigor mortis* and seems to call for the antithetical and infernal wisdom of Blake's proverb (in *The Marriage of Heaven and Hell*), "drive your cart and your plow over the bones of the dead."

It is here that Hesse's valuation of "classic" works of art in his eighteenth-century life (written the same year as the final version of the "Introduction") provides an illuminating interpretive gloss. In his discussion of the impact of leading Pietist theologians on the Swabian Knecht, the narrator of the Fourth Life casts "a sidelong glance" at the efforts of the Glass Bead Game to translate humanity's greatest cultural achievements into its "hieroglyphics" (163). He is very much tempted to bring the ideas of "figures like Bengel and Oetinger" (whom Hesse much admired) into the game, but he grants reluctantly that this is not feasible because their impact, which was "subterranean" and local, has been forgotten, while that of a contemporary of theirs like Voltaire was spectacular and cosmopolitan and has thus been enshrined in the game. The problem with the game's narrow and exclusive canon is that the forgotten and "subterranean" works and ideas may ultimately be more important and valuable than those that have been admitted into Castalia's pantheon of the mind, just as these obscure German thinkers (and their "occult master," Jakob Boehme) working in the literary underground of the Enlightenment (like Blake in England), may be possessed of more imaginative force than the well-known but rather limited works of that polemical freethinker and citizen of the world, Voltaire.

These startling comments in the unfinished Fourth Life are subversive of the entire value system on which Castalia and the Bead Game are founded. Through the narrator (whose reference to the game identifies him as the Castalian Knecht), Hesse voices the Romantic and

> heretical opinion . . . that the classic manifestations of the spirit are to be valued by no means higher than those that are subterranean and anonymous, but on the contrary, that all classicists and all classic works are not donors and creators, but rather consumers of the spiritual heritage, and that it is precisely the unclassical and frequently nameless movements that constitute the true source of power and that preserve and increase the cultural inheritance. All classical authors stand at an end, are inheritors and consumers, and an efflorescence like Mozart's contains alongside that radiance which brings us joy always its opposite as well, namely, the saddening intuition that at such a peak an old, slow, and noble process of growth is not being renewed but exhausted and spent. (166)

This anti-Castalian reflection—which, incidentally, contains a probing insight into the cultural dynamics of canon formation that has only recently become a major concern of contemporary criticism—is an incisive exposé of the questionable nature of the Castalian cult of the "classic," and of the deeper meaning of its belated and unproductive frame of mind that the Magister Ludi (who as a student supposedly authored these sentiments) transcends at the peak of his Castalian career.

Another important element of the "Introduction," and one that has understandably appealed to Marxist critics, is the witty attack on the first half of the twentieth century as the Age of the Feuilleton. With his fiction of a Castalian scholar living in a dated future and looking incredulously back at the low point of our century, Hesse employs the trick perspective of the satirist that is meant to shock us into seeing ourselves as we really are. What is remarkable about the fourth and final version of the "Introduction" (from which all direct allusions to the political events of the 1930s were expunged) is how applicable and relevant it is to the cultural situation of the West in the later twentieth century. Hesse was more farsighted than he realized, for television, public relations, and the mass media have perfected many of the features identified by the historian Plinius Ziegenhals (Goatneck) in his anatomy of the Age of the Feuilleton.

Just as this "emphatically bourgeois" era was given to "an almost untrammeled individualism" (9–10), so our popular culture has reached new lows in its celebration of the deviant, the bizarre, and the perverse; just as its *feuilletons* "were a source of mental pabulum for the reader in want of culture" and "reported, or rather, 'chatted' about, a thousand-and-one items of knowledge" (11), so our media specialize in conveying a numbing flow of trivia; just as its papers were fond of "interviews with well-known personalities on current problems" (12), so our celebrated talk show hosts know how to satisfy the public's curiosity by linking "a well-known name with a subject of current interest" and to interview, "for example . . . popular actors, dancers, gymnasts, aviators, or even poets . . . on the benefits and drawbacks of being a bachelor, or on the presumptive causes of financial crises" (12). Like that of the Age of the Feuilleton, so the popular journalism of our time, from *People Magazine* and *Life Styles of the Rich and Famous* to highly rated national news broadcasts and "infotainment" shows, knows how to capitalize on "the anecdotal, historical, psychological, erotic, and other stuff" that is "the catchword of the moment" (12) in order to garner higher viewer ratings.

Much of our popular literature also "bears the mark of mass goods rapidly and irresponsibly turned out" (12). The trade in lecturing by "celebrated university professors" has its counterpart in some of our colleges and universities whose course listings also serve up a "gigantic consumption of empty whimsies," though Hesse's satirical lecture titles, "The Role of the Lapdog in the Lives of Great Courtesans" and "Friedrich Nietzsche and Women's Fashions of 1870," are perhaps a little too highbrow for what has gone on under the name of higher education on some campuses during the last two decades.

In sum, some of the larger cultural ills that Hesse targets with his satire in the context of the 1930s are very much with us in our time and have, if anything, multiplied apace, including "the dreadful devaluation of the Word" (14) in a consumer society of material and cultural overproduction, the abandonment of moral and intellectual standards, the rule of the demagogue and the celebrity, and, in a larger sense, "the dreary mechanization of life, the profound debasement of morality, and the decline of faith among nations, the inauthenticity of art" (15). Admittedly next to the miasma of the Age of the Feuilleton and its contemporary equivalents, the Castalian world with all its limitations and its deeper problematic can take on, in moments of revulsion, the near-utopian attractions of a country in romance.

Hesse's Bridging of Polarities

The exemplary figure of the Magister Ludi is Hesse's principal "incarnation" in the Castalian "Life," but many of the other characters, as Mileck has shown in some detail,[82] are also partial self-portraits, including the Music Master, Plinio Designori, the Elder Brother, and Master Alexander. Even those antithetical figures, Fritz Tegularius and Pater Jacobus, who are modeled on Nietzsche and Jacob Burckhardt respectively, refer us back to Hesse: the former to the young poet enamored of the philosopher's writings, the latter to the older author who had learned from the famous historian of the Italian Renaissance to look at human life through the lens of history and to see, as he acknowledged in 1943, his "utopia, Castalia, in its relativity."[83] Still other characters such as Knecht's friend Carlo Ferromonte and the Magister Ludi who precedes him in office, Thomas von der

Trave, are teasing allusions to real persons: the former is Hesse's nephew Karl Isenberg (Ironmountain) who helped him with musical studies for the Fourth Life; the latter points (with a measure of ironic circumspection) to Thomas Mann, the more famous and honored colleague (born near the river Trave) who strongly encouraged Hesse to finish *The Glass Bead Game* and who nominated him for the Nobel Prize after its publication.[84] Through Knecht's varied dealings with these other characters Hesse sets up an intricate autobiographical overview that in effect takes in different areas of his experience and periods of his life.

The key to the Magister Ludi's personality lies in the paradox that he is the non-Castalian Castalian par excellence. From his first entry into the elite schools he is one of the "lucky" ones who, as the narrator observes on several occasions, by virtue of his talents and strength of character—and without any careerism on his part—is bound for success in a system that targets him for rapid advancement and positions of increased responsibility. In fact, his academic career is the inverse of Hesse's at Maulbronn, which was as brief and unlucky as Knecht's was long and spectacular. Under the auspices of the confessional imagination, Hesse scripts a wish-fulfillment *vita* of what might have been.[85] Yet this fortune's minion who rises so effortlessly and so early to the peak of the Castalian pyramid is never a pure Castalian, but always something more and other. He has an extra dimension, a certain surplus of talent and energy, which enables him to succeed within the system but preserves him from being wholly absorbed or defined by it.

It is this non-Castalian aspect of Knecht that emerges more clearly with every rereading of the book. Despite the narrator's dry account, it is evident from the opening paragraphs that *Eigensinn* is the leitmotif of Knecht's life: "Like every man of importance he had his *daimonion* and his *amor fati*" (36). Young Knecht is also one of the fortunate ones, unlike young Hesse, whose inner demon "manifests itself . . . free from somberness and fanaticism" (37). Even if the narrator is not quite capable of understanding these urges from within, Hesse gets his point across well enough by occasional reminders—for instance, the later mention of "a certain inner independence, a self-reliance [*Eigensinn*] that by no means barred or hampered him from serving, but demanded that he serve only the highest master" (119–

120). Knecht's insistent though highly controlled self-will is what impels him to leave Castalia at the peak of his tenure as Magister Ludi. Field calls attention to the fact that he "possesses . . . the Faustian quality of striving" that he formulates in his poem "Stages" (or "Steps")[86] once he has become fully aware of the dynamic informing his life. Even the Magister Ludi's final "step" beyond Castalia contains an autobiographical reference back to the failure of the unruly fourteen-year-old who ran away from Maulbronn—only this time, as E. R. Curtius observes, "its signs are reversed from negative to positive."[87] The Maulbronn escapade had branded Hesse with the mark of the outcast and the rebel, the prodigal and the failure; now, almost a lifetime later, his dream of Joseph Knecht propels him to the most honored position in an academic hierarchy similar to the one at whose hands he suffered such a precipitate defeat—only to have him turn his back on it because it fails to satisfy his deepest needs. Hence the ironic autobiographical burden of Hesse's compensatory plot of the academic road not traveled is that it leads him in the end right back to where in a sense he has been all along: on the narrow path of his *daimonion* and *amor fati*.

Though understandable, the complaint of many early readers and critics of *The Glass Bead Game* that the end of Knecht's life makes for a disappointing anticlimax is largely unfounded insofar as it ignores the carefully developed pattern that shows convincingly that the talents and inclinations that initially draw Knecht to Castalia are ultimately also those that launch him beyond it. It is indeed remarkable that every one of the twelve chapters of his biography contains at least one significant (and sometimes polemically voiced) anti-Castalian counter-perspective, and that in the aggregate these place an increasing stress on the non-Castalian side of Knecht—to the point where his need for a self-realization beyond Castalia emerges, in the last third, as the focal point and final aspiration of his life. Like the holy city of Yeats's "Sailing to Byzantium" (1927), the spirit-temple of Castalia is the artifice of eternity, and its high priests become for a time the singing masters of Knecht's soul. Yet like the older Yeats, the older Hesse cannot long abide a static perfection beyond "what is past, or passing, or to come," which inhibits and must in turn yield to his Romantic need for *becoming*. What is already implicit in the early chapters—that Knecht is not fully at home in Castalia—becomes explicit by Chapter 7, "The Two Poles." His higher sense of homelessness is poignantly expressed in the poem ("Stages") whose verses come to him as the haunting *credo* of his life at the crucial juncture of his impending resignation.

There is a delicious irony in the fact that Knecht's literal-minded biographer allows for the element of poetry that marks Hessean autobiography with the reminder, "we must not forget that the writing of history—however dryly it is being done and however sincere the desire for objectivity—remains literature. History's third dimension is always fiction" (31). Like those of the earlier incarnations, the autobiographical legend of the Castalian life also turns on a spirit-call inherent in the momentous encounter with a master. The opening note of that "life" become "legend"—whose chronicler from the start posits "a clear succession of stages" and dismisses the possibility that Knecht's "death could have been a matter of pure chance" (38)—is the Music Master's interview with the boy Knecht at the Latin school at Berolfingen. The "symbolic . . . call" that Knecht receives is not primarily to Castalia the pedagogic institution, but to the ideal—"the realm of Mind" (39)—on which it is founded. In the larger scheme of *The Glass Bead Game* the sacramental "voice of his vocation" that Knecht hears is really the first stage of what he later comes to define as the "core . . . experience" (46) of "awakening." At this early juncture the desire to serve that is roused in him does not conflict but largely coincides with the expectations of the Order on whose lowest rung he will be positioned as an elite student at Escholz. For now, Castalia fosters his inner powers, and provides the appropriate setting for his intellectual development.

Knecht's "election" by the Music Master reveals that the experience of "awakening" as a fateful movement or "evolution" (47) from one stage to the next is a mixed blessing that entails not only the sweet "moments of supreme rejoicing and radiant self-assurance" at shedding the dead skin of an outgrown past, but brings with it as well "something akin to guilt" at being thus singled out.[88] Indeed, in the poignant memoir Hesse wrote in 1936 for his brother Hans (who had committed suicide that year), he explicitly analyzes "awakening" as a crucial experience of his adolescence. He recalls vividly how, at the age of thirteen or fourteen, he had felt a sudden sense of superiority while observing the radiant expression of childish joy on his (five-years-younger) brother's face as the latter opened his Christmas presents: the "core and meaning" of this charged moment is the realization, analogous to the Christian *felix culpa*, that his own childhood is over: "I saw and suddenly knew that I was no longer a child; I was older and more clever than Hans, but also meaner and colder." The truth that the boy Hesse could only sense and that the adult writer can consciously recollect and formulate—"that there is no process of growth that does not also contain an element of dying"[89]— also informs the narrative of Knecht's life and is crystallized in the concluding sentiment of "Stages," that life is a perpetual leavetaking.

The opening chapter already points Knecht beyond Castalia in two different ways that will be repeated and varied throughout the remainder of the narrative. The first of these is his ambivalent attitude to those students who are dismissed from the elite school. Despite the fact that the adolescent soon feels very much in his own element at Escholz, he cannot accept at face value the authorities' evaluation that the expelled scholars have simply failed, but is troubled by the thought that their return to "the world" is not necessarily a "relapse" or "a fall," but may well be "a leap forward and a positive act" (59). In these early reservations we can see the germ of the later Magister Ludi who resigns his office. As Knecht confides to his mentor, the appeal of those who are sent down is that of the rebellious angel Lucifer—and when he explains the attraction the idea of "leaping" holds for him, he already anticipates the meaning of his final leap into the mountain lake as a positive and existential act: "I do wish that if ever the time comes and it proves necessary, that I too will be able to free myself and leap, only not backward into something inferior, but forward and into something higher" (63).

Knecht's second pointer beyond Castalia is, ironically, the very Master who was responsible for his entry into its elite schools. His first and foremost Castalian mentor, the Magister Musicae, is an exception, like the Elder Brother, to the Castalian mentality, for his values ultimately transcend the intellectual establishment in which he plays such a prominent role. In light of his conversations with his young protégé it is not surprising that he too finds a way of passing beyond Castalia: like the Elder Brother, and unlike Knecht, he will rise above it from within, through the mysterious metamorphosis of his silent and smiling end, which the Castalian officials either ignore or write off as senility, but which Knecht fathoms and endorses to the full. From the start this serene sage helps to gird Knecht for his later trials of self-will and "awakening" by insisting that he should seek not "a perfect doctrine" but a perfection of his self: "the deity is within *you*, not in ideas and books. Truth is lived, not taught" (69). His valorizing of the person over the system reflects Hesse's idea of the self as a process of becoming; his wisdom, which is Hesse's own, points beyond all institutional embodiments of that ideal, for like the Blake who wrote "less than All cannot satisfy Man," Hesse invokes a higher totality and unity of being that he identifies as our true goal: "Each one of us is merely one human being, merely an experiment, a way-station. But each of us should be on the way toward perfection, should be striving to reach the center, not the periphery" (68). As this Master puts it eloquently, those who pursue "true being" may not appear passionate in the eyes of the world, "because the flame of their fervor cannot always be seen," yet they "are burning with subdued fires" as they "direct the maximum force of their desires toward the center" (69).

The non-Castalian side of Knecht's personality evident in the opening chapter is subsequently defined and strengthened in a dialectical interplay with his Castalian education. His erstwhile sympathy for expelled students comes back to haunt him within the inner circle of the Waldzell elite through the guest student Plinio Designori's vehement anti-Castalian rhetoric that it becomes his lot to rebut. Under the watchful eye of the Music Master the same headstrong Knecht who resolutely refused to knuckle under to Headmaster Zbinden's demand that he not devote all his free time to musical studies is now cast as the public defender of Castalia, a role that forces him to look into Plinio's criticisms, as well as undertake "an intensive study of the fundamentals of the prevailing system in Castalia and in the Order" (84).

In their spirited exchanges, the "two principles" of Castalia and the world, mind and nature, "had become embodied in Knecht and Designori" (91), yet beneath this "dialectical interplay" and "sonata movement on two themes" (80), each is secretly drawn to the position of the other. Plinio ends up confiding to Joseph that he is "infatuated with" the Order (93), and Knecht right at the beginning of their friendship confesses to the Music Master that he finds Plinio's rhetoric appealing: "Presumably it is the voice of nature and it runs utterly counter to my education and the outlook customary among us. When Plinio calls our teachers and Masters a priestly caste and us a pack of spoon-fed eunuchs, he is of course using coarse and exaggerated language, but there may well be some truth to what he says" (83). These debates are a more polemical version of some of the earlier dialogues between Narcissus and Goldmund—in fact, in a manuscript fragment Hesse links Plinio directly with Goldmund and permits a more telling attack on Castalia than any of those in the final version when he has him quote from memory Goldmund's last words to Narcissus. Plinio, who had come across this "tawdry novel from the Age of the Feuilleton" in his grandfather's library (note Hesse's self-persiflage), exclaims, "certainly you all have fathers, fathers galore, you live in a world of fathers and teachers. But you do not have a mother." Knecht's tempered reply shows his intuition of a reality more profound than Castalia: what matters is not whether one still has one's biological mother, but rather whether one knows about "the Mothers, whether one has a relationship to the depths and primal sources of life."[90]

Because Knecht is strengthened through these public debates in his ability to think critically and independently, Plinio acts as an unwitting midwife to his non-Castalian proclivities, which now in late adolescence are also evident in his writing of poetry in a community that regards this (not unlike the student Hesse's teachers) "as the most impossible, ridiculous, and prohibited of conceivable acts" (92). As the narrator admits, what may be Knecht's "measure of concession to Plinio's world" also has "an element of rebellion against certain unwritten laws of Castalia." That Knecht's creative writing may also be an expression of his sexual urges is only obliquely hinted at in the mention of the "traces of profound upheaval and crisis" (92) discernible in his poetry. The narrator, who shares his Order's (and the later Hesse's) disinterest in matters sexual, notes cavalierly (at the beginning of Chapter 3) that although there is no marriage in Castalia, the elite students do have sexual liaisons, courtesy of the daughters of the province's ordinary citizens: they marry late and take the young Castalians as eager lovers in the interim. This "love," writes the author of two unhappy marriages, "is not governed by a morality directed toward marriage" (98). The fact that the Order does not allow for love between the sexes, but only for the relief of an occasional coupling, is also evident in an early manuscript variant (circa 1932–1933) that describes Knecht leaving the Order's precincts several times a year "in order to sleep with" a "veiled" woman: females who appear thus signal that they are available either because they have not found a suitable mate or because they are subject to periodic relapses "from the restraints of culture to the chaos of their instincts."[91]   We are not surprised to discover that the Knecht who has developed his powers of independent thinking in his arguments with Designori goes on a long and solitary quest during his subsequent years of "free" study in order to test the validity of the Bead Game by tracing back the sign language of a single game to its original sources. Though the Game passes his exacting scrutiny, his insight that its "dark interior . . . points down into the One and All" again pushes beyond Castalia, for "one who had experienced the ultimate meaning of the Game within himself would by that fact no longer be a player" (107). Nor is it strange that Knecht becomes for several months the student of the Elder Brother who has transformed himself into a Chinese recluse, and whose "bamboo grove" serves as "the scene of [Knecht's] I Ching studies" (111). Knecht later sums up this crucial period as "the beginning of [his] awakening," because his encounter with this second mentor strengthens his non-Castalian thinking at a time when, as the narrator puts its rather circumspectly, "the concepts and categories . . . of the . . . Castalian hierarchy became for him more and more relative matters" (117).

The Elder Brother is Hesse's ironic portrait of himself as the recluse of Montagnola as well as his tribute to the I Ching (the Book of Changes, which he studied and consulted in Richard Wilhelm's translation) and the Taoist tradition from Lao-Tzu to Chuang-Tzu, with which he had built up a considerable familiarity over the years. Hesse the man of changes could readily relate to the root-idea of change expressed by the "I" of the I Ching, two of whose sixty-four hexagrams are directly imported into The Glass Bead Game. The studies of Adrian Hsia and of Ursula Chi clearly demonstrate the significance of China for the later Hesse, and the detailed analyses of Chi show how extensively and esoterically he works both the Confucian and the Taoist traditions, and their common foundation, the Book of Changes, into The Glass Bead Game.[92] In addition to the developed references in his novel to the great Chinese wisdom book, Hesse also indicates his acquaintance with the exegetical tradition associated with it in a manuscript jotting to the effect that, of Knecht's writings, the only item to have appeared in print is a scholarly disquisition on "the pre-Confucian commentaries to the *I Ching*."[93]

What Knecht gains from his stay with the Elder Brother—the realization that there is a spiritual and cultural tradition far older than the one that has shaped his outlook—reinforces his growing awareness of a world beyond Castalia. The Elder Brother also presents an alternative "to all the dubiousness of the Game," namely, the escape into "a self-sufficient and beautiful kind of perfection" (119). Yet Knecht does not see this as a viable posture for himself, for as Chi points out, Knecht's "Confucian side," his active striving for knowledge that brings him to this Taoist hermit, can admire but not endorse a "renunciation of the present and the future in favor of something perfect enough, but past" (119). (In that respect this Castalian eccentric is the Chinese equivalent of the yogi of the "Indian Life.") Though the hermit's graceful rituals of goldfish pond and fountain, *I Ching* studies, meditation, and calligraphy are very attractive to Knecht, his bamboo grove is only a way station for the journeyer who will remain open to the past, but not at the expense of the future, and whose exemplary path, as Chi points out, will combine the ethical and this-worldly impulses of Confucian thought with the mystical and purely contemplative counterpole represented by Lao-Tzu.[94]

As yet another instrument of Knecht's "awakening," however, the Elder Brother does cast an ironic light on the intellectual and aesthetic world of the Bead Game players. When (in keeping with the Youthful Folly hexagram) Knecht expresses the wish "to incorporate the system of the *I Ching* into the Glass Bead Game," the sage laughingly replies, "anyone can create a pretty little bamboo garden in the world. But I doubt that the gardener would succeed in incorporating the world into his bamboo grove" (117). As Hsia has observed, the crucial difference between the symbolic language of the *I Ching* and that of the Bead Game is that the former encompasses the whole cosmos with its cycles of change, whereas the latter only aspires to capture the larger whole of the intellectual world.[95] The Elder Brother's aphorism says the same thing: the Bead Game is the bamboo garden, whereas the *I Ching* is the world. Thus in his sly way he points Knecht beyond the microcosm of the game to the macrocosm governed by the "I" principle of cyclic change and polarity that is denied or minimized by the Castalians.

In this respect Knecht's encounter with the Elder Brother makes for a logical transition to the next stage of his "awakening," and paves the way for his first journey outside the Order. This stage is presided over by a new mentor and sage, Pater Jacobus, who in his own (and distinctively Western) way also embodies the knowledge of the laws of change that govern the world and that are codified in the esoteric hexagrams of the Chinese Book of Changes. The relationship between Knecht and Jacobus re-enacts at a higher level the earlier dialectic between Knecht and Plinio Designori. This Benedictine monk and seasoned man of the world submits Castalia to a less vehement yet more authoritative critique. The meeting ground between these two is not only their mutual interest in music and in eighteenth-century Pietists, but also in what each can teach the other about his respective order and outlook. The pedagogic charm of the situation is that both can play by turns the respective roles of student and teacher, with the older Pater taking the more commanding position by virtue of his scholarly eminence and because he is being wooed by the young Castalian emissary to further the Order's desire to establish official relations with the Catholic church. Knecht's "mission" at the Mariafels monastery—which takes place under the appropriate Wanderer hexagram of the *I Ching*—introduces him to a vastly older and rival cultural tradition that, unlike the Castalian, is fully conscious of its historic position in the world, and to a mentor whose teachings as well as striking personality throw the limitations of the Bead Game players into graphic relief. While Knecht's patient introduction to and defense of Castalia succeeds in mitigating the scholarly monk's strong prejudice against it as "a blasphemous imitation" of "Christian models" (147) and even earns his grudging recognition of it as "an attempt to create an aristocracy of the spirit" (154), Knecht comes in turn to accept the possibility that "Castalian culture was merely a secularized and transitory offshoot of Christian culture . . . which would someday be reabsorbed by its parent" (156).[96]

The Burckhardtian view of history that Knecht assimilates from his tutorials with Jacobus and that is a decisive factor in his subsequent development is not only anti-Castalian but also informed by an animus against Hegel's interpretation of history as the dialectical march of *Geist*: "Father Jacobus made no bones about his profound mistrust of all philosophies of history" (184). The eminent scholar and church politician who "experienced history not as an intellectual discipline, but as reality, as life," is open to all the accidents and contingencies of a flesh-and-blood world in which individual human beings seek to play their part: "He had used the position in which fate had placed him not just to warm himself at the cozy fires of contemplative existence; he had allowed the winds of the world to blow through his scholar's den and admitted the perils and forebodings of the age into his heart" (173). If this is also the later Hesse's ideal, what his young hero learns at Mariafels is to "see the present and his own life as historical realities" (150). Like the Marx who ridicules the German idealist thinkers for moving "in the realm of 'pure spirit', '" of which "the Hegelian philosophy of history [with its illusion of "the hegemony of the spirit"] is the last consequence," and who turns Hegel's (upside–down) dialectic right side up by insisting that "in direct contrast to German philosophy" he sets out "from real, active men" and "real life,"[97] Pater Jacobus attacks the Castalians for having "distilled a kind of world history to suit [their] tastes," one that is "bloodless" and "lacking reality" in its insistence on "nothing but the history of ideas and of art" (150). Knecht's new realism under the impact of Jacobus also leads him "to see many aspects of [Castalia's] history in the proper light for the first time and to discover its roots in the general history of nations" (175).

Knecht brings this new outlook back to Castalia and later makes it the basis of his warning (in "The Circular Letter") to the Order for its disregard of political and historical realities. His mission to the Benedictines also makes him aware of his friend Tegularius's "difficult" character as not just an individual but a Castalian symptom: after the latter's short visit to Mariafels, where he had felt utterly out of his element, Pater Jacobus offers his evaluation of "an inexperienced, overbred, weakly, and nevertheless . . . arrogant kind of person" (179) that Knecht comes to identify as the prototype of "a Castalia . . . that might come into being in the future" if it is not "rejuvenated and revitalized" (249). Hesse's late nineteenth-century version here of genius as an admixture of "great gifts" and "sickliness" (247) is surely as much a heightened portrait of certain features of his younger self as it is his final assessment of Nietzsche—including "states of low vitality, periods of insomnia and nervous aches . . . spells of melancholy, a hunger for solitude, fear of duties and responsibilities, and . . . thoughts of suicide" (130). What is more, the account of Fritz's Bead Games as "in structure almost pure monologues, reflecting the imperiled but brilliant life of the author's mind like a perfect self-portrait" as well as dialectical struggles "fading out in questioning and doubt" (132), suggests aspects of Hesse's writings up through *Steppenwolf*. Thus Pater Jacobus is a corrective fictional lens through which the later Hessean self that is Knecht takes a hard if still sympathetic look at the moody outsider and solitary genius who is at once an "embodiment of the finest gifts to be found in Castalia" and "a portent of the demoralization and downfall of those abilities" (249).

Hesse's careful contrast between the neurasthenic Tegularius and the vigorous Pater is further developed through the arguments about history between Tegularius and Knecht. In precisely the type of thinking attacked by Marx as "the German ideology," Tegularius separates political history, as the mere "struggle for power" and "a subject altogether unfit for study by a Castalian" (254), from "real history," that is, "the timeless history of the Mind" (255). In fact, his willful disregard includes an obvious slap at the followers of Marx as "a sect fairly widespread in the nineteenth or twentieth century" by whom "the arts and religions were regarded as mere façades, so-called ideologies erected above a human race concerned solely with hunger and feeding" (255). To Knecht's objection, "doesn't the history of thought, of culture and the arts, have some kind of connection with the rest of history?" he answers, "absolutely not" (255). Even if Knecht (like his author) is no adherent of Marx's dialectical materialism, his reply to his friend's one-sided claims about ideas and the life of the mind is consistent with the anti-Hegelian Marx who wants to ground the transcendental abstractions of the German idealists back into "where speculation ends—in real life."[98] Knecht grants the Castalians' "great good fortune" of being able to live in a timeless world of ideas (even if, as he points out, "the only creativity" they "have left is preserving" the works of the past), but he also objects, "not everyone can spend his entire life breathing, eating, and drinking nothing but abstractions. History has one great advantage over things a Waldzell tutor feels to be worthy of his interest: it deals with reality. Abstractions are fine, but I think people also have to breathe air and eat bread" (256). Though the Marxist agenda of a proletarian revolution is clearly not Hesse's, the anti-idealist thinking that the later Hesse (with his Burckhardtian view of history) shares with Marx is the function of a secular humanism that emerges as the driving force of Knecht's life and that, it must be stressed, does not clash with but is in fact closely connected with his growing need for self-realization.

Knecht's new maturity and independence of mind after his return from Mariafels are signs that his long Castalian apprenticeship is behind him. His growing mastery is also evident in his ability to exert a decisive influence on others, and especially the young, from Anton, the Benedictine novice, to endangered Castalians like Tegularius (for whom he serves as a steadying force) and the student Petrus (whom he restores to a productive life in the Order after Petrus has painted himself into a corner with his futile cult of the departed Music Master). And in the last act of his life, he ministers to the needs of the distressed Designori family. Finally, the "legend" that has accrued around the figure of Knecht is of course proof positive of his greater impact on others, of which the narrator's scholarly labor of love is, at the remove of several generations, the latest instance.

Yet another sign of Knecht's coming into his own is his gaining the first prize, during his last year at Mariafels, in the annual Bead Game competition of the Waldzell elite: though by inclination Knecht is, like Tegularius, a "champion" of the "psychological method of Game construction" that does "not display perfection to the outward eye," the game he puts together to show his mastery is primarily a "formal" one (177–178). These descriptions serve not only to characterize Knecht's first but also Hesse's final prize-winning entry, one in which he demonstrates his mastery by refraining from "the psychological method . . . of construction" that "would have been closer to his inclinations," but opts instead for "a Game modern and personal enough in its structure and themes, but of transparently clear, classical composition and strictly symmetrical development in the vein of the old masters" (177).

The unusual circumstances that result in Knecht's sudden elevation to the peak of the Castalian hierarchy provide an object lesson in the challenges and difficulties he will have to surmount in his new position. Significantly, the death of Knecht's predecessor, Thomas von der Trave, also becomes, like the later death of Knecht, the stuff of Castalian legend. But the essential difference between these legends is that Knecht is able to control his fate and consolidate his authority right from the beginning of his tenure as Magister Ludi, whereas his predecessor is ultimately undone not by the mortal illness that overtakes him just before the celebration of his last annual game, but by his earlier choice of an official "deputy" who is not fit to assume the burdens of an office so unexpectedly thrust upon him—and for whose failure the dying Magister must, according to the Castalian code, assume full responsibility.

Hesse wrote in 1939 that "the animal and the demon within humanity always returns again to kill and to torture,"[99] and in reading the episode of Master Thomas and his unfortunate "Shadow" we are shocked to discover that this is true even in Castalia. Through his error of judgment in choosing what turns out to be an insufficient deputy, Master Thomas has in fact created a target for the hidden cruelty of the inner circle of the Castalian elite: "Their reverence for the Master was balanced by their malice for his Shadow; they wanted Bertram to fail even if the Master himself had to suffer as well" (193). Therefore the thematic link between this episode and "The Rainmaker" is the sacrificial death of a scapegoat—save that these overcultivated Bead Game players are more refined in their hidden cruelty than their primitive ancestors. When Knecht reprimands Tegularius and his cohort for their ritual shunning of Bertram—for letting him flounder in "a frigid atmosphere of isolation" (193) in his hour of need—his friend's callous indifference shocks him into recognizing the true meaning of this "sacrifice": "Bertram had been fully condemned by his judges and would not return" (195). And if Bertram's (rumored) death in the mountains presents a parallel with Knecht's end, his fall "from a cliff" (196), unlike Knecht's leap into the mountain lake, is not a life-affirming act but the suicidal step of one who has lost his place—and his face—in the Castalian Order.

When Knecht grasps the deeper meaning of his predecessor's unfortunate end, his resolve to avoid a similar defeat as Magister Ludi is evident in his desire to gain firm control over the arrogant inner circle of the Bead Game players by initially devoting nearly all of his energy and attention to them.[100] The challenge inherent in this task is epitomized in the narrator's use of one of the oldest of tropes, that of "a rider [who] masters a thoroughbred horse" (206). Once Knecht has gained the upper hand and presides unchallenged, "a Master, a sovereign and servant, a perfect instrument" (211), he is in a sense already ripe to leave his position and move on to further challenges. However, before he can come to a conscious realization of this through his growing attraction to teaching the very young (and his related insight that "the expression Magister Ludi . . . had originally been simply the name for the schoolmaster," 219), he first must give a sustained demonstration of his powers through a series of brilliant annual Bead Games, debuting, appropriately enough, with one based "on the ancient ritual Confucian pattern . . . of a Chinese house" as the symbol of cosmic order (224).[101]

Knecht's eventual resignation is already implicit in his decision right at the start of his term in office not to continue in it if it should ever prove to be a burden rather than a challenge. Another important clue to his later departure is the mysterious "transfiguration" of the Music Master, whose smiling death also becomes the subject of "a swarm" of later "legends" (239). These pointers to Knecht's future come, ironically, in the single chapter allotted to his years "In Office," a fact that also suggests that the focus of "The Life of Magister Ludi Joseph Knecht" is more on his non-Castalian than his Castalian side. Before proceeding to the final phase of that life, however, the narrator devotes a separate chapter to a schematic overview of "the two poles" of Knecht's personality—the "cultivation of the mind" versus the "instincts" and "impulses" of "his own heart" (244). This chapter serves as an interpretive frame for the "most unusual" and, for some, "scandalous end" of the Magister Ludi as "not mere chance or misfortune but a wholly logical outcome of what went before" (243).

Knecht's renewed friendship, after a lapse of many years, with Plinio Designori is instrumental in the final stage of his "awakening." The conversations between them also reveal that Knecht's departure from Castalia is not simply a defection from or renunciation of its basic principles, for, like his death soon after, these take place under the sign of "Belpunt" ("Beautiful Bridge"): the man of "two poles" will not sacrifice one—the mind— for the other—nature. Rather he will attempt to bridge the gap by moving toward the middle, that is, by acting as an intermediary between Castalia and a world beyond it that have become increasingly alienated from each other. In Plinio's bitter confession that he has failed in his ambition "to bring Castalia and the world together" (274) Knecht hears a challenge that shapes his own resolve to succeed where his friend has failed. Designori has fallen between the cracks of the *vita activa* and the *vita contemplativa*, being at home neither in the marriage and the career of liberal politics into which he had thrown himself in rebellion against his patrician background, nor in the Castalia through whose elite schools he has passed. The voice of his mid–life despair reaches Knecht "at the right moment" as "a kind of call," one that corresponds to an "insistent desire" within himself (285), and that now leads him back *to* the greater world *from* which his initial call to the pedagogic province had taken him. Appropriately, Knecht's final "awakening," like his first, is associated with music, which Knecht, now taking the lead, plays to soothe the battered Plinio. At the verge of quitting his Castalian office he reconciles his old friend with the life of the mind, and in so doing is already taking the first step toward the reconciliation between Castalia and the world that is the goal of the last stage of his life.

The style of Knecht's departure from Castalia shows his balanced character, for though his decision amounts to a bold "leap into a new life" (306) and a "breaking away" (307) from the old, it has none of the irrational and compulsive quality that had marked the wayward episodes of Hesse's youth. The "legend" of Knecht's resignation and death shows to what extent Hesse has moderated and rationalized the promptings of self-will when seen next to the demonic extremes of *Demian*. Knecht's reply to Master Alexander's suggestion that he may be "the victim of mysterious voices, whether of divine or diabolic origin," demonstrates that the author of *The Glass Bead Game* has shifted his interpretation of the meaning of the inner voice from a religious to an existential one: "No, I never thought of those awakenings as manifestations of a god or daimon or some absolute truth. What gives these experiences their weight and persuasiveness is not their truth, their sublime origin, their divinity or anything of the sort, but their reality. They are tremendously real" (365). A somewhat earlier Knechtian reflection also stresses the personal character of "awakening" as not an approach to "truth" or a movement "to the center of the world," but rather one "into the center of [one's] individuality" (351).

The Knecht who wants to leave Castalia is enough of a pragmatist to realize that he needs a "springboard" for his "leap" (309), and that his crossing to the world requires a "bridge"—both of which Designori will provide. Nor does the Magister who has mastered the "formal" style of game construction provoke an open break with the Order, but succeeds in taking his leave according to the letter of its regulations. He asserts his self-will, that is, by beating the legalists at their own game, and slips Castalia's nets without tearing a single mesh. The stringent critique of his official "Circular Letter" to the directorate is no mere bureaucratic formality but an assertion of his nonconformist viewpoint as he reminds these Castalian high priests of the founding principles of their hierarchy and their blindness to the realities of history and politics. Yet his prophetic ruffling of their feathers has a comic side to it as well, for it is partly a schoolboy's prank, as is evident when Tegularius's reading of the draft of his contribution to the document is "often . . . interrupted by peals of laughter on the part of both" (318). The humorous element carries right through to Knecht's confrontation with Master Alexander, who is caught so totally off guard by the Magister Ludi's unannounced visit that he has to resort to emergency breathing exercises to deal with the shock of his colleague's sudden resignation. What Knecht explains as a carefully considered "course of self-will" (356), the mind-boggled president of the Order, the epitome of the genteel but limited Castalian, can only interpret as the "totally un-Castalian" act of a deserter and "defector" (356) who is, as he puts it in shocked words that underscore the comedy of his incomprehension, "running amok or going berserk" (362).

The best readings of the book's unexpected concluding sequence all draw attention to a symbolism so rich in implication (in terms of Hesse's life and art) as to defy interpretation. Hesse the master of mystification orchestrates a powerful final movement that is consistently ambiguous, yet does so without making us feel that he is not fully in control of his material. In the closing episode everything is stark and elemental, yet nothing is one-dimensional or elementary. Thus even the setting of dawn and morning has the secondary suggestion of a "journey to the East"; because death overtakes Knecht as he swims toward the rising sun, the motifs of beginning and ending are brought together in his drowning, which is at once a *going-under (Untergang)* and a crossing-over *(Übergang)*.

The hinge on which this complex ending turns is the developing relationship between Knecht and Tito Designori, which is a significant variation of the central teacher-student paradigm of all the Knecht Lives. Here master and pupil confront each other as equals because each is in a sense initiated into the world of the other. Indeed, this time the former is even willing to follow the lead of the latter, for Knecht drowns in pursuit of his new charge in a sacrificial act that results from a challenge (to race to the other side of the lake) that he feels he cannot ignore if he is to keep Tito's trust. Of course, Knecht doesn't know that his plunge into what he discovers to be ice-cold water will result in his death, but he consciously *chooses* to take the risk of meeting "head-on" (393) the boy's dare in spite of physical warning signs (his vertigo and irregular heartbeat at such an elevated altitude).[102] Indeed, to drive home the point of the teacher following the student, Hesse writes that Knecht "threw himself into the water at the same spot where his pupil had dived" (393).

Plinio's high-spirited challenge is one Knecht dare not refuse because of what had been revealed in the boy's ritual homage to the rising sun. In this Lawrencian display, Knecht quite properly sees no mere throwback to a mindless paganism, but the boy's rare gifts as evident in his unconscious tribute to "the earth mother" and his "festive sacrifice" to the elements ("mountain, lake, and sky") that Tito's "outspread arms" embrace (390). What Tito pays such spontaneous homage to is the totality of those forces earlier celebrated in the Rainmaker's matriarchal culture and now denied or minimized by Castalia's exclusively logocentric outlook. The "priestly solemnity" of Tito's ecstatic dawn dance makes Knecht realize the difficulty inherent in his final mission to bridge the gulf between Castalia and the world, Mind and Nature, for Designori's self-willed son emerges as a much more formidable opposite than his father had once proved for the young defender of Castalia, "more remote from culture, more pagan . . . more alien, more elusive, less obedient to any summons" (391).

Yet Tito the born aristocrat has felt from the first a summons in his meeting with the Magister, whom he recognizes as an embodiment of "intellectual aristocracy" and spiritual nobility, which "to serve . . . might be a duty and honor for him" (387). Knecht judges correctly that Tito's dawn dance is in fact not an act of rebellion or a rejection of him, but is rather the proud youth's uncanny self-revelation as well as a ritual offering of "his devout soul as a sacrifice to the sun and the gods, and no less to the man he admired and feared" (39). In thus "presenting himself in a new light" to Knecht as "alien and entirely his equal" (392), Tito introduces Knecht to the maternal source and ground of (his) being, and at the same time calls upon the Master to initiate and guide him into the paternal cult of Mind. Still, the complex relationship between the two should not be reduced to a bald allegory of Mind versus Nature, because it is important to remember that Tito, despite his unruly temperament, is receptive to the call of Mind, just as Knecht, the non-Castalian Castalian, is open to the forces of Nature and Instinct that play such an important role in his final "awakening."

The account of Knecht's transactions with and larger impact on the Designori family is in fact an intricate autobiographical scenario that refers us to different periods and aspects of Hesse's life. The dead-locked marriage between Plinio and his wife bears some resemblance to Hesse's first marriage (and to the earlier fictional portrait of it in *Rosshalde*), but more importantly, the central figure of Tito is Hesse's final fictional treatment of that passionate child of nature, mother's son, and rebel against paternal authority that he himself had been. In the charged encounter between Knecht and Tito, then, two Hessean selves from opposite ends of the human life cycle are engaged in a final dialectical struggle and confessional psychomachia. When viewed in such a light the Romantic myth of the child being the father of the man takes on a new meaning in *The Glass Bead Game*, at whose close the man (Hesse) seeks to gain spiritual authority over the child who fathered him. Conversely, the burden of guilt and responsibility at Knecht's death that Tito senses in "a premonitory shudder of awe" as a force that will "utterly change him and his life" (394), runs a significant change on still another and more famous father-son myth, for it inverts the Christian pattern of the son sacrificed by the father in order to show a (Socrates-like?) father figure who ends up sacrificing himself for the son—and in so doing, motivates him to take the path of Mind.

If in this respect Hesse's ending points to Tito as the symbol of a potential synthesis of the polarity of mind and nature, something that is also suggested by the youth's androgynous appeal, Hesse the student of the *I Ching* knows that life is subject to the laws of contingency and the cycles of change, and wisely leaves the question of Tito's future open. One might wish, as Mileck does, that Hesse had followed up the promise of "the balanced interplay of spirituality and physicality" inherent in Tito by adding "the Tito story to his continuum of tales."[103] To such a consummation desired by some, Hesse might properly reply with the closing sentence of *Crime and Punishment*: "All that might be the subject of a new tale, but our present one is ended."

The manner of Knecht's death itself constitutes Hesse's recognition of the world of contingency, for if on a deeper level his drowning does not violate the pattern of "awakening," on another level it is as "realistic" as a newspaper headline, and as pointless an accident as the death (due to a faulty bathroom fan) of a saintly Thomas Merton on his journey to the East. To view Knecht's death, however, as a defeat of the purpose of his final "step" beyond Castalia is surely a misprision of the legend of his life as a process of becoming, a Faustian striving for something that can never be fully realized but whose value is on that account not diminished or nullified. Knecht's end at "Belpunt" under the sign of the rising sun is not an undoing but the active fulfillment of his life's meaning. The author of *The Glass Bead Game* shares with the game's players a predilection for "developing in counterpoint, and finally harmoniously combining two hostile themes or ideas," as well as a dislike for "Games with discordant, negative, or skeptical conclusions" (30). Too often in the past, Hesse's games had fallen short of harmonious outcomes, but in his final performance or magisterial confession, everything points away from such a "skeptical" or "forbidden" end (30). The greater synthesis provisionally adumbrated through the concluding movement of the book might well take as its cachet the Zen Buddhist parable cited in an essay Hesse wrote not long before his death: when a Zen Master is asked by an emperor, "what is the ultimate meaning of the sacred truth?" the Master replies, "wide open space—nothing of it sacred."[104]

The Glass Bead Game's attempt to bridge the eternal antinomies is also "open"—to the three dimensions of time, as well as to the great cultural traditions of West and East. In the concluding chapter it is the later Hesse's Romantic and existential sense that (to paraphrase Shakespeare) *becoming* ripe is all that accounts for the dynamic thrust of Knecht's self-will breaking through and transcending the geometric stasis of the closed sphere that is Castalia. Unlike the Music Master whose dying is a subsiding into mystical serenity, Knecht ends the career of his aspiring soul with an active ethical commitment to a world of fellow humans. The evolutionary momentum of Knecht's "stages" results in the cultural "boundary breaking" by "a renegade self" that has recently been identified as a basic feature of Romantic thought, a mode of "transgression" that involves taking a "risk" in the attempt "to rediscover a comprehensive *wholeness* which could preserve . . . an autonomous self . . . allied with an infinite organic universe."[105] Indeed, the idea of risk inherent in Knecht's *leap* beyond Castalia and his *plunge* into the alpine lake is as existential as it is Romantic, for as an expression of post-Enlightenment process thinking, it also resembles—despite Hesse's (later) negative reaction to the philosopher—Heidegger's notion of *Dasein* (Existence) as *Geworfenheit* (Thrownness).[106]

The spiral is the most appropriate sign for Knecht's last stage because his return to the "world" and the "native soil" (370—the German text reads *Mutterboden* = mother ground) of human life should not be viewed as a regression, but rather as the path of the higher self.[107] This upward movement implicit in the spatial metaphor of "Stages"—as Knecht puts it to Master Alexander, "one more stage had been left behind; I had passed through another area, another space, which this time was Castalia" (371)—is closely linked with the visual and verbal symbolism of "Belpunt" (the Designori vacation home in the mountains) as a bridging of multiple polarities. The initial reaction of the unmagistered Magister is that of a joyful release from the burdens of his high office. Like Wordsworth's romantic footjourney at the beginning of *The Prelude*, Knecht's at the close of *The Glass Bead Game* suggests a happy return to the spontaneous pleasures of childhood and the seasonal rhythms of nature, but only as these are experienced by an adult fully conscious of making a transition to a new phase of his life. Knecht's enjoyment of "this bright and cheerful September afternoon" that fills him "like a strong drink" (376) is also the Goethean experience of repeated puberty that marks the lives of truly creative individuals.

It is highly significant that at this point Hesse reintroduces the motif of the wooden flute, an instrument that in the eighteenth-century Fourth Life is associated with Knecht's father (who, as we saw, has his being in the mother world). Knecht plays a melody on "this naive, childish-looking instrument": "With pleasure, he felt the smooth wand between his fingers and reflected that aside from the clothes on his body this toy flute was the only piece of property he had allowed himself to take from Waldzell" (377–378).[108] Like the Swabian youth who (after having finished his theological education at Tübingen) looks forward to a joyful homecoming to the forests, fountains, and music of his childhood, the older Knecht of this autumnal excursion is also experiencing a return, but at a higher level, to the very wellsprings of his life.

The sense of release from a burdened past that initiates the final movement of *The Glass Bead Game* is, however, only the necessary prelude to a more fitting occupation. If Knecht's mission of teaching a single if difficult youth does not strike us as a major project, it is nevertheless the modest beginning of greater things to come. As Knecht had earlier assured the anxious Designoris, their problem child "has good blood and high endowments . . . What is missing is the harmony of these forces" (311). The teacher in Knecht looks forward to the task of forming the discordant elements of Tito's personality into a harmonious whole as a pleasant one—like gardening, to which it is compared (384). In undertaking it, he wants "to heal and make good" (389) the breach between Castalia and the world so painfully evident in the failed life of Tito's father. He knows that it will require all of his wisdom and patience to "gradually bring the boy to an awareness of his gifts and powers, and at the same time nourish him in that noble curiosity . . . from which springs love for the sciences, the humanities, the arts" (388). And Knecht is also aware of the high stakes inherent in the challenge that awaits him, because Tito "was not just any talented young man whom he had to awaken and train," but "the only son of a wealthy and influential patrician

family" (388). Here we see the larger pedagogic goal—Eastern and
Western, Confucian and Socratic—of the Magister Ludi who lays
down his office to take up the calling of bringing the world of ideas
and politics, of mind and history, together by educating a youth destined by his birth as well as his talents to be "a future leader, one of
the social and political shapers of the country" (388).

The concluding episode of Knecht's death represents a symmetrical arrangement of the perennial antitheses of Hesse's life and art,
and does so with a culminating overview that projects the polar tensions of Knecht's life as a balanced set of complementarities in and
through a symbolic landscape. The concatenation of images and metaphors here is also richly allusive in its reference back to a host of
earlier motifs and moments that constitute *The Glass Bead Game*'s
greater design. Hilde Cohn may have been the first to point out the
connection between Knecht's visit to the Elder Brother and his death
through the reappearance of the constituent elements of the Mong
("Youthful Folly") hexagram ("above mountain, below water,"
115).[109] And more recently Ursula Chi has demonstrated that the depiction of Knecht's drowning contains hidden allusions to the polar
opposites of Chinese thought, Confucius and Lao-Tzu, and "their
common root, the *I Ching*," and what is more, that the surface of the
mountain lake is transformed into a dramatic Yin and Yang symbol
at the moment when the rising sun divides it into areas of shadow
and light. According to her, the figurative arrangement of the death
scene "unfolds . . . the great archetypal images of the *I Ching*"
(mountain, water, fire, sky, lake).[110] Critics who view the book primarily as an affirmation of Western values[111] are not so much wrong
as they are expressing a half-truth, because the totalizing imagination
at work in *The Glass Bead Game* incorporates elements of both traditions, and if the "legend" of Knecht's death refers us back to Chinese
sages, it surely also contains a covert pointer to perhaps the most
famous Western man of wisdom, Socrates.

In the emblematic landscape of "Beautiful Bridge," many opposites
meet, and Knecht-Hesse has (in Wordsworth's sense) become the ultimate Borderer positioned at the great divide of polar realms: Night
and Day, Light and Dark, Apollo and Dionysus, Youth and Age, Nature and Mind, Logos and Eros, Life and Death, Beginning and Ending. In his long career as a writer Hesse never came closer to standing

at the center of his being or of his world than in this culminating moment of a lifetime's dream in which his own features are made over into a larger trope of humanity. From its elevated perspective, his life's work as a writer of autobiographical fiction is in a sense finished, yet everything is still possible, and all questions remain to be answered.

To extrapolate—at the risk of radical oversimplification—the autobiographical agenda of what is surely one of the great self-encounters in modern literature, Hesse's double move in *The Glass Bead Game* is (1) provisionally to project his dream or ideal through the fiction of Castalia and the Bead Game players and (2) to submit this ideal, through the figure of Joseph Knecht, to a searching critique that turns on the dynamic of historical change and the requirements of individual development. Hesse not only gives fictional form to his utopian longings for a much better world as an alternative to the political nightmare of the 1930s, but he imagines himself living in this world, with the ironic result that he finds himself forced to deconstruct it: he defects from his own utopia in order to remain true to himself. Despite his persistent need during the later 1920s and the decade of the 1930s to lose himself in the service of a higher (religio-aesthetic) ideal, he discovers that the true locus of the authentically and irreducibly *human* is the living individual. When in the end he finds himself ill at ease within the confines of his splendid Castalian spirit-dome, he champions, through the process thinking that is "Stages," the Romantic-existential need for "transcendence" and boundary breaking. In so doing he also shows with the "legend" of Knecht's final incarnation that, as Belhalfaoui has put it, "the genuinely 'revolutionary' deed" is performed by the great individual.[112]

Therefore despite his best efforts to the contrary, Hesse remained a Romantic iconoclast who ends up reaffirming in the conclusion of *The Glass Bead Game* his lifelong creed of *Eigensinn*, of attending to one's inner voice, and marching according to the different drummer of one's *daimon*. The fundamental paradox of his final phase is that the book that was meant to be the enshrinement of the goal of Unbecoming (*Entwerden*) turns out to privilege the path of Becoming

(*Werden*), and emerges as the fictional home of the unbecoming and forever renegade self. Yet as the mysterious finale of his last novel suggests, the serene faith of the older Hesse is that this wayward and prodigal self can never be truly lost, for its movement is always and already "toward the sacred center."[113]

EPILOGUE

WHO IS HE?

After resigning from his office as Magister Ludi, Knecht confides to Plinio Designori, "now that I have liberated myself from officialdom, I am much drawn to the idea of using my leisure and good spirits to write a book—or rather, a booklet, a little thing for friends and for those who share my views." "The subject," he continues, "would not matter," only the tone, which would be "a proper mean between the solemn and the intimate, earnestness and jest, a tone not of instruction, but of friendly communication and discourse on various things I think I have learned."[1] This vision of the leisurely *littérateur* is also a preview of the Hesse who after the completion of *The Glass Bead Game* became essentially a writer of occasional pieces—of commemorative essays and poems, prose sketches, circular letters (for friends and relatives), and autobiographical reminiscences of various kinds. The bulk of this material is not available in English, but "For Marulla" and "Events in the Engadine" (1953, included in *Autobiographical Writings*) are representative of the older Hesse's reflective prose. Like that of Joseph Knecht, his own magisterial career was essentially behind him—even as, ironically, the award of the Nobel Prize (1946) brought him new recognition and carried his name beyond the German-speaking world.

How can we characterize Hesse's larger achievement as a confessional writer? With his dialectical interweaving of Poetry and Truth, and his transformation of Life (*Leben*) into Art (*Kunst*) in a literary career that extends over more than four decades, Hesse deserves to be called the Goethe of modern autobiography. Like Goethe, Hesse reflects in the magic mirror of his (admittedly still more subjective) confessional imagination not only his own features but also summons up a symbolic and many-layered portrait of his (very different) age. His is an enormous autobiographical prose poem whose relevance is supported by the astonishing response it has found among different groups of readers at different times and in different parts of the world. Even if, as Ziolkowski has recently written, "the Hesse fashion in the U.S. is over; it has been talked to death and analyzed *ad nauseam*,"[2] there is no reason why the author who has been in vogue several times since World War I may not be so again at some point with a new generation—and probably in a different cultural context and for different reasons.

Which of his works will survive in the long run? Certainly *Steppenwolf* and *The Glass Bead Game* promise to have a permanent place in the canon of world literature; and at a level just below that, *Demian*, *Siddhartha*, and *Narcissus and Goldmund* will most likely continue to find an appreciative audience for the foreseeable future. And in the German-speaking countries, some of his prolific pre-*Demian* writings (especially some of the very readable Gerbersau stories) will maintain their popularity with a broad reading public. Hesse himself was not given to such prognostications, but in his old age he could afford to be wryly modest about his writings because he obviously knew that he had "arrived" in that greater literary arena where (to use a metaphor from *Steppenwolf*) the Immortals abide. In that regard he had fulfilled the fond dream of all autobiographers, whatever their professed intentions: the phoenix-miracle of textual immortality.

Since at least the mid-1920s Hesse faced up to the truth that his most authentic *being* is his being-in-the-text, and that the very richness of his writing is in a sense the correlative of the impoverishment of his experience. A diary excerpt of 1955 (some seven years before his death) may serve as his final meditation on this larger issue. In this poignant entry Hesse records his ambivalent response to hearing on the radio a reading from *Klingsor's Last Summer*. As he listens to this public broadcast of a work of which he has only a fragmentary recollection, memories of "the burning summer of 1919, the first after the War, the first of [his] new life in the Ticino" rise up from the "abyss" of the forgotten past.³ Moreover, his encounter with the flamboyant narrative of his earlier self, recited in someone else's voice, brings him a heightened experience of that characteristic sense of *dédoublement de soi* shared (in different versions) by many autobiographers: "during the entire reading I saw myself double . . . as the one who had experienced the Klingsor summer . . . and as the other one who had, almost simultaneously, written it." The writer of now-advanced years who suffers from a weak heart and who, despite a good night's sleep, feels dizzy and utterly exhausted, experiences the ambivalent feelings—the curse and the blessing—inherent in a textual confrontation with a younger self at the very peak of its powers and surrounded by friends "nearly all of whom have long been at rest in their graves and are forgotten."

After such a sense of irremediable loss, what gain? After such bittersweet knowledge that moves the heart with the "sad and glowing magic of that which is transient," what consolation? Only the phoenix-mystery of the autobiographer's self buried alive, yet forever able to rise from the ashes of his past, the marvel of "that which has not passed away . . . its secret persistence, its secret eternity, its possibility of being awakened in memory, its being buried alive in the for-ever conjurable word!"

Of course Hesse knows that there is always a difference between this more-real-than-life fiction of the self and the mere biographical presence of the autobiographer who has authored it. Or to put all this another way, the greater enigma of the inexplicable and irreducible self still looms large for the aged Hesse who had spent the better part of his life in a seriatim effort to fathom that strange entity. Like the Montaigne who poses the classical question of the autobiographer as *homo sapiens*—"what do I know?"⁴—Hesse asks (with a typical ironic elusiveness evident in the grammatical shift from the first person to the third) the crucial question of the modern autobiographer as *homo existens*—"who am I?": "And who is he lying on the sofa, lightly swayed by vertigo and enchanted by the storyteller and his tale; an extinguished old man much less real than his self-portrait conjured up from the depths of time?"

Who is he, indeed?
All of, and none of, his words.

NOTES

Chapter I: The Confessional Imagination

1. Friedrich Schlegel, *Dialogue on Poetry and Literary Aphorisms*, trans. E. Behler and R. Struc (University Park: Pennsylvania State University Press, 1969), 81, 100.
2. For comprehensive accounts of the emergence of a historical view of the self, see Karl J. Weintraub, "Autobiography and Historical Consciousness," *Critical Inquiry* 1 (1975): 821–848, and *The Value of the Individual: Self and Circumstance in Autobiography* (Chicago: University of Chicago Press, 1978), as well as Eugene L. Stelzig, *All Shades of Consciousness: Wordsworth's Poetry and the Self in Time* (The Hague: Mouton, 1975), 12–53.
3. Schlegel, *Dialogue on Poetry*, 103. Jerome H. Buckley's *The Turning Key: Autobiography and the Subjective Impulse* (Cambridge: Harvard University Press, 1984), which appeared after this chapter was written, offers a broad historical survey of modern (mostly British) autobiography as a function of "the subjective impulse." For a discussion of subjectivity as a problem for Romantic writers, see Eugene L. Stelzig, "Romantic Subjectivity: Disease or Fortunate Fall?" in *English and German Romanticism: Cross-Currents and Controversies*, ed. J. Pipkin (Heidelberg: Carl Winter Verlag, 1985), 153–168.
4. Roy Pascal, *Design and Truth in Autobiography* (London: Routledge and Kegan Paul, 1960), 36, 39, 47.
5. Weintraub, *The Value of the Individual*, xv.
6. In *Season of Youth: The Bildungsroman from Dickens to Golding* (Cambridge: Harvard University Press, 1974), Buckley stresses that "most of the English *Bildungsromane* are highly autobiographical," and suggests that the novel of education was "perhaps the most successful of autobiographical forms, because the most oblique and richly creative" (viii, 27).
7. Jean Guéhenno, *Grandeur et misère d'un esprit*, vol. 2 of *Jean-Jacques: Histoire d'une conscience*, 2nd ed. (Paris: Gallimard, 1962), 44–47, 290–292.
8. Georg Misch, *Von der Renaissance bis zu den autobiographischen Hauptwerken des 18.*

und 19. Jahrhunderts, vol. 4, pt. 2 of *Geschichte der Autobiographie* (Frankfurt: Verlag Schulte-Bumke, 1969), 858, 859, 848.

9. Georges Gusdorf, "Conditions et limites de l'autobiographie," in *Formen der Selbstdarstellung*, ed. G. Reichenkron and E. Haase (Berlin: Duncker und Humblot, 1956), 105–123. For a recent selection of important articles (including Gusdorf's and some others cited in this chapter), see *Autobiography: Essays Theoretical and Critical*, ed. James Olney (Princeton: Princeton University Press, 1980).

10. Pascal, *Design and Truth*, 9, 16.

11. Pascal, *Design and Truth*, 175–177.

12. Alfred Kazin, "Autobiography as Narrative," *Michigan Quarterly Review* 3 (1964): 212; John Sturrock, "The New Model Autobiographer," *New Literary History* 9 (1977): 52, 62. For a more conservative position, see Barret J. Mandel, who claims that the autobiographer "may never falsify his facts for a fictional purpose," "The Autobiographer's Art," *Journal of Aesthetics and Art Criticism* 27 (1968): 220.

13. Philippe Lejeune, *Le Pacte autobiographique* (Paris: Editions du Seuil, 1975), 33. See also Jeffrey Mehlman, *A Structural Study of Autobiography: Proust, Leiris, Sartre, Levi-Strauss* (Ithaca: Cornell University Press, 1974). Mehlman offers no generic discussion of modern autobiography, a term he uses loosely to describe both autobiographies and confessional novels. See also the special issue of *Modern Language Notes* 93 (1978) on "Autobiography and the Problem of the Subject."

14. A good example is Louis A. Renza, "The Veto of Imagination: A Theory of Autobiography," *New Literary History* 9 (1977): 1–26. Renza claims "that autobiography is neither fictive nor non-fictive, not even a mixture of the two. We might view it instead as a unique, self-defining mode of self-referential expression, one that allows, then inhibits, the project of self-presentification" (22).

15. Johann Wolfgang von Goethe, *Aus meinem Leben: Dichtung und Wahrheit*, vol. 5 of *Werke* (Munich: Winkler Verlag, 1973), 256.

16. Sturrock, "The New Model Autobiographer," 56–59.

17. Jean-Jacques Rousseau, *Les Confessions*, ed. Jacques Voisine (Paris: Garnier, 1964), 790, 322.

18. Guéhenno, *Jean-Jacques*, vol. 2, 292, 290.

19. A good example of this is the first dream analyzed in *The Interpretation of Dreams* (chap. 2, dream of July 23–24, 1895): Freud's account of his dream of examining Irma is full of striking sexual-phallic imagery whose significance he refuses to consider in his interpretation of the Irma sequence as wish-fulfillment. For a Freudian discussion of this dream that also develops its "sexual themata," see Erik H. Erikson, "The Dream Specimen of Psychoanalysis," *Journal of the American Psychoanalytic Association* 2 (1954): 5–56.

20. Schlegel, *Dialogue on Poetry*, 104.

21. Misch, *Geschichte der Autobiographie*, vol. 4, pt. 2, 64; Buckley, *Season of Youth*, 24–25.

22. Lejeune, *Le Pacte autobiographique*, 20, 23, and "Autobiography in the Third Person," *New Literary History* 9 (1977): 33, 41–42.

23. Michel de Montaigne, *Essays and Selected Writings*, trans. and ed. Donald M. Frame (New York: St. Martin's Press, 1963), 281 (bk. 2, chap. 18).

24. T. S. Eliot, "Tradition and the Individual Talent," *The Norton Anthology of English Literature*, ed. M. H. Abrams, 4th ed. (New York: Norton, 1979), vol. 2, 2296, 2299.

25. Alfred Kazin, "The Self as History: Reflections on Autobiography," in *Telling Lives: The Biographer's Art*, ed. Marc Pachter (Washington: New Republic Books, 1979), 85–86.

26. Buckley, *Season of Youth*, viii.

27. Pascal, *Design and Truth*, 168, 175; Buckley, *Season of Youth*, 26.

28. Quoted in Buckley, *Season of Youth*, 23–24.

29. Flaubert's comments reveal his ambivalent authorial identification with and self-distancing from his heroine. As Jacques Suffel has noted in his introduction to the novel, " '*I am Madame Bovary*' he said. He also said: 'it is a totally invented story: I have put in it nothing of either my feelings or my existence' "; *Madame Bovary* (Paris: Garnier, 1966), 16.

30. Ralph R. Wuthenow, in *Das erinnerte Ich: Europäische Autobiographie und Selbstdarstellung im 18. Jahrhundert* (Munich: C. H. Beck Verlag, 1974), 203–210, suggests that Jean Paul's conjectural autobiography is a parody of *Poetry and Truth* and of the prevalence of the genre in eighteenth-century German literature. Jean Paul's assertion, "I can even turn the present into a past into which I gaze back with longing, and the future into a present which I experience intimately in all its parts" (Wuthenow, 242), demonstrates this writer's innovative conception of "autobiography" as a fictional device.

31. Pascal, *Design and Truth*, 177.

32. Peter Axthelm, *The Modern Confessional Novel* (New Haven: Yale University Press, 1967), 11.

33. Francois-René Chateaubriand, *Atala, René* (Paris: Garnier, 1964), 175.

34. Buckley, *Season of Youth*, 25.

35. William Howarth, "Some Principles of Autobiography," *New Literary History* 5 (1974): 381.

36. Robert Jay Lifton, *History and Human Survival* (New York: Random House, 1970), 311–331.

37. Goethe, *Poetry and Truth*, *Werke*, vol. 5, 528.

38. As Stephen Spender has written, "in literature the autobiographical . . . is no longer the writer's experience: it becomes everyone's." "Confessions and Autobiography," *The Making of a Poem* (London: Hamish Hamilton, 1955), 65.

39. A risk, indeed, which some contemporary theorists have been willing to take, most impressively so James Olney, whose seminal exploration of "the philosophy and psychology of autobiography" considers the genre not in historical or formal terms, but more fundamentally "in relation to the vital impulse to order that has always caused man to create and that, in the end, determines both the nature and the force of what he creates." *Metaphors of Self: The Meaning of Autobiography* (Princeton: Princeton University Press, 1972), vii, 4.

40. Elizabeth W. Bruss, *Autobiographical Acts: The Changing Situation of a Literary Genre* (Baltimore: Johns Hopkins University Press, 1976). Bruss seeks to define autobiography "as an act rather than a form" in the context of "illocutionary speech act theory developed by philosophers of language" (5, 19). Two recent major books that appeared after this chapter was written build on Bruss's premise of autobiography as an act: in *Figures of Autobiography: The Language of Self-Writing in Victorian and Modern England* (Berkeley: University of California Press, 1983), Avrom Fleishman places the "emphasis on the activity rather than the corpus" because "*Autobiography* seems to refer from the outset to the writing process rather than the results" (39); Paul John Eakin, in *Fictions in Autobiography: Studies in the Art of Self-Invention* (Princeton: Princeton University Press, 1985), focuses on "the autobiographical act" in selected twentieth-century writers as one in which "autobiographical truth is not a fixed but an evolving content in an intricate process of self-discovery and self-creation" (1). In Eakin's subtle developmental model, this act turns on "the moment of language in which the self first finds its being" and which is "both a re-enactment and an extension of earlier phases of identity formation" (209, 226).

Chapter II: Life *as* Writing

1. Keats, letter of February 19, 1819: "Shakespeare led a life of Allegory: his works are the comments on it." In *English Romantic Writers*, ed. David Perkins (New York: Harcourt, 1967), 1222.

2. Goethe, conversation of January 26, 1826, in Johann Peter Eckermann, *Gespräche mit Goethe* (Munich: Goldmann Verlag, n.d.), 115.

3. Stelzig, "Romantic Subjectivity: Disease or Fortunate Fall?" (cited in Chapter I, note 3).

4. Eliot, "Tradition and the Individual Talent" (cited in Chapter I, note 24), 2296, 2299.

5. Flaubert, in *Documents of Modern Literary Realism*, ed. George J. Becker (Princeton: Princeton University Press, 1963), 95, 91, 94.

6. Olney, *Metaphors of Self* (cited in Chapter I, note 39); Flaubert, cited in Chapter I, note 29 (Suffel, Preface to *Madame Bovary*).

7. William Hazlitt, "On the Character of Rousseau," in Perkins, *English Romantic Writers*, 618.

8. GB I, 22, letter of May 1896 (the two preceding quotations are also from this letter).

9. MB, 111, 112.

10. Ziolkowski, Introduction, AW, viii.

11. Hesse chose this phrase (from an aphorism by Novalis) as the joint title (1931) of several works written under the impact of psychoanalysis.

12. GB I, 65, letter of November 5, 1899.

13. GB I, 436–437.

14. GB II, 154, letter of October 14, 1926.

15. GB II, 155, letter of November 11, 1926.

16. "Journal 1920–1921," AS, 120–121.
17. AS, 122.
18. AS, 124.
19. AS, 124.
20. GB I, 470.
21. Gusdorf, "Conditions et limites de l'autobiographie" (cited in Chapter I, note 9).
22. GB I, 412.
23. Hesse, *Die Morgenlandfahrt* (The journey to the East) (Frankfurt: Suhrkamp Verlag, 1969), 38, 122.
24. I am indebted in my use of these terms to James Olney's Introduction (6) to *Autobiography: Essays Theoretical and Critical* (cited in Chapter I, note 9).
25. Vladimir Nabokov, *Speak, Memory: An Autobiography Revisited* (New York: Paragon Books, 1966), 310.
26. GB II, 178, letter of June 1927.
27. AW, 60, 61–62, 62.
28. AW, 5.
29. GB I, 443, letter of January 26, 1920.
30. GW, vol. 11, 82, 80–81.
31. AS, 122.
32. AW, 288, 289.
33. Mileck, xii.
34. Gay, review of *Hermann Hesse: Pilgrim of Crisis*, by Ralph Freedman, in *The New York Times Book Review*, January 21, 1979.
35. AB, 52, letter of May 4, 1931.
36. GW, vol. 1, 119.

Chapter III: Self-Will

1. Hesse, "Self-Will," in *If the War Goes On: Reflections on War and Politics*, trans. Ralph Manheim (New York: Farrar, Straus and Giroux, 1971), 79. (Subsequent references to this collection are to this edition and will appear in the text as *War*.) The literal German version of the last phrase ("his own 'will' ") is "the sense of his 'own'."
2. More than a decade earlier Hesse had recommended the reading of Emerson to a young relative (Paul Gundert) because "even though he [Emerson] doesn't offer the absolute truth [which] no philosopher can . . . he writes about human matters in a human way and with much delicacy." GB I, 135, letter of July 23, 1906.
3. "Concerning *Zarathustra's Return*," AS, 114, 115.
4. Ball, 161.
5. *Hermann Hesse: Politik des Gewissens*, ed. Volker Michels, 2 vols. (1972, 1977), Suhrkamp Verlag.
6. For Hesse's shifts in attitude to the war, see Mileck, 72 ff. As Mileck notes, the result of Hesse's "awakening" of 1916 was that by 1917, "an indecisive apologist for his country and for himself now became a resolute censor . . . Hesse emerged as a determined Jeremiah" (76).

7. GB II, 245, letter of January 31, 1930.

8. GB II, 330–331, letter of March 28, 1932.

9. GB II, 508.

10. AB, 100, letter of March 1933.

11. AB, 101, 102.

12. "Hate Letters," AS, 153–154.

13. GB II, 213, letter of April 9, 1929.

14. AB, 111, letter of ca. 1933.

15. GB II, 295, letter of November 1931. Further citations of this letter are given in the text.

16. "From a Journal of July 1933," AS, 183–196.

17. AB, 81, letter of 1932 (no precise date given).

18. AB, 262, letter of January 5, 1949.

19. *Kindheit und Jugend vor Neunzehnhundert: Hermann Hesse in Briefen und Lebenszeug-nissen 1877–1895*, ed. Ninon Hesse (Frankfurt: Suhrkamp Verlag, 1966). Further citations of this volume will appear in the text as *Youth*.

20. For a brief sketch of this remarkable woman and her unusual life, see Freedman, 18–26.

21. *Marie Hesse: Ein Lebensbild in Briefen und Tagebüchern*, ed. Adele Gundert (1934; rpt. Frankfurt: Suhrkamp Verlag, 1977), 159; hereafter cited in the text as MH.

22. J. D. Salinger, *The Catcher in the Rye*, chap. 18. Not surprisingly, when Hesse as an old man came to review the novel (in 1953), he praised it highly, especially Holden's noble and sensitive nature hiding behind a rough exterior; GW, vol. 12, 565–567.

23. Freedman, who amply documents this double pull in Hesse's life (particularly during the crisis years of the two great wars), observes that "his need to be accepted and at the same time to break away was as strong in the man in his sixties as it had been for the adolescent and child" (363).

24. AW, 11–12.

25. GB I, 11–12, letter of January 11–13, 1896.

26. AW, 15–16.

27. "Life Story Briefly Told," AW, 44, 45, 46, 46–47.

28. Heinz Lichtenstein, "Identity and Sexuality: A Study of Their Interrelationship in Man," *Journal of the American Psychoanalytic Association* 9 (1961): 208. I am indebted to Professor Norman Holland for drawing my attention to Lichtenstein's theory, and for sending me a copy of the above article, as well as copies of some of his own writings on the subject. For a good example of Holland's application of "identity theme" to particular authors and works, see "Human Identity," *Critical Inquiry* 4 (1978): 451–469.

29. Freedman, 21.

30. Ball, 42–43, 65.

31. In the dedication of the poem "To My Mother" (written between 1899 and 1902): "I had too much to tell you / Too long I dwelt in a foreign land / And yet you

were the one who could understand / Me the best through all my days." *Hermann Hesse: Die Gedichte*, 2 vols. (Frankfurt: Suhrkamp Verlag, 1977), vol. 1, 204.

32. GB II, 408, letter of December 5, 1933.
33. AB, 42, letter of December 17, 1930.
34. AW, 55.
35. Foreword to "From German Self Biographies," MS in Hermann Hesse Collection (Nachlass), Schiller-Nationalmuseum, Marbach am Neckar, West Germany.
36. GB I, 445, letter of February 28, 1920.
37. AB, 203, letter of May 1943.
38. Ziolkowski, chap. 4, pp. 52 ff.; Abrams, *Natural Supernaturalism: Tradition and Revolution in Romantic Literature* (New York: Norton, 1971).
39. MB, 189.
40. Ziolkowski, 57.
41. MB, 192.
42. MB, 193.
43. GB II, 256, letter of November 1930.
44. GB II, 342, letter of summer 1932; AB, 364, letter of January 9, 1951.
45. MB, 193 (translation slightly modified).
46. AB, 101, letter of mid-March 1933; 467, letter of June 8, 1956.
47. Edel, "The Figure Under the Carpet," in *Telling Lives: The Biographer's Art*, 24–25 (cited in Chapter I, note 25).
48. AB, 260, letter of January 5, 1949; 309, letter of February 1950.

Chapter IV: Autobiographical Beginnings

1. Hesse's notation in a business calendar of 1899; Hermann Hesse Collection, Schiller-Nationalmuseum, Marbach am Neckar, West Germany.
2. Hesse, *Childhood and Youth Before 1900* (cited in Chapter III, note 19), 466, 474.
3. GB I, 38.
4. GB I, 39, letter of August 27, 1898.
5. Hesse, *Die Gedichte* (cited in Chapter III, note 31), vol. 1, 41.
6. GB I, 48, letter of December 2, 1898.
7. *Eine Stunde hinter Mitternacht*, GW, vol. 1, 159, 165, 170.
8. GW, vol. 1, 181, 182.
9. GW, vol. 1, 202, 207.
10. Hesse, *Hinterlassene Schriften und Gedichte von Hermann Lauscher* (first edition), later shortened to *Hermann Lauscher*, GW, vol. 1, 217. Further citations of *Lauscher* will appear in the text.
11. Cited in Unseld, 15.
12. Freedman, 85.
13. As Mileck has observed, it "is our only example of the beautifully simple and sober narrative style that Hesse had managed to achieve before he began to assume the heroic pose of the suffering aesthete" (29).
14. Quoted by Unseld, 19.

15. Freedman, 109–111.
16. Ball, 103.
17. GB I, 109, letter of October 25, 1903.
18. GB I, 115, letter of January 10, 1904.
19. Hesse in an open letter to French students in *Neue Zürcher Zeitung*, August 4, 1951, quoted in Unseld, 20.
20. Hans Jürg Lüthi, *Hermann Hesse: Natur und Geist* (Stuttgart: Kohlhammer Verlag, 1970), 16; Fritz Böttger, *Hermann Hesse: Leben, Werk, Zeit* (Berlin: Verlag der Nation, 1974), 104.
21. Hesse, *Peter Camenzind*, trans. Michael Roloff (New York: Farrar, Straus & Giroux, 1969). Subsequent citations of the novel are of this edition and translation and will appear in the text.
22. Freedman, 99–102, 113.
23. AW, 48.
24. Boulby, 39–46.
25. "Encounters with the Past" (1953), GW, vol. 10, 352.
26. Ball, 52.
27. Hesse, *Beneath the Wheel*, trans. Michael Roloff (New York: Bantam Books, 1970), 67. Further citations of the novel are of this edition and translation and will appear in the text.
28. Hesse, *Childhood and Youth Before 1900*, 189.

Chapter V: Domestic Fictions

1. "On Moving to a New House," AW, 235, 232.
2. GB I, 124, 125, letters of September 2 and 11, 1904.
3. For a summary of Keller's influence on Hesse's "Gerbersau" cycle, see Boulby, 69–71.
4. Mileck, 57.
5. Since the bulk of Hesse's Gaienhofen stories have not been translated into English, I will limit myself to a number of those available in Hesse, *Stories of Five Decades*, ed. Theodore Ziolkowski, trans. Ralph Manheim (New York: Bantam Books, 1974). Unless otherwise noted, all citations of Hesse's prewar stories are of this edition and translation and will appear in the text.
6. As Mark Boulby does with his strictures on "Hesse's defects as a stylist in these years," 71.
7. Walter Benjamin, letter of July 30, 1913; quoted in Unseld, 31.
8. The link to Eichendorff is made explicit when Knulp (in the first part) whistles the famous Eichendorff lyric, "The Broken Ring," *Knulp*, GW, vol. 4, 449.
9. Hesse, unpublished letter of January 1954, quoted by Unseld, 45–46. In this letter Hesse also acknowledges the sentimentality of his conception of Knulp.
10. GB I, 163, 210, letters of December 15, 1909, and June 6, 1912.
11. GW, vol. 4, 462.
12. Boulby, 79.

13. GW, vol. 4, 514, 515.
14. GW, vol. 4, 437, 524.
15. Theodor Heuss's review of *Gertrude*, quoted in GB I, 508; Hesse's reply, GB I, 183, letter of November 17, 1910.
16. Freedman judges *Gertrude* the "most substantial work of the time in Basel and Gaienhofen" (138), whereas Field (35) asserts that "the mood of the work is insipid and sentimental."
17. George Wallis Field, *Hermann Hesse: Kommentar zu sämtlichen Werken*, 2nd ed. (Stuttgart: Verlag Hans-Dieter Heinz, 1979), 81.
18. Hesse, *Gertrude*, trans. Hilda Rosner (New York: Farrar, Straus & Giroux, 1969), 177, 122, 89, 235. Subsequent citations of the novel are of this edition and translation and will appear in the text.
19. In an unpublished letter of December 1910 Hesse grants that Gertrude is "less a character than a symbol" necessary for Kuhn's development; quoted in Unseld, 32.
20. I have modified Rosner's translation ("his loneliness had become inveterate to him") because it omits the important wolf simile.
21. Marie Hesse, unpublished letter of June 15, 1899; quoted in English translation by Mileck, 19.
22. Mileck, 19.
23. I have somewhat modified Rosner's translation to give a more accurate version of Hesse's text.
24. Kuhn's deformed leg (a consequence of his sledding accident) may be Hesse's unconscious parallel to Oedipus (whose name literally means "sore foot").
25. Hesse, *Rosshalde*, trans. Ralph Manheim (New York: Farrar, Straus & Giroux, 1970), 84. Subsequent citations of the novel are of this edition and translation and will appear in the text.
26. GB I, 242, letter of March 16, 1914.
27. GB I, 183–184, letter of November 17, 1910.
28. GW, vol. 11, 30, letter of 1942.

Chapter VI: Hesse's Marriage of Heaven and Hell

1. AW, 51–52.
2. See Mileck, 71–72, for the "ambiguity of [Hesse's] political posture" in the early part of World War I.
3. Freedman, 167.
4. GB I, 271, 255, letters of April/March 1915 and December 26, 1914.
5. Hesse, "O Friends, Not These Tones!" (September 1914), *If the War Goes On* (cited in Chapter III, note 1), 11, 12, 14, 13. Hesse's title is a pointed citation of the opening of Schiller's famous ode "To Joy," which Beethoven used for the chorale of his Ninth Symphony.
6. "Life Story Briefly Told," AW, 50.
7. Mileck, 101.

8. Ball, 143. See Freedman, 187–88, for a summary of Hesse's relationship with his analyst. Freedman notes that Lang's daughter unfortunately destroyed his notebooks after his death in 1945.

9. MB, 48–49.

10. AW, 53–54.

11. GB I, 325, 414, letters of May 21, 1916 (from the Sonnmatt sanatorium in Lucerne), and August 24, 1919.

12. GB I, 424, letter of fall 1919.

13. GB I, 384, 457, letters of June 7, 1917, and August 14, 1920.

14. "Life Story Briefly Told," AW, 54.

15. In his excellent critical overview of Hesse's *Märchen*, George Wallis Field notes that in these (the bulk of which were written during the war) Hesse is concerned with the related issues of probing the unconscious, restoring the "ideals and psychological insights" of the German Romantics (especially Novalis), and lifting "the veil of his own childhood experiences"; "Hermann Hesses moderne Märchen," in *Hermann Hesse Heute*, ed. Adrian Hsia (Bonn: Bouvier, 1980), 204–231.

16. Mileck, 101. Hesse's letter about Jung (of ca. April 1950) was first printed in *The Psychoanalytic Review* (Fall 1963) and is reprinted in English translation in C. G. Jung, *Letters*, ed. Gerhard Adler, trans. R.F.C. Hull, Bollingen Series (Princeton: Princeton University Press, 1973), vol. 1, 575.

17. Mileck, 115.

18. *Märchen*, GW, vol. 6, 67, 69. Subsequent citations of Hesse's *Märchen* are of this edition and will appear in the text.

19. Erich Neumann, *The Origins and History of Consciousness*, trans. R.F.C. Hull, Bollingen Series (Princeton: Princeton University Press, 1970), 43.

20. Neumann, *Origins and History*, 45.

21. Mileck, 118.

22. GB I, 455, 416; letters of summer 1920 and August 27, 1919; GB II, 210, letter of February 1929.

23. M.-L. von Franz, "The Process of Individuation," in *Man and His Symbols*, ed. C. G. Jung (London: Aldus Books, 1964), 186.

24. Hesse, *Demian: The Story of Emil Sinclair's Youth*, trans. Michael Roloff and Michael Lebeck (New York: Bantam, 1966), 90. Subsequent citations of the novel are of this edition and translation and will appear in the text.

25. C. G. Jung, *Letters*, vol. 1, 573–574, letter of December 3, 1919.

26. Mileck, 103.

27. Jung, *Letters*, vol. 1, 552, letter of March 24, 1950.

28. Hesse, letter of ca. April 1950, in Jung, *Letters*, vol. 1, 575.

29. For a summary of the influence of the nineteenth-century Swiss anthropologist Bachofen on *Demian*, see Ziolkowski, 111–113.

30. Ziolkowski, 106.

31. Hesse, *Stories of Five Decades* (cited in Chapter V, note 5), 260; MB, 70.

32. C. G. Jung, *Symbols of Transformation*, vol. 5 of *The Collected Works*, 2nd ed., ed.

William McGuire et al., Bollingen Series (Princeton: Princeton University Press, 1967), 124.

33. Ziolkowski, 137; Hans Jürg Lüthi, *Hermann Hesse: Natur und Geist* (cited in Chapter IV, note 20), 44.

34. Boulby, 120.

35. Jeffrey Sammons, "Hermann Hesse and the Over-Thirty Germanist," in *Hermann Hesse: A Collection of Critical Essays*, ed. Theodore Ziolkowski (Englewood Cliffs: Prentice-Hall, 1973), 132.

36. Heinz Stolte, *Hermann Hesse: Weltscheu und Lebensliebe* (Hamburg: Hansa Verlag, 1971), 111, 119.

37. Sigmund Freud, *Civilization and Its Discontents*, trans. James Strachey (New York: Norton, n.d.), 91.

38. MB, 91. Further citations of the Dostoevsky essays are of this edition and will appear in the text.

39. GB I, 430, letter of December 12, 1919.

40. D. H. Lawrence, "Foreword," *Women in Love* (New York: Viking, 1960), vii. The Lawrence quotations that follow immediately in the text are also from the "Foreword" (vii–viii).

41. Freedman, 179, 182.

42. Hesse, *A Child's Heart*, in *Klingsor's Last Summer*, trans. Richard and Clara Winston (New York: Farrar, Straus & Giroux, 1970), 4. Subsequent citations of the novella are of this edition and translation and will appear in the text. I prefer the literal translation (*A Child's Soul*) of the German title (*Kinderseele*).

43. Boulby, 96.

44. "Artists and Psychoanalysis," MB, 49.

Chapter VII: Ticino Legends of Saints and Sinners

1. Hesse, *Wandering: Notes and Sketches*, trans. James Wright (New York: Farrar, Straus & Giroux, 1972), 5–6.

2. GB I, 405, letter of July 2, 1919.

3. AS, 130.

4. "Journal 1920–1921," AS, 130.

5. "Life Story Briefly Told," AW, 56.

6. GB I, 412, 437, letters of August 8, 1919, and January 5, 1920.

7. Hesse, "Self-Communion," in *Materialen zu Hermann Hesses "Siddhartha,"* vol. 2, ed. Volker Michels (Frankfurt: Suhrkamp Verlag, 1974), 360–363. Subsequently this volume will be cited as MATSID2.

8. In the essay cited in the previous note Hesse claims that he is "at a further remove from every truth than ever before," MATSID2, 360.

9. "Journal 1920–1921," AS, 122.

10. For example, Boulby calls it "probably one of the most ruthlessly direct and merciless pieces of self-exposure in the whole range of modern German literature"

(130), and Mileck similarly describes it as "perhaps . . . the most ruthless of Hesse's many self-exposures" (242).

11. Field has objected that "the psychoanalytic and mystic-philosophical" perspectives are not harmonized; *Hermann Hesse: Kommentar* (cited in Chapter V, note 17).

12. Hesse, *Klein and Wagner*, in *Klingsor's Last Summer*, trans. Richard and Clara Winston (New York: Farrar, Straus & Giroux, 1971), 49. Subsequent citations of *Klein and Wagner* are of this edition and translation and will appear in the text.

13. Hesse, "From Martin's Journal," in *Materialen zu Hermann Hesses "Siddhartha,"* vol. 1, ed. Volker Michels (Frankfurt: Suhrkamp Verlag, 1975), 300–304. Subsequently this volume will be cited as MATSID1.

14. GW, vol. 12, 284.

15. MATSID1, 202.

16. AS, 132–133.

17. AS, 124.

18. GB I, 424, letter of ca. fall 1919.

19. Freedman, 213; Field, 69.

20. Richard Sheppard, "German Expressionism," in *Modernism 1890–1930*, ed. Malcolm Bradbury and James McFarlane (New York: Penguin Books, 1976), 278.

21. Hesse, *Klingsor's Last Summer* (see note 12), 187–188. Subsequent citations of this novella are of this edition and translation and will appear in the text.

22. MATSID1, 192, letter of ca. December 1919.

23. "Klingsor Sends His Friend Thu Fu a Poem," GW vol. 5, 346.

24. AB, 45, letter of April 6, 1953.

25. "Journal 1920–1921," AS, 130.

26. "Journal 1920–1921," 119.

27. "Journal 1920–1921," 129–130.

28. MB, 177.

29. MB, 176; Mileck, 160.

30. Freedman, 225. As Freedman notes (224), we know next to nothing "about the content of these sessions," save that Hesse found them very trying.

31. AS, 146.

32. MATSID1, 112. See also Ziolkowski, 146–147.

33. GB II, 56, letter of April 6, 1923.

34. Ziolkowski, 161.

35. For such specialized yet illuminating readings of *Siddhartha* in terms of its Indian and Chinese elements respectively, see Adrian Hsia, *Hermann Hesse und China: Darstellungen, Materialen, und Interpretationen* (Frankfurt: Suhrkamp Verlag, 1974), 237–248; and Vridhagiri Ganeshan, "Siddhartha und Indien," MATSID2, 225–254.

36. GW, vol. 11, 50.

37. GB II, 48, letter of February 3, 1923.

38. Ziolkowski, 153.

39. GB II, 52, 55, letters of February 10 and March 12, 1923.

40. GB II, 96, letter of June 18, 1925.

41. Ball, 147–151.

42. Ball, 151; Freedman, 217.

43. Field, 81.

44. Hesse, *Siddhartha*, trans. Hilda Rosner (New York: Bantam, 1971), 3. Subsequent citations of the novel are of this edition and translation and will appear in the text.

45. Cf., Boulby has emphasized that "*Siddhartha* discloses finally and unmistakably the significance of hagiography, of the saintly *vita*, as a formal conditioning factor in Hesse's work," 152.

46. AS, 137.

47. MATSID1, 98, letter of February 23, 1920.

48. GB I, 468, letter of March 23, 1921.

49. MB, 385–386.

50. Freedman, 217, MATSID1, 86–91.

51. GB I, 480 (letter of November 11, 1921); MATSID1, 152, letter of February 1922.

52. Hsia, *Hesse und China*, 240, 246.

53. Hsia cites the Confucian saying, "thus like this river everything flows on day and night without cease" (*Hesse und China*, 244).

54. Ziolkowski, 166–167. Hans Jürg Lüthi's claim that the river represents the mother world that is otherwise absent in the novel (*Hermann Hesse: Natur und Geist* [cited in Chapter IV, note 20], 68) misses the mark twice, because the mother world is symbolized not by the river but by Kamala and the world of the senses.

55. Boulby has drawn attention to the "very interesting . . . change of [authorial] standpoint" (157) in the last chapter.

Chapter VIII: Live(d) Fantasies

1. Hesse, "Thoughts about Reading," in *Materialen zu Hermann Hesses "Der Steppen-wolf,"* ed. Volker Michels (Frankfurt: Suhrkamp Verlag, 1975), 59. Subsequently this volume will be cited as MATSTEP.

2. AW, 167–168. Subsequent citations of *A Guest at the Spa* are of this edition and will appear in the text.

3. This and the immediately following excerpts are from the "Kareno" episode in *Klingsor's Last Summer*, 174–176 (cited in Chapter VII, note 12), a fictional account of Hesse's visit to the Wengers and their "palazzo" in Carona with a group of friends, including "Agosto and Ersilia" (read Hugo and Emmy Ball). Freedman plays down the sex appeal of this highly "embellished" (211) portrait of Ruth, and views the initial relationship as "the attraction of a father of three sons to a daughter" (247). Yet Hesse's erotically charged description of this "Queen" clearly points to the sexual rather than the parental character of his attraction.

4. Hesse, *Piktors Verwandlungen*, ed. Volker Michels (Frankfurt: Insel Verlag, 1975), 9–11. Subsequent citations of *Piktor's Metamorphoses* are of this edition and will appear in the text.

5. Michels, Epilogue to *Piktors Verwandlungen*, 82. Michels believes that Hesse's re-

lationship with Ruth played a role, like his sessions with Jung, in enabling him to complete *Siddhartha*.

6. Mileck, 220.
7. Freedman, 248.
8. MATSTEP, 43, letter of April 1, 1925.
9. GB II, 132, letter of February 19, 1926.
10. *Journey to Nuremberg*, AW, 182. Subsequent citations of this travelogue are of this edition and will appear in the text.
11. "From the Journal of One Who Has Been Derailed," MATSTEP, 201.
12. This last sentence is probably a veiled criticism of Jung.
13. GB II, 155, letter of November 10, 1926.
14. GB II, 154.
15. In the letter of January 7, 1926 (GB II, 128–129) which serves as the epigraph of this Chapter, Hesse mentions, "I have a friend here (the Pistorius of *Demian*) with whom I am travelling these [inner] paths."
16. "From the Journal of One Who Has Been Derailed," MATSTEP, 199–202.
17. Freedman, 243.
18. Freedman, 277.
19. Mileck, 175–179.
20. Mann, Introduction to (the first American edition of) *Demian* (cited in Chapter VI, note 24), ix.
21. GB II, 159 (letter of December 22, 1926); MATSTEP, 121 (letter of July 8, 1927); AB, 75 (letter of October 1932).
22. Ziolkowski, 189–195.
23. GB II, 178, letter of June 1927.
24. MATSTEP, 106.
25. Freedman, 283.
26. Sarton, *Journal of a Solitude* (New York: Norton, 1977), 143.
27. GB II, 62, 152, letters of June 26, 1923, and October 13, 1926.
28. "Excursion into the City" (December 1925), MATSTEP, 53–54.
29. MATSTEP, 63, letter of February 17, 1926.
30. MATSTEP, 65, letter of March 17, 1926.
31. Hubacher, MATSTEP, 65–66. The German for one-step, *Wonnestep*, is a pun (*Wonne* = delight).
32. The 1928 edition is available in a bilingual edition, *Crisis: Pages from a Diary*, trans. Ralph Manheim (New York: Farrar, Straus & Giroux, 1975). The text I use is that included in MATSTEP, 161–195. Subsequent citations of *Crisis* are of this edition and will appear in the text.
33. For a developed discussion of the relationship of these poems to the novel, see my article, "The Aesthetics of Confession: Hermann Hesse's *Crisis* Poems in the Context of the *Steppenwolf* Period," *Criticism* 21 (1979): 49–70.
34. Hesse, *Steppenwolf*, trans. Basil Creighton, rev. Joseph Mileck and Horst Frenz (New York: Bantam Books, 1969), 77. Subsequent citations of the novel are of this edition and translation and will appear in the text.

35. See Ziolkowski, 200–206, for the impact of the German Romantic *Märchen* on *Steppenwolf*.

36. Freedman in his discussion of *Steppenwolf* points to "the mirror" as "Hesse's most explicit device, and in the way he used it, also his most significant invention" (294).

37. In the German text this phrase also appears beneath the title of the Steppenwolf Treatise, though in the English translation it is omitted.

38. MATSTEP, 143, letter of November 13, 1930.

39. Ziolkowski, 189.

40. Montaigne, *Essays and Selected Writings* (cited in Chapter I, note 23), 315 (bk. 3, chap. 2).

41. Harry's mention of "an unusually strong tincture of laudanum" in his "medicine chest" as an infrequent remedy for "physical pain" (of which he now makes "a little freer use") must refer to Hesse's own practice during the Steppenwolf years. While the counterculture generation of the sixties, under the enthusiastic sponsorship of Timothy Leary, was willing to extend honorary membership to the author of *Steppenwolf* in the psychedelic brotherhood, Mileck rightly cautions that "whether or not Hesse had recourse to drugs for other than medicinal purposes during his critical Steppenwolf period is debatable" (181).

42. "With These Hands," MATSTEP, 194.

43. Ziolkowski observes that "not the least indication—it must be stressed—justifies us to assume that a murder has taken place on the realistic level" (220); Mileck also emphasizes the "imaginary" character of the murder (192).

44. Heinz Stolte, *Hermann Hesse* (cited in Chapter VI, note 36), 205; Fritz Böttger, *Hermann Hesse* (cited in Chapter IV, note 20), 330; Mileck, 192.

45. Boulby, 200; Ziolkowski 220; Hans Jürg Lüthi, *Hermann Hesse* (cited in Chapter IV, note 20), 86; Rix Weaver, *Spinning on a Dream Thread: Hermann Hesse, His Life and Work and His Contact with C. G. Jung* (Perth: Wyvern Publications, 1977), 162.

46. GB II, 332, letter of April 3, 1932.

47. Freedman credits Hesse's relationship with Ninon as "the greatest impulse for the new burst of creativity" (318).

48. Whereas Ziolkowski judges it "the most imperfect of Hesse's later novels" and complains of "symbolism flattened into allegory" and of the "structural flaw" of the near-exclusive narrative focus on Goldmund (228, 232, 239), and Boulby notes "a certain weariness of the artistic imagination" (211), Freedman praises it as "one of the most revealing but also one of the most beautiful novels Hesse ever wrote" (315), and Lüthi commends it as Hesse's most beautiful version "of a finally achieved harmony born out of suffering" (*Hermann Hesse*, 91).

49. Mileck, 205.

50. Boulby, 230, 231.

51. Hesse, *Narcissus and Goldmund*, trans. Ursule Molinaro (New York: Bantam Books, 1971), 312, 311. Subsequent citations of the novel are of this edition and translation and will appear in the text.

52. Freedman, 324; AB, 29, letter of August 9, 1929 (I cite Boulby's translation, 237).

53. Freedman (317) has suggested that it is "highly probable" that there is a "connection" between Hesse's friendship with Ball and the friendship between Narcissus and Goldmund.
54. Ziolkowski, 240.
55. GB II, 167, letter of ca. 1927.
56. GB II, 276, letter of April 1931.

Chapter IX: Home to the Un-becoming Self

1. Freedman, 332–333.
2. GB II, 284–285, letter of ca. May/June 1931.
3. GB II, 373, letter of January 1933.
4. GB II, 282, letter of May 1931.
5. Heinz Stolte, *Hermann Hesse* (cited in Chapter VI, note 36), 227.
6. Hesse, *The Journey to the East*, trans. Hilda Rosner (New York: Farrar, Straus & Giroux, 1973), 24. Subsequent citations of the novel are of this translation and edition and will appear in the text.
7. Mileck, 227. Mileck's is the most thorough tracing of the biographical, literary, and historical allusions in Hesse's novel (see 217–233).
8. Mileck, 233; Ziolkowski, 263–264.
9. This phrase from Bachofen is quoted by Ziolkowski in his discussion of Leo, 279.
10. The rendering of *Psychokratie* as "psychiatry" (6) is an obvious mistranslation.
11. Quoted in Unseld, 132, 108.
12. GB II, 404, letter of October 1933.
13. GB II, 362, letter of January 26, 1933.
14. Hesse in a statement of 1932 (quoted by Unseld, 144).
15. Mileck, 215; GB II, 299, letter of November 24, 1931.
16. Samuel Beckett, *Company* (New York: Grove Press, 1980), 48, 46.
17. As some critics have noted: cf., Mileck, 218; Ziolkowski, 262.
18. "A Bit of Theology" (1932) MB, 189.
19. Boulby makes the penetrating remark that "perhaps the deepest idea Hesse's works have yet expressed" is "that failure on the Way is in the last resort impossible, since each relapse . . . is itself but part of the Way" (258).
20. As several critics have noted, the final sentence of this excerpt echoes the words of John the Baptist about Christ (John 3:30).
21. Fleishman, *Figures of Autobiography* (cited in Chapter I, note 40), 33.
22. Cf. Freedman's observation, "if the figure of the sensualist Goldmund harks back to Hesse's previous work, the figure of Narcissus dominates his last two important books," 335.
23. *Materialen zu Hermann Hesses "Das Glasperlenspiel,"* vol. 1, ed. Volker Michels (Frankfurt: Suhrkamp Verlag, 1973), 117. Subsequently this volume will be cited as MATGBG1.
24. Mileck, 122.
25. "Bird," GW, vol. 6, 463, 468.

26. For instance, Boulby calls it "a very elusive work indeed" (267); and Field notes "the density of its enigmatic and esoteric allusions," "Goethe and *Das Glasperlenspiel*: Reflections on 'Alterswerke'," *German Life and Letters* 23 (1969): 100–101.

27. MATGBG1, 55, letter of April 1932.

28. Hans Mayer, "Hesses 'Glasperlenspiel' oder die Wiederbegegnung," *Materialen zu Hermann Hesses "Das Glasperlenspiel*," vol. 2, ed. Volker Michels (Frankfurt: Suhrkamp Verlag, 1974), 158. Subsequently this volume will be cited as MATGBG2.

29. Ziolkowski, 283, 294; Boulby, 267, 300.

30. Freedman, 367; Joachim Kaiser, "Science fiction der Innerlichkeit," MATGBG2, 219; Osman Dürrani, " 'Cosmic Laughter' or the Importance of Being Ironical: Reflections on the Narrator of Hermann Hesse's *Glasperlenspiel*," *German Life and Letters* 34 (1981): 398.

31. Mann, "For Hermann Hesse's Seventieth Birthday," MATGBG1, 276.

32. *The Glass Bead Game*, trans. Richard and Clara Winston (New York: Bantam Books, 1970), 78. Subsequent citations of the novel are of this translation and edition and will appear in the text.

33. Oskar Seidlin, "Hermann Hesse: The Exorcism of the Demon," *Hesse: A Collection of Critical Essays* (cited in Chapter VI, note 35); Boulby, 265.

34. Mayer, "Hesses *Glasperlenspiel*," MATGBG2, 163, 168; Hesse, MATGBG1, 302, letter of July 1961. Field ("Zur Genesis des Glasperlenspiels," MATGBG2, 182–183) notes that he can find no evidence that Hesse actually read Hegel, but suggests the possibility that the parallels between the Bead Game and Hegel's dialectic may be based on Hesse's reading of a commemorative newspaper essay on Hegel by an acquaintance (Otto Engel) that appeared in 1931.

35. MATGBG1, 170.

36. Boulby, 267.

37. Peter Suhrkamp, "On Hesse's Seventieth Birthday," MATGBG1, 168.

38. Bruno Hesse, "Father in Conversation," MATGBG1, 289.

39. MATGBG1, 294, letter of January 1955; Mileck, 255.

40. GW, vol. 12, 192. Subsequent citations of Hesse's Goethe essays are of this edition and will appear in the text.

41. Early outline of *The Glass Bead Game*, MATGBG1, 314.

42. MATGBG1, 295–296.

43. Martin Pfeifer, "Der emanzipierte Kastalier: Zur Entstehung und Rezeption des *Glasperlenspiels*," MATGBG2, 305.

44. For a summary of this *cause célèbre*, see Mileck, 248–253. Will Vesper's attack, from which I have quoted, appeared in *Die Neue Literatur* (in April 1936) and is reprinted in full in MATGBG1, 153–159. It is a curious irony indeed that Vesper's literary remains are now housed in the same building and in close physical proximity to the Hesse collection in the Schiller-Nationalmuseum.

45. "From a Journal of 1933," AS, 190. Subsequent citations of this journal will appear in the text.

46. Freedman, 369. During the Nazi era, *Steppenwolf*, *Narcissus and Goldmund* (because of the account of a pogrom in the "Rebekka" episode), and some of the political

332 NOTES TO CHAPTER IX

essays of the World War I period were not allowed to be reprinted (MATGBG1, 176).

47. MATGBG1, 225, letter of December 14, 1942.
48. MATGBG1, 115, letter of May 5, 1935.
49. In his 1934 preface to the third version Hesse states that it was completed in the early summer of 1932 (MATGBG1, 8); Mileck, however, dates it (on the basis of an unpublished note by Hesse to Ninon) as finished in January 1933 (285).
50. Third version of the "Introduction" to the Glass Bead Game, MATGBG1, 19–20.
51. AB, 138 (letter of February 23, 1935); "Besinnung," MATGBGI, 87–88.
52. MB, 191.
53. GB II, 459 (unmailed letter of March 3, 1935); MATGBGI, 115 (letter of March 3, 1935).
54. Ziolkowski, 294, 336–337; Boulby, 265–266; Field, 152.
55. MATGBGI, 284–285, letter of 1949 or 1950.
56. Barbara Belhalfaoui, "Utopische Glasperlenspiele . . . Oder ist Hesses Roman eine Utopie," *Deutsche Vierteljahrschrift für Literaturwissenschaft und Geistesgeschichte* 55 (1981): 127.
57. My major sources for this chronological overview are MATGBGI, and Mileck, 258–263.
58. MATGBGI, 98, letter of October 17, 1934.
59. The exception is "The Circular Letter" (chap. 11), of which a draft was sent to Suhrkamp in September 1938.
60. Mileck, 263.
61. MATGBGI, 80, letter of early 1934.
62. MATGBGI, 198, letter of October 1938.
63. MATGBG2, 323 (letter of August 26, 1931); MATGB1, 200, 190, 91, letters of December 1938; July 28, 1938; May 1934.
64. MATGB1, 193, 295, letters of fall 1938 and January 1955.
65. MATGBG1, 253, 60, letters of September 1943 and March 22, 1933.
66. MATGBG1, 80, 181, 219, 232, letters of spring 1934, July 1937, ca. 1941–1942, November 1, 1943.
67. "Hours in the Garden," MATGBG1, 119–120. Subsequent citations of the poem are of this edition and will appear in the text.
68. I am here relying on Pfeifer's summary of and quotations from the *Spiegel* article on Hesse ("Der emanzipierte Kastalier," MATGBG2, 295).
69. MATGBG1, 61, 91, letters of January 28, 1933, and May 1934.
70. MATGBG1, 101, letter of January 17, 1935.
71. MATGBG1, 233, 232, letters of late 1943 and January 11, 1943.
72. MATGBG1, 314.
73. *The Encyclopedia of Philosophy* (1967; rpt. New York: Macmillan Co. and The Free Press, 1972), vol. 1, 234–235. For a summary of Bachofen's influence on Hesse, see Ziolkowski, 111–113.
74. For this reason it seems to me that Ursula Chi [*Die Weisheit Chinas und "Das Glasperlenspiel"* (Frankfurt: Suhrkamp, 1976), 144–146] is wrong in ultimately rejecting

Hegelian readings of the novel because, as she argues, Hesse's version of the dialectic is not Hegelian but polar in the Chinese sense, and because he allows for progress only in the spiritual development of the individual but not at the level of human history or society. As Roger C. Norton has concluded, if we consider the series of Knecht's incarnations, we find "in combination with concepts of historicity and cyclicity, also a belief . . . that a linear progress can take place within the realms of culture and intellect, if not in social and political institutions" [*Hermann Hesse's Futuristic Idealism: The Glass Bead Game and its Predecessors* (Frankfurt: Lang Verlag, 1973), 130].

75. MATGBG1, letter of October 18, 1940.

76. Hilde D. Cohn, "The Symbolic End of Hermann Hesse's *Glasperlenspiel*," *Modern Language Quarterly* 11 (1950): 353–354.

77. Hesse's description of the star shower is based on "something wonderful" he had witnessed in 1933 (MATGBG2, 324).

78. Field, 164. Chi (in *Die Weisheit Chinas*) repeatedly points to the importance of both these sages on Hesse's conception of Knecht's life and of the Bead Game; and Adrian Hsia in his chapter on *The Glass Bead Game* [in *Hermann Hesse und China* (cited in Chapter VII, note 35), 272–299] also signals Taoist as well as Confucian elements in Hesse's novel.

79. Roger Norton (*Hesse's Futuristic Idealism*, 128) has pointed out that this tale "presents a striking parallel to the Magister Ludi's final journey outside the order."

80. Hesse, "The Eighteenth-Century Swabian Life" ("Schwäbischer Lebenslauf aus dem 18. Jahrhundert"), *Josef Knechts Lebensläufe* (Frankfurt: Suhrkamp Verlag, 1977), 109. Subsequent citations of the Fourth Life will be of this edition and will appear in the text.

81. Boulby (313–315) has noted this and several other parallels between the Fourth Life and Knecht's Castalian career.

82. Mileck, 266–277.

83. MATGBG1, 232, letter of November 1, 1943.

84. Erhard Friedrichsmayer has concluded that "Hesse's ambivalent attitude toward Mann" becomes in the book "the opportunity to stake his claim for his art vis-à-vis Mann's, to assert himself over his admired and more famous 'older brother'," "The Bertram Episode in Hesse's *Glass Bead Game*," *Germanic Review* 49 (1974): 297.

85. As Ernst Robert Curtius has pointed out, "what had, as a neurotic conflict, been a stumbling block [for the adolescent Hesse] becomes . . . a building block," "Hermann Hesse," *Hesse: A Collection of Critical Essays* (cited in note 33), 49.

86. Field, 161.

87. Curtius, "Hermann Hesse," 49–50.

88. Despite the obvious differences in character and setting, Hesse's account of Knecht's mixed feelings after his "election" is similar to Dickens's account of Pip's reaction to the announcement of his "great expectations," including the use of the crucial clothing metaphor: "the clothing he had worn . . . could be discarded at last. A new suit was waiting for him" (49).

89.   "Memories of Hans," MATGBG1, 345.

90.   Manuscript variant of *The Glass Bead Game*, MATGBG1, 318.

91.   "The Veiled Women," manuscript variant of *The Glass Bead Game*, MATGBG1, 319.

92.   Hsia concludes (*Hermann Hesse und China*, 281) that the symbolic language of the Bead Game is based in part on the principle of Chinese ideograms and "appears to be a modified version of the system of the *I Ching*." Chi argues (*Die Weisheit Chinas*, 90 ff.) that Knecht's biography is structured around four *I Ching* hexagrams that are "of decisive importance for the interpretation of Knecht's life and death": Mong = Youthful Folly (no. 4), Lu = Wanderer (no. 56), Ting = The Caldron (no. 50), Wei Chi = Before the Completion (no. 64). She concludes that the latter two, which she deduces from the first two, explicitly present in the novel, are part of Hesse's larger esoteric plan. Her deduction of Ting follows logically from the moving line in the Youthful Folly hexagram (*The Glass Bead Game*, 115–116) and is thus demonstrably intended by Hesse; her derivation of the fourth hexagram (as the motif of Knecht's final stage) is more suggestive than conclusive.

93.   Manuscript variant of *The Glass Bead Game*, MATGBG1, 325.

94.   Chi, *Die Weisheit Chinas*, 119, 137.

95.   Hsia, *Hesse und China*, 282.

96.   Such passages show the late Hesse's admiration of Catholicism "as a form and tradition, as a culture preserving and creating power" superior (in that respect) to the Protestant denominations (AB, 183, letter of October 1939). Hesse also wrote that though he is "not a Catholic, perhaps not even a Christian," it should be apparent from the accounts of Goldmund's and Knecht's stays in monasteries that he has "a great admiration" of the idea of monastic orders and monks (MATGBG1, 293, letter of October 1954).

97.   Karl Marx, *The German Ideology*, in *The Marx-Engels Reader*, 2nd. ed. Robert C. Tucker (New York: Norton, 1978), 166, 175, 154, 155.

98.   Marx, *The German Ideology*, in *The Marx-Engels Reader*, 155.

99.   AB, 183, letter of October 1939.

100.   In his (ingenious if not fully convincing) analysis of the Bertram episode in terms of the Jungian concept of the Shadow, Friedrichsmayer ("The Bertram Episode in Hesse's *Glass Bead Game*," 292) notes the significance of Knecht not appointing a deputy himself, but having "the elite choose one for him" as a way of preventing the danger of being "assailed through his deputy."

101.   Mileck's claim that Knecht's "seven grand annual games are counterpart to the seven major tales written by Hesse from *Demian* to *Die Morgenlandfahrt*" (275) probably makes for too literal a parallel.

102.   Thus the objection of Kenneth Negus ["On the Death of Joseph Knecht in Hermann Hesse's *Glasperlenspiel*," *Monatshefte* 53 (1961): 393] that neither Tito, nor Knecht, nor the reader is "aware . . . of Knecht's *intention* to make the sacrifice" is ultimately beside the point.

103.   Mileck, 307, 309. Barbara Belhalfaoui writes that "the greatest wisdom" of the book is that "everything remains open, everything possible" ("Utopische Glas-

perlenspiele," 134), and Reso Karalaschwili draws attention to the fact that the "open ending" is not peculiar to Hesse but is "one of the characteristics of the modern novel" ("Joseph Knechts Tod," MATGBB2, 232).

104. "Joseph Knecht to Carlo Ferromonte" (1960), MATGBG1, 335.

105. Philip Gilbertson, "Boundaries and the Self in Romanticism," *English and German Romanticism: Cross-Currents and Controversies* (cited in Chapter I, note 3), 145, 151.

106. In July 1952 (AB, 396) Hesse wrote that he finds "*Geworfensein* [sic] as the philosophy of our day" unsatisfactory. In any event, I do not mean to suggest that this resemblance (between Knecht's "leap" and Heidegger's concept) is a matter of Heidegger influencing Hesse, but rather that it is a function of both men sharing a common heritage and inspiration in the process thinking of German Romanticism (Cf., Heidegger's writings on Hölderlin). For a helpful overview of the complex issue of Hesse's relationship to Romanticism and Existentialism, see Ziolkowski, 342–361 ("Between Romanticism and Existentialism").

107. Christian Immo Schneider rightly cautions against turning the (by now standard) reading of Knecht's departure from Castalia as a return to the world of the mother (cf., Boulby, 319, Lüthi, *Hermann Hesse*, 136; Norton, *Hesse's Futuristic Idealism*, 117) into a "*magna mater* interpretation," since "nowhere in *The Glass Bead Game* is the search for the mother" the life-problem it was for Goldmund ("Josef Knechts Abschied und Neubeginn," MATGBG2, 282–283).

108. Boulby has pointed to the presence of the flute as "an erotic symbol" in both "The Legend" and Knecht's eighteenth-century life (311–312).

109. Cohn, "The Symbolic End of Hesse's *Glasperlenspiel*," 335. For a revealing analysis of Hesse's use of the *I Ching* symbolism as proof that "the pattern of Knecht's destiny is not broken but fulfilled by his death," see J. C. Middleton, "An Enigma Transformed in Hermann Hesse's *Glasperlenspiel*," *German Life and Letters* 10 (1956–1957): 298–302.

110. Chi, *Die Weisheit Chinas*, 197–200.

111. Cf., Curtius writes that "*Das Glasperlenspiel* is a western book" and that Knecht's "departure" is "the heroic setting-out of the Nordic man whom Oriental absorption does not restrain" ("Hermann Hesse," 49–50). In Chi's balanced reading, Joseph Knecht is "the ideal . . . human being, who combines the virtues of the East with those of the West" (*Die Weisheit Chinas*, 208).

112. Belhalfaoui, "Utopische Glasperlenspiele," 129–130.

113. My translation of the concluding phrase ("nach der heiligen Mitte hin") of the poem (supposedly written by Knecht), "The Glass Bead Game" (English text, 412).

Epilogue: Who Is He?

1. Hesse, *The Glass Bead Game* (cited in Chapter IX, note 32), 384, 385.

2. Theodore Ziolkowski, "Hermann Hesse in den U.S.A.," *Hermann Hesse Heute*, ed. Adrian Hsia (cited in Chapter VI, note 15).

3. This and the remaining Hesse quotations are from "Pages from a 1955 Journal," entry of March 13; *Gesammelte Schriften*, vol. 7 (Berlin: Suhrkamp Verlag, 1958), 936–937.

4. *Montaigne's Essays and Selected Writings* (cited in Chapter I, note 23), 231 (bk. 2, chap. 12).

INDEX

Abrams, M. H., *Natural Supernaturalism*, 73

adolescence, 55, 66–67, 96–103, 118–19, 155, 179, 229, 278, 289–90; in *Knulp*, 119; in *The Glass Bead Game*, 292

aestheticism, 81–85, 120, 125, 134, 233–35

"alterbiography," 10, 12, 23

amor fati, 47, 54, 134, 141, 287–88

Angst, 155–56, 165

animals, in short fiction, 113

Apollonian/Dionysian split, in *Rosshalde*, 126

art and artists, 52–53, 121, 124, 166, 170–71, 212, 214, 223, 231–37, 255; in *Gertrude*, 120–21; in *Narcissus and Goldmund*, 225–28; in *The Glass Bead Game*, 283

art as confession (*Kunst als Bekenntnis*), 28, 30, 163, 190, 196–97, 206

art/life, 6, 7, 9, 21, 34–35, 106, 125–26, 134, 139, 162, 228, 252

art/religion, 32–33, 160, 278–79

asceticism, 96, 208

associative style, 140

Augustine, St., *The Confessions*, 16–18, 32–33, 143–44, 182

authenticity (*Aufrichtigkeit*), in modern autobiography, 28, 196

authority, paternal, 56, 57, 60, 68, 70, 97, 156–57; spiritual, 299, 304

autobiographical fiction, 13, 14, 16, 33–34, 36, 202, 237, 248, 289

autobiography, 3, 5, 7–8, 10–17, 20–24, 34–35, 41–42, 134, 159, 196–97, 203, 223, 228, 243–44, 246–48, 256, 312; and biography, 8–10, 34–35; as literature, 6, 8, 10, 23; as self-disguise, 241; in *Demian*, 144; in *Märchen*, 136; in *Steppenwolf*, 209; in *The Journey to the East*, 240

autobiography/fiction, 6–10, 13–16, 20–24, 42, 273

"awakening," in *Siddhartha*, 178–82; in *The Glass Bead Game*, 274, 289–91, 293–95, 300–305

Axthelm, Peter, 18

Bachofen, J. J., 142, 324n29; *Grave Symbolism of the Ancients*, 240; *The Law of the Mother*, 270

Ball, Hugo, 132, 194, 203, 227, 229; *Hermann Hesse*, 35, 48, 69, 88, 95, 97, 132, 177, 203

Barns, John, 68

Basel, 81, 193–94, 201

Beckett, Samuel, *Company*, 242–43

becoming, 3, 4, 20–21, 41, 78, 192, 281, 288, 291, 305, 309–10

being, 167, 170. *See also* true being; writing as being

being/becoming, 4, 281

Belhalfaoui, Barbara, 309, 334n103

Benjamin, Walter, 107

Bern, 114

Bernoulli, Maria ("Mia"), 95, 105, 131, 138, 194
Bible, 143, 166
Bildung (education), 19, 72
Bildungsroman, 4, 6, 13, 19, 139, 315n6
biography, 78, 203; and autobiography, 8–10, 34–35
birth imagery, 145–46, 149, 154. *See also* new self; rebirth
Blake, William, 47, 72–74, 139, 142, 144, 256, 291; "Augeries of Innocence," 268; *The Marriage of Heaven and Hell*, 130, 152, 283
Blumhardt, Pr. Christoph, 60
Bodmer, Hans and Elsie, 238
Boehme, Jakob, 284
Böttger, Fritz, 89, 329n44
Boulby, Mark, 96, 118, 149, 156, 224, 227, 251–53, 263, 322nn3, 6; 325n10, 327nn45, 55; 329nn45, 48, 50; 331n36, 333n81, 335nn107, 108
Brahmanism, 74
Brontë, Charlotte, *Jane Eyre*, 5
Bruss, Elizabeth, 23, 318n40
Buckley, Jerome H., 4, 13, 15, 16, 20, 315nn3, 6; 317nn26, 34
Buddhism, 74; in *Siddhartha*, 177, 179–80
Burckhardt, Jacob, *Reflections on World History*, 272, 286, 295–96, 298

Calw, remembered, 117, 155
Catholic church, in *The Glass Bead Game*, 283, 295, 334n96
challenge, in *The Glass Bead Game*, 300–303, 306–7
change, 41, 293–95, 305, 309
Chateaubriand, *René*, 19–20
Chi, Ursula, 293, 294, 308, 332n74, 333n78, 334nn92, 94
childhood, 55–57, 64, 67, 83, 85–86, 90, 117, 126, 132, 140, 174–75, 289–90, 324n15; in *A Child's Soul*, 155–58; in *Demian*, 143; in *Knulp*, 119; in mother *Märchen*, 136–38; in *Peter Camenzind*, 95; loss of, 114; return to, 102, 215, 306–7
Childhood and Youth Before 1900, 55–56, 59–64, 67, 71, 76, 97, 155

China, 71, 174, 183–84, 254, 276–77, 293–94
Christianity, 62–63, 71, 115, 142, 183, 218, 295
Cioran, E. M., 25
city life, 201–4
civilization, 114. *See also* culture
classicism, 282–85
Cohn, Hilde, 273, 308
Coleridge, Samuel Taylor, 265
Communism, 49, 52–53
community, 64–65, 76, 108, 112, 275
confession, 4–6, 11, 14–15, 28, 32, 37, 134, 160, 162, 188–89, 197; in *Crisis*, 206; in *Demian*, 143, 147, 149; in *Gertrude*, 122–23; in *Klein and Wagner*, 168; in *Klingsor's Last Summer*, 172; in *Knulp*, 117; in "Robert Aghion," 114; in *Steppenwolf*, 209, 220, 222; in *The Journey to the East*, 242, 249
confessional aesthetics, 195
confessional fiction, 3, 11, 13–24, 30–31, 42, 93, 124, 190–91; and autobiography, 13–14, 20–24, 42
confessional imagination, 4, 18, 21–24, 149, 203, 287, 312; in *Narcissus and Goldmund*, 225, 237; in *Steppenwolf*, 222
confessional persona, 17, 19, 165, 181
confessional writing, 35, 97, 139, 156, 169, 198, 311–12
confessions of belief, in poems, 82, 259, 268
Confucius, 184, 276, 293, 294, 327n53, 333n78
conscience, 43–47, 50, 53, 71–72, 131, 143, 155, 258, 279
creative process, in *Narcissus and Goldmund*, 232–33
creativity, 224, 230–33, 297
criticism, 7, 222, 250–51, 268
cult of Mind (*Geist*), in *The Glass Bead Game*, 271, 273–75, 280, 304
cult of the past, in *The Glass Bead Game*, 283
culture, 153, 253, 255, 262, 266, 269, 273, 278; in *The Glass Bead Game*, 278, 281–86, 295, 297; popular, 285; Western, 172–73

Curtius, Ernst Robert, 288, 333*nn*85, 87; 335*n*111

daemon image, 146–48
daimon (Socratic concept), 65, 143, 222, 287–88, 309
dancing, 205
"dark"/"light" worlds, 144, 146, 150, 161–62, 279
death, in *Beneath the Wheel*, 104; in *Klein and Wagner*, 165, 168; in *Klingsor's Last Summer*, 171; in *Narcissus and Goldmund*, 225–27, 230, 234–37; in *Steppenwolf*, 221–22; in *The Glass Bead Game*, 275, 303, 305, 308; in "Walter Kömpff," 111
Demian, 31, 36, 44–45, 99, 103, 114, 116, 130, 132–36, 139–54, 157, 160, 162, 312; "Beatrice" chapter, 144, 146; compared to *Siddhartha*, 176; compared to *Steppenwolf*, 211, 217; "Frau Eva" sequence, 146–48
"demon" self, 155
depression, 162, 204
De Quincey, Thomas, 8
despair, 63, 88, 110–11, 128, 165, 188, 193, 221, 227, 242, 244, 246
Dickens, Charles, *David Copperfield*, 137; *Great Expectations*, 11, 333*n*88
disobedience, 66
divided self, 164, 188–89, 195, 198, 200–201, 214, 219–21, 224, 228, 234, 237, 248
domestic life, 106, 117–18, 124
Dostoevsky, Feodor, 17–19, 50, 134, 152–53
doubt, 243–45, 247
drama, Romantic, 4
dreams, 133, 136–40, 144, 147, 163–64, 203, 235
drugs, 219, 329*n*41
duality, 189, 191, 198, 223, 226, 252

Eakin, Paul John, 318*n*40
Eastern philosophy and religion, 71–73, 162, 167, 175–76
Edel, Leon, 78
education, 286, 307. *See also Bildung*

ego, 21, 64
Eichendorff, Joseph, Freiherr von, 117, 322*n*8
Eigensinn (self-will), 43–79, 99, 109–10, 114, 132, 142, 145, 176–79, 229, 253, 287–88, 291, 301–6, 309
Eliot, T. S., 15, 25, 145
elitism, 76–77, 242, 261, 304
embourgeoisement, 107, 124, 130
Emerson, Ralph Waldo, 44
Englert, Josef, 170
epiphany, 166, 180, 233
Erikson, Erik H., 316*n*19
eros, 16, 144, 217, 220–23, 228, 249–50
eros/logos, 221–23, 231, 236, 261, 282
escape, 67, 100, 109, 117–18, 163–64, 209, 256. *See also* suicide, as escape; travel, as escape
essay, Romantic, 4
ethics, 45, 50, 262
Eve figure, 102, 225
Everyman, 213
existentialism, 165–66, 301–2, 309
Expressionism, 169, 172

"fable" concept, 21–22
fact/fiction, 6–8, 16, 84, 208. *See also* poetry and truth
Faesi, Robert, 266
fairy tales. *See Märchen*
faith, 69, 71, 74, 176, 246–47, 261, 269, 310
fall of man, 73–74, 114, 143, 290
family, 86, 106, 108, 124, 131; in *Peter Camenzind*, 94–95; in *Rosshalde*, 126, 128; influence, 174–75
family romance (Freudian), 86, 94, 123, 155, 279
fantasy, 17, 84, 146
fascism, 259, 261
fate, 146
father figure, 85–86, 126; in *A Child's Soul*, 155–58; in *Beneath the Wheel*, 97–98; in *Demian*, 150; in *Narcissus and Goldmund*, 229; in *Peter Camenzind*, 93–94; in *Siddhartha*, 177; in *The Glass Bead Game*, 304
father-son conflict, 56, 154, 158, 177, 231

father-son myth, 119, 304
father world (*Geist*), 155, 177, 180, 231, 236, 260, 270, 273, 279–80. *See also* logos; Mind
felix culpa. See fall of man
"fever muse," 82
fiction, 5, 7, 15, 133, 223, 289. *See also* fact/fiction
fictions of the self, 18, 22, 36, 37, 41, 141, 202, 252, 269, 313
Field, George Wallis, 120, 169, 178, 263, 276, 288, 324*n*15, 326*n*11
fire imagery, 170, 225–26, 267
Fischer, Samuel, 35, 87
Flaubert, Gustave, 16, 17, 26, 199–200, 317*n*29
Fleishman, Avrom, 248, 318*n*40
flute image, 280, 307
folk tradition, 105, 117–18
form, in autobiography, 13; in *Steppenwolf*, 202
framing devices, in *Steppenwolf*, 209, 211
Francis, St., 71, 90, 92, 106
Franz, M.-L. von, 324*n*23
Freedman, Ralph, *Hermann Hesse*, 40, 68, 84, 88, 95, 131, 169, 175, 177, 199, 201, 203, 227, 251, 256, 320*nn*20, 23, 29; 323*n*3, 324*n*8, 329*nn*36, 47, 48, 52; 330*n*53
freedom, 110, 131, 160, 239
French, Marilyn, *The Women's Room*, 14
Freud, Sigmund, 28–29, 56, 134–35, 147, 158, 220, 227, 232, 256; *Civilization and Its Discontents*, 152; *Group Psychology and the Analysis of the Ego*, 44; *The Interpretation of Dreams*, 5, 12
Freudian symbolism, 156–58
Friedrichsmayer, Erhard, 333*n*84, 334*n*100
friendship, 91–92, 99, 101, 121, 291, 300
Frühromantiker (early German Romantics), 29, 72, 85
future, 262

Gaienhofen, 105–7, 120, 124
Ganeshan, Vridhagiri, 326*n*35
gardening, 267–68, 307
Gay, Peter, 40
Geist, 87, 199, 251–52, 254, 260–61, 268–

69, 272, 283, 296. *See also* logos; Mind
genius, nature of, 214, 297
Gerbersau, 119
German nationalism, 257
German Prisoners of War Welfare Organization, 132
German Romantics, 29, 37, 78–79, 80–81, 84, 85, 107, 133–34, 141, 196, 324*n*15
Geworfenheit, 167
Gnosticism, 141–45
God within, 47, 73–75, 136, 167, 176, 291
Goebbels, Joseph, 262
Goethe, Johann Wolfgang von, 4, 25, 27, 65, 72, 143, 187, 254; as seen in *Steppenwolf*, 216, 218; *Faust*, 214; *From My Life: Poetry and Truth*, 4–8, 13, 18, 20, 22; *Sufferings of Young Werther*, 4–5, 18–19, 21–22, 92, 108; *West-Eastern Divan*, 255; *Wilhelm Meister*, 4
"golden track," 212–13, 217
Guéhenno, Jean, 6, 12
guilt, 163, 164, 166, 169, 208, 304
Gundert, Dr. Hermann, 57, 59, 70, 174
Gusdorf, Georges, 6, 34

hagiography, 106, 178, 327*n*45
Hazlitt, William, 26
heaven, 218
hedonism, 182
Hegel, Georg Wilhelm Friedrich, 142, 219, 251–52, 272, 296, 333*n*74
Heidegger, Martin, 167, 306, 335*n*106
Hesse, Bruno, 253
Hesse, Hans, 289
Hesse, Hermann, "A Bit of Theology," 73, 260; *A Child's Soul*, 154–58; *A Glance at Chaos*, 152; *A Guest at the Spa*, 188–89, 198–201; "A Man by the Name of Ziegler," 113; "A Poet's Preface to His Selected Works," 28; "A Work Night," 36; *An Hour Behind Midnight*, 82–83, 123; "Artists and Psychoanalysis," 133; *Autobiographical Writings*, 311; *Beneath the Wheel*, 55, 66–67, 95–104, 149–50, 235, 278; biographies, 106; "Bird" (*Vogel*), 250; "Childhood of the Magician," 36, 65, 138; *Crisis*, 188, 197–98, 203, 206–8; *Demian*, 31, 36, 44–45, 99, 103, 114, 116, 130, 132–36, 139–54, 157,

160, 162, 312; Dostoevsky essays, 154, 171; "Events in the Engadine," 38, 311; fairy tales, 134–39, 240; "For Marulla," 311; "From a Journal of 1933," 53, 256–59; *From India*, 175; "From Martin's Journal," 164; "From the Journal of One Who Has Been Derailed," 195, 198, 210, 328*n*11; "Gerbersau" stories, 106–17; *Gertrude*, 119–24; "Goethe and Bettina," 254; "Gratitude to Goethe," 254; "Hours in the Garden," 267–68; *If the War Goes On*, 44–48, 319*n*1, 323*n*5; "Inside and Outside," 143; "Journal of 1900," 84; "Journal [of] 1920–1921," 31–32, 38, 160, 167–68, 174–75, 180, 182, 230, 243; *Journey to Nuremberg*, 188, 195–96, 201; *Klein and Wagner*, 32, 160–69, 220; *Klingsor's Last Summer*, 160–61, 169–73, 186, 190–91, 312, 327*n*3; *Knulp*, 117–19; "Letter to a Communist," 51–53; "Life Story Briefly Told," 35, 66–67, 71–72, 96, 130, 133; *Märchen*, 135–39, 240; "Memories of Hans," 289–90; "My Belief," 174, 176; *Narcissus and Goldmund*, 36, 38, 188, 224–37, 292, 312, 331*n*46; "Pages from a 1955 Journal," 312; *Peter Camenzind*, 87–95, 120; *Piktor's Metamorphoses*, 191–93; *Politics of Conscience*, 48; "Reflection" ("Besinnung"), 259–61; "Robert Aghion," 114–17, 175; *Romantic Songs*, 81–82; *Rosshalde*, 106–7, 120, 124–29, 142, 159; "Self-Communion," 161, 325*nn*7, 8; *Siddhartha*, 141, 167, 173–87, 191, 192, 312, 327–28*n*5; "Stages," 41–42, 288–90, 306, 309; *Steppenwolf*, 113, 136, 164, 188, 193–98, 201–24, 246, 266, 312, 331*n*46; "Tao," 183; "The Brothers Karamazov, or the Decline of Europe," 143, 153; "The City," 113–14; "The Cyclone," 114; *The Glass Bead Game*, 178, 185, 238, 246, 250–70, 273–312; "The Homecoming," 109–13; *The Journey to the East*, 34, 170, 239–50, 252; "The Latin Scholar," 109; *The Literary Remains of Hermann Lauscher*, 83–87; "The Marble Works," 108–9; *The Steppenwolf: Excerpts from a Diary in Verse*, 206; "The Wolf," 113; "Thoughts about Reading," 188–89; "Thoughts on *The Idiot*," 152; "To My Mother," 320–21*n*31; "Walter Kömpff," 109–11; *Wandering*, 159; *Zarathustra's Return*, 44, 46–48

Hesse, Johannes, 57–60, 63, 86–87, 93, 131, 155, 158, 177, 229, 231; "Lao-Tzu as a Pre-Christian Witness to the Truth," 183

Hess, Maria. *See* Bernoulli, Maria

Hesse, Marie Gundert, 55, 57–60, 68–70, 82–83, 85–87, 93, 95, 97, 123, 136, 280, 320*nn*20, 21

Hesse, Martin, 131

Hesse, Ninon (Ausländer) Dolbin, 64, 190, 224, 238–40, 265; epilogue to *Childhood and Youth Before 1900*, 56

Hesse, Ruth Wenger. *See* Wenger, Ruth

Hinduism, 174

history, 52, 153, 253, 255, 269, 272, 286, 289, 296–98, 302

Hitler, Adolf, 151, 258–59, 262, 275–76; *Mein Kampf*, 10

Hoffmann, E.T.A., 84, 240

Holland, Norman, 67

home, 95, 107, 208, 218, 249

homicidal fantasy, 200, 207, 221–23

homology, in biography, 9–10, 12

hope, 281

Howarth, William, 20

Hsia, Adrian, 183, 293, 294, 326*n*35, 327*nn*52, 53; 333*n*78, 334*nn*92, 95

Hubacher, Hermann, 205–6

human evil, 275

humanism, 46, 78, 213

humanization, 73–75, 176, 178, 186, 215, 245, 247, 260. *See also* individuation

humor, 188, 201, 268; in *A Guest at the Spa*, 198, 215; in *Siddhartha*, 178, 186; in *Steppenwolf*, 211, 214–15, 219, 223; in *The Glass Bead Game*, 302

Ibsen, *Peer Gynt*, 21

I Ching, 293–95, 293*n*, 308, 334*n*92, 335*n*109

idealist aesthetic, 235–36

identity, 17, 21, 41, 61, 68, 111, 161, 164, 185, 207; in *Knulp*, 118–19; in *Narcissus and Goldmund*, 224; in *Steppenwolf*, 210

identity crisis, adolescent, 55, 66, 97, 103, 118–19, 155, 179, 229; of confessional writer, 190
identity of opposites, 186, 193, 225, 308
identity theme, 67–70, 77–78
ideology, 296–97
imagination, 6–8, 90, 135, 143, 212, 218, 235, 239, 249, 267–68, 271. *See also* confessional imagination
impersonality, 15, 25–26, 253–54
independence, 99, 287, 298, 306
India, 71, 114–17, 174–76, 277
individual, 65, 110, 140, 167, 302, 309; and community, 253
individual conscience, 43–47, 50, 53, 71
individualism, 45, 47, 50–54, 71–77, 122, 163, 177
individuation, Jungian theory of, 29, 66, 74–75, 132, 136, 140, 144–46, 176, 215–16
influences, 56, 90, 107, 135, 141–42, 256, 276
inner/outer worlds, 140, 144, 214, 218–19, 249, 274
inner self, 29, 133, 140–43, 146, 148, 161–62, 202, 219
inner voice, 44–46, 54, 111, 177, 273–74, 301, 309. *See also* individual conscience
intellect, 212, 261, 304
irony, 12, 84, 98, 101, 109, 112, 200, 209, 219, 223, 251, 252, 282, 289
Isenberg, Karl, 286–87
isolation, 96, 204, 268

Jung, Carl Gustav, 28–29, 132–33, 135, 139–44, 175, 197, 327n5, 328n12; mother myth, 147; scheme of individuation, 74–75, 217, 222; *Septem Sermones*, 141; *Symbols of Transformation*, 144

Kafka, Franz, 22, 256
Kama Sutra, 181
Karalaschwili, Reso, 335n103
Kazin, Alfred, 7, 15
Keats, John, 25, 234–35
Keller, Gottfried, 88, 106, 322n3
Kierkegaard, 18, 165
Künstlerroman, 4, 120

Lang, Dr. Josef B., 36, 132, 133, 139, 141, 197, 240, 324n8
language, 37, 39
Lao-Tzu, 183, 293, 333n78
Lawrence, D. H., 56, 72, 83, 153–54; *Sons and Lovers*, 17, 19, 279; *Women in Love*, 154
legend, 100, 203, 299–301
Lejeune, Philippe, 7, 13–14
letters to readers, 76–77, 80
Lichtenstein, Heinz, 67–68, 320n28
life/art, 6–7, 9, 21, 34–35, 106, 125–26, 134, 139, 162, 228, 252
life of the mind, 262, 267–69, 301
Lifton, Robert Jay, 21
"light"/"dark" worlds, 144, 146, 150, 161–62, 279
literary imagination (*Dichtung*), 16
literature, as confession, 32; popular, 286; role of, 134
logos, 259, 261, 268–69. *See also* Geist; Mind
logos/eros, 221–23, 231, 236, 261, 282
loneliness, 121–22, 128
love, 64, 109, 117, 225; of nature, leading to love of man, 91–92
loyalty/apostasy, 246–47
Lüthi, Hans Jürg, 89, 327n54, 329n45

madness/sanity, in *Steppenwolf*, 210
male/female images, reversed, 280
Mandel, Barret J., 316n12
Mann, Thomas, 202, 251, 257, 258, 286–87, 333n84
Märchen, 84, 134, 192, 209, 250, 324nn15, 18; 329n35
marriage, Hesse's, 105–7, 122, 124, 127–29, 131, 150, 163, 168–69, 190, 192–94, 204, 222, 238–39; in *Demian*, 150; in *Gertrude*, 122; in *Klein and Wagner*, 168–69; in *The Glass Bead Game*, 280, 292–93
Marxism, 49, 51–53, 258, 272, 296–98
März (magazine), 106
mass media, 285
mass movements, 50, 53
Maugham, Somerset, *Of Human Bondage*, 16
Maulbronn school, 60, 64, 97, 99–102, 287–88

Mayer, Hans, 251–52
meditation, 267–68, 277
Mehlman, Jeffrey, 316n13
memory, 9
Michels, Volker, 191, 327nn4, 5
middle class, 107, 109, 124, 130, 163, 199, 209–11, 214, 216
Middleton, J. C., 335n109
mid-life crisis, 188, 194, 206, 208
Mileck, Joseph, 39, 106, 123, 135, 141, 174, 192, 202, 222, 224, 242, 250, 254, 286, 300n, 305, 319n6, 321n13, 323nn2, 7; 326n10, 329nn41, 43, 49; 330nn7, 8, 15, 24; 331n44, 332nn49, 57, 60; 334nn101, 103
Mind (Geist), 155, 218, 230, 236, 261–62, 267–69, 271, 275–76, 289, 297, 301, 304, 305
Mind/Nature, 206, 300–301, 303
mirror images, 198, 203; in Klein and Wagner, 163, 165, 168; in Klingsor's Last Summer, 172; in Steppenwolf, 209–10, 214, 219, 221, 329n36
Misch, Georg, 6, 13
modernism, 15, 139, 144, 171, 202, 214, 219, 241, 245
Moilliet, Louis, 170, 240
Montagnola, 160–62, 169, 190–91, 238
Montaigne, 15, 219, 313
mother image, 83, 134–36; in A Child's Soul, 154; in An Hour Behind Midnight, 82; in Demian, 147–48, 150; in Gertrude, 123; in Märchen, 136; in Narcissus and Goldmund, 225, 237; in Peter Camenzind, 92–94; in Rosshalde, 126–27; in Steppenwolf, 217; in The Literary Remains of Hermann Lauscher, 86
mother myth, 82–83, 119, 136–37, 140, 143, 147–49, 153, 155, 217, 225–26, 237
mother world (Natur), 90, 98, 104, 137, 139, 150, 177, 231, 236, 260, 270, 273, 279–80, 303, 335n107
mother Märchen, 135–39
Mozart, Wolfgang Amadeus, as seen in Steppenwolf, 221, 223–24
music, 167–68, 185, 202; in The Glass Bead Game, 275, 279–82, 301
mysticism, 185
myth, 140, 250

Nabokov, Vladimir, Speak, Memory, 23, 34, 242
Narcissus motif, 149
narrative idiom, 107, 109
nature, 85, 88–91, 93, 98, 104, 107, 108, 113–15, 118, 138, 150, 271, 273
Nature/Mind, 153, 215, 260, 273, 279, 291–93, 304–5
Nazi regime (National Socialism), 151, 238–39, 256–58, 261, 266
Negus, Kenneth, 334n102
Neue Rundschau (journal), 264
new self, Jungian concept of, 145–46, 148, 161, 214, 216
Nietzsche, Friedrich Wilhelm, 18, 44, 46–47, 71, 121, 134, 142–43, 232, 286, 297; autobiography, 172; Ecce Homo, 196; The Birth of Tragedy, 232
Nobel Prize (1946), 287, 311
nonconformity, 64, 71–72
nonviolence, 49
Norton, Roger C., 333nn74, 79
Novalis (Friedrich von Hardenberg), 29, 80, 84–85, 146; Heinrich von Ofterdingen, 16, 21, 138, 171, 240

obedience, 44, 46, 54
objectivity/subjectivity, 4, 7, 9–10, 15, 17, 20, 25–27, 31, 178, 213, 219
Oedipus complex, Freudian, 83, 94, 123, 126, 134–35, 150, 156, 158
Olney, James, 34, 317n39, 318n6, 319n24
Orientalism, 175
Orwell, George (Eric Blair), "Politics and the English Language," 262
outsider, artist as, 64, 120, 129, 204, 209, 214

pacifism, 49
painting, 161, 194
paradox, 281
Paris Daily (newspaper), 256
Pascal, Roy, 3, 7, 16, 18
passive resistance, 179
perfection, in The Glass Bead Game, 288, 291, 294
persona, confessional, 17, 19, 165, 181; in Beneath the Wheel, 97; in Gertrude, 120

personality (*Persönlichkeit*), 51, 253–54
personal myth, 134, 141
personal/suprapersonal, 253–56, 269
personas, confessional, 17, 19, 165, 181; in *Beneath the Wheel*, 97; in *Gertrude*, 120
perspectives, multiple, 18–19, 189, 209–10, 281–82
perspectivism, 209–10, 244
"petit cénacle," in Tübingen, 84
Pfeifer, Martin, 256, 331*n*43, 332*n*68
"Phantasie," 6
Pietism, 32, 71, 144, 264, 284, 295
Plath, Sylvia, *The Bell Jar*, 5, 14, 18
Plato, 218, 261
poetry, 4, 88, 106, 293
poetry and truth, 5, 8–9, 13, 21, 23, 55, 125, 203, 211–12, 244, 247, 312
polarities, 175, 178, 189, 242, 295, 306
political refugees, 258, 265
popular culture, 285
prodigal son theme, in *Demian*, 143–44; in *Knulp*, 119; in *Narcissus and Goldmund*, 230–31
progress, 271, 332–33*n*74
propaganda, 50–51, 256–57, 262
Protestantism, 71–72, 142; secularized, 78–79
pseudonym, 139
psychoanalysis, 29–30, 48, 95, 132–42, 154, 158, 160–62, 168, 175, 196–97, 256
psychobiography, 214–15
psychobiology, 140
psychomachia, of *Klein and Wagner*, 164, 168
psychopathology, 163
publicity, 204, 241

quest romance, 138, 249, 293

readers, 12, 76, 241, 251, 257–58
reading, 80, 188–89
realism, 88, 158, 296
rebellion, 55, 67, 110, 292
rebirth, 148, 153. *See also* birth imagery; new self
reincarnation, 253–54
religion, 69–75, 115–16, 140, 169, 176–77, 183, 185
religion/art, 32–33, 160, 278–79

religion of art, 81, 84
Renza, Louis, 316*n*14
resistance, 98–99, 110
Richter, Jean Paul, 18
river symbol, in *Siddhartha*, 167, 178, 183–85, 187
Romanticism, 3, 4, 29, 95, 73, 74, 80–85, 89, 90, 107, 138, 143–44, 171, 205, 209, 216, 218, 245, 271, 288. *See also* German Romantics
romantic love, 117
Rossetti, Dante Gabriel, 83; "Beata Beatrix," 146
Rousseau, Jean-Jacques, and confessional writing, 89, 189; *The Confessions*, 3, 4, 6, 10-13, 18, 20, 32–33, 56, 147, 156, 182, 219

sacrifice, 69–70, 275, 299
saints, 168, 178
Salinger, J. D., *The Catcher in the Rye*, 5, 19, 63, 320*n*22
Sammons, Jeffrey, 151
sarcasm, 109
Sarton, May, 204
satire, 109, 285–86
Schiller, Friedrich von, "To Joy," 323*n*5
Schlegel, Friedrich von, 3, 13
Schneider, Christian Immo, 335*n*107
Schoeck, Othmar, 240
school, 55, 66, 96–101, 119, 150
"school" literature, 96
Schopenhauer, Arthur, 167
secular humanism, 298
Seidlin, Oskar, 251–52
self, 3–4, 13–14, 17–19, 21, 31, 37, 39, 41, 47–48, 64–65, 72–73, 94, 99, 103, 111, 132, 134, 136, 141, 144–45, 149, 155, 161–62, 164–65, 172, 179, 180, 182, 185, 200, 203, 209–11, 214, 220, 223–24, 228, 248, 252, 291, 306, 310, 313; divided, 195, 198, 200–201, 219–21, 224, 228, 234, 237, 248
self-awareness, 164
self-criticism, 134, 264
self-disguise, 12, 36, 251
self-encounters, 96, 146, 209, 216, 221
self-expression, 15, 36
self-fictionalization, 18, 22, 36, 37, 41, 141, 202, 252, 269, 313

self-image, 37, 66, 68, 71, 134, 160–61, 193, 209–10, 215–16, 219–20, 254, 267
self-integration, 193, 199
self-knowledge, 207, 209, 214, 216, 245
self-projections, 149, 168
self-realization, 94, 140, 160–61, 163, 176, 178, 185, 222–23, 235, 272, 283, 288, 298
self-renewal, 178, 188, 193. *See also* "awakening"; new self; rebirth
self-revelation, 189, 222, 304
self-sacrifice, 69–70, 275
self-transformation, 14, 130
self-understanding, 210, 247. *See also* self-knowledge
self-will. *See Eigensinn*
sentimentality, in *A Guest at the Spa*, 200; in *Klingsor's Last Summer*, 171; in *Knulp*, 117; in *Steppenwolf*, 215–16
service to the Mind (*Dienst am Geist*), in *The Glass Bead Game*, 261, 269, 272–79, 289; in *The Journey to the East*, 247
sexuality, 102–3, 146–48, 150, 168, 181, 218
Sheppard, Richard, 169
signification of self, 15
sincerity, in autobiography, 11, 12
"Sinclair, Emil," pseud., 139
social criticism, 109
socialism, 49
Socrates, 142, 308
Spender, Stephen, 317*n*38
Spiegel, Der (magazine), 267–68
Spirit, 252, 268–69, 272, 296
spirit-call, 277–79, 289
spirit/nature, 184. *See also* Nature/Mind
spiritual growth, 74–75
spirituality, 70, 283
spiritual traditions, 176
Stelzig, Eugene L., 315*nn*2, 3; 328*n*33
Steppenwolf, 113, 136, 164, 188, 193–98, 201–24, 246, 266, 312, 331*n*46; Haller's Records, 209; "The Immortals" (poem), 216; The Magic Theater, 213–15, 219–22; "The Steppenwolf" (poem), 216; The Steppenwolf Treatise, 19, 209, 213–16, 220
Stetten, 61–63
Stolte, Heinz, 151, 329*n*44
striving, Faustian, 288, 305

Sturrock, John, 7, 8
Sturzenegger, Hans, 106
style, in early stories, 107, 109; in *Klingsor's Last Summer*, 171–72; in *Rosshalde*, 125; in *Steppenwolf*, 195–96, 202, 211; in *The Glass Bead Game*, 251; influenced by Jung, 140; mature, 265
stylization of experience, 13
Styron, W., *Confessions of Nat Turner*, 5
subjectivity/objectivity, 4, 7, 9–10, 15, 19–20, 25–27, 31, 178, 213, 219
success, 88, 106–7, 130, 195, 241
Suffel, Jacques, 317*n*29
suffering, role of, 92, 119–20, 184, 245–46
Suhrkamp, Peter, 253, 257
suicidal tendency, 55, 62, 121, 182, 215
suicide, as apotheosis, 165; as escape, 109, 164, 209, 215; in *Klein and Wagner*, 164–67; in *Steppenwolf*, 193–94; in "The Marble Works," 109; in "Walter Kömpff," 111
suprapersonal, 253–56, 269
Swift, Jonathan, 113, 262, 283
Switzerland, 257
symbol, defined, 144
symbolism, 22, 36, 143–45, 150, 153–55; Freudian, 156–58; Gnostic, 153; in *A Child's Soul*, 156; in *Demian*, 141–43, 145; in *Knulp*, 119; in "Lulu," 84–85; in *Märchen*, 135–39; in *Narcissus and Goldmund*, 225; in *Piktor's Metamorphoses*, 192; in *Rosshalde*, 126; in *Siddhartha*, 175, 178, 183–85; in *Steppenwolf*, 113, 199–200, 217; in "The Cyclone," 114; in *The Glass Bead Game*, 273, 294, 302–3, 306; in *The Journey to the East*, 246; Jungian, 141, 144

Taoism, 174–75, 183, 254, 293, 294, 333*n*78, 334*n*92
Tao Te Ching, 183
teacher-student relationships, in *The Glass Bead Game* biographies, 273–74
Teilhard de Chardin, Pierre, 74–75
teleology, 8
The Glass Bead Game, 178, 185, 238, 250–70, 273–312; Fourth (Swabian) Life, 264, 278–84; "Introduction," 258–59, 263–64, 281–82, 285; poems, 265; "The

The Glass Bead Game (cont.)
  Father Confessor'' (second life), 264, 276–77; ''The Indian Life'' (third life), 264, 277–78; ''The Rainmaker,'' 264, 270–75, 299
theology, nontheological, in *The Glass Bead Game*, 283
Third Reich, 256–61, 265–66
Thoreau, Henry David, 20, 45
Thurber, James, ''The Secret Life of Walter Mitty,'' 16
Ticino fictions, 172
time, reality of, 186–87
Tolstoy, Count Leo, 105, 235
transcendence, 217, 309
transformations, in *Piktor's Metamorphoses* and *Siddhartha*, 192
transience, 226–27
travel, as escape, 106, 117–18, 127
true being, 165, 291, 312
''true confessions,'' 17
''true'' self, 28, 39
truth, 6, 9, 244, 261–62, 291
truthfulness, in biography, 6, 207
Tübingen, 80–81, 84

un-becoming (*Entwerden*), 185, 253, 309–10
unconscious, 117, 133–34, 136, 140, 152–54, 158, 168, 211, 220, 273, 324n15
unity of being, 75, 161, 166, 168, 178, 185–86, 200, 261, 274, 291
utopias, 65, 266–67, 286, 309

Vesper, Will, 256, 331n44
viewpoints, multiple. *See* perspectives, multiple
Vivos Voco (literary journal), 183
Voltaire, 284

war, 131, 139, 150–51, 153, 266
water image, 161, 184. *See also* river symbol
''way within'' (*Weg nach innen*), 29, 154, 160
Weaver, Rix, 222
Weintraub, Karl, 4, 315nn2, 5
Wenger, Lisa, 190
Wenger, Ruth, 170, 190–94, 208, 327–28nn3, 5
Whitman, Walt, Song of Myself, 20
wholeness. *See* unity of being
Wiegand, Heinrich, 51
wisdom, 183, 186, 238, 252, 254, 291
wisdom books, 174, 186, 253, 294
wish-fulfillment, 123, 247, 287
wit, 207, 211. *See also* humor
wolf motif, 199–200
women, relationship to, 92, 190–93, 217, 233; view of, in *Klingsor's Last Summer*, 171–72
Wordsworth, William, 4; ''Anecdote for Fathers,'' 157; ''Expostulation and Reply,'' 166; ''Intimations of Immortality,'' 245, 247; *The Prelude*, 6, 10–11, 13, 57, 89–90, 165, 306; *The Recluse*, 265
World War I, 45–51, 131, 143–44, 149–50, 154, 171
writer, role of, 131
writing, 23, 30, 80; as being, 34–35, 227, 312; compared to painting, 37
Wuthenow, Ralph R., 317n30

Yeats, William Butler, 81, 138, 288

Ziolkowski, 29, 73–74, 142, 147, 175–76, 184, 194, 202, 213, 240, 251, 263, 312; 329nn35, 43, 48; 335n106
Zürich, 144, 201